Humana Festival 2008
The Complete Plays

D0167861

Humana Inc., headquartered in Louisville, Kentucky, is one of the nation's largest publicly traded health and supplemental benefits companies, with approximately 11.5 million medical members. Humana is a full-service benefits solutions company, offering a wide array of health and supplementary benefit plans for employer groups, government programs and individuals.

The Humana Foundation was established in 1981 as the philanthropic arm of Humana Inc. It is a private foundation that supports and nurtures charitable activities that promote healthy lives and healthy communities.

Humana Festival 2008
The Complete Plays

Edited by
Adrien-Alice Hansel and Amy Wegener

Playscripts, Inc.

New York, NY

Published by Playscripts, Inc.
450 Seventh Avenue, Suite 809
New York, New York, 10123
www.playscripts.com

Cover Design by Matt Dobson
Cover Image by Tomer Hanuka
Text Design and Layout by Jason Pizzarello

First Edition: April 2009
10 9 8 7 6 5 4 3 2 1

LCCN: 95650734
ISSN: 1935-4452

ISBN-13: 978-0-9709046-8-3

Contents

Acknowledgments

The editors wish to thank the following persons for their invaluable assistance in compiling this volume:

Jennifer Bielstein
Cathy Colliver
Julie Felise Dubiner
Matt Dobson
Leslie Hankins
Charles Haugland
Kory Kelly
Devon LaBelle
Rachel Lerner-Ley
Sarah Lunnie
Marc Masterson
Brendan Pelsue
Jeff Rodgers
Emily Ruddock
Zan Sawyer-Dailey
James Seacat
Kyle Shepherd
Wanda Snyder

Judy Boals
Val Day
Joshua Harmon
Morgan Jenness
Carl Mulert
Olivier Sultan
Chris Till
Derek Zasky
Cathy Zimmerman

Actors Theatre of Louisville Staff
Humana Festival 2008

Artistic Director .... Marc Masterson
Managing Director ....Jennifer Bielstein

ADMINISTRATION

Budget and Management
General Manager .... Jeffrey S. Rodgers
Human Resources Coordinator .... Cora Brown
Systems Manager ....Dottie Krebs

Business Office
Executive Secretary .... Wanda Snyder

Communications
Director .... James Seacat
Marketing Manager ....Cathy Colliver
Media & Publicity Coordinator ....Kyle Shepherd
Community Relations Coordinator ....Babs W. Freibert
Group Sales Manager .... Sarah Peters
Festival/Events Coordinator .... Katherine Bilby
Outbound Sales Manager .... Lynda Sylvester
Communications Associate ....Leslie Hankins
Group Sales Assistant Manager .... J. Stephen Smith
Graphics Coordinator .... Matt Dobson
Mail Services .... Alan Meyer

Development
Director ....Christen McDonough Boone
Manager of Foundation and
Government Relations .... Michael K. Brooks, Jr.
Manager of Patron Relations .... Trish Pugh Jones
Manager of Corporate Relations .... Jamie Paradis
Coordinator ....Julia M. Leist
Coordinator of Patron Relations ....Gretchen Abrahamsen

Finance
Director .... Peggy Shake
Accounting Assistants ....Shirley Bruce, Brunhilda Williams-Curington

Ticket Sales
Director ....Kim McKercher
Senior Box Office Manager ....Saundra Blakeney
Training Manager ....Steve Clark

Subscriptions Manager..Julie Gallegos
Customer Service ....Cheryl Anderson, Amanda Blair,
Kristy Kannapell, Nathaniel Nobbe,
Biz Parker, Dav Yendler

Operations
Director.. Mike Schüssler-Williams
Housekeeping Supervisor..Jesse Miller
Assistant Manager... Barry Witt
Maintenance Staff ....Bruce Foley, Allan Reed
Receptionist...Dot King
Housekeeping Staff...................................... LaTonya Brown, Robert Bryant,
Pat Duncan, Tyree Hampton,
Sidney Lawaun, Christie Palmer, Sharon Sloan

Volunteer and Audience Relations
Director... Allison Hammons
House Managers...Megan Alexander, Adela Chipe,
Elizabeth Cooley, Darnell Johnson,
Jennifer Nichols, Kyle Sawyer-Dailey
Coat Check Attendants..................................Dana Cooley, Charles Haugland,
Drake Nichols, Cory Vaughn

ARTISTIC AND PRODUCTION
Associate Artistic Director ....Sean Daniels
Production Manager...Frazier W. Marsh
Associate Director .... Zan Sawyer-Dailey
Artistic Manager... Emily Ruddock
Production Stage Manager.. Paul Mills Holmes
Resident Stage Manager.......................................Debra Anne Gasper
Company Manager.. Ashleigh Pugh

Resident Designers
Scenic Designer.. Paul Owen
Costume Designer .... Lorraine Venberg
Properties Director...Mark Walston
Lighting Designer..Brian J. Lilienthal
Sound Designer... Matt Callahan

Literary
Director of New Play Development....................Adrien-Alice Hansel
Literary Manager ....Amy Wegener
Resident Dramaturg...Julie Felise Dubiner
Playwright-in-Residence..Naomi Wallace

Education
Director...Katie Blackerby

Associate Director ....Jess Jung
New Voices Playwriting Coordinator..................................Lee Look

Design and Technology

Technical Director..Michael J. Bowen
Assistant Technical Director..................................Justin Hagovsky
Technical Production Assistant.....................Rebecca Price-Sanders
Shop Foreman.. Alexis Tucker
Lead Carpenters .... Marshall Spratt, Pierre Vendette
Carpenters ....Charles Ames, Braden Blauser, Ryan Harvey,
Noah Johnson, Javan Roy-Bachman
Deck Carpenter ....Amy Jonas
Stage Operations Supervisor... Emily Meyer
Design Assistant.. Brenda Ellis
Scenic Charge ....Kieran Wathen
Scenic Artist...John Andrew Dropp
Props Master.......................... Doc Manning, Adriane Binky Donley
Props Soft Goods Artisan.......................................Deanna Hilleman
Props Carpenter..Joe Cunningham
Props Artisans .... William Griffith, Eric Barnes,
Richard Taylor, Scott Rygalski
Props Journeyman ....Sarah Heck*
Costume Shop Manager..................................... Margret Fenske
Costume Crafts..Shari Cochran
Drapers.....................................Shana Lincoln, Barbara Niederer
First Hands................................... Karen Merrill, Jessica Allison
Stitchers .... Christie L. Johnson, Bonnie Jonus,
Stacey B. Squires, Mary Lee Younger
Design Assistant..Susan Neason
Costume Journeyman... Emily Ganfield*
Wig and Make-up Designer...Kelly Meurer
Pamela Brown Wardrobe Mistress.....................Angela Marie Logsdon
Bingham Wardrobe Mistress...Christy Smith
Victor Jory Wardrobe Mistress.....................................Elizabeth Olin
Media Technologist ....Jason Czaja
Sound Engineer.. Paul Doyle
Associate Sound Designer..Benjamin Marcum
Sound Technicians............... Anna Caramanna*, Jessica Collins, Adam Smith
Lighting Supervisor..Paul Werner
Assistant Lighting Supervisor ....Nick Dent
First Electrician .... Derek Easton
Deck Electrician..Lauren Scattolini
Board Operators / Swing Electricians ....Rob Brodersen, Kat Seaton
Lighting Journeyman..Danielle Clifford

Apprentice/Intern Company

Director..Will MacAdams
Associate Director ....Michael Legg

Apprentices

Cheyenne Christian, Nicholas Combs, Thomas Jerome Ferguson, Elizabeth Gilbert, Katie Gould, Nathan Gregory, Jessica Lauren Howell, Jesimiel Jenkins, Jay J. Lee, Andy Lutz, Brandie Moore, Genesis Oliver, Bing Putney, Ashley Robinson, Matthew Sa, Christopher Scheer, Emily Scott, Sarah Sexton, Yuko Takeda, Dara Jade Tiller, José Urbino, Teresa Wentzell

Interns

Apprentice/Intern Company...Halima Flynn
Communications...............................Andrew Keith Nusz, Brittany M. Riley
Directing.. Dav Yendler
Education ....Stephanie Ong, Ganelle Paxton
Festival...Lindsey Palmer
Literary.. Charles Haugland, Devon LaBelle
Scenic .... Mike Boone
Stage Management...................................... Melissa Blair, Erica Sartini,
Chris Steffan, Megan Thompson
Properties ....Elliot Cornett, Taj Whitesell
Wig and Make-Up.. Kelsey Caulum

*Paul Owen Fellow

Special Thanks

Louisville Comprehensive Care MS Center for *Becky Shaw*
Brown Hotel for *Becky Shaw*
Dr. Perelmuter Orthodontics for *Game On*

Actors Theatre's company doctors:
Dr. Andrew Mickler, F.A.C.S.
Dr. Edwin Hopson, DC, CSCS
Dr. April Hopson, DC
Dr. Bill Breuer, MCH, DC, FAPHP

Actors Theatre of Louisville was founded in 1964 by Richard Block in association with Ewel Cornett. Jon Jory was Producing Director from 1969 to 2000.

Alexander Speer, Executive Director, ended his 40-year tenure at Actors Theatre in 2006.

Foreword

In the thirty-two years since the Humana Festival was founded, the American theatre has seen a lot of change. At the birth of the Festival, few regional theatres were producing new work and finished scripts languished on the shelves of producers. But recent years have seen an explosion of new plays produced in theatres large and small throughout the country. The Humana Festival is by its nature a bellwether of this change, and the varied plays in this publication demonstrate the powerful creativity of contemporary playwrights working in a wide range of styles, as well as new models for the ways that plays reach our stages and find audiences beyond the Festival.

At the close of this Humana Festival in April 2008, three of the plays were already slated for New York productions, and a number of these works have since made their way to venues around the nation. Before premiering here in Louisville, the plays' developmental journeys were rich and varied, several made possible by valuable webs of institutional support. Gina Gionfriddo's sharp comedy *Becky Shaw* sprang from an Actors Theatre of Louisville commission and enjoyed a fairly typical path from an initial draft to a first reading with actors, then next draft to workshop before beginning rehearsals in Louisville for its premiere production. On the other hand, *This Beautiful City*—written by Steven Cosson and Jim Lewis, with music by Michael Friedman—evolved through a network of partners which included their own company, The Civilians, as well as Colorado College, the Sundance Theatre Lab, Playwrights Horizons, and the Center Theatre Group. Before its premiere at Actors Theatre, it had already found subsequent productions at Studio Theatre in Washington, D.C. and Center Theatre Group's Kirk Douglas Theatre in Los Angeles. Marc Bamuthi Joseph's *the break/s* had an unusually long list of developmental partners, and reached its premiere via an exciting alliance between Actors Theatre and the Walker Arts Center in Minneapolis—primarily a museum and arts presenter. At the time of this writing, *the break/s* has been performed in dozens of cities.

Lee Blessing returned to Louisville with his play *Great Falls*, marking a twenty-six year history with Actors Theatre and seven productions since the world premiere of his play *Oldtimers Game* in 1982. As an early play by a young writer, Carly Mensch's *All Hail Hurricane Gordo* exemplifies this same spirit of discovery. The Cleveland Play House co-produced *Gordo* with Actors Theatre, and the play has already found its second audience in Ohio. Jennifer Haley's *Neighborhood 3: Requisition of Doom* came to our stage following a workshop production at Brown University, and was featured at the 2008 Summer Play Festival in New York City.

As regional theatres have changed the scope, focus and range of our work over the last three decades, innovative small and mid-sized companies like The Civilians have played an increasingly important role in supporting playwrights at all stages of development and production. Increasingly, arts presenters are finding new markets for plays—as with *the break/s*—that can tour throughout the country, and institutional theatre companies are partnering to offer developmental paths that increase the likelihood of a work finding additional audiences. Many of the larger not-for-profit companies based in New York have reached out to regional theatres in new ways. These varied paths to production—first and subsequent—are great news for the American playwright and for the Humana Festival of New American Plays, as the work that has begun on our stages heads out around the country and the world.

—*Marc Masterson*
Artistic Director
Actors Theatre of Louisville

Editors' Note

It's February 2008, and we're stepping off the elevator onto the fifth floor at Actors Theatre of Louisville, where Humana Festival rehearsals are in full swing. Between Market Street on one side and Main Street on the other, along the century-old hallway of a renovated furniture store, an array of doors lead to various rooms—and on this particular day at the height of festival preparations, there's a different play rehearsing in each. Behind every door, there's a different world: from a suburb invaded by zombies to an Evangelical church service, from the imagined house of the rock star Prince to a roadside in the Great Northwest. Across each threshold, there's a playwright and director, cast and creative team exploring the terrain of that world, learning its language, mapping its parameters and possibilities. Standing in this hallway, the energy emanating from these rooms is palpable. As dramaturgs who've spent the last nine months reading, advocating and preparing for the premieres of these plays, this is the kind of energy we live for—so we regard with exhilaration the theatrical landscapes that the festival playwrights' diverse imaginations have unleashed in these corridors.

Soon, strains of music can be heard from one room where a sound designer has joined the process, and a playwright and her cast emerge laughing from another. A properties designer hurries by with a custom-built piece of rehearsal furniture. Another writer sits talking with a director, comparing notes after their first run-through of the entire play. It's just another day during the Humana Festival, but it's not hard to retain a sense of wonder, both in this collective enterprise, and in the accomplishments of the individual writers gathered here.

Before audiences witness the collision of stories, styles and voices that is the Humana Festival of New American Plays, our theatre must bring this marvelous multiplicity of writers' visions to life. From the beginning of February, a new play begins rehearsals every four or five days, so that by the end of the month Actors Theatre is buzzing with activity. Those of us staffers who work on more than one project experience the juxtaposition of plays in a very tangible way, perhaps becoming immersed in one playwright's concoction in the morning, and another writer's play the same afternoon. Racing from room to room, we see that every process has a different kind of path as the collaborators confer and productions take shape. The writers listen intently to their work, and as the text becomes embodied in three dimensions, the choices made during a first production are important steps in its development. There are often script changes, if the writers so choose—for some, new scenes or substantially reworked sections; for others, smaller refinements that bring the world subtly into sharper focus. There are design decisions to be honed and directorial brushstrokes that realize the unique tone of each work.

But at the end of the day, the plays themselves really are the thing, the playwrights' imaginations our guides. So as we come full circle to where we began—with the texts—it's with vivid memories of these plays in process and as our audiences experienced them for the first time, and with admiration for the extraordinary constellation of voices that the 2008 Humana Festival brought together.

Even in the intimate confines of a windowless rehearsal room, where we first saw two remarkable performances take shape, Lee Blessing's *Great Falls* conjured the grandeur of some of America's most breathtaking territory, as its characters embarked on a road trip through Nebraska, South Dakota, Wyoming and Montana. As the play begins, we find a middle-aged man in the driver's seat of his car, waxing poetic about the scenery while his angry teenage passenger accuses him of kidnapping her. As it turns out, the man is the young woman's stepfather, now divorced from her mother. Hoping to retrieve something from their past together, he's striking out on the open road with his fuming companion. But she's not going to make it easy for him to find the brand of self-acceptance or forgiveness that he hopes for, instead pushing them both to traverse a much more difficult territory. "The play is a fictional piece," says Blessing, "but it's drawn from any number of marriages and divorces I've known—friends who've gone through all sorts of difficulties when they broke up, and different kinds of fractured families." As this pair make their way across broken and beautiful landscapes, the play gradually reveals the stories of these two travelers—of who they are to one another and what they've lost. Along the way, Blessing unfolds the tale of their shattered connection with moving complexity.

Questions of familial bonds and responsibilities drive Carly Mensch's nimble comic drama *All Hail Hurricane Gordo*, the tale of adult siblings abandoned by their parents long ago, and left to their own devices in the family home that has now become a kind of decrepit bachelor pad. Chaz looks out for his brother Gordo, initially to keep Child Protective Services away and keep them together, but also because Gordo's erratic behavior seems to indicate that he cannot function in the world outside. (For instance, he dons a football helmet and charges at people when upset—just one of the adrenaline-fueled moments performed with gusto by an agile Louisville cast.) When caretaker Chaz decides to expand their small world by inviting a tenant into their house—India, a fierce young woman dealing with her own family issues—the delicate balance of brotherly love and interdependence is shaken. "With my plays I tend to take two different worlds and then just smash them into each other," says Mensch. "I was playing around with the idea of how people are torn between the things they are given and the things they choose—the family you're born into and your second family, the one that you create with a stranger." As he senses Chaz's restlessness, Gordo is terrified of change; will Chaz remain his brother's keeper?

Fear and familial disconnection take a sinister tone in *Neighborhood 3: Requisition of Doom,* Jennifer Haley's tale of a subdivision where the appearance of control—of manicured lawns, identical houses and suburban serenity—belies a creeping sense of dread. Some local teens have become alarmingly addicted to an online horror video game that sends them running around a neighborhood that looks just like their own, butchering zombies in order to reach the Last Chapter. In tense encounters, with foreboding pitted against denial—and a good deal of dark humor—Haley deftly reveals her characters' dawning realization that the boundaries between the suburban world and its virtual mirror may be breaking down. In this chilling and slyly genre-bending meditation on addiction, avoidance and the nature of fear, ominous exchanges ratchet up the tension in each scene, much like advancing through the levels of a video game. Haley's treatment of character also takes a cue from gaming avatars, since her entire neighborhood is portrayed by four actors playing various mothers, fathers, sons and daughters whose relationships have been intricately mapped. Shifting personas and costumes from scene to scene with lightning-fast dexterity, the Humana Festival cast articulated individual characters as well as a whole community, creating composite images of family members who are almost never in agreement about reality. Despite warnings that something's coming, a heavy dose of denial keeps Haley's neighborhood moving toward its titular doom. "Ultimately it's about people trying desperately to communicate with each other, and being woefully incapable of it," says the playwright. "For me, that's the true horror."

The steady hum of rehearsal room activity often continued well into the evenings, thanks to Marc Bamuthi Joseph's *the break/s*—whose fusion of music and rhythm, dance, poetry and video elements played at a decibel level that could fill the fifth floor all on its own. Joined by music mixed and created live by DJ Excess and beatboxer/percussionist Tommy Shepherd a.k.a. Soulati, Joseph is the writer, dancer, and performer of this "travel diary recorded as dream." A story that keeps circling back to begin "in the middle," *the break/s* traces Joseph's journeys around the country and the world as a hip-hop artist crossing cultural lines, and grappling with questions of identity. He teaches in Wisconsin, Cuba and Bosnia, has an impromptu performance in Senegal, visits family in South Florida, attends the funeral of a former student in San Francisco, remembers meeting Jay-Z, and even imagines "chillin with Prince" in Minneapolis. With a poet's ear and dancer's grace, he details the struggles of perceiving and being perceived, of representing a culture and finding oneself out of context, and *the break/s* creates its own structure that reflects the impulses of hip-hop itself. "The design of the piece is to reimagine DJ Kool Herc at a party in the Bronx going from one record to the next—as he moves forward, continuing to reference music that he has played before," Joseph explains. "I'm trying to fade back and forth, mix back and forth from present to past, from Senegal to Miami, from the personal narrative to a macro perspective on race and identity. That makes this piece a work of hip-hop theatre. I'm trying to replicate the way that hip-hop acts in the moment."

The Civilians' grassroots investigations of American culture spring from the opinions and experience of everyday people. *This Beautiful City* took them to Colorado Springs, home of the unofficial headquarters of the American Evangelical movement. Co-writers Jim Lewis and Steven Cosson (who also directed), composer/lyricist Michael Friedman and actors from The Civilians traveled to Colorado in 2006 and spoke with people across the religious spectrum. Over the course of seven months—which included a divisive midterm election and the revelation that the pastor of the city's largest church had engaged in a three-year relationship with another man—these collaborators met face to face with the people they'd be portraying. Once in Louisville, their writing and rewriting continued, as did their research: Scouring the podcasts of the Coloradan churches they'd visited for new text; attending services and youth ministry concerts at a Louisville megachurch to give new cast members a sense of the worldview and worship of this movement. In Louisville as in Colorado, diverse religious communities opened their doors and engaged in conversations with the production team of *This Beautiful City*. And the company hopes to engender just such an exchange of ideas. "In the end," Cosson says, "my question for this play is: How is it possible that Evangelical and non-Evangelical America exist in totally different worlds? How are we all even Americans? One of our goals is to find a fundamental root, not where we all agree, but where we at least know the common questions we're seeking answers for."

Becky Shaw is a moral mystery with a crackerjack plot, equal parts ethical conundrum and unsettling comedy about the Darwinian cruelty of relationships. Suzanna doesn't know much about Becky when she sets her up on a blind date with her closest friend, Max. Suzanna's first sign of things to come is the dress Becky wears to the date. As Gina Gionfriddo's stage directions describe our first look at the eponymous Becky Shaw, she's wearing a "slightly puffy, pastel-colored cocktail dress. Maybe it's satin and bare. A great dress for another occasion…New Year's Eve, for example." The dress, and the work that Becky has put into choosing it, was the first image Gionfriddo had for the play: "It really evoked the humiliation of showing up in the wrong thing, and the dynamic of one person being very, very invested in a situation where other people aren't as invested." Striking the balance between making Becky plausibly sexy and awkwardly dressy fell to the ingenuity of director Peter DuBois and costume designer Jessica Ford, who scoured evening gowns and party dresses before hitting on a short champagne satin frock and prom-gorgeous hair. When the date with Max ends disastrously, and its fallout threatens to unhinge every other relationship in the play, an uncomfortably honest Becky forces Suzanna—and the other characters—to consider the ethical puzzle Gionfriddo poses: "The play asks to what extent Becky's desperation and investment obligates the other people to rise to the occasion. What do you owe a desperate stranger? What do you owe her when you invited her in?"

This year's ten-minute plays were no less dynamic for their brief rehearsal period and duration. Whether facing the challenge of translating a lullaby into Arabic or brainstorming another baguette sight gag, our rehearsal halls crackled with the energy of bringing these four plays to their first life. Michael Lew's exuberantly titled *In Paris You Will Find Many Baguettes but Only One True Love* follows the attempt of one heartbroken woman to be truly happy for a friend who's found the man of her dreams—a man who happens to be a mime. Rehearsals for *Tongue, Tied,* M. Thomas Cooper's two-actor, six-character play about a couple who give in to their sock puppets' baser desires (and find a little something in it for themselves), were equal parts character analysis and Twister game. In *One Short Sleepe,* Naomi Wallace explores the human fallout of the Lebanon war of 2007, in a college student's ode to spiders and his younger sister; rehearsals were spent balancing the enthusiasm of the eager entomologist with the emotional insight the bombing of his neighborhood brings him. *Dead Right* concerns a minor crisis in a well-worn relationship when one of the wife's acquaintances not only dies, but also is given a terrible obituary—a slight that launches a spousal argument about mortality, memory, and proper proofreading. One of the hardest finds for Elaine Jarvik's play was the music for the right NPR show—we settled on "Weekend Edition"—to set the scene for this touching comedy about how we see ourselves and how we hope to be remembered.

More than any other show in the 2008 Humana Festival, *Game On* assured that the rehearsal halls at Actors Theatre were almost always in use. The Acting Apprentice Company, twenty-two young professionals who join the theatre for the season to hone their performance skills while assisting behind the scenes, spend their days supporting rehearsals for the full-length shows and their evenings moving sets. During this festival, they also managed to rehearse the nineteen plays that make up *Game On,* mostly before ten in the morning or after ten at night. The adrenaline-inspired marathon proved a particularly apt method to rehearse this annual anthology, as the seven playwrights—Zakiyyah Alexander, Rolin Jones, Jon Spurney, Alice Tuan, Daryl Watson, Marisa Wegrzyn and Ken Weitzman—were commissioned by Actors Theatre to explore the pervasive effects of sports on American culture. From a comedy about what happens when the geeks make their own steroids to a budding romance on the stud farm for retired racehorses to the story of a reigning elementary school tetherball champion, these plays plumb the silly and the sublime while investigating America's love of sport, and what our affinity for both underdog and conqueror says about our culture.

As vividly as we can recall the dynamic conversations and hard work of so many that brought the 2008 Humana Festival plays before their first audiences, we know that these eleven world premieres were both culminations and beginnings in the lives of these scripts. Actors Theatre of Louisville joins a play's journey for several months, a brief and intense time along the playwright's long and arduous journey of writing and revision. A company of collaborators is brought into the mix, opening the experience to audiences—in the case of this festival, first a local audience and then a national one. Working in the theatre, we find ourselves always in the midst of this energizing cycle of arrivals and departures—at the end of a new play's Louisville run, which launches it into the wider cultural dialogue. And now, after a remarkable staff and a company of artists from around the country have brought these works to vibrant life in three dimensions, we return to where we began: with the playwrights' texts, and a reader's imagination.

—Amy Wegener and Adrien-Alice Hansel

GREAT FALLS

A PLAY IN SEVERAL TOWNS

by Lee Blessing

1

BIOGRAPHY

Lee Blessing's Actors Theatre of Louisville credits include *Down the Road, Riches, Independence, Nice People Dancing to Good Country Music,* and *Oldtimers Game,* plus various shorter pieces. Broadway: *A Walk in the Woods* (also performed in Moscow and London's West End). Off-Broadway: *A Body of Water, Going to St. Ives, Thief River, Chesapeake, Cobb, Down the Road,* and *Eleemosynary*; and *Fortinbras, Lake Street Extension, Two Rooms* and *Patient A* (Signature Theatre's 1992-93 season). Regional Theatre: World premieres of *Lonesome Hollow, The Scottish Play, Flag Day, Whores, Black Sheep,* and *The Winning Streak.* Current commissions include *Moderation* (Weissberger Group), *Perilous Night* (Denver Center Theatre) and Thornton Wilder's *Heaven's My Destination* (Cleveland Play House). Mr. Blessing heads the graduate playwriting program at Mason Gross School of the Arts, Rutgers University.

ACKNOWLEDGMENTS

Great Falls premiered at the Humana Festival of New American Plays in February 2008. It was directed by Lucie Tiberghien with the following cast:

MONKEY MAN	Tom Nelis
BITCH	Halley Wegryn Gross

and the following production staff:

Scenic Designer	Paul Owen
Costume Designer	Lorraine Venberg
Lighting Designer	Brian J. Lilienthal
Sound Designer	Matt Callahan
Properties Designer	Doc Manning
Original Music	Brian Callahan
Stage Manager	Kathy Preher
Production Assistant	Mary Spadoni
Dramaturg	Amy Wegener
Assistant Dramaturg	Devon LaBelle
Casting	Zan Sawyer-Dailey
Directing Assistant	Gaye Poole

Development support for *Great Falls* was provided by the Eugene O'Neill Theater Center during a residency at the National Playwrights Conference of 2005.

CAST OF CHARACTERS
MONKEY MAN, in the middle of his life
BITCH, at the start of hers

PLACE AND TIME
The Great Northwest. Now, more or less.

Halley Wegryn Gross and Tom Nelis
in *Great Falls*

32nd Annual Humana Festival of New American Plays
Actors Theatre of Louisville, 2008
Photo by Harlan Taylor

4

GREAT FALLS

WALL

MONKEY MAN *drives.* BITCH, *in the passenger seat, is rageful. A long beat before he speaks.*

MONKEY MAN. I love this whole part of the country. Not quite the table lands. Just before the table lands. The Great Plains. They're different up here. Hard to describe. Well, there's the Badlands. They have the Badlands up here.

(Pointing left out of the car.)

Just over there, in fact. One step and—boom! There you are: broken country. That's what they call it, broken country. Want to see the Badlands?

(As she continues to ignore him.)

Maybe on the way back. It's tremendous, though. I remember from when I was a kid. Like driving on the moon. Gorgeous, in its way.

BITCH. They're gonna rape you in prison.

MONKEY MAN. Hope you like this car. It's amazing you've never been in it before. Got it right after the...well, you know. At least we're roaming in style, eh? When I was a kid, ten or so, my folks took me on a trip out here. Did it all: Mt. Rushmore, Devil's Tower, Pompey's Pillar—you know what that is?

(No response.)

Little Bighorn. The Last Stand.

BITCH. Kidnappers get raped in prison. Especially if they kidnap children.

MONKEY MAN. You're not a child. And I didn't kidnap you. We're taking a drive, that's all. Spending time together. Having a talk. At least we would be, if you weren't taking the world's longest nap. Didn't you get any sleep last night?

BITCH. Sometimes they use objects. Various objects they carefully fashion in secret—or maybe right in your cell, right in front of you.

MONKEY MAN. I haven't committed a crime.

(After a beat.)

You'll like Wall Drug. My folks took me there. The Interstate wasn't finished yet. We went through Pierre, the old way. Wall Drug had signs like every two hundred feet for hundreds of miles in advance. "Wall Drug." "Visit Wall Drug."

(Pointing as they pass an actual sign.)

"Everything's at Wall Drug." Everything was, too. And it was all like wood, you know? Like it had been that way forever—ancient trading post. Bin after bin full of crap only kids and tourists could like. I didn't care about the crap; it was the wooden bins I loved. They have this old, yellow, orangey-brown sort of sheen—or gray.... The wood feels like velvet, it's been touched so much. Reshaped by all those fingers sliding over it for years.

BITCH. Spoons, sometimes. That's a foreign object they use. They could rape you with spoons.

MONKEY MAN. No one is going to jail.

BITCH. Or sometimes they make spoons into knives. Maybe it'll be knives.

MONKEY MAN. You're not being abducted.

BITCH. I'm not?

MONKEY MAN. No. You're not.

BITCH. You're such a loser. I just wanted to see how far you'd go. I thought, "Twenty miles, he'll turn around." Then I thought thirty, fifty, a hundred, three hundred—

MONKEY MAN. Damn it, no one's abducting you!

BITCH. (*Producing a cell phone.*) Then I can call Mom?

MONKEY MAN. Put that away! You said you wouldn't. You promised.

BITCH. Like you promised to turn around?

MONKEY MAN. Give me that!

BITCH. No way! It's mine!

MONKEY MAN. (*Grabbing for it.*) Give it! Right now!

BITCH. Watch where you're going!

> (*They're swerving. He jerks the wheel back from a close call, then drives on, chastened.*)

MONKEY MAN. I do not want you to call her.

BITCH. Is that an order? 'Cause if it's an order, then I'm being abducted, aren't I?

MONKEY MAN. Please.

BITCH. Wish denied.

> (*Punching in a number.*)

You could try overeating in prison, I suppose—get real fat. But some convicts like fat guys. Bigger the better. Wish I could be there to hear you scream.

> (*On phone.*)

Hello, Mom—? Guess who I'm with. Monkey Man. Yeah! We're in his car, driving west. He's making off with me.

MONKEY MAN. Gimme that!

(*Grabbing the cell phone from her.*)

Hello? Yeah, it's me. I'm not doing anything with her. I'm not making off with anybody. She's being theatrical. We're just— What? We're taking a drive. So we can have a *talk.* What do you mean? There's plenty of things to talk about, there's— What's it matter where we are? We're in my car. On a road somewhere.

BITCH. In South Dakota!

MONKEY MAN. Shut up!

(*On the phone.*)

What? No. She's just being— We're not in South Dakota. We're nowhere near—

BITCH. (*Shouting at the phone.*) We're in South Dakota! We're right next to the Badlands, and Wall Drug is—

(*With a quick look out the window.*)

—twelve-point-three miles away—!!

MONKEY MAN. (*On the phone.*) Don't call the police! Don't call the police. Just listen, okay? Can you? Can you just *listen* to me?!

(*With a dirty look at the grinning* BITCH.)

First of all, she's not a child. She's eighteen. Okay, she's a *week* from being eighteen. If she wants to be with me, she has every right. We ran into each other this morning. At her work. I came over from Lincoln for an appointment; I stopped for a bagel. I have bagels sometimes. I have a human right to have a fucking bagel, okay?! I'm not swearing. Sorry, I'm— She was on her break, having a smoke in the parking lot. I was on that stoop thing—or, you know, the ramp for the disabled. Yeah, very funny. Anyhow, we realized we had a lot to talk about. So we took a drive—

BITCH. He said I'd be back in *five minutes!!* My job is *toast!!*

MONKEY MAN. (*Covering the phone.*) Shut *up!*

(*On the phone.*)

What—? Who cares? It's a summer job. The money doesn't matter. I'll give her the money, for Christ's— I don't know, a couple days?

BITCH. We're driving to Oregon! Like Lewis and Clark!

MONKEY MAN. *Will you—?!*

(*On the phone.*)

I know. I know. It's a long way from Omaha. But sometimes I can't think— you know, *think*—unless I'm driving, or walking, or…I have to be in motion of some kind, or the blood doesn't—*you* remember. So anyway, it was just this idea that developed. While we *talked.* Okay, yes—more than a couple days. For God's sake, in the great scheme of things…I know. I know. I've just…lost a lot here—we all have—and talking this morning, we realized there may still be something to retrieve.

BITCH. Like my job.

MONKEY MAN. (*A harsh whisper.*) Your job is gone! I'll pay for your job!

(*On the phone.*)

So, look. Just…let us do this, okay? Just. Just relax, and we'll be home before you— Okay. Okay. Okay. Okay. I know what I did. You don't have to—

(*To* BITCH.)

She thinks I'm insane. She's angry. She never wanted to speak to me again, and suddenly here I am on the—

(*On the phone.*)

What? Okay. Okay. That does sound reasonable. I'll buy her things. Wall Drug's coming right up; we can— Sure, of course. I should have called right away. I'm sincerely sorry— No, you're completely…perfectly reasonable. You wouldn't be a responsible adult if you didn't…. No, no—go ahead, absolutely.

(*Handing her the phone.*)

She wants to know if you're being kidnapped.

(*As she stares at the phone, lights fade to black, then bounce up again. They're still driving. She now has a large, white plastic shopping bag on her lap. It's full of purchases and says, "Visit Wall Drug."*)

MONKEY MAN. That was fun, wasn't it?

BITCH. No.

MONKEY MAN. Don't know why they got rid of the wooden bins. I used to love those. So much plastic in there now. Didn't really feel like Wall Drug.

BITCH. It'll probably be a Wal-*Mart* next year. So what?

(*A beat. She fishes a pair of jeans from the shopping bag, starts removing tags.*)

MONKEY MAN. Did you get everything you needed?

BITCH. (*Pulling a stuffed rabbit with tiny antlers attached—a jackalope—from the bag.*) Pretty much.

(*Staring at the jackalope.*)

I need more toilet stuff.

MONKEY MAN. I'll get off at the next exit. It's been a long day. We can pick up whatever you need, find a motel—

BITCH. (*With sudden rage.*) You are not my FATHER, you fucking asshole!!!

MONKEY MAN. (*After a long beat.*) I never said I was.

BITCH. You're fucking Monkey Man! I know you read my diaries!

MONKEY MAN. I never did.

BITCH. I know you did.

MONKEY MAN. You can't "know" that, because I never did.

(*A long silence. They drive.*)

BITCH. I'm not staying in a motel with you.

MONKEY MAN. It doesn't have to be the same room. I was kind of hoping it could be—I mean, you know, twin beds—because after a few days it starts to add up. I'm still paying support for you and your brother, you know. Don't have to; it's my choice, but…. Plus I'll be paying you back for your job—

BITCH. You're so cheap. No wonder Mom left you.

MONKEY MAN. That's not why she left me.

BITCH. You had sexual fantasies about me.

MONKEY MAN. I did not.

BITCH. You're a man. You couldn't help yourself.

MONKEY MAN. I am a man. And I can help myself.

BITCH. You had sexual fantasies about everybody. That's what Mom says.

MONKEY MAN. Your mother is very angry.

BITCH. Someday they're going to make sexual fantasies a crime. People like you will go to prison for eternity and live them out with four hundred-pound serial killers who never shower.

MONKEY MAN. I'm very sorry for what your father—

BITCH. *Shut up!*

MONKEY MAN. (*After a beat.*) So where do you suggest we sleep tonight?

BITCH. In the car.

MONKEY MAN. In the *car?!* I'm not going to—! We'll get arrested.

BITCH. Want me to call the cops right now? 'Cause if you're abducting me—

MONKEY MAN. Okay, okay—! I could…I could look for a side road, I guess. Somewhere they don't patrol. But you won't be comfortable. It'll be cold.

BITCH. I'm calling the cops.

MONKEY MAN. Stop. Just stop, okay? We don't have to call anybody. There's a blanket in the trunk—

BITCH. I'm not sharing—

MONKEY MAN. That you can have. Christ. Don't know why I thought this was a good idea.

BITCH. What makes you think you think?

(*After a beat.*)

I've named my jackalope. Wanna hear?

MONKEY MAN. It's just that a motel would—

BITCH. *Wanna hear!?*

MONKEY MAN. Why do you suddenly get like you're seven years old when you're around me?

(*No response.*)

What's his name?

BITCH. Vicious Penis Destroyer.

(*Staring at the jackalope.*)

That's his name.

MONKEY MAN. So. This is going to be fun. We'll find a little...spot... down by some creek and hope we don't run into any sheriffs or psychotic ranchers. We can go to the bathroom in the underbrush, try not to disturb any rattlesnakes or black widows or Rocky Mountain jumping lice.... Then I'll get to shiver and be miserable all night while you take the only blanket. How's that sound? Will that help?

BITCH. It's a start.

(*Lights shift as scene ends.*)

THERMOPOLIS

> *The next evening.* MONKEY MAN *and* BITCH *stand facing twin beds in a cheap motel room.*

MONKEY MAN. Is this place all right?

BITCH. Compared to what?

MONKEY MAN. It's got everything we need. I think it's some kind of chain—

BITCH. Scrimpy-Lodge?

MONKEY MAN. Hasn't gone national. It's not the bottom tier. We can work our way up. Anyway, it's better than sleeping in the car last night. God, was I cold!

(*Stretching.*)

So. Another long day on the road. Can't believe we got all the way to Thermopolis. You like Wyoming? The sky seems so low here. I mean, 'cause the ground, you know, gets, um...higher.

(*After a beat.*)

Which bed do you want?

BITCH. There's a difference?

MONKEY MAN. Guess not.

BITCH. (*As he moves toward the bathroom.*) You don't want the one by the door?

MONKEY MAN. What?

BITCH. The one closer to the door? So I can't escape?

MONKEY MAN. Escape.

(*He goes in the bathroom, shutting the door. She goes to the TV, picks up the remote.*)

BITCH. Hey, Monkey Man! Want to watch TV?

MONKEY MAN. (*From the bathroom.*) No. Please. Not tonight. We've got things to talk about.

(*She drops the remote, wincing at his audible pissing.*)

BITCH. Yuck.

(*She picks a bed, sits on it, and rummages through her Wall Drug shopping bag, plus two more she's acquired. She pulls out the jackalope and puts it by her pillow.*)

MONKEY MAN. (*From the bathroom, as the toilet flushes.*) I'd rather we talked.

BITCH. Fine.

(*She pulls out an iPod, slips in the earphones and stretches her legs out on the bed.*)

MONKEY MAN. (*Still in the bathroom.*) This is better. We have things to say, right? Mind if I use your name? It'll be hard to discuss anything if I'm—

BITCH. (*Pulling out an earphone.*) What?

MONKEY MAN. (*From the bathroom.*) Can I use your name?

BITCH. (*Not angry—shouting so he can hear.*) Call me Bitch! That's what you think I am—that's what you call me!

(*She replaces the earphone. Tinny sound of the iPod playing fills the room. After a moment, he appears. He stares at her.*)

MONKEY MAN. I won't call you anything.

BITCH. (*Pulling out an earphone.*) What?

MONKEY MAN. Turn it off.

BITCH. No.

MONKEY MAN. We agreed, right? No music at night. You can use it in the car, but—

BITCH. You can't tell me when to—

MONKEY MAN. You spent the whole day doing that. Mile after mile all I got was—

(*Making the irritating, tinny sound of a turned-up iPod.*)

Thought my head was going to explode. It's not why we're out here. Put it away. Please? We're here to talk.

BITCH. And if I don't?

MONKEY MAN. I'll back the car over it.

(*She considers, then puts it back in the bag.*)

BITCH. Go out of the room.

MONKEY MAN. What do you mean? We're going to—

BITCH. Get out! I have to pee.

MONKEY MAN. Just shut the—

BITCH. I can't pee if I know you're out here. It's too loud. I could hear you the whole time.

MONKEY MAN. Oh...sorry. The fan's not working. Or maybe it was the other switch—

BITCH. Just go. Or I won't talk.

MONKEY MAN. Okay, okay— You didn't have much dinner. Want some food?

BITCH. No. Get cigarettes.

MONKEY MAN. You should eat more.

(She glares at him. He goes to the door, opens it.)

I'll be right back.

(He leaves. She stays sitting for a moment, then goes into the bathroom. The faint sound of her urinating can be heard, then the sound of a flush. She returns, picks up the remote, points it at the TV. She holds it poised for a moment, then puts it down without turning on the TV. She sits on her bed, pulls a pillow from under the cover and smells it.)

BITCH. *Shit.*

MONKEY MAN. *(Entering with cigarettes.)* What?

BITCH. This smells like B.O.!

MONKEY MAN. No, it doesn't.

BITCH. It smells old!

MONKEY MAN. They wash these all the—

BITCH. This one's *yours!*

MONKEY MAN. Okay. No big deal.

(He sighs, hands her the cigarettes. She opens the pack as he switches the pillows.)

You can't smoke in here.

BITCH. *What!?*

MONKEY MAN. You can't smoke in here. Non-smoking room. I asked for it.

BITCH. Pig fucker.

MONKEY MAN. Nevertheless.

(She rises, takes a cigarette and her lighter to the door. She lights up and blows the smoke outside.)

BITCH. So? What'll we talk about?

MONKEY MAN. Well...

BITCH. 'Cause there's nothing like talking all night in a motel in Buffalo Ass.

MONKEY MAN. Thermopolis.

BITCH. I mean, you keep saying that's why we're here. 'Cause we can't help ourselves from all this talking.

MONKEY MAN. Doesn't have to all be talk. Tomorrow we can explore the area.

BITCH. Explore the area?

MONKEY MAN. Sure.

(*Pulling a brochure from his pocket.*)

Here's a list of the top attractions in town—

BITCH. We're *staying?!*

MONKEY MAN. I did. When I was a kid. My folks brought me here. We stayed a couple days. And there's lots more here now—

BITCH. Like what?

MONKEY MAN. Like the largest mineral Hot Springs in the world.

BITCH. What's there?

MONKEY MAN. A hot springs.

(*Consulting the brochure.*)

And, it says, "Grass, trees—"

BITCH. *Grass* and *trees?*

MONKEY MAN. *And*...walkways, a path by the terraces—that's where the hot water runs over the stone and where it's held in cooling pools—and a walking bridge, a picnic area...It says, "Big Spring Fun for all ages." There's also a Dinosaur Center.

BITCH. Where's that?

MONKEY MAN. "One mile east of the traffic light—"

BITCH. *The* traffic light.

MONKEY MAN. And there's a Teddy Bear museum. It's actually three museums in one, it says. Teddy bears, quilts and, um...wax. Oh—and they've got a model railway and a...a barbed wire display. And it looks like the Chamber of Commerce is there, too.

(*She gives him a long look, then shakes her head at the pathetic description. She blows smoke into the room.*)

Or...I guess we could push on.

(*Putting down the brochure.*)

Sure you don't want to eat?

(*No response.*)

I'm getting a little nervous with you standing out there. Someone could see you.

BITCH. So?

MONKEY MAN. They could get the wrong idea. Older man, younger woman…. People are overly suspicious these days.

BITCH. You're my stepfather.

MONKEY MAN. They don't know that.

BITCH. What are they gonna assume? That you're kidnapping me?

(*She smokes in silence for a long moment, tosses the cigarette to the sidewalk, crushes it and comes back in.*)

If we're not going to talk, I'm going to bed.

MONKEY MAN. Bed? It's early.

BITCH. I'm *tired*. Are we going to talk? 'Cause I'll talk if you want to. If you really, *really* want to talk.

(*After a beat.*)

Thought so. Well. No rush, I guess.

(*She grabs one of her bags and goes into the bathroom. He sighs, tosses the brochure into a waste basket. After a moment, he moves toward the bathroom door.*)

MONKEY MAN. It's great to have a room though, isn't it? Better than last night, sleeping in the car. I'm tired myself. Lots of miles in just two days—

BITCH. (*Off.*) I'm in another room!

(*Sound of the shower turning on.*)

MONKEY MAN. Right. Sorry.

(*He sits on the end of his bed, sighs, takes off his shoes. Softly, he rehearses his half of a prospective conversation.*)

Divorce is no reason to lock people out of your life. Divorce is…normal, and natural, and more people do it than don't. So…. So why compound the damage? Why take sides, or pretend that one partner or the other is an ogre or…a villain of some sort, when the truth is *always* that it's *both* people's fault?

(*Nodding, as though someone is responding.*)

I know, I know. I did bad things. I did very unthinking and heartless things that came out of what was really—what was it? What was it really? It was *really*…. Arrested development, that's what it was. Emotionally, I was still a child. I was incapable of anything like real introspection, or real growth, or real…fidelity. But you know the worst thing I did? I can say this, now that we're being honest. Now that we're here, face to face. The worst thing wasn't going outside the marriage, it was…it was telling her. Because you can never do that. You can never think a thing like that will ever do any good—not the least, tiniest little grain of good. Because we're all weak. We're all...we're subject to it. She told me, your mother told me, when we were in the middle of breaking up, when we—

(*Looking at the bathroom door, then resuming.*)

—were in the middle of that entire mess of *shit* and *anger* and...shame...that she flirted with it. She was romanced by someone. Well, romanced—he was trying to...fuck her, and he was a friend of ours, a very charming and handsome.... What? No, I'm not going to say who it was. The point is, the *much larger* point—and this is when I realized it by the way, when it became *clear* to me—is that fidelity is not what people demand from each other in marriage. What we *demand*.... No, no—hear me out. What we demand is not to be humiliated. Which ninety-nine percent of the time means not to be told. "Honey, I almost slept with that guy. We were sitting, talking on the couch in his apartment. He was so attentive, he really seemed to care. And we'd had some wine—" No. No! "We made out for awhile. It was just kissing, but then—" *No!* We don't do this. We demand from each other not to do this. Because it's humiliating to sit in a conversation and be told that the person you give yourself to gives himself to...someone else—under any circumstance. And the point is, I know that *now*.

(*The shower turns off. He stares at the bathroom door, then continues, softer.*)

Because...and this is what it really is. Under everything. The essence of it. Unless you're having your spouse tailed twenty-four seven by the world's best detective agency, you can *never know for certain* if they've stayed faithful every minute of every day. But what you can know is if they've told you. That you can know. And the reason your mother and I divorced—I think anyway, this is definitely my interpretation—is that I told her. But I didn't have the affairs because I wanted out of the marriage. And I didn't tell her because I wanted out of the marriage. Honestly, that was never—at least until the very end, maybe—that was *never* the reason. I didn't want these revelations to end things. I wanted them to...change her. That she would hear these things, and they would wake something up in her. That she'd realize that I didn't enjoy these...*activities*, that I was in pain. Every day. I was in pain every day with her, and these...lapses, adventures—I don't know what to call them—were a kind of relief that instantly palled. Lost its appeal, became ugly and pointless, instantly, because I didn't love them.

BITCH. (*From the bathroom.*) The water smells like rotten eggs!

MONKEY MAN. What? I know. I think it's the hot springs.

BITCH. (*Off.*) What?

MONKEY MAN. It's the hot springs! I mean, I don't know. It's probably that.

(*She comes out of the bathroom. She's naked, except for panties and a towel.*)

BITCH. So you have no idea. That's what you mean.

(*She strides past him, belching as she goes, and sits on her bed. She pulls on her socks, making no great effort to preserve her modesty as she does so. He stares at her in surprise.*)

What are you staring at? I always wear socks to bed.

MONKEY MAN. You don't have any clothes on.

BITCH. This is how I sleep. If you don't want to see how I sleep, don't kidnap me.

(*Getting under the covers, stares at him.*)

How are you gonna sleep, in a parka?

(*No response.*)

You wear pajamas? Did you bring your pajamas when you abducted me?

(*He goes into the bathroom.*)

BITCH. (*Calling out.*) I saw you drooling!

(*She slips on an oversized t-shirt, picks up her cell phone and punches a button.*)

Hi, Mom? I'm fine. I'm *fine!* Since six hours ago? Yes, I'm fine. We're in Therm something, Thermos—I don't know. In a hotel. They've got hotels in Wyoming. It's very nice, if you must know. It's got a hot spring and every-thing. It's like a spa. He's spending lots of money. I think he's trying to buy my love. It's totally pathetic. What? No, he's in a room down the hall. No, I'm not going to get him, I'm too tired. Why do you always worry? He's a piece of shit; he's not gonna make me sympathize. God, you are so—! I'll call you to*morrow.* I'll call you tomorrow. I'll— Hey! *Hey.* Almost eighteen here, remember? If you do that, I'll never speak to you again. I mean it. Listen. No, listen to me. This is the grown-up voice. Right? Right. Okay, good night.

(*She hangs up. He comes out of the bathroom. He wears only boxer shorts.*)

MONKEY MAN. This is how I sleep.

BITCH. I can see why she left you.

MONKEY MAN. (*Glancing down at his body as she turns her back to go to sleep.*) What do you mean?

BITCH. Look at you. Can't believe she didn't vomit every time you—

MONKEY MAN. I'm just average. I'm not special…I'm not awful.

BITCH. You're old.

MONKEY MAN. (*Getting into his bed.*) Is that the awful part?

BITCH. Men are bad enough, but old men…

(*As she shudders at the thought.*)

You gonna read or something?

MONKEY MAN. No.

BITCH. Then turn off the light.

MONKEY MAN. (*Looking at the light next to the bed, not moving.*) I was thirteen when I was here before. We went to the hot springs. They didn't have all the stuff they have now, of course.

BITCH. The grass and trees?

MONKEY MAN. Mom hated it, said it stank. Which it did, of course. Just…overpowering. But even so, Dad and I climbed up to this place above the main spring. It was so beautiful. The water was the clearest I ever…well, it had to be, right? What could live in it? And the colors were…And all this heat just kind of flowed up from it in big waves, through the air. I could see where humans got their vision of hell, you know? So beautiful and…lethal. Strange to be someplace where the earth's so much hotter than everything else. Guess nobody's sleeping in the cold, cold ground around here, eh?

(*No response.*)

That was a great trip. I liked my parents best on trips. Wish we'd taken more trips with you and your brother. Bet you guys would have traveled well. Are you asleep?

BITCH. No, I'm thinking.

MONKEY MAN. About what?

BITCH. Who I hate more. You, or my father.

(*After a long beat.*)

Turn out the light.

(*He hesitates, then clicks the light off.*)

YELLOWSTONE

Late morning. The car. They're parked. MONKEY MAN's *behind the wheel. He stares ahead and to his left, anxious.* BITCH *calmly writes in a notebook.*

MONKEY MAN. We won't be able to see anything from here.

(*No response.*)

You have to go up. See the crowd up there? You have to sit with the crowd.

BITCH. I'm working. You go.

MONKEY MAN. It's no fun all alone. Can you see from that side?

BITCH. (*Not looking up.*) Yeah, I can see fine.

MONKEY MAN. Can we at least get out of the car?

BITCH. No! I don't want people staring at me.

MONKEY MAN. They're not staring at you. This is Yellowstone. They're looking at Old Faithful. At least they will be, in a second. Nobody cares about you. This place is unique on the whole planet.

BITCH. (*As she writes.*) It's a zoo for nerds. Besides, it smells like ass.

MONKEY MAN. You're not even going to look at it, are you? I swear, this carries perversity to a whole new level.

BITCH. I don't have to like what you like.

MONKEY MAN. I'm not saying you have to. But…at least do the world you were born into the honor of recognizing its wonders—

BITCH. Who's recognizing me?

MONKEY MAN. What?

BITCH. Who's recognizing me?

MONKEY MAN. I don't understand.

BITCH. That's right.

MONKEY MAN. (*His attention suddenly riveted.*) Oh, shit! There it is! There it is! Are you looking!?

> (*He quickly glances at her as she casts a brief, uninterested eye at the proceedings. Then he looks back at the show.*)

MONKEY MAN. (*Rapt, joyous.*) There she goes! There she goes! Isn't that fantastic?! There she goes! There she goes! There she goes!

> (*As he shouts, unseen by him,* BITCH *pulls a blanket out of one of her bags and puts it over her head. She's completely obscured.*)

Isn't that—!!?? Oh, my *God!* Isn't that—? Don't you *love* that?! Don't you just—?!

> (*He looks around and sees her under the blanket. He's shocked, speechless, staring at her. He looks again at the geyser, knowing it won't last long. He looks at her. He looks at the geyser. A long beat.*)

MONKEY MAN. (*Quietly, staring straight ahead.*) There she went.

> (*Still under the blanket, and without his happening to see, she puts her jackalope on top of her head and holds it there.*)

> (*Lights quickly down.*)

ANACONDA

Morning. Roadside picnic table. A stone retaining wall divides BITCH *and* MONKEY MAN *from the "view," which we see in the background: a butte, fronted by a distant, enormous, lone smokestack. They're nearly done with a fast food breakfast. She checks over what she's been writing in her notebook. He stares at the landscape, occasionally studying her as well. Sound of Interstate traffic below them.*

MONKEY MAN. What are you working on?

> (*No response.*)

Is it something new?

> (*No response.*)

You used to write some beautiful things. You always let me read them and—

(*Her look stops him in mid-comment.*)

Is your food okay?

(*As she belches.*)

Great. Great. Highest praise, from you. I remember.

(*No response.*)

Have you even looked at the view?

BITCH. You mean the big *cock?*

MONKEY MAN. It's not a…. It's not.

BITCH. It's not?

MONKEY MAN. It's the largest smelter stack in the world. At least it used to be. It's a superlative, is what it is. This trip is filled with superlatives. Mosts, biggests, onlys…. It's an amazing part of the country, if you'd—

BITCH. It's a great big smokestack in the middle of nowhere that looks like an enormous dong in a town named Anaconda that's even shaped like a snake. It's the most phallic place in the world Dad, and you brought me here. What's *with* you?

MONKEY MAN. I'm not your dad.

(*A beat.*)

It's on the freeway; it's not like we could avoid it. Last night we were in Butte—biggest hole in the world. You didn't say anything about that. Open-pit copper mine, smelter stack. It's just industry, it's—

BITCH. It's not on the freeway; it's ten miles off. You brought me here to show me that. Fucking perv.

MONKEY MAN. (*As she goes back to her notebook.*) I just remembered it, that's all. From when I was a kid. I wanted to see it again.

Watch your language.

BITCH. Watch your life.

MONKEY MAN. What's going on with you? I couldn't believe the act you pulled at Yellowstone yesterday.

BITCH. It was no act.

MONKEY MAN. It was insane, is what it was.

(*As she gives him a sharp look.*)

Okay, I'm sorry; I don't mean "insane." That's a ridiculous word. That word doesn't apply to you.

BITCH. Apply it. I don't care.

MONKEY MAN. But to put a blanket over your head—

BITCH. It was nice under there. Like the whole world was just me.

MONKEY MAN. And you liked that?

BITCH. Doesn't everybody? Anyhow, as far as I'm concerned, Old Faithful's just one more symbol on Monkey Man's Freudian tour of America. What did your folks say when they took you there? "Someday Son, you too will erupt every hour on the hour. 'Course, you'll need a lot of different women—"

MONKEY MAN. Will you shut up? God, you can be horrible sometimes.

(*Collecting the remains of the meal, stuffing it back into its paper sacks.*)

All I'm saying is you agreed to look at it. That's why we went.

BITCH. We went 'cause it was your car. Let me drive and see where we go.

MONKEY MAN. (*After a beat.*) What are you writing?

(*No response.*)

I remember when you brought me the first poem you ever wrote.

(*She stops writing. She starts again.*)

Wish I could afford to write poetry again. That's what Thomas Hardy did. All those novels were just to make enough money to go back to writing poems. I know how he felt. There's something about a novel. It gets so tired of itself by the end. It never resolves so much as...peters out. The fact that it ends at all feels like a flaw. Yet I know I have to end it. The reader's bored, we're both already thinking about the next one.

BITCH. Maybe if you were a better writer.

MONKEY MAN. Poems, though. They have to be perfect, or they can't exist. Perfect in every limb. If a word's out of place it's like a...lesion. So when you're making one, it feels like you're making something perfect, you know? Like you have that power.

BITCH. You could write a dirty limerick about the smokestack.

MONKEY MAN. What are you writing? I'd love to hear it.

BITCH. Why? Just another poem by the "insane" Bitch. Nothing special.

MONKEY MAN. Everything you write is special. That's why I like you.

BITCH. What if it wasn't special? Would you like me then?

MONKEY MAN. Of course I would. No matter how you wrote. I'd love you.

BITCH. You love everybody.

MONKEY MAN. No, I don't.

BITCH. Tell it to Mom.

MONKEY MAN. (*As she writes.*) Are you writing in a form, or free verse, or—?

BITCH. *I'm writing haikus! Shut up!*

MONKEY MAN. Haikus are great.

BITCH. Wanna hear one?

MONKEY MAN. Yeah.

BITCH. It's called "Dreams."

(*Reading.*)

> "I'm trying to decide
> How big a garbage bag I'll need
> When I trash all your dreams."

(*She laughs at his perplexed look.*)

That's not a real one. Here's a real one. It's called "Spider."

> "Spider I have let live,
> Protect the dark corner
> From my fears."

MONKEY MAN. That's great.

BITCH. Right.

MONKEY MAN. No, I mean it—that's really great. I love that. What's the syllable count?

BITCH. What?

MONKEY MAN. In the lines, I mean? It's not the classic number of syllables, is it?

BITCH. Who cares?

MONKEY MAN. Just hard to call it a haiku, if it's not—

BITCH. *Who—cares?*

MONKEY MAN. Right. You're right. It's beautiful. You're very talented.

BITCH. I know.

MONKEY MAN. Only wish I could say it was genetic.

BITCH. It is. I get it from Mom.

MONKEY MAN. (*Laughing despite himself.*) There's a…fresh perspective.

(*As she goes back to writing.*)

So. Lots to decide at this point. Have you been thinking?

BITCH. Yeah.

MONKEY MAN. Totally up to you. Completely your decision.

BITCH. I think—

MONKEY MAN. But before you say, I think it's important to mark a moment like this. Here we are, astride the Continental Divide so to speak— on our own, free to explore. We're talking, we're exploring, the Pacific Northwest is only a couple mountain ranges away—

BITCH. No.

MONKEY MAN. And—

(*After a beat.*)

And just like Lewis and Clark we could—

BITCH. No.

MONKEY MAN. We *could* see the Columbia River Gorge, and Astoria and Cannon Beach and—

BITCH. No.

MONKEY MAN. And the wide and endless…unswimmably cold…Pacific. It's west, it's the way of the future. Why not?

BITCH. I don't have time.

MONKEY MAN. We have months of time. It's summer. I'm a writer, for God's sake; no one needs me. You're going to college this fall. This is a great—

BITCH. It's where *you* went, when you were a little kid. It's where your parents took you, and you love it 'cause you *had* two parents. But I don't. So I'm not going there, 'cause I can't go there, 'cause I don't have two parents— *get* it? I've only got Mom, and she *hates* trips. We tried that a couple times and we were *all* miserable. And I don't want to see the ocean with you any more than I wanted to see Old Faithful with Old Faithless. So I didn't do that, and I'm not doing this—and I'm not going one more foot unless I—*drive!*

MONKEY MAN. (*After a beat.*) I had so much more to show you.

BITCH. Maybe we need a new tour guide.

MONKEY MAN. Do you think your brother's ever going to speak to me again?

BITCH. No.

MONKEY MAN. I know he's not speaking now, but he's only fourteen. He's got so much more growing up to—

BITCH. He cut up every picture of you in the house. They were all in this box, and Mom went to throw them away, and when she opened it, it was all just confetti.

(*After a beat.*)

Once he bought a book of yours.

MONKEY MAN. He did?

BITCH. And peed on it. When it dried out, he burned it.

MONKEY MAN. I should've adopted you guys; then I'd have some rights. Visitation.

BITCH. And you call me insane.

MONKEY MAN. That's not insane, that's…. That's not insane.

BITCH. What were you thinking?

MONKEY MAN. What?

BITCH. When you were with…. When you were with other women.

MONKEY MAN. I was not with that many other women. I was with three.

BITCH. All at once?

MONKEY MAN. Three women in eight years. Not exactly Don Juan material.

BITCH. Model of restraint. So? What were you thinking?

MONKEY MAN. It was complicated.

BITCH. Right.

MONKEY MAN. I'm not even sure I could— Why do you want to know?

BITCH. Thought as long as you took the trouble to bring me to Dickville, you must want to talk about it.

MONKEY MAN. There's a lot I need you to understand.

BITCH. Mom gave me the names, dates, places. We just have no idea what you were thinking.

MONKEY MAN. There was an interviewer on a book tour. Tulsa. I didn't know they had bookstores. They had a radio station though, and she interviewed me and was…taken with my work. A lot of women are taken with it. The style, the themes, whatever. They seem to think I capture something about them—

BITCH. Right.

MONKEY MAN. They proposition me. They do. Lonely, untouched… *under*touched…. Glad-to read-a-serious-voice-writing-about-other-lonely-untouched—

BITCH. You are such a sleaze—

MONKEY MAN. It's serious literature. I win prizes.

(*A beat.*)

I always said no. Even before I was with your mother. They were too vulnerable. My writing brought out these…I don't know, spiritual expectations in them. I didn't feel sufficient. It was like—

BITCH. (*Indicating the smokestack.*) Like your spiritual schlong would have to be as big as that?

MONKEY MAN. You really are a poet.

BITCH. So why'd you suddenly say yes?

MONKEY MAN. I don't know.

BITCH. Yes, you do.

MONKEY MAN. It was a few years into the marriage. Things with your mother had calmed down, so to speak, in the sex department—on their way to what ultimately would be a "dead calm." It just made her uncomfortable. She'd never say why, she wouldn't discuss it…. We were both too polite, or terrified or— You really want to hear about this?

(*As she stares at him.*)

It got so she didn't want anything…unusual in our relations. There was less foreplay, less—

BITCH. Oral sex?

MONKEY MAN. Among other things.

BITCH. So the woman in Tulsa blew you?

MONKEY MAN. Among other things. Do we really have to—?

BITCH. And what was Mom? Missionary? Lights out?

MONKEY MAN. Aren't you supposed to be saying, "too much information" about now?

BITCH. Knowledge is power.

MONKEY MAN. I think the real reason—what I was "thinking" as you say—was that I was becoming very afraid your mother would be the last woman I'd ever make love to. So I slept with this other woman—once, to take the pressure off. It wasn't because I loved your mother any less.

(*As* BITCH *laughs at him.*)

I loved her. I did.

BITCH. So you slept with two more women?

MONKEY MAN. Much later. You'd been doing all that therapy, bouncing off walls at five-hundred-dollar-a-day clinics, and she was utterly distracted by what was going on—

BITCH. So you thought you'd help out by looking up an old girlfriend—

MONKEY MAN. To *talk*. Just to talk. And she was an old colleague, not a girlfriend. We never actually dated.

(*Going on, with a sigh.*)

I was in L.A. for a conference. I looked her up. That was all. I just looked her up and—

BITCH. Did her.

MONKEY MAN. We were at funny places in our lives.

BITCH. You didn't leave her bedroom for a week. Mom was very grateful for the details, by the way.

MONKEY MAN. That wasn't my idea. She demanded specifics. She said she couldn't "heal" otherwise, or some shit.

BITCH. God, you're gullible.

MONKEY MAN. It's my special brand of charm, okay?

BITCH. And the last one?

MONKEY MAN. That was to get out of the marriage. I didn't know it then, but…. It was so I could tell her and…make her ask for a divorce.

BITCH. Why?

MONKEY MAN. 'Cause I couldn't ask for one. I felt too guilty, too *debilitated*—

BITCH. Too chickenshit.

(*After a beat.*)
Receptionist. Nice going.
MONKEY MAN. They call them associates at the publishing house. She had a variety of duties.
BITCH. Did you love her?
MONKEY MAN. 'Course not.
BITCH. Did you even like her?
MONKEY MAN. Not much.
BITCH. If you and Mom were having problems, why didn't you talk about it?
MONKEY MAN. I don't know. We told ourselves we weren't.
BITCH. You ever fight?
MONKEY MAN. No.
BITCH. Not even once? Didn't you want your marriage to get better?
MONKEY MAN. I didn't think it could. I didn't think…it deserved to.
BITCH. I got better. You never gave up on me.
MONKEY MAN. You're a writer. You always had that, no matter how crazy you got. It made me believe in you.
BITCH. And Mom?
MONKEY MAN. I remember when I told her about my affairs. I had the irrational idea that somehow she could hear about them and understand that I wasn't in love with these women. I was just so happy that two people could be in bed enjoying themselves, and there didn't have to be these enormous steamer trunks of baggage. That's what I wanted for us. I wanted that to be us. But I could never get it, because—
BITCH. She was abused.
MONKEY MAN. Yes. When she was little, by a relative—she *thinks*.
BITCH. Just like I was, by—
MONKEY MAN. (*With sudden violence.*) I *know!!* You think I don't know!? Jesus Christ, it's all I *hear!* You, your mom—for all I know, *her* mom. Maybe it goes back ten generations; what the hell's the *difference?!!* Your mother had a responsibility at *some point* to grow the fuck up and learn how to be a wife to me! I have a life, too—and I will not let *any*one dictate that I get no sex, no real intimacy with a partner 'til the day I fucking die! So I had affairs. I didn't have a million of 'em, but I had my share, and I am grateful for every one! Women deserve to be cheated on, 'cause they cheat men every day—every *fucking day!!*
(*After a silence.*)
I didn't mean that.
BITCH. Yes, you did.

MONKEY MAN. Bottom line is, I couldn't handle it. Life as a never-ending tragedy controlled by some...*event*...that occurred years before I ever showed up. I don't know who could face that. I couldn't; I cheated.

BITCH. You were a coward.

MONKEY MAN. I was *not* a coward, I was—

(*Stopping, under her intense gaze.*)

I was—

(*Hesitating again.*)

No one could expect me to...

(*Another beat, as she stares at him.*)

I was a coward.

BITCH. That's why you're divorced.

MONKEY MAN. Yes.

BITCH. That's why Mom doesn't ever want to speak to you.

MONKEY MAN. Yes.

BITCH. That's why this is your last trip with me. Ever.

(*He looks at her. She stares steadily back at him.*)

We're going back now. My way.

(*Holding out her hand.*)

Give me the keys.

(*Lights shift.*)

KALISPELL

The car. BITCH *drives.* MONKEY MAN *listens to her recite. He smiles from time to time.*

BITCH.   "Out of all the faces, I have picked your
                    Face. But why? It's just like the others.
                    Nice enough; nothing special. It could mean
                    A good person.

                    Or not.

                    Out of all the hearts, I have picked yours.
                    Sounds all right, when I lie on it.
                    How many lies are in it?

                    Out of all the hands, your hands.
                    Quiet. They haven't hurt me yet.

                    Your voice is soft. I know commands
                    Are coming, but for now...

I am so grateful for your face.
Without it, where would I know to look?
I can't even find the seam
Where it is attached to my face."

MONKEY MAN. That's amazing. When'd you write that?

BITCH. This winter.

MONKEY MAN. Terrific. What's it called again?

BITCH. "Face"?

MONKEY MAN. Right. Sorry. It should be published. It should be in a literary journal.

BITCH. It will. I mean, I've had a couple offers. I have to decide.

MONKEY MAN. Wow. You know how old I was before I got a poem published? You should only send to one magazine at a time, though.

BITCH. I know that now, thank you.

MONKEY MAN. 'Course. Sorry. Hey, it's beautiful up here. You chose a great road.

BITCH. It's the only one into the park.

MONKEY MAN. Kalispell was nice, wasn't it? Pretty town—way up in the mountains. They had a Scrimpy-Lodge; we could've stayed.

BITCH. Gotta keep moving.

MONKEY MAN. Or, I mean, we could always stay someplace better.

BITCH. Why switch now?

MONKEY MAN. Glacier National Park. Can't believe it. My folks took me here, you know.

BITCH. You said.

MONKEY MAN. I'm surprised you want to see it.

BITCH. It's my favorite park.

MONKEY MAN. How come?

BITCH. 'Cause it's disappearing. All the glaciers are melting. Glaciers are the whole reason they made a park. Used to be like a hundred and fifty of 'em; now there's only a few tiny ones left. Exhibit A for global warming.

MONKEY MAN. So that's why we're here? 'Cause you care about global warming?

BITCH. I don't give a rusty shit about global warming. I wish it'd warm up faster. I just like visual proof that the world really is going to hell.

MONKEY MAN. Anyway, I think it's nice you're taking me through such pretty country. There's a big lodge in the park, you know. Giant old WPA thing. Enormous inside—'course I was little then. Dark, all these giant timbers. And they have these animals, these taxidermized wild animals in glass cases you can walk all the way around. There was a Rocky Mountain goat and a Bighorn and…a buffalo? No, that would have been too big—

BITCH. I'm pregnant.

(*A silence. He looks at her. She looks straight ahead.*)

MONKEY MAN. How?

BITCH. The usual way.

MONKEY MAN. Does your mother know?

BITCH. No.

MONKEY MAN. When are you going to tell her?

(*After a beat.*)

Who…I mean, who…with…. Who's—?

BITCH. The father? I don't know.

MONKEY MAN. Of course you know.

BITCH. No. I don't.

(*A beat.*)

I was a virgin 'til a little while ago. I mean, I had a boyfriend. We messed around and everything like everybody else. We did a lot of stuff, mostly just to get him off—

MONKEY MAN. You don't have to get specific.

BITCH. Yes, I do. Anyhow, as virgins go, I was getting more "technical" all the time. Don't know why I was keeping it. Wasn't waiting to be in love or anything. But, given my special history, I guess I didn't…feel comfortable yet.

MONKEY MAN. No reason to rush. It's different for everyone.

BITCH. My boyfriend was totally frustrated. He wouldn't admit it, though. He was being sensitive, you know? I was getting pretty good at oral, but—

MONKEY MAN. Please—

BITCH. *But* it was obvious I was going to lose him if I didn't put out pretty soon, so—

MONKEY MAN. So he's the father?

BITCH. *Do I interrupt you?!!*

(*A beat.*)

I didn't know how I was going to be the first time. Since I was so "special." Since Dad had made me so special. I was afraid I'd get all insane and panicky with my boyfriend. So I asked a friend of his instead.

MONKEY MAN. You *what?*

BITCH. Kid we both knew, sort of. In our class, anyway. I told him I wanted to lose it: one-time thing, no biggie. I don't know why I picked him; I didn't like him. Maybe that's why. Anyhow, he said come on over, his folks were out of town. We could drink, smoke, loosen me up a little. Zip-zap, shouldn't take long.

MONKEY MAN. Maybe you shouldn't tell me all the—

BITCH. *And* he was right. It didn't. Blood on the towel—he *did* put down a towel. Blood all over my legs. I was so drunk and stoned, I barely remember it.

MONKEY MAN. First times are always—

BITCH. What I do remember is *his* friend.

MONKEY MAN. What?

BITCH. We were in the middle of doing it the second time. He insisted on a second time—even though I hurt, and there was blood all over—because, he said, he was always better the second time. I didn't want to, but he just rolled on top of me and was like, shut the fuck up, I'd get used to it. And he was bigger than me, and I couldn't push him off. So anyhow, in the middle of us doing it again, his friend came in the room.

MONKEY MAN. His friend? How do you mean—by accident?

BITCH. No, he called him up when I was in the bathroom. Said he should come over and "share the booty"—some pirate expression like that. They laughed about it while they took turns holding me down so each one of them could fuck me. The more I fought, the more they laughed. Oh, and his friend teased him for using a condom, so they both went bareback.

MONKEY MAN. Jesus. When was this? Who were they?

BITCH. My business.

MONKEY MAN. No, it's not! It's not just your— Did you tell your mom? The police?

BITCH. No.

MONKEY MAN. You should have gone directly to the police. Why didn't you?

BITCH. I don't know.

MONKEY MAN. You don't *know?*

BITCH. No, I don't! It was *my business!*

(*After a beat.*)

I just felt like going home. And that's what I did, after they threw me in the shower, and put my clothes back on, and told me to come back any time. I thought Mom'd be home, but she was out. I called up my boyfriend, and he came over. I was bawling and freaking out—total mess. He held me and said how he was going to kill those guys and everything, and I was saying don't be an idiot. And he was like, why would you do that? And I was like, it's my fucking business. And he said, no it's not—just like you—and we got into this real bad fight; we were like, yelling at each other, and he...this was really weird, I have no idea how this part happened, but he...he hit me.

MONKEY MAN. He *what—*?

BITCH. Just once. Really hard, though. Right in my face. Drew blood. I nearly blacked out. Then he got all scared and sorry and said he couldn't believe I let those guys rape me, when he would've been gentle if I'd only come to him. And I started screaming that I didn't "let" them, that they raped me—and he said he was sorry again, and by now he was holding me again and we were kind of on the couch and just lying there without talking for a long time, but he was shivering and freaking out like, you know, really bad but silently and…I don't know why, but I undid his pants and took him out…and he kind of stopped shivering, and…and we did it too.

MONKEY MAN. Oh, God. Honey—

BITCH. *DON'T CALL ME THAT!!* He didn't rape me; I let him. I don't know why. He was so fucking pitiful. Mom could've come home anytime.

(*After a long beat.*)

So. You see? I really don't know who the father is.

(*Another beat.*)

Why would it matter?

MONKEY MAN. (*Staring at her.*) Did you ever go to the police?

(*A beat.*)

What…what are you going to do about it?

BITCH. Get an abortion.

MONKEY MAN. Oh. Well. Under the circumstances, I guess that's… understandable.

BITCH. Glad you feel that way.

MONKEY MAN. Well—

BITCH. 'Cause you're going to help.

(*He stares at her. Lights shift as they get out of the "car." It disappears. They move into a dark and cavernous interior. Facing front, they walk in place. Projected behind is an image too small and dim to make out. It slowly grows as they walk. They seem to stare at it as they go.*)

MONKEY MAN. Fantastic drive. Going-to-the-Sun Road. Wonder why they named it that?

BITCH. Probably has something to do with going, and the sun?

MONKEY MAN. Thanks for driving slow. I could really see things.

BITCH. The glaciers are totally melting, aren't they?

MONKEY MAN. You were right; it's going to be beachfront property in Hell. Man, this lodge is *bigger* than I remember it.

(*Pointing ahead.*)

And look—it's still here. Isn't that great?

BITCH. If you say so.

MONKEY MAN. This place is so huge. Elemental. Smells like a forest that's been, I don't know…dead for a thousand years. You have to tell your mother.

BITCH. I'll never tell her. And you know why.

MONKEY MAN. Even she will understand that in some cases—

BITCH. *No.* She never will. You know that.

MONKEY MAN. Do they even have abortion in Montana?

BITCH. Yes.

(The projection is closer now. It's a Rocky Mountain goat—long, white shaggy hair, white goatee, short black horns—in a free-standing glass case. They stop and stare into the audience as though looking at the goat.)

MONKEY MAN. What do you need from me?

BITCH. Help.

MONKEY MAN. What do you mean? You mean like, money or—?

BITCH. *Help.* "H-E-L-P." I can spell it; you try.

(After a beat.)

I need someone to be there. I need…. What animal is this?

MONKEY MAN. Rocky Mountain goat.

BITCH. It's…white.

MONKEY MAN. Yeah.

BITCH. Let's look at the other one.

(They start walking, still facing the audience. The Rocky Mountain goat projection recedes.)

MONKEY MAN. Have you thought about having it?

BITCH. Right.

MONKEY MAN. I'm serious. You could put it up for adoption, or—

BITCH. I'm not having it.

(After a beat.)

Mom's not going to find out. Ever. That's the whole point.

(By now the projection of the Rocky Mountain goat has disappeared, only to be replaced by the slowly-growing projection of a Bighorn sheep in a similar glass case. They keep walking.)

MONKEY MAN. Things like this have a way of getting known.

BITCH. Are you going to tell her?

MONKEY MAN. Of course not.

BITCH. 'Cause if you ever did…

(Stopping.)

When I was thirteen, know what I did? I went downstairs in the middle of the night. I got a kitchen knife, a big one. Then I sneaked back up and stood outside your bedroom door. I was going to stab you. It's not like you did anything or anything, but I was going to kill you all the same. I was really crazy back then. Anyway, I didn't have the nerve. So I just went back to bed and cried. After a long time Mom came in, and I told her what I did.

MONKEY MAN. I know.

BITCH. You do?

MONKEY MAN. When she came back to bed, she told me.

BITCH. She said she wouldn't. What did you do?

MONKEY MAN. Nothing. We just lay there in the dark for awhile. Finally I asked if we could switch sides.

(*She smiles, despite herself. He smiles. She laughs softly for a moment. He joins in. Their laughter fades and they start walking again.*)

BITCH. There's a Planned Parenthood in Great Falls. We're going there tomorrow.

MONKEY MAN. Shouldn't we think about this more?

BITCH. No.

MONKEY MAN. I won't lie for you.

BITCH. You don't have to. You're my stepdad. We were out driving and thought we'd drop in for an abortion.

MONKEY MAN. You can't do this sort of thing frivolously.

BITCH. The adverb doesn't matter, Monkey Man. I can do this thing, and I'm going to.

(*A long beat as they finally stop before the now full-sized projection of the Bighorn sheep. Its enormous horns curl around its head. If it's feasible,* BITCH *and* MONKEY MAN *now turn left and "circle" the glass case. The image of the sheep in the projection revolves three hundred-sixty degrees as they go.*)

MONKEY MAN. What do I do? Wait in the car, or—?

BITCH. You come in with me. You say you're my stepdad, so I don't look so pitiful. So they know what kind of person's driving me home. *Geez!*

MONKEY MAN. What if they think I'm the...? You know, the...?

(*As she gives him a disgusted look.*)

They *could.*

BITCH. Like I'd have sex with my stepdad? Yuck!

MONKEY MAN. I'm just saying they could, that's all. Might make things harder for you. More to explain, all sorts of...suspicions.

BITCH. They're not going to suspect anything. People like us come in there all the time. Stop trying to weasel; you're so obvious. It'll be over before you know it.

MONKEY MAN. No. No. I can't do it. I can't walk in there with you. I can't even wait in the car. It's too...too—

BITCH. Too what?

MONKEY MAN. It's not that you don't have the right. You do. But…I'll keep it secret from your mother, but beyond that—

BITCH. Do this for me, and I won't cut you out of my life.

MONKEY MAN. (*Stopping, staring at her a long moment.*) Cut me out of your life.

(*He starts walking again. She hesitates, then catches up with him quickly.*)

BITCH. I can do it without you.

MONKEY MAN. Yeah, and you can also hitchhike to Great Falls.

BITCH. I will. I'm not afraid to. I just thought you might want to support me, you know?

MONKEY MAN. Not this way—okay?! Not this way. I'm not made to— It's not something I can do. You have no right to ask me. I didn't molest you, I didn't rape you, I didn't get you pregnant—

BITCH. I know.

MONKEY MAN. I wronged your mother, not you. There comes a time when I stop paying, you know? There just simply comes a time.

(*They finish the circle, stand staring at the projection of the Bighorn sheep.*)

Bighorn Sheep. God. I was such a little geek back then. There's a snapshot of me sitting right outside this lodge, feeding a chipmunk. I'm in these high-water pants, doofy sweatshirt. I'm wearing a tam-o-shanter my mom *knitted* for me. It was green, brown and yellow. Still get shivers whenever I see that picture. Hope it's one of the ones your brother cut up. Anyhow, there's no denying it—I was a total dork. Sometimes I wish I'd been executed right then. Bolt of lightning: world a better place. I wasn't though, was I?

BITCH. No.

MONKEY MAN. (*After a beat.*) Remember when I first met you and your brother? Your mother was so nervous. Ice cream parlor. You guys ordered banana splits and made the biggest mess I'd ever…. Your mom thought she'd never see me again.

BITCH. It was fun.

MONKEY MAN. Yeah. It was.

(*After a beat.*)

How far is it to Great Falls?

(*Lights shift.*)

GREAT FALLS

Sidewalk of a mini-mall, Great Falls, Montana. Midday. BITCH *stands smoking.* MONKEY MAN *has a bagful of donuts. He's eating one.*

MONKEY MAN. Donut?

BITCH. I'm not eating today. I'm having a procedure.

MONKEY MAN. Keep your strength up.

BITCH. You want me to choke on my own vomit?

MONKEY MAN. They don't put you all the way under. Do they?

BITCH. You are so dumb.

MONKEY MAN. I'm nervous. I eat when I'm nervous. I eat junk when I'm nervous.

BITCH. You eat junk all the time. It's a miracle you're alive.

MONKEY MAN. Thanks for caring.

BITCH. I didn't say it was a good miracle.

MONKEY MAN. Look at this place. Mini-mall in Great Falls, Montana: the sum of ten thousand years of Western Civilization. If there were any justice, fetuses would abort us.

BITCH. Will you shut up? You're here to help, remember? Let's go, we're going to be late.

MONKEY MAN. No rush. It's only a few blocks.

BITCH. I have an appointment. I want to be on time. There's probably stuff to fill out.

MONKEY MAN. They always keep you waiting anyway.

BITCH. I want to *go*. What's your *problem?*

MONKEY MAN. I just don't know why you want to hurry. There's lots to think about here.

BITCH. No. No. We're not reopening this.

MONKEY MAN. Why not? We've only been discussing it for a day.

BITCH. *We* are not making this decision. I've thought about it for almost three weeks, and I know what I'm going to do. Now, let's get in the car and—

(As she pulls the car keys from her pocket, he immediately snatches them away.)
GIVE ME THOSE!!

MONKEY MAN. I'll drive.

BITCH. You are not driving! *Give 'em!*

MONKEY MAN. I can drive a couple blocks.

BITCH. You won't take me there. You'll drive me to fucking Mongolia! I know how you operate.

MONKEY MAN. I will not.

BITCH. You'll kidnap me! You'll kidnap me, and take me someplace and try to brainwash me into having it.

MONKEY MAN. I do think we should talk about it more—

BITCH. *NO!!* I'm not going to be fucking kidnapped, you understand?! You're acting like I'm in a *cult!!*

MONKEY MAN. Let's get in the car—

BITCH. (*Knocking his donuts out of his hand.*) *STOP TRYING TO KIDNAP ME!!!*

> (*Suddenly from behind them we hear the heart-sinking broop of a lightly-tapped police siren. They freeze, then slowly look back. Lights shift as* BITCH *and* MONKEY MAN *move to opposite sides of the stage. A red flashing police light bounces over them as each talks to a Montana State Trooper—both of whom we do not see, of course. In these separate but simultaneous parking lot interrogations* BITCH *and* MONKEY MAN *can't hear each other. They speak as swiftly and convincingly as possible. The effect should be fast-paced and fragmentary. Clearly we're not hearing the entire conversations.*)

MONKEY MAN. I'm sorry, Officer. She lost her temper. She's just a teen-ager—

> (*Answering the Trooper's question.*)

What? Oh, almost eighteen—in fact, what day is it?

BITCH. I didn't mean kidnapping. Was I really saying kidnapping?

MONKEY MAN. She's my stepdaughter. We're traveling to the West Coast. No, just to…see it.

BITCH. We're going to Oregon. He's even letting me drive.

MONKEY MAN. I'm not kidnapping anybody. I know we have different last names. I told you, I'm her stepfather.

BITCH. He's lived with us since I was like, eight.

MONKEY MAN. We were having a little argument, that's all. Dispute about the itinerary. She wants to see Old Faithful, and I—

> (*Again, answering a question.*)

No, go ahead—call in. Run my name, my plate. It's not like I'm lying. No, I don't work for a living. I'm a writer.

BITCH. I'm a writer. I'm still in school, but I'm—

> (*Answering a question.*)

My mom? She's in Omaha. Probably at work. You want that number?

MONKEY MAN. *I* don't know if she has tattoos. Ask her.

BITCH. We always fight. The whole family. We fight like crazy. We love it.

MONKEY MAN. I'm really sorry if we alarmed anyone. She gets over-dramatic.

(Responding to an unheard comment.)

Yes, I guess…I do too.

BITCH. What are we doing in Great Falls? We're just traveling around. You know, looking at stuff and…stuff.

MONKEY MAN. Here in Great Falls? Oh, um…we just came to, uh…. We came to—

BITCH. See the Falls.

MONKEY MAN. We want to see the Falls. Mostly that's what we want to do. Just see the— You know, the Falls. And leave. Peacefully, quietly. Having …seen the Falls.

BITCH. We hear it's…great?

(A long beat. They turn and stare at each other. What has the other one said? Lights shift and they move to a pair of chairs in a waiting room—the reception area of Planned Parenthood. BITCH fills out a form on a clipboard that she balances on her knee. MONKEY MAN pages irritably through a local brochure.)

BITCH. You still mad?

(Silence.)

We should've told the truth right away, I guess. Wouldn't have wasted an hour at the police station.

(Silence.)

This clinic is nice though, isn't it? Sort of…I don't know, cheery.

(Silence.)

Wasn't it funny we both said we were here to see the Falls?

(Silence.)

I thought it was funny. Like ESP and stuff.

(Silence.)

Glad we talked 'em out of calling Mom. Lucky I turned eighteen, eh? Kinda weird though, getting arrested on my birthday.

MONKEY MAN. Can we talk about something else?

BITCH. What do you want to talk about?

(Silence.)

Thanks for paying for this, by the way. I'll pay you back when—

MONKEY MAN. No. No need.

BITCH. I mean it. You don't have to—

(Stopping as she notices his glare.)

Anyway, thanks.

(After a beat.)

What're you reading? Is it about Great Falls? Facts and stuff?

MONKEY MAN. Yeah.

BITCH. Read 'em to me.

(*As he looks at her.*)

I mean, please?

MONKEY MAN. (*Reading.*) "Great Falls is the first known community in Montana to elect an African-American."

BITCH. Wow. Glad they got past that one.

(*Silence.*)

Anything else?

MONKEY MAN. It's called "The Cataract City." It's home to the World's Shortest River.

BITCH. This is really an amazing part of the country.

MONKEY MAN. It certainly is.

BITCH. (*After a beat.*) It was going to be your grandkid, wasn't it? Or like, step-grandkid anyway. Is that why you're sad?

MONKEY MAN. I don't know why I'm sad.

BITCH. (*After a beat.*) Want to hear a haiku?

MONKEY MAN. Not right now.

BITCH. I hope they can do it all today. The doctor says they might.

(*After a beat.*)

Oh, and she knows your novels—isn't that great?

MONKEY MAN. I'm going to sit in the car.

BITCH. Please don't. Please? I don't want to sit here alone. I'm sorry if I—

MONKEY MAN. This is just too—

BITCH. Don't think about it. Read to me or something, okay? Just…read another fact.

(*Quietly,* MONKEY MAN *starts to cry. His crying builds until it's a steady sobbing.*)

It's okay. It really is okay. Honest. It is. Please stop. Can you stop?

(*Reaching for the magazine.*)

Come on, I'll read you a fact. There must be one that—

MONKEY MAN. *No!*

BITCH. (*Glancing at reception as he keeps crying.*)

They're looking over here.

(*Waving in the direction of the reception desk.*)

He's fine. He just loves me a lot, that's all.

(*Quietly, as he cries.*)
I hope there aren't any complications.
(*Lights shift.*)

MILES CITY

Another Scrimpy-Lodge motel room. BITCH *lies in shirt and shorts on one of the beds. She's got a serious fever. Sound of water running.* MONKEY MAN *calls from the bathroom.*

MONKEY MAN. (*From off, alarmed.*) I'll be right there! You okay?!

BITCH. Yeah...

MONKEY MAN. (*Entering with a wet washrag filled with ice.*) This should help. It's ice. It's cold.

(*Applying it to her forehead, wiping her face, etc.*)
There. That better? That feel better?

BITCH. Yeah...

MONKEY MAN. I don't understand it. You said you were feeling better. I wouldn't have checked in first if—

(*As she groans with pain.*)
What's going *on!?* You've been fine. You rested two whole days in Great Falls. Why are you getting sick now? We should go to a clinic.

BITCH. *No!* Don't want to...

MONKEY MAN. Why *not?!* You've been getting worse all day.

BITCH. I'm not sick—!

MONKEY MAN. Of course you're sick. You're burning up.

BITCH. I'm gonna get better—!

MONKEY MAN. How do you feel down there? You know, down...down there.

BITCH. Hurts.

MONKEY MAN. (*As he continues to apply the ice pack.*) I don't understand. It's Planned Parenthood. They know how to—they know what they're *doing.* We have to get you to a doctor—

BITCH. *No!* He's gonna get me. I can't go see a doctor—that's where he'll *look!*

MONKEY MAN. Who? That's where who'll look?

BITCH. My kid! My *kid!*

MONKEY MAN. Your what? Honey, you don't have a— Remember? We were in Great Falls. You don't have a—

BITCH. His *ghost!*

MONKEY MAN. What are you talking about?

BITCH. His ghost. His ghost is *after me!!*

(*She suddenly flails away from him and rolls halfway off the bed, as though trying to escape. He grabs her and holds her still.*)

MONKEY MAN. No, it's not! Honey, no—!!

BITCH. (*Suddenly convulsing with pain.*) Oh God, it *HURTS!!*

MONKEY MAN. It's all right. It's going to be all right. We're going to the doctor—

BITCH. Don't touch me! *Let go of me! You're raping me!!*

MONKEY MAN. (*Trying to get his arms under her so he can lift her up.*) I'm not raping you.

BITCH. (*Struggling weakly.*) You raped my Mom, and you're raping me!

MONKEY MAN. I didn't rape anybody.

BITCH. You rape me every day!

MONKEY MAN. (*Finally in control of her.*) You don't know what you're saying.

(*Lifting her in his arms.*)

We're going to the doctor.

BITCH. He'll be there. My boy'll be there. Ghost boy.

MONKEY MAN. No, he won't.

BITCH. (*Almost a whisper.*) Ghost…boy…

(*She faints.*)

MONKEY MAN. Oh, God. Oh, God. Oh, God. Oh, God. Oh, God…

(*He hurriedly carries her out to the car. Lights shift in the room. Same room, a day later. BITCH is in the bed, sleeping. She looks much better, but weak. MONKEY MAN sits in a chair, staring at her. Her eyes open.*)

BITCH. Have I been sleeping?

MONKEY MAN. Yes, dear.

BITCH. How long?

MONKEY MAN. Almost a day.

BITCH. (*Closing her eyes, smiling.*) I had chlamydia.

MONKEY MAN. Yes, honey—chlamydia. No one knew. It's nobody's fault.

BITCH. (*Detached, dreamily.*) I had a complication.

MONKEY MAN. It doesn't matter. You're going to be fine.

BITCH. I can't even spell it.

MONKEY MAN. The point is, they found it. One of those sick little bastards infected you. But you're getting well now. You don't have it anymore.

BITCH. (*Eyes still closed.*) No symptoms.

MONKEY MAN. That's right. That's why we didn't know.

BITCH. Little bugs got inside. When they opened my cervix.

MONKEY MAN. No one knew. It happens this way sometimes. You'll be fine now. You'll be just like new. It's a big town—Miles City. They had a good clinic.

BITCH. Are we in a Scrimpy-Lodge?

MONKEY MAN. Yes.

BITCH. Good.

(*To herself, a little sing-song.*)

Com-pli-CA-tion…

MONKEY MAN. Go back to sleep, sweetie.

BITCH. (*Eyes still closed, her dreamy smile broadening.*) I like being your sweetie.

MONKEY MAN. I like it, too.

BITCH. I like it, too.

(*She sleeps.*)

MONKEY MAN. So do I.

(*He stares at her. Lights shift. Same room, the next afternoon. MONKEY MAN sits in a chair, in the same clothes he wore a day before. BITCH is in the bathroom. We hear water rushing.*)

BITCH. (*Off.*) I'm just about ready. Are you ready?

MONKEY MAN. Yeah.

BITCH. (*Off.*) You can drive. I'm way too tired.

(*Off, after a beat.*)

Those antibiotics really work, don't they? Wish they could make a patch out of it or something. No one would ever get sick.

(*Off, after a beat.*)

What do you think? Is that a plan or what?

(*Entering, dressed for the road.*)

You didn't even change clothes.

MONKEY MAN. (*Absently, noticing.*) Oh…yeah. I'll be okay.

BITCH. If you say. We can stay another night, if you want. It's already afternoon. Mom doesn't need to see me that soon.

MONKEY MAN. No, no…I want to get on the road.

BITCH. (*Getting her shoes on.*) Scrimpy-Lodge is always going to make me think of you. Oh—by the way, thanks for saving my life.

MONKEY MAN. That's okay. I didn't—

BITCH. Should've said that before, I guess.

MONKEY MAN. It's fine. Glad I could…glad I could help.

(*He watches as she puts her toiletries into one of her bags and rearranges her things.*)

BITCH. Wonder which one of 'em had chlamydia. Probably all of 'em. Suppose I'll tell 'em when I get back. Maybe.

MONKEY MAN. Who's Ghost boy?

BITCH. What?

MONKEY MAN. Ghost boy. You kept talking about some Ghost boy when you were...when you had your fever.

BITCH. Yeah, I was like, delirious.

MONKEY MAN. So who was he?

(After a beat.)

Sounded like he was...

BITCH. What? I was hallucinating. I said a ton of shit.

MONKEY MAN. Yes, but this sounded like...you know.

BITCH. I know what?

MONKEY MAN. The kid you would've had.

BITCH. *(Shrugging.)* What's it matter? We should go.

MONKEY MAN. It's just that...usually when someone talks about an unborn...I mean, if no one knows its sex, then usually.... People tend to say "it." Don't they? I mean...But you said "he."

BITCH. I have no idea what you're talking about. Can we get going please?

MONKEY MAN. You said he would haunt you. You said he.

(A silence. As she shrugs.)

Did you know?

(After a beat.)

Is that possible?

BITCH. Are you even packed?

MONKEY MAN. How'd you know it was a boy? They couldn't do a sonogram that early.

BITCH. Twenty-first Century, Monkey Man. Age of information.

MONKEY MAN. What does that mean? Honey—

BITCH. *Bitch.*

MONKEY MAN. What does that mean? Are there other ways? It's just that you seemed so scared of it.... The ghost, I mean.

BITCH. Why do you care what I'm scared of? My nightmares are my business. It's not like you ever cared.

MONKEY MAN. I cared. Your mother always—

BITCH. Sat up with me—right. That's 'cause she's my *real mom*. Can we get *going?!*

MONKEY MAN. You knew what its gender was. You knew. How—?

BITCH. For a thousand dollars you can find out a lot of stuff.

MONKEY MAN. A thousand? Where'd you get so much—?

BITCH. Have you ever seen me spend my own money? Not everybody's like you. Some people save.

MONKEY MAN. What were you saving for?

BITCH. I don't know. In case I needed to disappear—from Dad or something. Felt good knowing I had it.

MONKEY MAN. You saved a thousand dollars?

BITCH. More than that.

MONKEY MAN. So…somehow you found out. When?

BITCH. Seven weeks. It's like a blood test. They analyze all this crap and stuff. Takes a couple days. I went to a friend's doctor, so Mom wouldn't know.

MONKEY MAN. Why would you spend all that? If you were just going to—?

BITCH. I wasn't sure what I was going to do, okay? I wanted to know first. I just…. It was important to know.

MONKEY MAN. It was a boy.

BITCH. It was a fetus.

MONKEY MAN. Male. Would you have had it, if it'd been a girl?

BITCH. Can we go now?

MONKEY MAN. I want to know.

BITCH. Why?

MONKEY MAN. I don't know. I mean…. It's important.

BITCH. No, it isn't.

MONKEY MAN. Of course it is.

(*After a beat.*)

I helped you do this. If it was just because it was the wrong gender—

BITCH. It's not your *business!*

MONKEY MAN. You keep *saying* that. Like it means something. Like I have no rights. I have rights. We've shared our lives. We've been each other's business for a long time. No one is absolutely alone. No one! I have business in your life—!

BITCH. *So does everybody!* That's what my boyfriend thought. That's what his friend thought. So did his friend's friend. So did Dad. I was all their business —every part of me. Dad especially. I was his business before I even knew what that meant. I couldn't remember it then, but I did later—way too late, in treatment. He used to just stand there in my bedroom door, in his pajamas. He wouldn't move at first. He'd just take it out and let it bob around like some big, red-nosed clown. He didn't say a word. He didn't have to. He was tucking me in—

MONKEY MAN. Don't—

BITCH. Don't what?! I thought I was your business. You know how I felt? In treatment I mean, when I first remembered that? I felt safe. Just finally knowing what it was, knowing that was never going to happen again—that Dad was gone, and he'd moved far away, and I'd never have to see him again and I had a new dad who would never hurt me in a million years.

(*After a beat.*)

Sometimes I wish I could know what I felt when I was little, though. Do little kids feel anything? What do you think? Maybe not. Maybe it's like fishing or something. Remember when you took me fishing? I was big, but I wouldn't bait my own hook. You got mad and said the worm doesn't feel a thing—and the fish doesn't either. I was a teenager, and you told me that.

MONKEY MAN. Please—

BITCH. I knew you were lying, but did you? What do you think Mom felt when you told her the stuff you did? Think she felt anything?

(*After a beat.*)

When you were my stepdad and you were like so good for Mom for so long, I almost used to think boys were possible. You know, possible human beings? But they're not, are they? They're really not.

MONKEY MAN. So you killed him?

BITCH. It. I killed it.

MONKEY MAN. (*After a silence.*) Can we go now?

(*Lights shift.*)

FREMONT

The side of the road. Early morning. MONKEY MAN *stands under a sign that says, "FREMONT pop. 25,198." He's alone, staring into the low sun. Unseen, a lone car passes.* BITCH *enters. She looks disheveled.*

MONKEY MAN. You woke up.

BITCH. How long have we been here?

MONKEY MAN. Not long.

BITCH. (*As another lone car passes.*) Where are we?

MONKEY MAN. Fremont.

BITCH. Almost home.

MONKEY MAN. Less than an hour.

BITCH. Why'd we stop?

MONKEY MAN. Stretching my legs.

BITCH. We drive all night?

MONKEY MAN. Mm-hm.

BITCH. We could've stopped.

MONKEY MAN. I thought about it. Saw a Scrimpy-Lodge in Sioux Falls. Almost gave in.

BITCH. Did you get tired?

MONKEY MAN. Yeah.

BITCH. I can drive from now on if you want. I feel good enough.

MONKEY MAN. Really?

BITCH. Yeah.

> (*As another lone car passes, he takes out his car keys. He hands them to her. She smiles.*)

MONKEY MAN. Happy Birthday, by the way. Forgot to say so at the time.

BITCH. Thanks. Don't feel any different.

MONKEY MAN. I do. Anyway, now you can vote, enlist—whatever.

BITCH. So this is my present then? That I get to drive home?

MONKEY MAN. Actually, you get to have the car.

BITCH. What?

> (*A beat.*)

Don't kid.

MONKEY MAN. I'm not. I'm giving it to you.

BITCH. (*Amazed, as a semi passes.*) Why?

MONKEY MAN. You need a car. That one you're driving—

BITCH. This is like, *brand new.*

MONKEY MAN. Well, you can make it old. I probably owe it to you, anyway.

BITCH. Why?

MONKEY MAN. I owe something to somebody. Why not this?

BITCH. (*As a car passes.*) This is stupid.

MONKEY MAN. You don't like it?

BITCH. You're not supposed to do this.

MONKEY MAN. Why not?

> (*After a beat.*)

Is it that when we get back, you and I might not see each other anymore? Is it?

BITCH. Yeah.

MONKEY MAN. That's okay. It's yours anyway.

BITCH. Mom won't let me.

MONKEY MAN. Take it down, talk to her. Tell her no strings; tell her I insist. I'll send you the title in a couple days. She'll go for that. But tell her it's yours, not hers. That's my only condition. Fair enough?

BITCH. (*Nodding, as another semi passes.*) All that stuff I said yesterday? I didn't mean—

MONKEY MAN. You were right. You're an adult. It's your business.

BITCH. Should we get going?

MONKEY MAN. You go on. I'll get home my own way.

BITCH. What? But—

MONKEY MAN. Go ahead. I've got a lot of thinking to do. This is a good spot to split up. I'm headed to Lincoln anyway.

BITCH. How will you get there?

MONKEY MAN. Walk, probably.

BITCH. It's like fifty miles.

MONKEY MAN. I've got something in my head. Maybe I'll start writing it. Keep whatever's in the car. It's not important.

BITCH. Dad—

MONKEY MAN. Stepdad. Ex. Monkey Man.

BITCH. This isn't fair.

MONKEY MAN. Why not? There's a map in there. You can find your way.

BITCH. You're not saying good-bye right.

MONKEY MAN. No one can. Not in this family, anyway.

(*As a car passes.*)

I wish I could do you good without doing you harm. I can't, that's all.

BITCH. I wrote you a haiku. Before I started like, hallucinating. Want to hear?

MONKEY MAN. No.

BITCH. It's really good.

MONKEY MAN. Save it.

(*Two semis pass. She looks at the car keys in her hand, then quickly at him. She turns and goes. He stares after her.*)

Thank you!

(*The car door slams. The engine starts. Sound of the car pulling out. He watches awhile, staring into the early morning sun. After a moment, he starts walking in the direction the car has gone. Lights fade.*)

End of Play

TONGUE, TIED

by M. Thomas Cooper

BIOGRAPHY

M. Thomas Cooper has studied literature and theatre at Oregon State University, the University of Oregon, San Francisco State University and Portland State University. He's had a number of short plays presented in conjunction with the Ashland 10-Minute Play Festival, Theatre in the Grove and Portland State University. In 2005, his play *Rising* was a finalist for the Northwest Playwright Award. His first novel, *42*, was published in June 2008 by Ooligan Press.

ACKNOWLEDGMENTS

Tongue, Tied premiered at the Humana Festival of New American Plays in March 2008. It was directed by Marc Masterson with the following cast:

TINA .... Emily Ackerman
TOM .... Stephen Plunkett

and the following production staff:

Scenic Designer .... Paul Owen
Costume Designer... Susan Neason
Lighting Designer.. Paul Werner
Sound Designer.. Benjamin Marcum
Properties Designer .... Mark Walston
Stage Manager.. Debra Anne Gasper
Assistant Stage Manager............................Captain Kate Murphy
Dramaturg.. Adrien-Alice Hansel
Assistant Dramaturg...Devon LaBelle

CAST OF CHARACTERS

TINA: A young woman with different colored socks on each hand.
Her socks are:

Jean-Claude	Left Hand
Latisha	Right Hand

TOM: A young man with different colored socks on each hand.
His socks are:

Mr. Chan	Left Hand
Sven	Right Hand

PLACE

A psychiatrist's waiting room.

Emily Ackerman and Stephen Plunkett
in *Tongue, Tied*

32nd Annual Humana Festival of New American Plays
Actors Theatre of Louisville, 2008
Photo by Harlan Taylor

TONGUE, TIED

A psychiatrist's waiting room. TINA *sits, hands hidden behind her, waiting. After a moment her right hand jumps.*

TINA. Stop it.

(*Again her right hand jumps.*)

I said, STOP IT.

(*Again her right hand jumps.*)

Latisha! Damn it! I said, STOP!

(TINA *begins struggling to keep her right hand behind her.*)

No…no…I said…. NO. No-no-no-no no-no. Latisha…!

(TINA's *right hand—*LATISHA*—bolts out and looks around.*)

LATISHA. Girl, how many times have I told you? You gotta stop keepin' us down like that. Look at this bright, crazy world you're trying to keep us from. Just look at it! Ain't it amazin'?!

TINA. Latisha, you know I'm not trying to keep you down. I'm attempting to live an ordinary and relatively content life.

LATISHA. Ain't we all, Sista. Ain't we all.

TINA. And having a black woman, who happens…

LATISHA. A proud, powerful woman of color. Thank you.

TINA. Exactly. A proud, powerful woman of color, who happens to be a sock, living on my hand…

LATISHA. Hey, you can't just blame me. I thought there was also some hot, little piece of French crème brûlée dancin' on your other mitten?

(*A slight pause as* TINA *fights with her left hand.*)

Ain't that right?

(*More struggling and then* TINA's *left hand—*JEAN-CLAUDE*—bursts forth.*)

JEAN-CLAUDE. *Bien sur! Parceque* we will revolt and lop your pretty bourgeois head off!

LATISHA. Jean-Claude, why do you always opt for overdramatic reactionism, when intelligent discourse can…

JEAN-CLAUDE. Latisha, you and your intelligent discourse can suck my left…

TINA. People, people, people…please! Can we not simply sit here and get along? Isn't that what I've been attempting? To coordinate vast and diametrically opposed perspectives since I acquired you two.

JEAN-CLAUDE. Acquired? More like forced encampment.

LATISHA. Yeah, acquired my big beautiful ass. If I remember right, some dude named Matt dumped your skinny rump and you were all…

JEAN-CLAUDE. …Oh, boo-hoo. Oh, boo-hoo. Look at me I'm all alone.

LATISHA. No one loves me. I wish I weren't soooo forlorn. Soooo despondent, dejected and alone.

TINA. I didn't say…

JEAN-CLAUDE. *Mon cher*, I'm afraid you did. And *voilà*, we is *ici*.

LATISHA. That's right. We're here and there's no way you can blame us.

TINA. Yes, well…. It might be different if you two didn't bicker and argue so much. I might be able to enjoy your company. However…

(TOM *enters. His hands are thrust deep in his jacket pockets.* TINA *hides her hands behind her.* TOM *sits. A long, long uncomfortable silence. A few twitches from both their respective backs and pockets.*)

Can you believe how hot it is?

TOM. I know. Why just the other day I could swear I saw a dog burst into flames. A dog didn't actually catch fire…

TINA. It seems like it's a million degrees out there. I don't really mean a million degrees…

TINA / TOM. That'd be crazy.

(TINA *and* TOM *struggle to keep their hands hidden. However, to no avail. Simultaneously* LATISHA, JEAN-CLAUDE, MR. CHAN, *and* SVEN *leap out.*)

SVEN. Tom, if I'm not mistaken, keeping any part of your consciousness purposefully in the dark, regardless how unwanted, is perhaps not the best coping mechanism.

MR. CHAN. I've no idea what he just said, but I will agree with it.

JEAN-CLAUDE. *Mademoiselle*, what'd I say about your bourgeois head?

LATISHA. Girl, are you not thinkin'? Keep this up I'll help the little Frenchie.

JEAN-CLAUDE. Little? Moi? I'll have you know my nickname is *Mont Blanc*.

SVEN. *Mont Blanc?*

LATISHA. And who is this cutie? Hello.

(TINA *and* TOM *shove their hands away.*)

TOM. My father was a magician in the Tibetan army during the occupation of New Zealand in 1972.

TINA. I'm an entertainer. My show is in Vegas.

TOM. Every night he would entertain the troops with magic and vaudeville.

TINA. I inherited my act from a crazy, one-legged aunt who raised me after my parents were devoured by bunnies on a Tuesday during a solar eclipse.

TOM. Then during the month the natives call Rama-rama a witch doctor cast a spell on his socks.

TINA. My one-legged aunt was very strict and hated fingerprints on anything, /thus I became conditioned to wear socks on my hands.

TOM. *(Overlapping at /)* The next morning Sven and Mr. Chan had arrived— invariably I have inherited the curse.

TINA / TOM. Honestly, I'm not crazy.

> *(Beat. Gradually* LATISHA, JEAN-CLAUDE, SVEN, *and* MR. CHAN *slip out of the shadows.)*

TINA. I'm…. I'm Tina.

TOM. Hello. I'm Tom.

JEAN-CLAUDE. And I'm a turtle dove.

MR. CHAN. Tom, if you want, I'll kick his ass. Now.

SVEN. Violence is the first choice of the ignorant.

MR. CHAN. And after French-frying Frenchie, I'll teach Sven about the philosophy of the fist.

JEAN-CLAUDE. From a hospital bed. Prepare to be Jean-Clobbered.

LATISHA. Is that Tom with one M, or two?

TOM. Just…just one.

LATISHA. Ain't goin'ta do. Don't you know the ladies like things double-sized?

TINA. Latisha! I thought we agreed you wouldn't…

TOM. Well, I…. I guess I'm willing to add a letter…

JEAN-CLAUDE. Ah, what a pansy, he'll change anything—even his name—at the drop of a hat.

TOM. No, but for the right woman I'm willing to…

JEAN-CLAUDE. Boo! Now you can change your panties, too. Hahahaha-haha!

MR. CHAN. Let me kick his ass. Let me beat that French smirk off his…

TOM. Mr. Chan, no. No. Remember the song? The song Mr. Chan…the song…. War?

MR. CHAN. War? *(Singing.)* What's it good for?

TOM. Absolutely nothing.

JEAN-CLAUDE. Singing, little pansy, I would make *pâté* out of you.

SVEN. Ignore him, Mr. Chan. His anger and frustration is from not having found love.

LATISHA. I knew there was a reason I liked you. *(Singing.)* War?! What's it good for?

MR. CHAN. *(Singing.)* Absolutely nothing!

LATISHA. Say it again!

MR. CHAN. *(Singing.)* Absolutely nothing!

LATISHA. Mr. Chan you rock. Come here, honey!

MR. CHAN. This bee is bringing the honey, baby! Bzzzzzz...

(LATISHA *and* MR. CHAN *begin kissing.*)

TINA. She's always like this.

TOM. Yeah, Mr. Chan has a tendency towards the ladies.

(Suddenly, JEAN-CLAUDE *and* SVEN *lunge at one another. They, too, begin kissing.)*

TINA. It...it must be the heat.

TOM. Uh, yeah...yeah...the...the heat. *(Beat.)* So...so, what brings you here to Doctor DeMarco's?

TINA. Um. The.... Uh.... Honestly? Latisha and Jean-Claude. What about you?

TOM. Me too. Mr. Chan and Sven.

(Beat as TINA *and* TOM *watch the puppets necking.)*

TINA. Love 'em, but.... *(Beat.)* Your...your father wasn't a magician with the Tibetan army, was he?

TOM. No. And you don't have a crazy, one-legged aunt?

TINA. No.

TOM. And your parents probably weren't eaten by bunnies during a solar eclipse? *(Beat.)* You know, I just want to be normal. I want to be able to get a coffee and not worry if Sven is going to complain about holding the scalding cup, let alone his snide comments about the caffeine, the sugar, and the creamer.

(SVEN *breaks from* JEAN-CLAUDE.)

SVEN. It's a vasoconstrictor. Don't blame me if you have a massive coronary some lonely night while watching *Desperate Housewives.*

(SVEN *and* JEAN-CLAUDE *resume kissing.*)

TINA. Yes, normal would be nice. Like picking flowers without Jean-Claude calling me *une pansy de la fleur du mal.* Or Latisha complaining about her allergies.

TOM. Hey, pollen is nothing to laugh...about. I've...I've allergies, too.

TINA. Confession: I bloat up like a balloon if I even see shellfish.

TOM. Mr. Chan too—regular Goodyear Blimp.

TINA. Jean-Claude's afraid of heights. You should hear him wail like a baby when I pick apples.

> (JEAN-CLAUDE *breaks from* SVEN. MR. CHAN *and* LATISHA *stop kissing to listen.*)

JEAN-CLAUDE. I do not wail—I weep. I weep from the realization that life is fleeting, and your picking an apple is the perfect representation of a life lived and lost. Regardless how perfect the fruit, Death shall eat it to the core and, ultimately, cast it aside for the ants and worms to finish. Life is a mime at a convention for the blind.

> (*Beat. All ponder.* MR. CHAN *and* LATISHA, JEAN-CLAUDE *and* SVEN *lunge back together, kissing more desperately. Beat.*)

TOM. It's gotta be the heat.

TINA. Do you think we should try and stop them?

TOM. This is the most time I've had to myself in months. Not…not to imply that you're not great company, but…

TINA. No, no. I know exactly what you mean.

> (*Beat.*)

TOM. It's weird, isn't it?

TINA. Incredibly. (*Beat.*) There's got to be a way to get rid of them, don't you think?

TOM. Have you tried doing giant loads of laundry?

TINA. My record is ten in one day—lost two pairs of jeans, three blouses, a sweatshirt, and a skirt I didn't even wash.

TOM. My golden retriever, Mr. Snickers, will chew a lead pipe before them. They blow out the matches, and refuse to go near moving machinery parts. They curl into the fetal position any time I get near scissors, or knives. I've even attempted to talk to a surgeon…

TINA. About…amputation?

> (*Beat as* LATISHA, MR. CHAN, SVEN, *and* JEAN-CLAUDE *hover threateningly.*)

TOM. Yes.

TINA. Uh…uh, can you believe how hot it is?

TOM. I've always hated hot weather.

TINA. Me too. The humid stillness causes the sweat to collect at the nape of your neck and behind your knees.

TOM. And forces your underwear to crawl up your crack…

> (LATISHA *and* MR. CHAN, SVEN *and* JEAN-CLAUDE *return to necking.*)

TINA. And you can't sleep at night with the windows open…

TOM. Because the creepy man in the bushes is going to…

TINA. Crawl through the window.

TOM. Exactly.

TOM / TINA. It drives me crazy.

> (*Beat.*)

TOM. Crazy.

TINA. Crazy.

TOM. You're crazy.

TINA. I'm not crazy. You're crazy.

TOM. Nooo.

> (*Beat.*)

TOM / TINA. We're crazy.

> (LATISHA *and* MR. CHAN *separate, post-coital.*)

MR. CHAN. Man without horse doesn't buy saddle.

LATISHA. Yeah, you don't kill the rooster if the hen's happy.

TOM. Well…Sven, when he's brooding over the chessboard with a glass of Akvavit does claim…

> (SVEN *disengages from* JEAN-CLAUDE.)

SVEN. If time and space are relative, it would seem prudent to assume "reality" is also relative. Therefore, one could postulate each individual has their own inherent reality, thus providing the possibility to surmise those without talking socks on their hands are the minority. And, in regards to genetics, anomalies often…

JEAN-CLAUDE. Often fuse opposing poles together, like *amour. N'est pas?*

TOM. Of course, there's the conundrum…what happens to us when they're gone?

TINA. We return to…to…

JEAN-CLAUDE. Weeping.

SVEN. Brooding.

TOM. You…you weep?

TINA. Life is a mime at a convention for the blind. (*Beat.*) And you? You brood?

TOM. Time. Space. Relativity. Sweet, sad, silent…consuming…oblivion.

TINA. I-crochet. I-disdain-green-M & M's. I-prefer-tea-to-coffee. I-fear…

LATISHA. Girl, will you shut up and kiss the one-M fool!

MR. CHAN. Yeah, Tom, thump her with those thin lips.

LATISHA. Kiss him!

> (*Beat.*)

JEAN-CLAUDE. Weep not and…slip your hand…slowly…here.

SVEN. Glide past the dark despair…and…settle…here.

(*Beat.*)

TINA. But…but we could be doomed. Doomed to…lonely, ice cream nights of *Desperate Housewives*.

TOM. We…we could.

JEAN-CLAUDE. *Oui?*

TOM. We—you and I. Not *oui*.

TINA. Right. You and I. Not *oui*. (*Beat.*)

MR. CHAN. We.

LATISHA. We. (*Beat.*)

TINA. We.

SVEN. *Oui.*

LATISHA. We.

MR. CHAN. *Oui.*

SVEN. Wee-wee.

TOM. *Oui.*

TOM / TINA. We…

(*Beat.*)

TOM. I mean, they seem to have done pretty well. Right?

(LATISHA, MR. CHAN, SVEN *and* JEAN-CLAUDE *nod in agreement.*)

Why can't we?

TINA. All we…us can do is…is try.

TOM. *Oui?*

TINA. Yes. *Oui*. Us and…every…

TOM / TINA. One…

(TINA *and* TOM *tentatively kiss. Gradually they continue with enthusiasm.* LATISHA, MR. CHAN, JEAN-CLAUDE *and* SVEN *watch, turn to the audience, take a bow and resume kissing as the lights fade.*)

End of Play

The Civilians'

THIS BEAUTIFUL CITY

written by Steven Cosson and Jim Lewis
- music and lyrics by Michael Friedman

From interviews conducted by Emily Ackerman,
Marsha Stephanie Blake, Brad Heberlee, Stephen Plunkett,
Alison Weller, and the authors

57

BIOGRAPHIES

Steven Cosson founded The Civilians in 2001. With the company: co-writer and director of *Paris Commune*, which was recently produced at the Public Theater, and previously at La Jolla Playhouse; co-writer and director of *This Beautiful City* which premiered at the 2008 Humana Festival with productions at Studio Theatre, Center Theatre Group's Kirk Douglas Theatre and The Vineyard Theatre; writer/director of the long-running hit *Gone Missing* (*New York Times* critic Charles Isherwood's Best of 2007 list), published by Dramatists Play Service; *(I Am) Nobody's Lunch* (2006 Fringe First award at Edinburgh) published by Oberon Books in the UK; and director of the company-created *Canard, Canard, Goose?* The Civilians have also been produced at American Repertory Theatre, Actors Theatre of Louisville, HBO's Aspen Comedy Festival, London's Gate Theatre and Soho Theatre among many others. Mr. Cosson has directed and developed many new plays including Neal Bell's *Shadow of Himself*, Mat Smart's *13th of Paris*, Tommy Smith's *Air Conditioning*, Anne Washburn's *Communist Dracula Pageant*, the world premiere of Peter Morris' *Square Root of Minus One*; the U.S. premiere of Martin Crimp's *Attempts on Her Life*, the U.S. premiere of Sarah Kane's *Phaedra's Love*; also *The Time of Your Life, Serious Money, The Importance of Being Earnest,* and *Guys and Dolls*. Mr. Cosson has been a Fulbright Scholar in Colombia, a MacDowell Fellow, and Resident Director at New Dramatists. The Civilians won an Obie in 2004.

Michael Friedman. Composer/lyricist for The Civilians' *(I Am) Nobody's Lunch, Gone Missing* and *Canard, Canard, Goose?* Music/lyrics for *The Brand New Kid, Bloody Bloody Andrew Jackson, God's Ear, In the Bubble,* and *Saved.* With Steven Cosson, he is the co-author of *Paris Commune.* Mr. Friedman's work has been seen at New York Shakespeare Festival/Public Theater, New York Theatre Workshop, Playwrights Horizons, The Roundabout Theatre Company, Second Stage, Soho Rep, Theater for a New Audience, Signature Theatre, The Acting Company, and regionally at The Kennedy Center, Huntington Theatre Company, La Jolla Playhouse, Hartford Stage, American Repertory Theatre, Berkeley Repertory Theatre, Dallas Theatre Center and Williamstown Theatre Festival. Also London's Soho and Gate Theatres and the Edinburgh Festival. Film: *On Common Ground* and *Affair Game.* Artistic Associate, New York Theatre Workshop; Princeton University Hodder fellow; MacDowell Fellow and 2007 Obie Award for Sustained Excellence.

Jim Lewis won Tony and Drama Desk nominations for Best Book for a Musical for his adaptation of Gabriel Garcia Marquez's *Chronicle of a Death Foretold.* Also with Graciela Daniele, he wrote *Dangerous Games* and *Tango Apaisionado.* Other credits include Ballet Hispanico's *Nightclub* (libretto);

58

Philip Glass' *Les Enfants Terribles* (narration); and Paul Dresher's *The Tyrant* (libretto) while his translations include Ionesco's *The Chairs* and Ibsen's *Lady From The Sea*. Mr. Lewis also served as production dramaturg for *PastFOR-WARD* (with Mikhail Baryshnikov); Anna Deavere Smith's *House Arrest*; Lincoln Center's WOZA AFRIKA Festival; *Waste* (Obie winner); *Cymbeline* (with Bartlett Sher); and *STILL/HERE* at BAM (2003) He was the program director at The American Center in Paris and a resident dramaturg for Guthrie Theater, Second Stage Theatre and INTAR Theatre. Mr. Lewis' most recent show, *Fela!*, with Bill T. Jones, completed a sold-out run Off-Broadway at 37 Arts and moves to Broadway Spring 2009.

ACKNOWLEDGMENTS

This Beautiful City premiered at the Humana Festival of New American Plays in March 2008. It was directed by Steven Cosson with the following cast:

YOUNG WOMAN "God's Grace,"
T-GIRL CHRISTIAN, others ....Emily Ackerman

EMMANUEL CHOIR MEMBER,
BEN REYNOLDS, NEW PASTOR
AT EMMANUEL, others ....Marsha Stephanie Blake

NEW LIFE ASSOCIATE PASTOR,
FAIRNESS AND EQUAILTY
WORKER, others.....................................Brad Heberlee

FAIRNESS AND EQUALITY LEADER,
RHOP MEMBER.. Dori Legg

ALT WRITER,
MILITARY RELIGIOUS FREEDOM
ACTIVIST, RHOP LEADER, others.................. Ian Brennan

TAG PASTOR, PRIEST,
MARCUS HAGGARD, others......................Stephen Plunkett

ENSEMBLE............................ Elizabeth Gilbert, Katie Gould,
Andy Lutz, Bing Putney,
Ashley Robinson, Matthew Sa

and the following production staff:

Scenic/Video Designer ....Debra Booth
Costume Designer..............................Lorraine Venberg
Lighting Designer................................Deb Sullivan
Sound Designer ....Matt Callahan
Properties Designer ....Adriane Binky Donley
Video Coordinator ....Jason Czaja

Musical Director .... Scott Anthony
Choreographer .... Chase Brock
Stage Manager .... Debra Anne Gasper
Production Assistant .... Melissa Miller
Dramaturgs .... Adrien-Alice Hansel, Jocelyn Clarke
Assistant Dramaturg .... Devon LaBelle
Casting .... Emily Ruddock
Directing Assistant .... Rebecca Easton

For The Civilians:

Dramaturg .... Jocelyn Clarke
Research Dramaturgs .... Jana Goold,
Abigail Katz, Donya Washington
Associate Research Dramaturgs .... Ari Agbabian,
Li Cornfeld, Zac Kline,
Michele Travis
Associate Producer .... Jess Chayes

Presented in collaboration with The Studio Theatre, Washington, D.C.

Following the production at the Humana Festival of New American Plays, the script was subsequently revised. The version included in this anthology was produced at Center Theatre Group's Kirk Douglas Theatre opening September 28, 2008.

This Beautiful City was commissioned and developed by The Civilians, (Steven Cosson, Artistic Director; Kyle Gorden, Producing Director), with the assistance of the Sundance Institute, Colorado College and Center Theatre Group. Development supported in part by the National Endowment for the Arts and Z-Space Studio, San Francisco, California. World premiere co-produced in the 2008 Humana Festival of New American Plays at Actors Theatre of Louisville and by The Studio Theatre in Washington, D.C., as part of its 2008 Opening Our Doors Initiative.

This Beautiful City was developed in a residency January 8 through February 14, 2007, at Colorado College (Tom Lindblade, Drama and Dance Department Chair), with Chris Benz, Katherine E. Dawson, Ellen J Evers, Christine Gonzalez, Vincent Gumlich, Alexandra Hesbrook, Robin Hutchins, Hugh Johnson, Elizabeth Kancilia, Annie Kelvie, Sarah Lee, Meghan Murrah and Adam Stone.

TIME AND PLACE

Colorado Springs, Colorado. Leading up to, and after, the 2006 election.

"Work for the well-being of the city where I have sent you, and pray to the Lord for this. For if it is well with the city you live in, it will be well with you."

—JEREMIAH 29:7 (NLV.)

The Ensemble
in *This Beautiful City*

32nd Annual Humana Festival of New American Plays
Actors Theatre of Louisville, 2008
Photo by Harlan Taylor

THIS BEAUTIFUL CITY

ACT I

Scene 1: Cowboys

A member of the company enters and speaks to the audience.

EVANGELICAL WOMAN. (*Laughs.*) The reason why you've come to Colorado Springs? Well, if you if you want me to give you my initial you want me to give you my version? Ok here's my version. You are part of this…theater company from New York that produces plays to depict uh real-life real scenarios or real situations and you are looking to write a play from interviews with real people about the fundamentalist Christians in Colorado Springs and what that looks like to the outside world. Is that right? Pretty good, huh?

(*Music starts.*)

Ok, then, can I ask you a pretty forward question? Ok, um. Is there a particular slant that you would like to put on…the reason I ask is for example when I sit beside someone on an airplane you know, I try to avoid conversation because people have their ideas: "right wing fundamental evangelical" and I want to say if your whole belief of who we are is is formed through the media then let me buy you lunch. Look, this isn't something you can just understand right off. Come spend some time with us and see some of the CRAZY things happening here like helping a lot of people and a lot of families in this city lead better lives and then we can talk.

(*The rest of the company has entered. Three of them sing as a cowboy trio.*)

SONG: COWBOYS

IT'S SO LONG DOWN THIS LONELY HIGHWAY
SUCH A LONG LONG WAY WE HAVE TO GO
AND WE SING OUR SONGS TO THOSE WHO LISTEN
AND TO THOSE WHO STRIVE TO KNOW

NEW LIFE YOUNG WOMAN. I was living in Nebraska, don't ask my why, and I heard about the school of worship at New Life. So I packed up my '84 Toyota Tercel, which should not have been driven for more than like an hour anywhere. And I got as far as Denver. I said I made it this far, I can tow it the rest of the way!

SAVED MAN. So I was visiting my cousin in Colorado Springs. And my cousin, she was so different, 'cause she used to be an acid freak back in the day. So I went to church with her and that was the first time I ever really prayed. I was all by myself. And I said, God, if you're real, prove it. And someone put his hand on my shoulder and said "just believe I'm real." The room was empty. But it was a hand. I felt it. Freaked me out. I kept a diary at the time and it said, I need to get out of Colorado before Jesus gets me! So I got on a bus and went to San Francisco. Because Jesus couldn't possibly be in San Francisco.

> HOW COULD WE STOP OUR VOICES?
> HOW COULD WE CHANGE OUR TUNE?
> IT'S SO LONG DOWN THIS LONELY HIGHWAY
> BUT WE WILL BE THERE SOON.

NEW LIFE YOUNG WOMAN. I think the feeling is that God is definitely doing something in this City. It may not be on the scale of.... "This is the valley of Armageddon," but God definitely has a plan. God led people to this city that was full of like satanic things and all this...junk...and they obeyed God's voice and now we have a different Springs.

SAVED MAN. But then I told my cousin I wanted to get saved. I didn't want to go down to the altar. I was still a little— (*Gesture meaning uncomfortable.*) So she got two friends and we went to Baskin Robbins—ordered ice cream and stood in a circle and prayed. And I asked Jesus Christ to come into my life. (*Pause.*) And then we ate ice cream.

NEW LIFE YOUNG WOMAN. For a lot of people it's gonna start here, and it's gonna take them on missions all around the world. So I guess this place is pretty much a Mecca, you know?

> WHEN WE FOUND THAT WE WERE GETTING OLDER
> AND OUR MINDS WOULD WANDER IN THE NIGHT
> WELL WE FOUND OUR FAITH WAS GETTING BOLDER
> THAN SOME PEOPLE FELT WAS RIGHT.

ATHEIST ACTIVIST. Well I've pretty much lived here all my life.

(*She stops the music with a look.*)

We're atheists, and my business is Evolve Fish. You know, the little Darwin fish that have legs? We've got a shop and we do mail order. And when we first started, we would get death threats, phone calls at two in the morning. When we bought our house we chose a high elevation so people just couldn't come up and we thought about where the windows are. I'm ok with it. I'm up for the fight. But it's hard on our daughter. She's seven. And she's afraid that if her friends find out we don't believe that they won't be her friends anymore. And what do I tell her?

(*Music starts back up.*)

Colorado Springs was always a conservative military town but back in the 80s it got more and more religious. And there is a *big* difference! But you know they've seeded the military here with born-agains. Like with the cadets at the

Air Force Academy. You know, if someone wants to be an off-the-edge snake handler I don't care!

(*Music gets louder.*)

But when they endanger my life, and they endanger the lives of my children and my country because they let this insanity take hold, then I'm scared!

> HOW COULD WE STOP OUR VOICES?
> HOW COULD WE CHANGE OUR TUNE?
> IT'S SO LONG DOWN THIS LONELY HIGHWAY
> BUT WE WILL BE THERE SOON.

COLORADO WRANGLER. Well, we're the Colorado Wranglers. We used to be a five-piece cowboy band and we worked at the Flying W Chuck Wagon Dinner. But then.... You know we're Christians, right? We got the call from God, and we had to leave there, so now there are three of us. I'm not blaming anybody, but as we got older and older we got bolder and bolder in our faith. The Flying W is a secular place, and we started pushing the envelope and talking about the Lord, and the people there started saying, y'all are doin' too much, and they told us to pray about it. And we prayed about it, and God told us to leave. It wasn't a hard decision, when God tells you to do something, you do it.

TAG PASTOR. Well I came here from Washington right after college, and well...

(*Sings.*)

> IN COLLEGE I PARTIED ALL OF THE TIME.
> GIRLS GIRLS JUST CONSTANTLY
> THINKING LOTS OF MONEY A NICE HOUSE
> I USED TO WANT A BIG BIG BOAT.
> EVERYTHING WAS GREAT.
> JUST WHAT YOU'D WANT
> EXCEPT I STARTED THINKING ABOUT DEATH
> YOU KNOW YOU LIVE FOR SIXTY, SEVENTY YEARS
> MAYBE EIGHTY, NINETY IF YOU'RE LUCKY
> AND THEN WHAT?
> WHAT WAS IT FOR?
> THINKIN' BOUT MONEY
> GETTING A NICE HOUSE?
> AND A BIG BIG BOAT?
> I WAS LYING IN BED ONE MORNING WITH MY GIRL-
>   FRIEND.
> SHE WAS HOT.
> SHE WANTED TO GET MARRIED.
> AND SHE TURNED TO ME AND SAID
> IS THIS GOING ANYWHERE

AND I FELT GOD PULLING ON MY HEART.
AND I SAID NO. NO
AND I LEFT
MAN SHE WAS GORGEOUS.

WHAT WAS I THINKING?!
THEN I STOPPED DRINKING

GROUP A

WHEN THE SPIRIT COMES FOR YOU A'CALLING
AND YOU HEAR THAT VOICE FROM UP ABOVE
WELL YOU CAN'T JUST GO ON WITH YOUR BUSINESS
NO YOU HAVE TO GO WITH LOVE
DON'T LET THEM STOP YOUR SINGING
WHEREVER YOU MAY ROAM
IT'S SO LONG DOWN THIS LONELY HIGHWAY
TIL YOU HAVE REACHED YOUR HOME.

TAG PASTOR (*Simultaneous.*)

AND I WENT HOME AND I STARTED TO PRAY.
I CLOSED MY EYES AND I STARTED TO SAY.
GOD IF YOU ARE THERE YOU KNOW SAY SOMETHING
PLEASE SAY SOMETHING.
AND FOR A MOMENT I FELT NOT A THING.
BUT THEN I HEARD IT THE VOICE OF THE LORD.
I FOUND THE ANSWER
IF YOU LEARN TO LISTEN GOD WILL SPEAK TO YOU.
I LIVE THE WAY I LIVE BECAUSE I
I WANT TO BE CLOSE TO MY GOD AND
I AM A CHRISTIAN BECAUSE I LOVE GOD.
I LOVE TO SPEND EVERY MINUTE WITH HIM.
I LOVE TO SPEND TIME ALONE WITH HIM.
I DON'T NEED MONEY SUCCESS OR A BIG BOAT
OR A BIG BOAT. YOU KNOW?

Scene 2: Two Coffee Shops

One of the actors, wearing a Ranger costume, displays the book A Trails Guide to Pikes Peak Country.

TRAILS GUIDE. *A Trails Guide to Pikes Peak Country.* This comprehensive guide is designed to answer all your questions, and more. But if you want to know why Colorado Springs has become so famous for its scenic beauty and outdoor recreation, you'll just have to get out and experience it firsthand. So use this guidebook as you would a walking, talking human one—to help orient you during your stay in the Colorado Rockies.

(ASSOCIATE PASTOR *in a coffee shop at New Life Church.*)

ASSOCIATE PASTOR. Did you have a hard time finding me here? Yeah if it's your first time you can get lost at New Life. Yeah, this coffee shop is inside the World Prayer Center. Next door is New Life's main worship center, and the building past that is the Theater which is mostly used by the twentysomething ministry. (*Question.*) Well sure I guess New Life is a megachurch. But it doesn't feel big. It feels like you know everybody. So what are you guys doing exactly? Huh. No that doesn't sound too weird. Seriously, at New Life we've got an open-door policy. That's always been a big thing for Pastor Ted. So what do you want to know? (*Question.*) Well New Life started about twenty-five years ago. Yeah well when Ted Haggard first came to Colorado, he went on a prayer fasting retreat. Just to spend some time alone with God up in the mountains. He pitched his tent and prayed and fasted. And he had a vision for a church, a big church impacting the community. So then Ted and Gayle started New Life in their basement yeah with like lawn chairs and people sitting on buckets. Or at least so goes the story. Maybe one guy sat on a bucket once. I don't know. But then it moved to a Holiday Inn or something and then over the years, more and more Evangelicals were moving to the Springs and New Life kept growing and now it's yeah, the congregation is 14,000. It's pretty amazing.

(ALT WRITER *at a different coffee shop in downtown Colorado Springs.*)

ALT WRITER. It was like a zombie movie or something. To me. Right after I went to college, the Evangelicals just sorta invaded. Though you wouldn't necessarily notice it here in downtown, the Christians tend to live out there in the sprawl.

(*Downtown coffee shop is set up.*)

Yeah isn't this place great? Thank god there's still a few places that aren't a Starbucks or a Borders. So what do you want to know? ...Well, I grew up in Colorado Springs. I left, but then my wife and I moved back with our son to be near my mom. And my stepdad, who's my dad's lover. No, my dad's dead. And my mom's a lesbian. Yeah. *Yeah.* (*Laughs.*) So, I came home in 2001 and around that time New Life was getting huge—Ted Haggard—and, you know, they built that monstrosity of a building out there. (*Clarifying.*) In the north. (*Pointing.*) This way. No, that's.... Look, let me help you, it's easy. You've got the Rockies and Pikes Peak in the west, right, so that'll always be there to orient you, you'll see them wherever you are. And then in the northeast in the middle of nothing, there's New Life and Focus on the Family— Focus on the Family? James Dobson? It's like the biggest conservative Christian media empire in the world. Yeah. Did you like, read anything before you came here? Ok, so also up north on the other side of the highway you've got the Air Force Academy. And south is Fort Carson. Ent Air Force Base is due east and inside the mountain is NORAD. Right NORAD! Yeah, yeah *War Games.* Totally. And then here in downtown you've got the hippy kids at Colorado College and all the rest of us. Yeah to the Christians downtown is like Satan's personal den of iniquity.

ASSOCIATE PASTOR. So yeah, as New Life was growing, Pastor Ted really encouraged the church to look outward to the whole city. To follow Christ's example it's not just about taking care of your own. You know, you've got to consider other people. And so Pastor Ted really put this idea of city transformation into the church's DNA.

ALT WRITER. The way my mom tells it, before all the Evangelicals moved in, Colorado Springs was very live and let live. But what happened was: in the 80s this city had a housing market crash, which basically triggered a recession here, and what the city leaders did was, they brought in Evangelical nonprofits to jumpstart the economy. Yeah! Then New Life exploded, Focus on the Family relocated here, amendment two happened, which banned any kind of gay rights. This is back in 1992. Colorado got boycotted. And that was it, Colorado was the Hate State and we were Jesus Springs. It was like, I'm from here?

ASSOCIATE PASTOR. City transformation? Well, it just means improving people's lives, making it so that they have successful families, that they are doing their jobs well, serving their neighbors. And there's any number of ways to do that: there's volunteer projects of course and prayer, intercessory prayer. Like prayer walking. Like I might prayer walk through Colorado College and just ask God to help those kids be safe, whatever. Or it can be more strategic prayer, like when Ted will lead a more targeted prayer session in a troubled part of downtown. If it can help people, that's a good thing. (*Interviewer needs help.*) So have you gone to a service yet? You haven't? Yeah, sure you should go. Tonight's Wednesday so that's TAG, the youth ministry. (*Question.*) Yeah, go. You'll blend right in.

Scene 3: Tag

TAG at New Life Church. New Life band and singers perform as part of the service.

SONG: THIS BEAUTIFUL CITY

WE ARE DESPERATE FOR YOU
WE ARE HUNGRY FOR YOU
WE ARE EMPTY WITHOUT YOU
HERE IN THE MIDDLE OF NOWHERE

WILL YOU FILL US WITH YOUR LOVE
WILL YOU SHOW US YOUR PLAN
WILL YOU SHOW US THE WAY TO MAKE YOUR
BEAUTIFUL CITY

WHERE ARE WE GOING
HOW DO WE GET THERE
WHAT IS YOUR PLAN FOR THIS
THIS THIS BEAUTIFUL CITY

WHERE ARE WE GOING
HOW DO WE GET THERE
WHAT IS YOUR PLAN FOR THIS
THIS THIS BEAUTIFUL CITY

(*The* TAG PASTOR *speaks to a large audience of teenagers.*)

TAG PASTOR. You guys, you guys here at TAG, you're the next generation for New Life Church. But what have we become? A country club. You
come here and you dance and you sing and you rock out and you see your
friends, but where is God in that? Where is prayer? So we're going to change
the formula of youth ministry. You know, the great band and the catchy
tunes, the bright lights and the cool technical effects, the funny preacher who
contorts his body. But see, the church needs to be a place where people
make a choice. And you need to make a choice about God. How many
people here tonight are ready and willing to make that choice? Just, I promise
I won't make you feel weird or uncomfortable. Well, maybe. But raise your
hands, raise them up in the air, how many out there OK I see one over there
one over there raise your hands up high...

(*He proceeds to call out each person with a hand raised.*)

Ok, leaders I just.... I just want you to pray with them. (*To audience.*) You
know what I need from TAG right now? I need you guys to resolve to love
Jesus and show him that you know in your heart why he was crucified. Can
you do that? And we're gonna make it so that if you have to say no you have
to say no to my face. Or your group leader's face. Your group leader is gonna
be the romance to your groove. Now, if you're a visitor tonight you're
probably thinking "What in the world did I get myself into? I gotta get outta
here." But we're not gonna force you. This is not about force. Come to
Christ with me tonight. Let me take you on an awesome journey. Let's walk
this walk together. Everybody, everybody in the room, ask Jesus to come to
you. Come to me Jesus. Pour into me. Fill me with your awesome love. I
want to be your disciple. I want to worship you and praise you and be loved
by you. Everybody say yes. Yes! Yes! Yes! Yes! Come to us Lord. We need
you. We need you. Say cleanse me, Lord! Do something new in me!!

(*Music swells, the kids in the imagined audience are getting saved.*)

Stay with me, now. Stay with me. We're gonna end on time today, don't
worry. Just everyone be silent. Everybody be silent for a moment and get to
know God.

(*Silence.*)

Scene 4: A Beautiful Place

ASSOCIATE PASTOR. So what did you think? Did it freak you out? It can be pretty intense for a first-time visitor. (*Question.*) Well, yeah the conversion experience is a big part of being an Evangelical. (*Question.*) Well, the definition Pastor Ted uses for the media is that an Evangelical is someone who believes that Jesus was the son of God, the Bible is the inerrant word of God, and we must be born again. (*Question.*) Which means...well, it's not about finding out who you are. It's about finding who He is and what He wants for your life. I mean, we're all born as selfish creatures. Being born again means you let that part of your life die so that you can really live. (*Question.*) Yeah, right that's the "new life."

ALT WRITER. But this is a beautiful place. The Mountains. It's beautiful. Did you know Katherine Lee Bates wrote the words to "America The Beautiful" here? From the top of Pikes Peak looking back on the Great Plains. Yeah, she did. This town could have been like Santa Fe. And now it's like I'm living in Middle Earth or something. Like everyone here's always sort of..."Mordor is over there and we're all just outside the gates living in the shadows of Mordor." You know? I guess my point is that I think so much of the power of the Evangelicals is imaginary. But we *give them* their power 'cause people are afraid. You know, like the local printers here will refuse to print something if they think it'll offend Focus on the Family. 'Cause Focus will find out and cancel their orders. And that's a lot of money. So yeah Dobson and their ilk—they're bullies. But it only works if people allow themselves to be bullied. People just roll over and bam they give up their freedom. Here, you want to see something. I started this paper called the *Toilet Paper.* And the first feature we did was this thing called The Church Kicker. So we would just pick a church and go and kick it, and then write a caption about why we kicked it. Take a look:

> (ALT WRITER *shows Church Kicker pictures as projections and performs the captions.*)

"These are just a few of the butt-ugly, strip-mall/warehouse/former-movie-theater variety of churches that litter Colorado Springs and deserve to be kicked."

> (*Projection.*)

"St. Mary's Church gets a kick for saying political candidates are accountable for their positions on gay rights or a woman's right to choose, but that war is not a moral issue."

> (*Projection.*)

"The Church Kicker is in rehab this month so we had to call in the Sculpture Puncher. Fortunately there were lots of ugly public sculptures in downtown Colorado Springs that needed their asses kicked."

> (*Projection.*)

"These little ninjas are giving a furious kick to the seventeen-million dollar, Super-Wal-Mart-sized New Life Church. They think Pastor Ted Haggard is on a crusade to erode the separation of church and state when he should be focused on being a compassionate Christian." Hey, do you want a Church Kicker T-shirt?

ASSOCIATE PASTOR. You know, it's funny to me how liberals are so quick to size up Christians as bigoted and hateful, when really that's what I hear so much from them. It doesn't strike me as very tolerant to bash someone else's beliefs.

ALT WRITER. Look I'm not talking about their beliefs per se. But I think they would agree their beliefs are absolute. Well absolute belief is stupid where matters of civil law are concerned. Our society is governed by the Constitution, not the Bible. So I think that absolute beliefs should be reserved for spiritual matters and not be imposed on those who don't share those beliefs.

ASSOCIATE PASTOR. Well I think most Christians would agree with that. I know I do. But the first amendment gives me just as much right to publicly express my views. And when it comes to politics, I think every citizen should be involved in the political system. Are liberals saying we shouldn't be involved because we're Christian or really is it because they don't agree with us? I mean, I don't hear so many complaints about Reverend Jesse Jackson getting involved in politics.

ALT WRITER. OK, bottom line, you don't believe in evolution? Don't be a scientist. You don't believe in abortion? Don't do it. You don't believe in homosexuality? Don't do it. You want to restrict the rights of other people in this city? FUCK YOU.

Scene 5: Email from Ted

TRAILS GUIDE. A great many people can share the wilderness if everyone shows a little consideration. Good manners are essential to the kindly and relaxed atmosphere that visitors are seeking. Avoid shouting, never throw rocks, and if you meet horses move to the side and let them pass. And please, please pack out your garbage. Anything that you try to hide or bury will only be dug up by animals and scattered around.

SONG: AN EMAIL FROM TED HAGGARD

> FROM: *TED.HAGGARD@NEWLIFECHURCH.ORG*
> DEAR NEW LIFE CHURCH,
> YESTERDAY A SMALL TEAM OF EVANGELICAL LEADERS AND MYSELF MET WITH BENJAMIN NETANYAHU

AND IN TWO HOURS WE'LL MEET PRIME MINISTER
ARIEL SHARON.
THEN WE'RE HEADING BACK TO THE UNITED STATES
BUT I WANTED YOU TO SEE THIS EMAIL ABOUT SOME
UPCOMING MEDIA ATTENTION
SO YOU CAN HELP ME.
BARBARA WALTERS IS WORKING ON A STORY ABOUT
HEAVEN
AND WILL INTERVIEW ME
AND GET SOME SUPPORTING SHOTS FROM THE
CHURCH.
SINCE WE BELIEVE IN HEAVEN, WE ARE, IN FACT, A
GOOD SOURCE.
OKAY, TOMORROW WE HAVE A MEETING IN WASH-
INGTON,
THEN ON FRIDAY WE'LL FLY TO NEW YORK
TO APPEAR ON *THE O'REILLY FACTOR.*
THEN WE'LL ZIP HOME TO BE WITH YOU ON SUNDAY.
SAINTS, I NEED YOUR STRENGTH.
I LOVE YOU!
AND I LOVE BEING YOUR PASTOR,
LOVE, TED

Scene 6: Fairness and Equality

Outside in a park/playground we meet a member of New Life, a YOUNG
WOMAN, *with her small kids nearby.*

YOUNG WOMAN—GOD'S GRACE. Thanks for meeting me here. I just
had to get the kids out of the house. What? (*Looking over at kids at playground.*)
Oh, they're fine. Ok, so I wanted to start the group at New Life, because I
felt that Christians in general, have like this real nasty view towards homosexuality. I called my group "God's Grace and Homosexuality." Anyhow, I
think it is important to have a forum where we could come together and
discuss our love of these people but also not compromise our values. I just
wanted to talk about it, you know? I mean there's got to be some middle
ground between saying "You're a sinner and you're going to hell" and "Oh,
everything you do is fine with me." Yeah. I was kind of shocked that only
two people showed up—I don't know. I felt like people were afraid to come.
But who nowadays doesn't have someone in their life who's gay! My father is
gay. He just celebrated his ten-year anniversary of his union. Yeah. My
husband has learned to respect my dad. To be kind. But he doesn't want my
dad staying at the house if he brings his lover with him. And my dad doesn't
ask anymore. 'Cause you know for a long time my dad didn't respect our
boundaries—you know please! Don't make out with your boyfriend on the

couch in front of my children! It's not OK! I don't want to have that talk
with them just yet! Yeah, he thought that because he was in love, and after all
God is love, then we should just respect it. You know? (*Looking at kids.*) Oh,
guys! *Behave,* ok? Excuse me.

> (*Staff from Coloradans for Fairness and Equality and walking down the tree-
> lined sidewalks of a residential neighborhood. They ring a doorbell and a door
> opens.*)

FAIRNESS WORKER. (*Male.*) Hi, we're walking around your neighborhood today handing out information about Referendum I. It extends equal
state rights to same-sex couples as those that are afforded to married
couples. Ok.

FAIRNESS LEADER. (*Female.*) Would you like to take a flyer? Great.
Thanks.

> (*Door closes.*)

Can we talk in between houses is that ok? Ok, so there is a LOT going on
here with the mid-term elections, and I don't know what it's like in New
York but here along with voting for Congress, etc. there are a lot of other
initiatives on the ballot. And this year there are actually *two* ballot initiatives
dealing with same-sex couples. Our campaign Referendum I, would make it
law that same-sex couples could have the same basic rights as married couples. And I'm in charge of the Colorado Springs campaign. Now the other
initiative, Amendment 43, that one would ban gay marriage in the state
constitution. And of course that campaign has the support of New Life and
Focus on the Family. Have you tried to talk to anyone at Focus? (*Laughs.*)
Yeah I didn't think they'd let you into the Death Star. Are you confused?
Referendum I: good for the gays. Amendment 43: bad for the gays. Does
that make—? You got it? Ok. Good. (*Laughs.*)

> (PRIEST *enters.*)

PRIEST. What we are trying to do is prevent them from DESTROYING
the identity of marriage. Because once you change what marriage fundamen-
tally is, you have destroyed it. So with this marriage amendment, we Catho-
lics got together with the Evangelicals. And I'll hear criticism of why are you
getting involved in politics—well let me tell you something...*there is no
separation of church and state.* The First Amendment prohibits the government
from establishing a state religion, that's quite different. If you look for the
phrase "separation of church and state" you will not find those words in the
Constitution. It's in some letters that Madison wrote but it is *not* in the
Constitution.

FAIRNESS WORKER. And this marriage amendment thing is happening
on the federal level too. Yeah, they're trying to put it in the U.S. Constitution. Ted Haggard's campaigning for that one too. You know Ted's President of the National Association of Evangelicals, which represents like

whatever 30 million people? So Ted talks to the White House once a week. Yeah, the President calls *him.*

FAIRNESS LEADER. It's funny, with this job friends of mine from out of town will ask me, "Well you're not gay why do you care?" Because that's how we think, right? We each care about our own issues. Well the Christian Right, they don't think like that. And I'm not necessarily talking about all the goobers who go to New Life; I'm talking about their *politicized* leaders 'kay? They've got a big picture and it has to do with big things like dismantling social programs and privatizing public education 'cause the more they can dismantle the more people need the church to provide those services. Those "Faith-Based Initiatives," that's billions of taxpayer dollars. And what do you think that means for the Christian leaders? Power and money. It's about power and money. And this gay marriage panic is just a means to an end for them. (*To* WORKER.) Do you want to do this one?

FAIRNESS WORKER. Sure.

(*Rings bell.*)

Hi we're handing out some information about Referendum I, it's not gay marriage—

(*Back to the church office.*)

PRIEST. It's gay marriage is what it is. And they don't say that and that's the stealth of it. It's the camel getting his nose under the tent. God started with marriage. It is the most sacred foundation of life. It's how He created the world and the ARROGANCE of those who would try to change that! That is government pretending to play God. They'll argue it's about rights but it's not, it's *temptation.* You see, evil has no power. Remember *Star Wars?* The Emperor had no power. It's only through Darth Vader. In the Garden of Eden the snake had no power, so all he can do is tempt Eve to eat of the tree. Abortion, stem-cell research, gay marriage, all that stuff is ultimately no different than in the Garden of Eden (*Whispering.*) "Eat the fruit. You can be like God. You can make the rules."

(*Back to the sidewalk.*)

FAIRNESS WORKER. Well, yeah as a matter of fact I am gay.

(*Door slams.*)

We get that a lot. It might be worse today because we're interrupting the Broncos game. Me? I'm a Celtic Wiccan. I grew up in a Christian family, but we never really went to church, the closest I got was Exodus International which was like living in a church.... What? Oh it's is like straight camp, it's where you go to recover from being a homosexual. ANYTHING is possible if you believe in Jesus enough, you know, it doesn't work obviously. They even showed us straight porn, like to say, this is what you should like, but...yeah but then if you like it too much I'm sure they'd send you off to porn camp.

FAIRNESS LEADER. Oh I know where you should go! This church here around the corner, Emmanuel Baptist it's the biggest black church in Colorado Springs. The pastor's name's Ben Reynolds. He wants to support us but he said to his congregation: I want to sign on as a supporter of Referendum I, but I won't do it without you. (*Question.*) No. They're pretty evenly divided. Just go over there: Ben Reynolds, Emmanuel Baptist. It's right there.

Scene 7: Emmanuel Baptist

Near the altar at Emmanuel Baptist. The EMMANUEL CHOIR MEM-BER, *an older African-American Woman.*

EMMANUEL CHOIR MEMBER. So. You want to know about Emmanuel? You know I sing in the sanctuary choir. I get up there and I'm directing the choir. What's hurt this church was that Pastor Reynolds was bringing in a lot of homosexuals and putting 'em up on that pulpit saying "Oh they anointed by God." And I kept saying "Lord, something's not right here. Something's not right." And it was eating at my spirit inside, I couldn't rest. So then I noticed with the AIDS ministry that was going on here at Emmanuel, it was getting outta hand. Like one evening, Pastor Reynolds said he wanted the whole choir back after the last service, to sing for *another* service to support the AIDS ministry…. And I look out in the audience and I say "Oh, we ain't got a lot a Emmanuel members out there. We got a lot of whites. And they homosexuals." So where the cross is, they had fifty candles on the table, and they said y'all come up and burn a candle for somebody you know done died a AIDS. So I'm looking at them, "Yup you gay, you gay, yup you gay." Ain't none of them members from here.

(TGIRL CHRISTIAN *enters and lights a candle.*)

But what blew me away was Over Six Foot Blondie. I call him Over Six Foot Blondie. He was dressed in women clothing. He had on this long blonde wig. And I looked at his feet. And I looked over where Reynolds was and I looked at the choir and I looked at everyone up there on stage and I said, "Holy Spirit, don't tell me I'm the only one up here that recognize that's a man dressed as a woman." I said "Holy Spirit, tell me I'm not the only one up here that recognize that that's a man dressed as a woman." (*Starts to laugh.*) I guess I'm the only one that see this.

T-GIRL CHRISTIAN. Oh, we Trans-Girls are in the basement of the basement. And here, most people don't even understand what it is to be transsexual; they just think we're drag queens that won't quit. And the Gay community doesn't like us 'cause they think we are sell-out 'cause we want to be girls. Then on the opposite side the lesbians (*Blows air through lips.*) because you ain't one of us…. (*Makes vampire cross with fingers.*) Oh no! Even if I was post-op, and had all the "whoop-de-doo." So it's like living in the middle of nowhere, and you have no people and no country, that's what it's like.

And well, living in this city…. (*Question.*) No, I was not out, when I came to Colorado Springs. I was married, had a wife and a family. When we got here we were very conservative Christians. We joined one of these big churches. We became small group leaders. We did all that. And a lot of those people at Focus on the Family. I was their Sunday School teacher! (*Laughs.*)

And yes, I was against the GLT community. I was like Ted Haggard more or less. I was saying, "That's sin." Until my mind got expanded, and I faced up to all the bad I was doing to my own community—that's something I'm doing penance for now and will never be able to pay back. Some Christians will be nice and say well God would accept you as you are but he's too kind to leave you this way. Yes and that's their nice way of saying that you need to *change.* And I'm like, "Sorry. Been there done that. Bought that t-shirt, burnt it and bought a blouse!"

But I almost walked away from God. I was gone for nine months. Because I didn't think God could love someone like me. But then there was a friend of mine, she's a T-girl and her name is Katherine, and it's funny 'cause her last name really is Paradise. Katherine Paradise. And she showed me this website:

> (*Projection: Grace and Lace Letter International, an Evangelical Christian Newsletter for Crossdressers, Transgendered and Transsexuals.*)

And it brought forth arguments from scripture—and I said this is Great! I can still be a Christian! And it lit me up! And that ended my nine months away from God. I said, I don't have to run anymore! You know what? Why should I? These conservative people are renegades, and they have hijacked the ship of Christianity and they are heading it towards the rocks!

Scene 8: End Times

SONG: END TIMES

THE CRAZY WEATHER
I THINK THIS CRAZY WEATHER IS DEFINITELY A SIGN
INCREASE IN KNOWLEDGE
THAT'S TALKED ABOUT IN BOOK OF REVELATION
AND THE WARS
THERE'S A WAR IN THE SPIRIT REALM
I CAN SEE IT

I WAS WORKING AS A WAITRESS
AND THIS BARTENDER GAVE ME
THIS BOOK ABOUT THE END TIMES
AND AFTER I READ IT I THOUGHT

THE CLOCK IS TICKING
SOMETHING'S COMING

AND IF IT'S COMING NOW
I'M GOING STRAIGHT TO HELL

YOU SEE THESE MOVIES
ALL THESE MOVIES
WHERE NEW YORK IS COVERED IN ICE
OR A TIDAL WAVE
ALL THESE DISASTERS
PEOPLE HAVE SEEN THIS STUFF
SO WHEN THEY LOOK OUT THEIR WINDOW AND SEE
A PLAGUE OF LOCUSTS
A PLAGUE OF FROGS
THE COAST OF CALIFORNIA COVERED IN BLOOD
IT'S NOT GONNA FREAK PEOPLE OUT THAT MUCH

THE CLOCK IS TICKING
THE CLOCK IS TICKING
SOMETHING'S COMING
SOMETHING'S COMING

IT'S SO EXCITING
BECAUSE GOD IS RAISING UP A NEW GENERATION
AND WE FEEL LIKE CHRISTMAS IS COMING
BUT GIVE ME ONE MORE DAY
GIVE ME ONE MORE HOUR
TO SAVE ANOTHER SOUL
'CAUSE THERE'S NOT MUCH TIME
'TIL THE TIME ARRIVES
WHEN THE BATTLE IS
WON WHEN MY FATHER WILL SHOW ME WHAT MY LIFE
    IS FOR
THAT THERE IS MORE TO COME THAN WE COULD
    EVER KNOW
YES THERE IS MORE TO COME THAN WE COULD EVER
    KNOW
GIVE ME ONE MORE DAY
GIVE ME ONE MORE HOUR
END TIMES ARE COMING
END TIMES ARE COMING

Scene 9: Air Force Academy

Three AIR FORCE CADETS *being interviewed together at the Air Force Academy.*

CADET C. There's not one group, there's tons of Christian groups that meet here at the Air Force Academy.

CADET A. Yeah, like FCA—Fellowship for Christian Athletes, The Navigators, Campus Crusade for Christ, YWAM—that's Youth With a Mission—

CADET B. And tonight after this, there's God Chasers.

CADET C. And a lot of cadets go to New Life on Friday nights. It's just on the other side of the highway and they send buses.

CADET A. I actually came to Colorado Springs originally to do the missions training program at New Life, and from there it was kind of a natural move for me to come here. I absolutely believe that God needs people in every part of society. Having graduated from the Air Force Academy will give me a huge platform to be able to influence other people's lives through God.

    (Question.)

CADET C. Tonight? Well tonight I think we're talking about the right way to share our faith with others.

CADET B. That means like...well, we call it the good news. I don't know. People do reject Christ on occasion but it doesn't need to be ugly like you can still be friends with them. Jesus was friends with sinners. We are called to be their friends and try to make them eternal friends. That's *why* we're friends with them.

CADET C. But here at the Academy. It is uh a sensitive environment like a few years ago there was a religious intolerance scandal—

CADET A. But a lot of the stuff that, that they were accusing Evangelicals of at the Academy were things that Evangelicals had nothing to do with.

CADET B. It wasn't necessarily someone trying to convey the Gospel of Christ—

CADET C. No one here would say "you f-ing Christ killer, you blah blah blah," I mean, no one, we're not gonna do that.

CADET B. We don't even think that.

CADET A. But I think there would be a lot less conflict if we were allowed to just openly discuss things. Just talk like we're doing now. But we can't talk about it, because uh, there are legal issues involved and that has a lot to do with uh Mikey Weinstein in particular,

CADET B. Who's the father—

CADET A. Of a cadet here.

    (The MILITARY RELIGIOUS FREEDOM ACTIVIST *enters. He is in a different location.)*

MILITARY ACTIVIST. Look, I don't know what you're going for with your show if you're shooting for G or PG 'cause with me you're going to get the R version and maybe some X. Ok? Ok. So, for the record, I was Air Force, one son is still at the Academy in Colorado Springs. All my kids are Air Force. And, you know, I spent fourteen years in, so in my immediate family, we have a hundred and fifteen years, combined active military service. So, um, I think I know a little of what I'm talking about. And let me tell you, the line between the church and the state's armed forces has been completely dissolved. Go back to your hometown paper and read the July 12, 2005, front page of *The New York Times.* General Richardson, the number two ranking chaplain in the Air Force, makes an astonishing fucking statement. Front page *New York Times.* It's the Air Force's official policy to evangelize anyone who comes into the service who is "unchurched." You know, my wife and I have three kids in the U.S. Air Force. And we're Jewish. Now, do our kids fall in this category being unchurched? And if so, Air Force, are you going to exercise your fucking right to evangelize them?

CADET A. Now, Evangelicals messed up their *tactics* tons of times.

CADET C. Yeah, some people have gotten outside the love. Because to evangelize someone shouldn't be just I'm right and you're wrong and you need to do this. Rather than, dude, I love you, and here's the truth man, and I really love you and I really hope you come to the right decision.

MILITARY ACTIVIST. But this Evangelical problem it's not just the Air Force Academy. It's the Marine Corps, Navy, Army. Have you seen the Christian Embassy video? They're one of these parachurch organizations and their targets are the leaders—Pentagon officials, foreign ambassadors, diplomats you name it. So in this Christian Embassy video, there are generals, admirals, senior people, *in their uniforms,* in the Pentagon, saying they serve God first then the country. I mean, it's supposed to be the fucking Pentagon, not the Pentecostagon.

CADET A. And really I think now it's almost like you get in trouble for practicing your Christian faith. People just need to calm down and realize, you know, that Christians are gonna be here, and we would never proselytize, but we reserve the right to evangelize to the unchurched. I mean, that's a part of our religion.

MILITARY ACTIVIST. Look, *I do not care what they believe.* Even though these are people that believe that Jack Benny, Dr. Seuss, Gandhi and Anne Frank are burning in an eternal fiery lake of hell. (*Question.*) Jack Benny? He was Jewish. And last I heard Anne Frank was. If you want to believe that little girl is roasting in hell, I'll support with my last fiber of my being under our social contract your right to believe that. But if you try to engage in the power of the state, and in the armed forces, and have my government tell me who are the children of the greater God and who are the children of the lesser God, I will fucking kill you or I will go down trying.

Scene 10: Doubting Thomas

TRAILS GUIDE. Whether you're a hiker, biker, fisherman, equestrian or cross-country skier, these tips will help you to safely prepare for what lies ahead. Because there are some real dangers in the mountains—though not always the ones you might imagine.

SONG: DOUBTING THOMAS

> THE DEVIL HAS A MAP
> THE CITY WILL NOT HIDE YOU
> AND YOUR SCARS REVEAL ALL THE SECRETS
> YOU HAVE CONCEALED
>
> YOUR BODY IS A TRAP
> THERE IS A TICKING BOMB INSIDE YOU
> CAN YOU KILL THIS THING INSIDE YOU THAT YOU
>   FEEL
>
> WHEN THE DEVIL MAKES HIS HOME
> IN THE GARDEN OF THE GODS
> HE FILLS YOU WITH THESE DOUBTS
> AND SAYS THAT HE KNOWS YOU, HE KNOWS YOU
>
> THOMAS HAD HIS DOUBTS
> THOMAS SAID TO THE APOSTLES
> CAN WE SERIOUSLY BELIEVE
> THAT THE LORD HAS RISEN AGAIN
>
> IN THIS CITY OF SIN
> THIS CITY OF FOSSILS
> CITY OF DARKNESS AND LIES
> OF FALLIBLE MEN
>
> BUT THEN JESUS CAME TO HIM
> AND SAID HERE I AM REVEALED
> DON'T YOU SEE ME HERE EXPOSED
> YOU KNOW ME YOU KNOW ME
>
> JESUS CAME TO THOMAS AND SAID TOUCH MY
>   WOUNDS
> THOMAS KNEW IT WAS JESUS WHEN HE TOUCHED HIS
>   WOUNDS
> AND NOW I'M READY
> NOW I'M READY TO SHOW THEM
>
> GARDEN OF THE GODS
> YOU BEAUTIFUL CITY

YOU GROW UNITL THE HORIZON
IS OUT OF SIGHT

WHERE THE SKY MEETS THE LAND
WHERE HEAVEN MEETS THE EARTH
CITY ON A HILL
I AM WAITING FOR THE LIGHT

LET THERE BE NOTHING HIDDEN IN MY LIFE
I DON'T WANT ANY DARKNESS IN MY LIFE
LET THERE BE NO DARKNESS IN MY LIFE

BUT LATE AT NIGHT I'M SO TIRED
I'M SO TIRED AND YOU NEED YOU NEED YOU KNOW
WAIT
WHERE I WAS GOING WITH THIS
IF YOU LOOK AT THE DEVIL THEN THE DEVIL LOOKS
AT YOU
IF YOU LOOK AT THE DEVIL THEN THE DEVIL LOOKS
BACK AT YOU

Scene 11: Spiritual Warfare

At home with YOUNG WOMAN, *in her kitchen.*

YOUNG WOMAN—GOD'S GRACE. We came from a Christian background. My father's father was a minister, so it was really a shock for all of us when my dad came out of the closet. So after my parents divorced, I moved out here to live with my dad actually. I was just a kid and I wanted my dad you know? I wanted him to keep loving me. But then my dad's boyfriend moved in. And I was put on the back burner; he didn't need me. So I just went wild and did whatever I wanted to. I actually met my husband when I'd just turned 16 and within a few months I was living with him. My dad was like, whatever! A week after I turned 17, my dad signed for us to get married, and then left for California. Yeah my dad left right after. Really fast right after.

(Kids in the distant background.)

Guys. Guys. Keep it down please Mom is talking to someone. Anyhow, my husband and I lived in Manitou Springs then. (*A little quieter.*) There was constant drug use, for lack of a better way to put it. I can probably count the days of sobriety on two hands. My husband and I had a really short bout with crystal meth. And it must have been the grace of God, 'cause I've heard that it's really hard to get off of. And the day before, a Saturday night, my husband and I were actually at a strip club, a local strip club, and we were doing coke with a bunch of strippers—I dunno, it was a party night. We had a babysitter. And I guess I had just been very gently hearing God calling to me, because the next morning I got up, and I got the kids dressed, and I walked them to this church down the road, Revolution Church. Just like that, and it was funny. I mean, look where I'd been just a few hours before. And it was unlike anything I had ever been to. They had like strobe lights and a smoke machine and a disco ball! And the people there were my age and they had tattoos! And I was sitting there with my boys, and I felt that I just didn't realize that I had missed God! And I said, God, who am I to you? And He just revealed to me, "You are my daughter. You are the one who pleases me." And in a way it made me ashamed. But at the same time He just lifted that burden off of me. He freed me, and just revealed to me that it was ok. And it made His heart ache every time I made a poor choice, but He loved me nonetheless, and He wasn't willing to let me go. (*Wipes away tears.*) To think of where I was four years ago. Now I can see how selfish that life was, and today I'm just so thankful. But at the same time, there is this sadness that washes over me because, the clock is ticking and we need more time. Like, I used to work as a senior companion, and I worked for this gentleman for a few years. And I got the call one day that he had died, and it just, really to this day, I regret that I never…that I was too afraid to say anything. I have a really vivid imagination. And to think of him in terror, and in hell for the rest of all eternity…. He was such a beautiful man. (*Wipes away tears.*) I'm sorry when God is consuming me I just start to leak.

You know it's funny, that day if I had just walked into some boring church, I would still be sitting on the couch smoking pot. We really liked Revolution and are still really good friends with the leaders, but it went from being a church to being a 24-hour house of prayer. Just prayer. All the time. By the time we left it had gone from like a hundred and fifty members to twelve or something. We just needed more of a community. That's when we chose New Life. Yeah, Revolution House of Prayer. RHOP, right. Oh you've been there? What did you think?

(*We go to RHOP, a House of Prayer headquartered in a small office building. We meet an RHOP MEMBER, a woman with a dramatic blonde hairstyle and striking eye make-up, and the RHOP LEADER, a man in his late thirties wearing a sporty Fila-style jacket.*)

RHOP MEMBER. Oh gosh (*Laughs.*) I'm not good at interviews. What am I doing here? (*Laughs.*)

RHOP LEADER. So of all the churches you've been to is this one by far the most bizarre?

RHOP MEMBER. You don't think we're weird? We're more down to earth than you probably think. I don't think of myself as a religious freak, I just never have. But if I see a woman in your play with a big bee hairdo and Tammy Faye make-up, I'm going to know it's me.

RHOP LEADER. Now we're…well obviously we're not a church like New Life. We're more like Special Forces. See here at RHOP we're all about revival. Hey if you guys can come back next week we're going to do a revival night. We're going to do some worship here and then we're headed for an intensive session in the Cave. We take everyone into this cave for about four hours, it's pitch black you can totally come if you like.

(*Interviewer declines.*)

Ok. You can decide later. But definitely come around for the first part here, you can just observe and see what we do.

(*Interviewer responds.*)

RHOP MEMBER. Oh…you know if you're going to be talking to Christians you really shouldn't say you want to be a fly on the wall. That's Beelzebub. (*Laughs.*) Yeah *Lord of the Flies*. He sneaks in as a fly on the wall. (*Laughing.*) So you don't want to say that.

RHOP LEADER. Have you read Ted Haggard's book *Primary Purpose?* Ok then, same idea. What Ted did in Colorado Springs in the 90s that's what we're trying to do here. And what I see here for Manitou Springs is the entire city as a church. I know it sounds impossible, but God's given us a vision of a church that encompasses the whole city. (*Question.*) You mean are there people who wouldn't like that to happen? That's why the warfare is necessary. (*Question.*) Huh? Well, bombs and missiles. (*Big laugh.*) No, just kidding. It's not like that at all. It's spiritual warfare.

RHOP MEMBER. Yeah, people misunderstand our rhetoric. What we MEAN is that we're praying and the violence is in the spiritual realm.

RHOP LEADER. Right, the Bible says we wrestle not against flesh and blood but against principalities, so we're not fighting people, we're fighting the invisible forces of the enemy.

RHOP MEMBER. Principalities? Like in the Bible, it tells you, there's all these different kinds of angelic forces, well same idea. There's a hierarchy of demonic forces. So a principality's like a high-ranking demon. They have authority over a territory. Right, right like a governor. There are stronghold demonic spirits, which is a sort of an anti-Christ, there's bondage spirits, controlling spirits, there are stealth spirits, death spirits, spirit of divination, jealousy, perverted spirits, reducing spirits, unclean spirits, Basilik, Bashan, Molech, Jezebel, Leviathan, Favian see so everything goes under a stronghold. I'm blowing you away, aren't I?

RHOP LEADER. But talking kingdom of God stuff, when the kingdom of God is established, you know it will be a kingdom, it's not a democracy, and there will be people, more than likely, unless everyone gets saved, which I would love, that really just won't like it. And this is where it gets hard. It gets hard for people to separate the battle and the person.

(EMMANUEL CHOIR MEMBER *back at her interview at Emmanuel.*)

EMMANUEL CHOIR MEMBER. You got Satan in the pulpit. Well you let Satan up there 'cause he entertaining you. Well, I had already started. Way

over a year ago. Paying attention, always paid attention to what's going on in
the pulpit. And then—Pastor Reynolds he gets up there and he make his
announcement and he tells us that he's homosexual, and he's coming up with
all kinda justification for people to accept his lifestyle. Well, I'm sick of your
lifestyle. When you wanna take your lifestyle and goin' throw it on somebody, and gonna make demand somebody accept you—and tell us that we
should be supporting this this this Referendum. Demand somebody give you
a health right—give you a— You ain't entitled to nothing! You can call me
anything you want to, I could care less what you call me, because I'll tell you
exactly wh-what I know and what I been taught is the word of God. It is one
man, one woman. And you will never change that. So we put Reynolds out.
And scripture tell you, you better do that. You better put 'em out. But you
put 'em out to be a Christian who has strayed. And he belongs to Satan. And
while he's at Satan, the Lord is hoping he will change himself before the time
end and he will come back. And it clearly gives us instructions, when that
person repent. We are to restore them back. But after I read it in the paper.
With his picture on the front page. Front page. I WILL NOT REPENT.
Okay. See ya. Hello Satan. 'Cause if you do not repent, oh, you goin' to hell,
homeboy.

SONG: DEMONS AND ANGELS

> THERE ARE SPIRITS ALL AROUND
> DON'T YOU SEE THEM?
> AND THEY SIT IN PRINCIPALITIES.
> SO MANY SPIRITS ALL AROUND.
> CAN'T YOU SEE THEM
> AND THEY WALK AMONG US
> THEY WALK AMONG US.
> MY SON IS SCREAMING IN THE MIDDLE OF THE NIGHT
> MAMA MAMA IT'S RIGHT THERE!
> RIGHT THERE! RIGHT THERE!
> HE SEES A DEMON IN THE MIDDLE OF THE NIGHT
> IT WAS TRYING TO KILL HIM, IT WANTS TO TAKE HIM

GROUP A.

> OH, WHAT CAN WE DO
> WHAT CAN WE DO
> TO CAST THE DEVIL OUT
> CONTINUE TO PRAY IN JESUS' NAME
> I SAY TO YOU BE GONE NOW

GROUP B.

> SPIRITS OF WILL
> SPIRITS OF PRESENCE,
> SPIRITS OF SPEECH,

SPIRITS OF KNOWLEDGE,
SPIRITS OF STEALTH
SPIRITS OF ANGER
SPIRITS OF LUST
SPIRITS PERVERTED.
SPIRITS OF LOVE.
SPIRITS OF DEATH.

RHOP MEMBER. And a lot of people just think of spiritual warfare as oh, I pray and the devil goes away. But it is a very real battle. It's God versus the devil and that's the way it's been since the foundation of the Earth.

THERE WAS A GIRL ON A PRAYER RETREAT
INTO WITCHCRAFT AND THE DARK
WE WERE PRAYING FOR DELIVERANCE
FROM THE DEMON IN THIS GIRL

THE HOLY SPIRIT OF THE LORD IT HIT SO HARD
THAT THE GIRL FELL ON THE GROUND
I HEARD THE SPIRIT OF THE DEMON CRYING OUT
"I'M INVITED HERE, THIS IS MY HOME, MY HOME"

GROUP A.
OH, WHAT DO YOU DO
WHAT DO YOU DO
TO CAST THE DEVIL OUT
CONTINUE TO PRAY IN JESUS NAME
I COMMAND YOU TO BE GONE NOW

GROUP B.
SPIRITS OF WILL
SPIRITS OF PRESENCE,
SPIRITS OF SPEECH,
SPIRITS OF KNOWLEDGE,
SPIRITS OF STEALTH
SPIRITS OF ANGER
SPIRITS OF LUST
SPIRITS PERVERTED.
SPIRITS OF LOVE.
SPIRITS OF DEATH.

EMMANUEL CHOIR MEMBER. My prayers had been that anything evil that stands in the pulpit, I don't care where they at, Lord, let them be exposed. And then the next week. The next week! I hear the gay guy on the radio. Coming outta Denver. And he's saying he had a, a three-year relationship with some pastor "Right down there at Colorado Springs!" He wouldn't call his name. And I'm thinking, you ain't exposing Reynolds. He was already in the paper. So you must be talking about another new one. And then he says, "He's big. Like president of something." So I knew it. He was talking about someone at New Life.

End of Act One

ACT II

Scene 1: Freedom

TRAILS GUIDE. With the proper precautions, and a solid plan, the hiker who reaches the top of Pikes Peak is well rewarded for the effort. But in the euphoria of having reached the summit, with its panoramic vistas of Colorado Springs and the plains stretched out eight thousand feet below, don't forget you are only at the halfway point of your journey. You still have to get back down.

(*New Life Church.*)

SONG: FREEDOM

> THERE IS THIS BALCONY
> ON THE THIRTIETH FLOOR
> WHERE PEOPLE PARTY
> AND THROW BARBECUES
>
> THE BALCONY'S RAILING
> KEEPS YOU SECURE
> IT'S A BOUNDARY YOU WANT
> A BOUNDRY YOU USE
>
> YOU WANT YOUR FREEDOM
> YOU WANT YOUR FREEDOM BUT
> IT'S NOT THE ABILITY TO
> DO WHAT YOU CHOOSE
>
> THE ONLY FREEDOM
> IS ON THAT BALCONY
> GOD LAYS OUT HIS LAWS
> YOU LIVE IN HIS RULES
> THAT'S WHAT FREEDOM IS
>
> GOD IS NOT INTERESTED IN YOUR HAPPINESS
> GOD IS NOT INTERESTED IN YOUR HAPPINESS
> GOD IS NOT INTERESTED IN YOUR HAPPINESS
> HE JUST WANTS TO KEEP YOU FROM FALLING
> FROM FALLING FROM FALLING BUT

YOU FALL FOR SOMETHING
OUTSIDE THAT BALCONY
YOU GET ADDICTED AND IT KILLS YOU
YOU WALK AWAY FROM GOD
YOU MAKE YOUR CHOICES
YOU CALL THAT FREEDOM
YOU CALL THAT LIVING YOUR LIFE
BUT IT'S A SPIRITUAL DEATH
IT'S A PARADOX

ASSOCIATE PASTOR. Ok so tonight we're going to look at some of the teachings that Pastor Ted talked about this morning in Samuel. And because we're coming up on a midterm election, there are a number of issues here that are salient particularly to us as people of faith. So this sub-series is titled: "Freedom for All." Let us pray together. Heavenly Father we thank you for the privilege of discussing ideas freely, and we thank you that we're free to participate in the public process. And to defend our ideas as persuasively and boldly as we are able. In Jesus' name. Amen. AMEN. Ok...

So some of you might be thinking, we're people of faith we care about spiritual matters we don't care about politics, well let me tell you something: God made representative government. It's His idea. We talked about that in Samuel. And in Deuteronomy where God instructs Moses to create a body of leadership for the different tribes. So if our American government is the purest realization of God's idea of government that the world has yet seen, then we have a responsibility to participate in the political process. But just how do you do that? Well first and foremost—register and vote. Sounds simple enough, but voting is one of those things like flossing. You know, we're supposed to do it but lots of us don't because it's a hassle. Look, we as kingdom-minded people don't have the luxury of being too busy to register and vote. So if you're not registered to vote November 7, there's a table right out here in the hallway sponsored by Coloradans for Marriage, and they have registration cards, then you'll receive information in the mail telling you where to go and basically holding your hand to the election booth.

Now how does all this pass the "who cares" test? It's because right now there are some issues like whether marriage is simply a contract which our government can refit to suit our purposes or whether it is an institution created by God which predates the American experiment. Whether the rights of unborn children are going to be protected. Look women need to be free to have the right to choose how to live their lives which they SHOULD. But that babies ought not to have the right to choose is absolutely defying of logic. Look no people ought to be free to choose completely. And further-more, by defending marriage that doesn't mean we're restricting anyone's rights. I wouldn't dream of depriving any American of his or her constitutional rights. And listen, I am for every person, even gay people's, right to marry. One consenting adult member of the opposite sex. (*Laughs.*) OK we need to wrap up. Now, would you do me a favor? Uh, especially those who are glazed over or mildly offended that I've been talking about politics. Would you raise your right hand please? Humor me people. Repeat after me. OK, I hereby forgive you for talking about politics tonight. OK thank you. I'm holding you to that forgiveness.

Scene 2: Revelations

RHOP revival.

RHOP LEADER. Ok, first off I want to welcome those of you who are coming here to RHOP for your first revival. This House of Prayer's been challenged by God to bring about a spiritual transformation of this city and you know maybe not everybody's up to that kind of dedication but those of you who've stuck to it I know your hearts are ready to do God's work. Okay second thing is we've got some visitors here from New York City. They've come back just to see what we do so welcome them. Okay, we're gonna worship here for a bit and then we'll be ready to go to the Cave. We say to any demonic stronghold in anyone's life right now you must break…you must break…in Jesus' name you cannot remain you cannot control in Jesus name we declare freedom in Jesus' name in Jesus' name…in Jesus' name. Ok. (*Gesturing to the mic.*) Okay come up, anyone come up. Holy holy holy.

RHOP MEMBER. Lord God we ask that you bring light to this city. Lord God we welcome your revelations. We are listening Lord God we are waiting for your direction. We praise you Lord God. (*Speaking in tongues/prayer language.*) Avvon d- Nih- Oo' mal-choota-oo khai- tush-al-mein! Amen Lord God.

RHOP LEADER. (*To everyone.*) I'm feeling God urging us to a place of understanding that in order to light this city he's giving me a picture ooh-aah he's giving me a picture of a city and it's night and all of a sudden you can just see just quadrants of the city and lights are coming on in the homes and the streetlights are coming on there had been a blackout and it's just all of a sudden the lights are coming on—

(*Online sound. Projection: "Haggard Accused" and a chat icon indicating that we've jumped outside the revival into the Haggard story unfolding online.*)

ONLINE CHATTER. Oh My God! One week before the election, and this is delivered in a nicely ribboned Holiday gift box. Looks like Ted Haggard is a closet case and a meth queen to boot! In the words of Whitney: Merry Crystal-meth-mas! Check this out:

(*Actors switch out of their RHOP characters and play a REPORTER interviewing TED HAGGARD in the driveway outside of Haggard's home.*)

REPORTER. Pastor Haggard have you had a relationship with—

TED HAGGARD. I have not.

REPORTER. Any kind of gay relationship—

TED HAGGARD. I, I've never had a gay relationship with anybody and uh I, I'm steady with my wife. I'm faithful to my wife.

REPORTER. What about the accusations you tried to buy meth?

TED HAGGARD. I have never done drugs, ever. Not even in high school.

REPORTER. Uh. So you don't know Mike Jones?

TED HAGGARD. No, I do not know Mike Jones.

(*Back at the revival.*)

RHOP MEMBER. (*Praying with someone at the revival.*) Lord God don't hold back this man is strong give him all you got. Give it to him he can take it.

RHOP LEADER. (*Speaking to someone at the revival.*) I'm calling you to step out into a place where there's freedom and I'm getting a picture here. I'm just seeing the funniest thing like uh the *Sound of Music* of uh that lady Andrews just dancing in the flowers. I'm just seeing that in my mind, and God's saying I called you to freedom. I've got a word. God's saying he wants you to fall. He wants you to fall into his arms.

(*Back to the news. This time a* REPORTER *is interviewing* TED *who has stopped his car.* GAYLE HAGGARD *sits in the passenger seat.*)

TED HAGGARD. So, I've put myself on an extended…. What do we call it—suspension of my senior pastor's role. I resigned as President from the National Association of Evangelicals because both of those roles are based on trust. And right now my trust is questionable. And so…

REPORTER. The voice expert that is in Denver that was hired by KUSA has…

TED HAGGARD. Yes.

REPORTER. …matched now eighteen of the words left on the voicemail message.

TED HAGGARD. Yes. I did call him. I did call him.

REPORTER. And what did you call him about?

TED HAGGARD. I called him to buy some meth but I threw it away.

REPORTER. So you now admit you know Mike Jones?

TED HAGGARD. I went to him for—I went there for a massage. So— OK, we're late for our appointment. So—but thank you for your work.

(*Back at the revival.*)

RHOP LEADER. Ok, ok, ok, stay with me here. Now in the Cave it's gonna be totally dark, totally silent. We'll be there for about four hours but before we go I want to tell you some of the amazing things that can happen in the cave. This one time—now first you gotta imagine, it's a cave. And you can't see anybody. So there I was and all of a sudden…I saw a demon. And all it was was two red eyes. And…the Lord spoke to me and he said it was a mocking spirit. And…and I said "All right guys, I need you to renounce this spirit! Are you ready to break through this thing?" And they were:

ALL. Yes, yes, yes.

RHOP LEADER. I said, "This is what you need to do, every one of you has to cry out to God." And man…talk about a *change* 'cause it was:

(*The revival has morphed into a recreation of the* RHOP LEADER's *story*.)

ALL. "DEVIL YOU GET OUTTA MY LIFE!" "GET OUT OF MY LIFE! GET OUT GET OUT GET OUT GET OUT GET OUT! GOD I NEED YOU! COME GOD COME! COME! COME!"

(EMMANUEL CHOIR MEMBER *reappears*.)

EMMANUEL CHOIR MEMBER. I said, "Thank ya, Holy Spirit." 'Cause that was my prayer. Expose them! 'Cause I'm sick of them hiding behind your cloth. No. I ain't jumping for joy for none of 'em to fall, I'm jumping for joy that God restored my faith. Seeing his miracles work today! Dang all these miracles are happening and stuff. Every day!

Scene 3: New Life Church

At New Life worship service. This is the day after Ted Haggard's removal from the church, and only a few days after the scandal broke. The New Life band plays music.

TAG PASTOR. We've had a wonderful twenty-one years here at New Life Church. Pastor Ted said many times that we've been living a little slice of heaven. For the last couple days we've been living a little slice of hell, but heaven! Is! Our! Home! And if we all stay together, praise the holy spirit, and continue our work in this city, then we have another twenty years and more, I believe with all of my heart that New Life Church's best days are ahead of us!

(*Applause*.)

In the words of Pastor Ted: What is the purpose of New Life Church? To make it hard to go to hell in Colorado Springs. So let's turn this room into a house of prayer tonight. Cry out for this church cry out on behalf of the believers all over the nation who are wrestling with the same demons. Oh God, we bow our hearts to you! Lord Jesus we ask you to purge our hearts, to take all judgmental thoughts away. All bitterness! All anger! All fear! Lord God, we surrender all these things to you! God, we are so desperate for you, would you come, would you come and save us? Rescue us LORD JESUS! GOD!!!!!!!!!!!

SONG: TAKE ME THERE

> THE EYES OF A NATION,
> THE ENTIRE WORLD IS WATCHING
> THE REVELATION OF A
> NEW AGE THAT IS DAWNING
> A NEW AGE THAT IS DAWNING.
>
> WHAT IS THE PLAN FOR
> THIS PLACE, THIS TOWN, THIS CITY?
> WHO IS THE MAN FOR THE
> NEW AGE THAT IS DAWNING,
> THE NEW AGE THAT IS DAWNING?
>
> WHERE YOU WILL GO TAKE ME ALONG,
> TELL ME SHOW ME WHAT I'VE DONE WRONG
> TO YOU I DEDICATE THIS SONG.
>
> TO SOMEONE UP ABOVE
> WE LIFT OUR VOICE IN PRAYER
> PLEASE FILL US WITH YOUR LOVE AND TAKE US
>   THERE,
> I KNOW YOU'LL TAKE ME THERE!

ASSOCIATE PASTOR. God is not intimidated or threatened by sin. He has an incredible plan. And you're seeing it, you're watching it unfold, you're watching the gospel at work, it is His plan and He will not let us go. Today salvation is working!!

> WE HAD A VISION
> WE SAW THE PASSAGE IN THE NIGHT
> WE HAD A MISSION
> TO BRING THE CITY INTO LIGHT
> BRING THE CITY INTO LIGHT.
>
> I KNEW A STORY
> I THOUGHT THAT I HAD HEARD THE PLAN
> TO SHOW YOUR GLORY
> BUT DID WE REALLY UNDERSTAND?
> DID WE REALLY UNDERSTAND?
>
> WHERE YOU WILL GO TAKE ME ALONG,
> TELL ME SHOW ME WHAT I'VE DONE WRONG
> TO YOU I DEDICATE THIS SONG.
>
> TO SOMEONE UP ABOVE
> WE LIFT OUR VOICE IN PRAYER

PLEASE FILL US WITH YOUR LOVE AND TAKE US
THERE,
I KNOW YOU'LL TAKE ME THERE!

NEW LIFE WOMAN. God we want the churches of Colorado Springs to
be a light and shine forth like the dawn. We ask Lord Jesus for mercy in our
hearts, we hope that righteousness reigns in this city. God you have cut back
the tree tonight. God, continue to prune us so that we can stand before you,
spotless, radiant, and whole. God let there be no vile thing in me. (*Very
moved, in tears.*) God please be with us here. Please be with us.

(*Under.*) TAKE ME THERE.
TAKE ME THERE.
TAKE ME THERE.
TAKE ME THERE.

(*In the clear.*) I KNOW YOU'LL TAKE ME THERE.
I KNOW YOU'LL TAKE ME THERE.
I KNOW YOU'LL TAKE ME,
YOU'LL TAKE ME,
YOU'LL TAKE ME THERE.

I KNOW YOU'LL TAKE ME THERE.
I KNOW YOU'LL TAKE ME THERE.
I KNOW YOU'LL TAKE ME,
YOU'LL TAKE ME,
YOU'LL TAKE ME THERE.

I KNOW YOU'LL TAKE ME THERE.
I KNOW YOU'LL TAKE ME THERE.
I KNOW YOU'LL TAKE ME,
YOU'LL TAKE ME,
YOU'LL TAKE ME THERE.

TO SOMEONE UP ABOVE
WE LIFT OUR VOICE IN PRAYER
PLEASE FILL US WITH YOUR LOVE AND TAKE US
THERE,
I KNOW YOU'LL TAKE ME THERE!

TO SOMEONE UP ABOVE
WE LIFT OUR VOICE IN PRAYER
PLEASE FILL US WITH YOUR LOVE AND TAKE US
THERE.

Scene 4: Reverberations

The ALT WRITER *has entered at the end of "Take Me There." He opens a copy of his latest newspaper and reads from his own editorial.*

ALT WRITER. "Don't get me wrong: I was as surprised as anyone that Haggard actually got caught. Just because everyone knows you're a repressed hypocritical piece of shit doesn't necessarily mean you're stupid enough to get caught. But those of us who live in Colorado Springs knew something was up. And we knew because the church itself told us everything Haggard was hiding. If you've been to New Life and have even trace amounts of gaydar, then it doesn't come as any surprise that Ted Haggard turned out to be a meth-fueled queer bag. When my big, gay stepdad saw him on the news for the first time three years ago, his first comment was:

"'Well he's as gay as a box of birds.'"

(He closes the newspaper.)

A lot of people criticized my paper for gloating about his fall. I mean, of course, the guy's obviously tortured, I wish he could come out and be a happy person. I feel for his kids certainly, having grown up with the shame that I grew up with having two queer parents, you know, *until I got over it.* But they're the ones who made this political and you know, when they slip you wanna slide a little bed of nails underneath as they're going down.

(Online.)

VOICE-OVER. You must be logged in to leave a comment. Would you like to sign on now?

(Bloggers and online comments.)

BROOKE. I don't know about the rest of you, but this was one of the best weekends ever. I could watch Ted's confession on YouTube for the rest of my life and never stop smiling. I heard just now that Dobson is going to counsel him to stop his gay tendencies. Okay, dude, make someone NOT gay, go ahead. —Posted by Brooke, Boulder

WENDY. Well, I think what will be truly fascinating to observe is how the religious right reacts to this news? Will there be a call for unity or will they throw him to the wolves? —Wendy, Pittsburgh.

BROOKE. Wendy, click here:

CNN.COM. White House spokesperson Tony Fratto downplayed the pastor's connections to the Bush administration—

FRATTO. He had been on a couple of conference calls but was not a weekly participant in those calls.

CNN.COM. Fratto admitted that Haggard had been to the White House—

FRATTO. One or two times. But there have been a lot of people who come to the White House.

(At New Life Church. Q & A after the Sunday night service.)

NEW LIFE MEMBER. I was wondering if you could tell us how Ted is doing and his family? I'd like to know especially how his son Marcus is doing at the Boulder Street campus, and how can we pray for them.

ASSOCIATE PASTOR. Marcus Haggard preached a phenomenal message on Romans 8:28 I believe this morning, and I heard great reports about it. The building was full and the offering was good. And people (*Supportive shouts etc.*) and people are not fading or shrinking back. And, I talked to Pastor Ted and Gayle on...let's see...on Monday? Is that right? Monday night? They were very adamant that God is involved in their marriage, very aggressively saying to me, "we are going to do this right." And what I think is so interesting—now this doesn't in any way um, this doesn't make OK the things that were wrong—but even in repentance, Ted modeled how to do it right. How to be authentically submissive to authority—and how we can pray for them—

(Online.)

THE WHOLE TRUTH. HAHAHAHAHA I'm loving this thread. Ooooh, the poor boy has admitted to some "indiscretions." Out with it, Pastor Faggard! You've been smokin' the pole for years. And now you lost your job and your poor wife will need to be tested. Oh, to be a fly on the wall explaining this to the Mrs.! —Posted by The Whole Truth.

YOU GUYS ARE ALL HATEFUL. I can't believe how hateful you people are! —Posted by You Guys are All Hateful.

(In Denver.)

BEN REYNOLDS. What happened with me and Emmanuel Baptist? Well after I made my announcement they basically fired me. It was just that cut. Boom. Get outta here. (*Laughs.*) Well, and I'm laughing now, but this thing with Ted Haggard, it's a very sad thing. I just wish that he could have told his own story. Because that's what I did. I am the author. I mean, of course it is still at a price, 'cause here I am a vagabond on the streets of Denver.

But when I made the announcement one of the leading deacons said to me "I knew it all the time." And that's a very arrogant thing to say when someone tells such a dynamic truth as to expose their sexuality. Because you really don't know anything until a person tells the truth to you. So when I analyzed it, he was saying "We all knew. I mean, I think we all knew. But the nerve of you to speak that truth in here. We're angry because you spoke the truth." Because if you knew and I just told you, then really this ought to be a party. Like, whew, glad that's over with. Now can we move on to something else?

After all that I knew I had to leave some distance between Colorado Springs and me. And here in Denver it's still too close. I mean, I can be walking down the street and like, people have stopped me and they want to talk. And most think, "Oh my God, he's fallen from grace." (*Giggles.*) They don't know how happy I am. They just don't know. I'm like brand new. On a Saturday night, back then, as a pastor, three o'clock I was at home. Shut up with the windows drawn, hahaha, you know, praying honestly for the word. And now, while I continue to pray, I might be out on a Saturday night with a glass of wine. And I like my life that way. Free. I feel free. And I'm gay everywhere.

(Music starts.)

PHINKY. Dear Mrs. Haggard, I know what you are going through. My soon to be ex-husband came out of the closet eleven months ago. My S2BX was filled with self-loathing for years. Now that he's out, it's like a giant weight has been lifted from his shoulders. Maybe that was the sensation that I got when he told me. The weight left his shoulders and slammed me in the face. You might have felt the same way.

SONG: THE ORDER OF THINGS

> WOMEN ASK ME
> WHY THEY ARE LONELY
> THEY FEEL UNHAPPY AND UNFULFILLED
> THEY DON'T UNDERSTAND
> THAT THERE'S AN ORDER
> THAT THE CHILD
> TO THE FATHER
> AS THE WOMAN
> TO HER HUSBAND
> AS THE HUSBAND
> TO THE FAMILY
> TO OUR LEADERS
> AND TO GOD
> THIS SUBMISSION IS A GIFT
> THIS SUBMISSION IS A GIFT
>
> IT'S THE ORDER OF THINGS
> IT'S THE ORDER OF THINGS
> CAN'T YOU SEE THE ORDER OF THINGS
> IS KEEPING US TOGETHER

PHINKY. But the first thing you should know, being gay is not evil. Your husband's dishonesty is evil. The second thing you should know, homosexuality is not a disease to be cured. Going to spiritual "restoration" will not cure gayness. That sounds so Soviet, like going to a re-education camp. Geez.

> IS YOUR HEART BROKEN?
> MY HEART IS BROKEN
> AND YOU WONDER WHERE IS GOD
> WHAT YOU THOUGHT WAS PERFECT
> NOTHING HERE IS PERFECT

ONLY GOD IS PERFECT
BUT THAT IS THE TEST
MY TEST HAS BEGUN
SO WATCH ME
WATCH ME

AND I WILL PRAY
AND I WILL FOLLOW
AND I WILL OBEY
AND I WILL KNOW
AND I WILL LOVE HIM
AND THAT IS MY CALLING
THAT IS THE FREEDOM
THAT I KNOW

ALL YOU WOMEN
WHAT CONCESSIONS
AND WHAT COST
WOULD YOU BEAR
DO I QUESTION WHAT I'M GIVEN?
DO I ASK
WHAT IS IT FOR?
IT'S MY BURDEN
IT'S MY CALLING
IT'S MY POWER

PHINKY. I understand that you want to try and make the marriage work, but the odds are against you. I know I'm a stranger telling you how to live your life but Evangelicals have been telling Americans how to live their lives for years. I'm just returning the favor. Hopes and wishes, Phinky.

AND I WILL PRAY
AND I WILL FOLLOW
AND I WILL OBEY
AND I WILL KNOW

AND I WILL LOVE HIM
AND THAT IS MY CALLING
THAT IS THE FREEDOM
THAT I KNOW.

THAT IS THE FREEDOM
THAT I KNOW.

Scene 5: Free Yoself

Service at Emmanuel Baptist Church. Ben Reynolds' replacement is preaching.

NEW PASTOR AT EMMANUEL. God bless you. You may be seated. I'm ashamed a myself today Emmanuel. Since taking over this pulpit a few weeks ago from Ben Reynolds, sometimes I find myself givin in to weakness. Feeling tired. Wondering if God was going to be here to help me through this second sermon. After this morning's service, I let the devil sneak up on me. And Miss Wanda said, "What happened to you? You had you a melt-down while we was gone?"

So I come with the question. God, is that you? Have you ever been in a situation and been at a point in time and wondered if you miss God talking to you, or working on you? How can you miss a God that's that big? God is so big that you can't confine him. Bigger than everything we can see. HOW can you miss some God that this big? Amazing that sometime we don't recognize the answers to our prayers when God gives them to us.

But I say even Peter who walked with Jesus and prayed to God and was one of Jesus' disciples, even Peter when God spoke to him, said "I don't know if it's live, or if it's Memorex." I don't know if this thing is real, I don't know if this is God, I don't know if it's me. I don't know if it's a vision or if it's real. Maybe I shouldn't'ta eaten those pig feet last night and gone to bed." Is that you God? Nobody sittin next to you on the bus, Is that you God? Nobody sittin at the organ, is that you God? Ask him. Now if you will remember Peter finds himself in prison. Locked up and dealing with angels showing up and moving things and he makes the statement that I wasn't sure if it was God or if I was dreaming. Well, lemme help you. One way to recognize when God is at work is that God always frees us from something. Because Peter was in prison and the scripture says he was being guarded, four units of guards. Sixteen guards. But they didn't understand something. You may lock me up but you can't lock God out. (*Screams at the top of his lungs.*) God has a way of finding me and coming to where I am! Anybody in here ever felt despair in the middle of the night, and all of a sudden God found you and all your troubles just disappeared? Anybody in here ever been driving down the street in your car, all by yourself, and you stuck in traffic, and some kinda way God knew your plate number, found your car, entered in your car and blessed you where you was? ANYBODY IN HERE EVER BEEN IN THE PRESENCE OF GOD! You may lock me up, but you can't lock God outta my life! The text says Peter was locked in the prison. The angel came in and started the freeing process. Y'all gotta understand something, when God frees us, He takes us through a process. The angel walked in and the first thing the angel did was he walked up to Peter and touched him in his side. Get ready for the journey. Get up! Now, if some of you was Peter, you'd say wait, you want me to get up and dress myself? I got chains on my arms! But the scripture says when the angels gave Peter directions and Peter listened and got up and started to move, THE CHAINS FELL OFF! If you expect somebody to help you get outta your situation, you better get up and get moving. When you wake up get moving. Want to get a new job? Get up and put in an application. Looking for a mate to come to your house? Do yo hair! Dress yoself! Put on some nice clothes! Lose some weight! Wash your face! Put on make-up! Put on your best suit! Put on a tie! And get movin! It's a process and the process is, you can't be sleep in yo prison!

Who the Son has set free is free indeed. So stop looking at other folk to validate you. Stop it. If your phone don't ring, CALL YOSELF! STOP IT! If don't nobody lay hands on you, put your hands on your own head. BLESS YOSELF! STOP IT! GOD is your validator. Stop waiting for the morning edition of the paper to come out, to see if you made it through the night. Stop waiting for the morning edition of the paper to come out, to see if you made it through the night.

Scene 6: Plan B

TRAILS GUIDE. Many a greenhorn is fooled into believing that the Rockies are a paradise where all you need are a pair of sneakers, shorts and sunglasses. But then suddenly the weather changes and the unprepared hiker can freeze to death of hypothermia. So expect the unexpected, make a backup plan, and you must take along the minimal gear we recommend, even if the weather seems warm and sunny when you start, and even if the other members of your party complain.

(RHOP LEADER *is driving. He appears projected as a video podcast.*)

RHOP LEADER. All right…well I told you all I'd do a video podcast as I'm driving to Kansas City and here I am. My family and I are leaving the Springs, we're making a move, we need to get out to Kansas City, and maybe someone out there, God would lay it on their heart to pay our moving expenses. And you know we've carried this baby of-of-of city transformation in Manitou Springs for a very long time. That was Plan A. I'll tell ya what—I believe possibly, now I don't know for sure, but I believe POSSIBLY that me and my family, we have to go to Kansas City because Plan A failed. Possibly. Plan A was for us to see revival happen to the people in this city. I believe that was Plan A. I think Plan B is now that we have to leave and go find the people. I think Plan B's okay.

(*Coffee shops. Nighttime.* ASSOCIATE PASTOR *reads from his laptop and sings.*)

SONG: ANOTHER EMAIL FROM TED

FROM *TEDHAGGARD@GMAIL.COM*
DEAR FRIENDS:

> THANK YOU SO MUCH FOR WRITING.
> JESUS IS STARTING TO PUT ME BACK TOGETHER.
> HE AND HIS FOLLOWERS HAVE SAVED MY LIFE.
> THEY SENT GAYLE AND ME TO PHOENIX
> FOR A THREE WEEK PSYCHOLOGICAL INTENSIVE
> THREE WEEKS THAT GAVE ME THREE YEARS WORTH
> OF TREATMENT.

FAIRNESS LEADER. Yeah well we lost Ref I. And they passed the marriage amendment. Yeah. But I—and maybe this is just to save my psyche—but we lost by a narrow margin which does in some way acknowledge social progress. Ten years ago getting this close would have been *unthinkable*. So you know what? It's just a matter of time. I'm not that worried. I'm pissed off but I'm not worried.

> GAYLE AND I HAVE DECIDED TO MOVE FROM COLO-
> RADO SPRINGS TO GO BACK TO SCHOOL.
> WE LOVE COLORADO SPRINGS SO MUCH,
>
> AND WILL ALWAYS REGARD THE BELIEVERS AT NEW
> LIFE CHURCH AS FAMILY,
> BUT WE HAVE TO GO

FAIRNESS LEADER. But look, whatever happens next politically it's not like the evangelicals are going to go away. They don't have a three-year plan or a five-year plan. They have a one-hundred-year plan. And you know, other places might think they have the luxury to just ignore them. But in this town—we have no choice but to find the common ground. You don't make change by doing nothing and you don't make change by attacking people. You build relationships, you realize you have differences of opinion, but you also realize you can move forward— So Ted…well, actually he was one of the more reasonable and more engageable leaders of that movement. What terrifies me is how quickly the Evangelicals can make him just disappear.

> WE HAVEN'T DECIDED WHERE WE ARE MOVING BUT
> SO FAR HAVE BEEN OFFERED TWO PLACES,
> ONE IN IOWA
> AND ONE IN MISSOURI.
> WHERE WE PLAN TO GET ONLINE DEGREES IN
> PSYCHOLOGY
> SO WE CAN SERVE OTHERS THE REST OF OUR LIVES.

RHOP LEADER. So anyway, I look over to my left, white tundra. Nothing but snow. And I look over to my right, more white tundra. Is tundra the right word? Is a tundra a place where snow is? Or is a tundra more of a desert…or a jungle…. I don't know. But it's flat and it's white and I'm driving…. Probably no one's listening to this…but if you made it to the end, send me an e-mail.... Send me an e-mail and say "You know what? I made it to the end of that ridiculous podcast...as you were driving to Kansas City. If—if you're the first one to send me an e-mail. I'll send you a prize. It'll have no monetary value, but...email me. All right, I'll look forward to it. God help me. Kansas City, here I come.

> THANK YOU SO MUCH FOR YOUR LOVE AND PRAYERS DURING THIS HORRIFIC TIME OF TRANSITION.
> FOR THE LAST THREE MONTHS, I'VE BEEN PARALYZED BY SHAME.
> BUT AS GOD AND PEOPLE LIKE YOU FORGIVE ME, THE SUN IS STARTING TO RISE IN MY LIFE,
> I LOOK FORWARD TO COMMUNICATING WITH GREATER EASE.
> GOD BLESS,
> TED HAGGARD
> "WE ARE EASTER PEOPLE."

Scene 7: Seeing the People

T-GIRL CHRISTIAN. You know the odds for being transsexual it's supposed to be 1 in 10,000 I think. We got way more than that in this city. I mean we have way far exceeded the quota (*Laugh.*) There are four military instillations here. And all these boys went into the military and they're running from the fact that they are big t-girls! (*Laugh.*)

But I've known since I was three that I was supposed to be a girl, but something was wrong with the outer package. Before I transitioned, to full-time t-girl, I was a civil designer, which is like a step below a civil engineer. And I was good at my job. But, oh, I was pushing the limits going more androgynous, wearing earrings but not like these. (*Shows earrings.*) And finally I was enough is enough! I got to be me. But I was not going to just show up in my Easter dress and do shock and awe. So I called a business meeting, the principals at the company, every significant person. I had handouts, I explained what it is to be transgendered, and asked if there were any questions you know, my life is an open book. My supervisor said you are really brave, I never would have been able to do that. And I said what I need to know from you all is this OK for me to go full time—it's required for my surgery. They said they needed some time to think, and a week went by and they handed me my pink slip. They couldn't come out and say it per se. I called the labor commission and they said they had no protections for transgendered people. I lost everything. I lost my job, my church, my family, my fortune. For six months I was getting unemployment, but that's all they ever give you in Colorado, six months. Now only by the grace of the friends of mine, they're propping me up. Otherwise I'd be a bag lady by now. No shit. I'd be out in the street. My vision's horrible. I can't work at McDonalds, because I can hardly read the itty-bitty buttons on the cash register. But when I was at my job, if I had trouble seeing on the computer, I can zoom it up. Plus, to me, designing things, it's like playing Sim City. I love my job. It's like a video game to me. Designing stuff. Designing roads. I design a neighborhood and then a year later, there it is. They don't know I did it, but there's a warm place in my heart because I helped the city.

(Another actress performs the song.)

SONG: URBAN PLANNING

YOU DESIGN A NEIGHBORHOOD.
ONE YEAR LATER THERE IT IS.
OR A PLACE THAT WAS EMPTY
NOW A BRIDGE HERE
A ROAD THERE
SO YOU MAKE A CITY
SO YOU BUILD IT GENTLY
AND YOU SEE THAT WHEN IT GETS DONE
THERE'S A SIGN HERE
A PARK THERE
IT'S PARADISE.
YES IT'S PARADISE.
IT'S A PARADISE THAT YOU'VE MADE.
SO MY DOCTOR SAYS DRAW SOMETHING.
SO I DRAW A CITY.
'CAUSE I'VE ALWAYS LIKED CITIES.
I HAVE SINCE I WAS A KID.
SO HE TELLS ME IT'S BEAUTIFUL.
BUT WHERE ARE THE PEOPLE?
I HAD NEVER THOUGHT OF THE PEOPLE
THEY MOVE.
THEY GET IN THE WAY.
THEY GET IN THE WAY.
I'M LOOKING AT BUILDINGS.
HE SAYS THAT'S KIND OF AN ISSUE.
HAVE PEOPLE HURT YOU
HAVE PEOPLE HURT YOU A LOT?
BUT IT'S PARADISE.
BUT IT'S PARADISE.
ALMOST PARADISE.
THAT I'VE MADE.

T-GIRL CHRISTIAN. I'd never seen all that when I was trying to run from me. If I learned anything from all this hell I went through is now I see the people. Now I see the people. And this is a beautiful city. A lot of my friends say well why don't you just move it's just too ornery it's too hostile they don't want you here. You know what this is AMERICA, I like it here. I LIKE seeing Pikes Peak out of my front door. And I'll be doggonned if some guy is gonna to tell me where I can or can't live. The moment we have to run and hide and live in shadows that is the moment when we have lost our liberties. And it's NOT gonna happen, not on my watch. You didn't get permission from me to be who you are, so damn sure I'm not gonna get permission from you to be who I am.

Scene 8: Pikes Peak

Projection: The Colorado Springs Gazette.

GAZETTE. Ted Haggard is back in Colorado Springs though he's not saying why. "I can't talk to you. I am forbidden from talking to the media," Haggard said Saturday evening after answering the doorbell at his home. Haggard and his wife, Gayle, are still listed as the owners of the home that sits behind a gated entrance two miles from the megachurch Haggard founded in his basement.

(*Online sound. Projections of the* BLOGGERS' *words animated across the set.*)

ONLINE 1. Jesus Christ! Any more of this BS and we should file stalking charges on behalf of the entire city! Can the city place a restraining order on Ted Haggard?

ONLINE 2. Well, I say Thank God for Ted Haggard, New Life AND Focus on the Family! They made Colorado Springs an excellent city to live in for Christians. And if that helps keep the crud from moving here then we welcome it!

ONLINE 3. This website is a freakin' cyber Tower of Babel. We've got the voices of the illiterate, the nonsensical, the reformed drunkards and prostitutes (you know who you are), and the born-again self-proclaimed voices of truth. If all of you would just get the hell out of here we would have the best city on earth!

(*At New Life.*)

ASSOCIATE PASTOR. —and we will keep you informed as the process for choosing a new pastor finally—fingers crossed—comes to its conclusion. I know there were people out there who doubted that we couldn't weather this storm, but I think we can say now that this dark season has shown us— has *proven*—that this church was never about a man. This church belongs to God. Yes. Now, we have a special visitor here. Up from our Boulder Street campus, it is a privilege and a pleasure for us to hear from Pastor Marcus Haggard. Would you welcome him.

(*Applause.*)

MARCUS HAGGARD. Thank you. I'm guessing you're applauding because I dressed up for you all tonight. If somebody would've told me that you were all going to wear shorts and flip-flops, I'd wear what I wear on Sunday morning, which is shorts and flip-flops, and maybe fit in—but I pulled out my nice black shiny shoes and well, am I like booming? Or is that just the power of this awe-inspiring sound system? Am I good? Sorry, I'm not used to all this. Downtown at Boulder Street Church things are a little simpler.

Now, this church has been through all kinds of interesting hard times. And I'll tell you, with my dad, yeah in one paradigm it's the fall. Sure. But in another paradigm, he came alive. He's understanding God for the first time. Because, you know, we believe God is unconditional love, he's the only one who can love us completely for who we are, no matter what we've done and heal us. For so many years before my dad had been really distant. With the constant act, you know. Like he's got everything together. I don't think he even realized how distant he'd become. But now, for our family, my dad's finally realizing that he doesn't have to perform for us. Because we love him. It's that simple.

I wanted to share this with all of you because I've been thinking how we're afraid to embrace love. Genuine love. Because we're afraid of being exposed. How fascinating is it that the constant criticism of the church is that we aren't genuine? Why is that? Because we're afraid people will find out who we really are. People will find out that we're human. And we hurt. Because we get hurt. You and I get hurt in life. Welcome to planet Earth: innocent people die. Innocent people get hurt all the time.

(*Music starts. Actor playing* TRAILS GUIDE *enters.*)

TRAILS GUIDE. No guide, no map can guarantee you won't get lost. So for a safe trip to the Rockies heed these final words of advice: Never strike out alone; someone should always know where you're going. Use a compass to orient yourself, and keep looking back so you know what the trail looks like in reverse. But suppose you have lost the trail entirely. Do not panic. Virtually all people who get lost are eventually found, either alive or dead, so the idea is to stay alive no matter how long you have to stay lost.

SONG: PIKES PEAK

SHE WAS BORN TO A YANKEE FAMILY
SHE TAUGHT AND WROTE POETRY
BUT ALWAYS DREAMED OF WESTERN VISTAS

SHE TRAVELED TO COLORADO
THE JOURNEY WAS HARD AND SLOW
SHE WAS SO TIRED THAT SHE NEARLY MISSED THE VIEW

BUT UP ON TOP OF PIKES PEAK
THE SUN WAS SHINING DOWN
OVER AMERICA THE BEAUTIFUL
THE PURPLE MOUNTAINS AND THE FRUITED PLAIN
FROM FAR ABOVE THIS COUNTRY IS SO BEAUTIFUL

OH WEARY TRAVELER WHERE ARE YOU GOING?
ARE YOU STILL UP THERE ON THAT MOUNTAIN?
WERE YOU SEDUCED BY ALL THAT BEAUTY?
WHEN WILL YOU COME DOWN?

YOU GO TO THE MOUNTAINTOP
YOU STARE AT THE VIEW BELOW
THESE DAYS THE DRIVE JUST TAKES AN HOUR

THE SUBURBS THE SCHOOLS THE STOPLIGHTS
THINGS NONE OF THE POETS SHOW
WHAT DOES IT SAY TO YOU THIS POWER AND THIS
GLORY

GROUP A.
OH WEARY TRAVELER WHERE ARE YOU GOING?
ARE YOU STILL UP THERE ON THAT MOUNTAIN?
WERE YOU SEDUCED BY ALL THAT BEAUTY?
WHAT IS YOUR PLAN FOR THIS THIS THIS BEAUTIFUL
   CITY

GROUP B.
UP ON TOP OF PIKES PEAK
THE SUN WAS SHINING DOWN
OVER AMERICA THE BEAUTIFUL
THE PURPLE MOUNTAINS AND THE FRUITED PLAIN
FROM FAR ABOVE THIS COUNTRY IS SO BEAUTIFUL

GROUP C.
WHERE ARE WE GOING?
HOW DO WE GET THERE?
WHAT IS YOUR PLAN FOR THIS THIS THIS BEAUTIFUL
   CITY?
WHERE ARE WE GOING
HOW DO WE GET THERE
WHAT IS YOUR PLAN FOR THIS THIS THIS BEAUTIFUL
   CITY?

MARCUS HAGGARD. So do this: stop hiding. Be vulnerable. Sometimes it really hurts. But we've gotta dig deep with this. All of us have different stories. All of us have this stuff. But we don't want to be believers just on the surface. Let God show us how to be completely exposed. And help us to trust. So come on, let's all stand and pray.

End of Play

BECKY SHAW
by Gina Gionfriddo

BIOGRAPHY

Gina Gionfriddo's play, *After Ashley*, premiered in the 2004 Humana Festival. It was subsequently produced by The Vineyard Theatre in New York and by regional theatres throughout the country. Ms. Gionfriddo has received an Obie Award, a Guggenheim Fellowship and The Susan Smith Blackburn Prize. Her play *U.S. Drag* was presented Off-Broadway by The Stagefarm in February, 2008. She is currently at work on a new play commissioned by Playwrights Horizons. Ms. Gionfriddo is a writer/producer for the NBC series *Law & Order*. She has contributed essays on rock music to the literary journal *The Believer* and short fiction to *Canteen*. A graduate of the M.F.A. playwriting program at Brown University, she has taught writing at Brown, Providence College and Rhode Island College.

ACKNOWLEDGMENTS

Becky Shaw premiered at the Humana Festival of New American Plays in February 2008. It was directed by Peter DuBois with the following cast:

SUZANNA SLATER .... Mia Barron
MAX GARRETT .... David Wilson Barnes
SUSAN SLATER .... Janis Dardaris
ANDREW PORTER .... Davis Duffield
BECKY SHAW .... Annie Parisse

and the following production staff:

Scenic Designer .... Paul Owen
Costume Designer .... Jessica Ford
Lighting Designer .... Brian J. Lilienthal
Sound Designer .... Benjamin Marcum
Properties Designer .... Mark Walston
Festival Fight Supervisor .... Lee Look
Stage Manager .... Michael D. Domue
Production Assistant .... Mary Spadoni
Dramaturg .... Adrien-Alice Hansel
Assistant Dramaturg .... Charles Haugland
Casting .... Zan Sawyer-Dailey
Directing Assistant .... Dav Yendler

Commissioned by Actors Theatre of Louisville with the support of the Harold and Mimi Steinberg Charitable Trust.

CAST OF CHARACTERS
SUZANNA SLATER
MAX GARRETT
SUSAN SLATER
ANDREW PORTER
BECKY SHAW

TIME AND PLACE
Present day.

David Wilson Barnes and Mia Barron
in *Becky Shaw*

32nd Annual Humana Festival of New American Plays
Actors Theatre of Louisville, 2008
Photo by Harlan Taylor

BECKY SHAW

ACT I
Scene 1

A room at a mid-range hotel in New York City. SUZANNA, 34, on the made bed, watching TV. She looks tranced out, exhausted. She's wearing a black dress (plain and casual; nothing sexy or formal or funereal) and no makeup or jewelry. She's not putting any effort into her appearance these days and it shows. MAX, 35, lets himself into the room. Man on a mission, he's energized.

MAX. All right. It took me fifty fucking minutes, but your mother has agreed to walk ten paces from her room to your room to negotiate. *(He turns the TV off.)*

SUZANNA. I won't see her.

MAX. Excuse me?

SUZANNA. I won't see her.

MAX. You won't see her. So you're not just depressed, you're delusional. You think you're the Queen of England, I'm your manservant—

SUZANNA. No—

MAX. You're the fucking Wizard of Oz now; I prep your audience, you turn them away on some…wizardly whim—

SUZANNA. Why do you have a key to my room?

MAX. Because I paid for it.

SUZANNA. Did you pay for my mom's room, too?

MAX. Yes.

SUZANNA. Because we're poor now?

MAX. That's…what we're all gonna talk about. After you pull yourself together.

SUZANNA. I can't.

MAX. You have to. Negotiations are all about who has the biggest dick in the room. If you don't have a big dick, you gotta bluff. *(Pointing at her.)* Big dick, no tears.

SUZANNA. She's my mother. She knows I have no dick. And I'm grieving, Max. Neither of you appreciate that.

MAX. I appreciate it, but right now you gotta stop it.

SUZANNA. Max, she brought a…man with her. That is so insulting to my father.

MAX. Your father is dead, his feelings don't matter.

111

SUZANNA. Max!

MAX. Suzanna, you gotta pull it together. Clock strikes midnight you can regress. Light your vanilla candle and write in your dream journal. Until then, you're a soldier. Comb your hair. Fix yourself up.

SUZANNA. (*As she tries….*) In one of my textbooks for school, I read about these families…. Craziest thing, Max. When someone in the family is down or weak, the other family members do this thing called nurturing. Have you ever heard of that?

MAX. No.

(*There's a knock on the door. MAX springs to answer it.*)

No crying. Big dick.

(*MAX answers the door and escorts SUSAN SLATER, 60, into the room. She has MS and may use a cane. She's attractive, but there's a heaviness to her: the fatigue of endless fatigue. Her mind is sharp and she's cultivated a forceful manner to compensate for her physical disability.*)

MAX. OK. So. Clean slate. Last few hours never happened. I'd like to welcome my two favorite ladies to New York City. We're all so glad we're here because we love each other so much, etc. etc. Now. I'm gonna suggest that we stick to the original plan.

SUSAN. I never suggested otherwise.

SUZANNA. You brought Lester! The plan did not include Lester!

SUSAN. Suzanna, I am disabled. I can't travel alone.

SUZANNA. I offered to drive to Richmond and pick you up—

SUSAN. I don't feel safe in a car with you. I'm sorry if that hurts your feelings, but—

MAX. It hurts my feelings, Susan. I taught her to drive.

SUSAN. I'm not blaming you. Suzanna has assumed a somber attitude since her father died.

SUZANNA. So I can't drive?

SUSAN. You're sluggish. If a drunk driver is careening into my path, I don't want my life in your hands. I'm sorry.

MAX. Suzanna's attitude is not the point. Lester is not the point.

SUZANNA. Lester is the point! I am not going to discuss my father's estate with your…whatever he is to you in addition to being your house painter, I don't really want to know.

SUSAN. He's my lover.

SUZANNA. Oh, my God. How could you?

SUSAN. (*Anger brewing.*) Listen to me. Your father died six months…

SUZANNA. It was three months!

MAX. Four. It was four months; you're both liars.

SUSAN. You didn't lose a child or even a breast. Your father died of natural causes after a life well lived. That's not loss, it's transition.

SUZANNA. How can you…. It's a huge loss.

SUSAN. No. It's an old man dying peacefully. It's not tragic—

SUZANNA. He was my dad.

SUSAN. And you're an adult. This…. This is a costume.

SUZANNA. What—my clothes?

SUSAN. The black dress. You're infatuated with your grief. You think you've finally found something that will distinguish you.

MAX. OK, that's enough.

SUSAN. It's not a distinction, Suzanna. A parent's death…. It is the most common of milestones—

MAX. My proposal is that we keep to the plan. We go downstairs and have dinner. We talk facts and figures. Lester can join us for dessert.

SUSAN. No. I won't leave him sitting in the room while we have our nice dinner.

MAX. See…. *This* is the point. It's not going to be a nice dinner, Susan. We're here to talk about your finances—

SUSAN. I don't discuss money at the dinner table. You grew up in my household; you should know that.

MAX. Oh, no. No. You agreed to this!

SUSAN. I agreed to hear your opinions—

MAX. They're not opinions.

SUSAN. I'm perfectly willing to have a conversation about the estate, but not over dinner. (*To* SUZANNA.) Some women—Marilyn Monroe, Princess Diana—are sensual in their grief. You are not.

SUZANNA. Max!

MAX. Susan, please—

SUSAN. Do you disagree? Look at her.

MAX. Let me tell you something. Suzanna can be fixed. I'm not worried about Suzanna. Your financial health on the other hand—

SUSAN. Lester and I will meet you downstairs. We'll share a meal and some good wine. We'll talk business in the morning.

MAX. No! I don't have time in the morning, Susan! And you can't afford good wine.

SUSAN. (*After a beat.*) Are you enjoying this drama you've created?

MAX. I didn't create it; your husband created it. I am just the messenger.

SUSAN. This is terribly exhilarating for you. I can see it.

SUZANNA. Mom.

MAX. How can you…. You and Richard raised me, Susan. For all practical purposes, you're my parents.

SUSAN. And that only makes it crueler.

MAX. You think I take pleasure in this? I would be a monster—

SUSAN. Not a monster, a power monger. I know that look.

MAX. What look? This look?

SUSAN. That is the look you get when my family's stupidity offers you a foothold to gain power.

MAX. Anytime I can clean up after your family's stupidity, I am more than happy to do it.

SUZANNA. Stop it. What is this "your family," "my family." We're…. This is our family.

(*A difficult silence that* SUZANNA *rushes to fill….*)

How broke are we?

MAX. I think we should drink some alcohol.

SUSAN. Lester is hungry. And I won't talk about money over dinner. Whatever you want to say, you may say now or in the morning.

MAX. I have a full day tomorrow—

SUSAN. Then say it now. Cogently, please. Do not savor.

MAX. (*After a beat.*) The business hasn't turned a profit in nearly a decade. Richard burned through a lot of your savings patching holes, keeping it afloat. I think it was largely…sentimental on his part. It's an old family business. Understandably, he hoped the tide would turn…

SUZANNA. Are we broke?

MAX. No. But your savings are…thin. I have a plan I would like to propose—

SUSAN. I have a very hard time believing this, Max. Yoshi would certainly have told me if—

MAX. Yoshi lost his objectivity. He'll be the first to admit that…

SUSAN. Nonsense. He's a Japanese businessman. His objectivity is all he has.

SUZANNA. Mom, that's racist.

SUSAN. Send me the figures, I will show them to my financial advisor.

MAX. Your financial advisor is Yoshi.

SUSAN. Correct.

MAX. Yoshi no longer wishes to be involved.

SUSAN. Because you bullied him in your zeal to seize power. I'll bring him back.

MAX. There's no power to seize, Susan! (*Pause.*) Look. Yoshi asked me.... There was a loss of objectivity.

SUSAN. In your opinion...

MAX. In reality on planet Earth. Your husband was stupid about his money and his financial advisor was.... There was a romantic situation and I'm sorry.

SUSAN. (*After a beat.*) Oh, you are devious.

SUZANNA. Romantic?

SUSAN. He means homosexual.

MAX. I don't think we need to get into labels.

SUZANNA. Gay?

MAX. Bi. Let's say he was bi.

SUZANNA. You don't believe in bisexuality.

SUSAN. I'm very upset with you, Max.

MAX. Me?

SUSAN. (*Rising to leave.*) Lester and I will be having dinner privately and returning to Richmond.

MAX. Susan, you gotta face this.

SUSAN. (*To* MAX.) I hope you enjoyed yourself. You could have done this in an email as I begged you to do. (*To* SUZANNA.) You're welcome to join us for dinner if you're prepared to apologize to Lester for your dramatics earlier this evening.

SUZANNA. Mom, you need to stay with me and deal with this.

(SUSAN *looks back and forth...at* MAX, *at* SUZANNA. *Her gaze lands on* MAX.)

SUSAN. (*To* MAX.) No good deed goes unpunished. You...were a good deed.

MAX. I know that.

SUSAN. I took you into my home...

SUZANNA. Mom. Stop.

MAX. You did. I owe your family a debt and I'm ready to start repaying it tonight. Let me help you—

(SUSAN *makes a dismissive swipe at the air and starts walking to the door....*)

MAX. I manage money for a living, Susan. I make people rich. You could do worse than having me—

SUSAN. You.... You are a rich man...who puts his family in a two-star hotel. That's what you are.

(SUSAN *leaves, closing the door hard behind her.*)

MAX. You're going to have to hire someone to do this. There's too much history— (*After a beat.*) This is a three-star hotel.

SUZANNA. Max, I'm sorry.

MAX. I think the MS is catching up to her. Since when does she run from a shitstorm?

SUZANNA. She likes other people's shitstorms. This is too close.

MAX. Is that it? (*After a beat.*) You know…. The day of my mother's funeral, she bought me a suit. I'm ten years old, I'd met her, like…once. She took me to the fat child department at Sears. She said, "Your mother is dead and your father dresses you like a gay hustler."

SUZANNA. Max, that's awful. Why have you never told me that?

MAX. It was awful at the time, but…. She saved me from walking into my mother's funeral looking like a gay hustler. Everybody else was…blubbering all over themselves. She's the only person who had my back.

SUZANNA. What did your dad dress you in?

MAX. Green corduroy Toughskins pantsuit.

SUZANNA. Wow.

MAX. Your dad and Yoshi…. You either knew or you surmised. You barely reacted and given what a fucking drama queen you are…

SUZANNA. I was counting on a deathbed last scene where I would ask him.

MAX. You were saving the hard questions until he was too feeble to run?

SUZANNA. It's not like that. Did you know?

MAX. I knew there was something. A factor X that would explain him. I figured he was gay…or impotent…or he'd…killed someone and your mother had proof so he couldn't leave.

SUZANNA. God, I should have asked him.

MAX. He just would have denied it. He was a lying denying kinda guy.

SUZANNA. Don't say that.

MAX. He was a liar and a denier AND the greatest man I've ever known. (*Pause.*) Your parents complemented each other. Your father denied problems, your mother rubbed your face in them.

SUZANNA. He did not deny…. My father had an appropriate grasp of how much a child could handle.

MAX. Right. He lied.

SUZANNA. That's what parents are supposed to do, dumb-ass.

MAX. Lie to children?

SUZANNA. Yes! He lied to me about my mother's illness until I was old enough to deal with it, and that was a gift.

MAX. A gift?

SUZANNA. You can't tell an eight year old that her mother has MS.

MAX. Susie, he told you she was an alcoholic and she wasn't.

SUZANNA. He never said "alcoholic." He said, sometimes Mommy drinks too much and that makes her drop things. It was better—

MAX. (*Overlapping.*) Well. You're going to graduate school in psychology. Get some feedback on that episode and get back to me.

SUZANNA. Even now, I can't fault him, Max. No matter how bad the money is, it was an act of love to shield me from it. My father always knew how much I could handle.

MAX. Can I ask…. What *did* he think you could handle? You seem to have been kept in the dark about pretty much everything…

SUZANNA. He told me about the MS when I was thirteen.

MAX. OK. (*Pause.*) Did he come clean about Santa Claus or do you need me to—

SUZANNA. Fuck you, Max. There are times when lying is the most humane and loving thing you can do.

MAX. I see. Your father spends his life being "humane" and making everybody love him. He leaves me to be the asshole…

SUZANNA. I'm sorry. It's not fair to you—

MAX. No, it's fair. I owe him something. He was generous to me beyond all reason.

SUZANNA. He was generous to you because he adored you.

MAX. (*A doubting look, and then….*) Well. When my father and I showed up at your house to say my mother had died, both of your parents said, "I'm sorry, Matt."

SUZANNA. They said Max. You misheard them.

MAX. No, I didn't. What your mother said—

SUZANNA. —is not true.

MAX. It's fine. I know I was your dad's good deed. I mean…. It wasn't pure charity. He thought an orphan in the house would make your mother behave better.

SUZANNA. Well, that is true, but…. It didn't work, did it? She stayed evil and he kept you anyway. Because he loved you!

MAX. It was a bold move on your father's part. Adopting a child to shame his wife into being less abusive…. That took some balls.

SUZANNA. (*After a beat.*) Can I finish graduate school?

MAX. Yes. You're not rich anymore, but you're not the fucking Joads.

SUZANNA. So what do we do?

MAX. Sell the company. Sell the house. Your mother can get a nice, full-service apartment. They carry the groceries, they clean. The rest of her needs…. Lester can pick up the slack.

SUZANNA. Lester is the slack. He's not a "lover;" he's a rent boy.

MAX. Yes, he is and it's honest work.

SUZANNA. No, it isn't!

MAX. Lester will do everything your father did for your mother. Whatever his price, it's worth it.

SUZANNA. No.

MAX. What's your solution? You gonna move home and help her?

SUZANNA. God, no. She needs to hire someone.

MAX. The money isn't there, Suzanna. Her health is gonna decline and Lester is a decent guy…

SUZANNA. He's dumb and he's our age.

MAX. He's not dumb. He's a redneck, but he's a sort of…alternative redneck. He wants to make a movie.

SUZANNA. So that's why he's with her! Fuck that.

MAX. You want your freedom? Open your eyes. Your freedom is rent boys and redneck cinema.

SUZANNA. You're talking about prostitution.

MAX. Prostitution, marriage…. Same thing. It's two people coming together because each has something the other wants.

SUZANNA. Wait. You don't believe in love?

MAX. Sure I do. Love is a happy by-product of use.

SUZANNA. (*After a beat.*) A happy by-product of use? What the fuck does that mean?

MAX. Suzanna, we're animals! Love is just…. It's a feeling. Like hunger, like cold. It's a feeling that tells you what you need to survive. A sandwich, a sweater, an orphan, a…Lester.

SUZANNA. Stop calling yourself an orphan. Do you think all love is use or just romantic love?

MAX. All love. Your father, for example, paid our college tuition. We, in turn, loved him very much which God knows he needed.

SUZANNA. I hate when you do this.

MAX. Do what?

SUZANNA. Turn a beautiful thing to shit!

MAX. Understanding behavior is not "turning it to shit"!

SUZANNA. You're saying my father was generous with us because he couldn't love men? Is that it?

MAX. I think if your father had been more self-actualized, I'd have college loans. I do believe that.

SUZANNA. I don't. And now I want to stop talking about this.

MAX. You're getting a Ph.D. in psychology. How are you so totally unwilling to ask the hard questions?

SUZANNA. I ask them when it's necessary. When there's no problem.... It's like shoving your face in the toilet after you shit. You can do it, but it's not necessary.

MAX. Wow. You're gonna make an interesting therapist. (*After a beat.*) I'm proud of you. I just told you you're broke and you have a gay dad. And you're.... I feel like I can go to bed and not worry about you.

SUZANNA. You worry about me? Since when?

MAX. Of course, I worry about you. You're a mess.

SUZANNA. My father's only been dead three months. I think I'm doing pretty well considering.

MAX. It's four months! God. It's long enough to grieve. You have too much time on your hands—

SUZANNA. I'm in a Ph.D. program, Max!

MAX. In psychology. If you had gone to medical school like I told you to, you couldn't call me crying; you'd be too busy saving human lives.

SUZANNA. Am I inconveniencing you by calling? I'll stop.

MAX. Call me all you want, I can't help you. You need to take action.

SUZANNA. I'm in therapy.

MAX. That's not action, that's wallowing.

SUZANNA. What's your idea of action?

MAX. Uh.... Things you do outside your home that require you to move your limbs. You need to join some clubs...

SUZANNA. Clubs? What kind of clubs?

MAX. Clubs! The KKK, The Daughters of the American Revolution.... I don't fucking care. You need activities so that when you get mopey-mopey weepy-weepy, you can abort the thoughts. You can say, "I don't have time for this. I have a...barn raising I need to jog to."

SUZANNA. You're insane.

MAX. Actions abort thoughts.

SUZANNA. Max, cut me some slack. Dad was my anchor in the world. I feel totally untethered...

MAX. Right. You need to fucking tether yourself. Join like a...powder puff, girl-on-girl softball team. Do something!

SUZANNA. I don't know. I think maybe there's value in just...sitting with it. This feeling of floating alone in the universe. Maybe I'm supposed to learn something from it.

MAX. You've had four months. You haven't learned anything.

SUZANNA. I'm talking about life lessons, Max. It's not like learning Photoshop.

MAX. So when you call me at three a.m. saying you want to...be dead, I should say, "Be very still, Suzanna, and reflect on your pain." That doesn't help you!

SUZANNA. It's not either/or, Max. You can offer empathy...

MAX. You're paying a therapist for empathy and you're still calling me saying some very scary things...

SUZANNA. They're normal impulses and they pass.

MAX. I hope so. They're hard to listen to. I need to go to bed.

SUZANNA. Now? It's so early.

MAX. I go to work at seven. I need to be in bed by ten which gives me...just enough time for take-out and pornography.

SUZANNA. Let's order food here.

MAX. Can we watch pornography?

SUZANNA. I don't know. I feel like our father is sort of with us right now, like, in the room...

MAX. He wasn't "our father." I have an actual, living father who would be very hurt to hear you say that.

SUZANNA. How is he?

MAX. I don't want to talk about that.

SUZANNA. That bad, huh?

MAX. No.... It's just.... It's more complicated financial stuff.

SUZANNA. He's not gonna go to jail, is he?

MAX. It's enough family drama for one night.

SUZANNA. Sorry. Not only do we all dump our problems on you, they're not even interesting problems. It's all...math.

MAX. Math, I can do. A little Japanese man crying all over me in a Starbucks, I can't—

SUZANNA. Yoshi! Wow. Was he super sad?

MAX. Oh, yeah. (*After a beat.*) I want you to call your mother tomorrow and suggest that someone other than me—

SUZANNA. Let's give it a few days to sink in. But I will call her.

MAX. You have to. I know you're in your...sad Buddhist phase, but time is money.

SUZANNA. I'll call her.

MAX. (*After a beat.*) So, let's pick some activities. Right now. Al-Anon, Unitarianism, The Green Party...what are you gonna do?

SUZANNA. I don't know. There's a grad school ski trip. Next week.

MAX. Go.

SUZANNA. I don't ski. It's cheap, though.

MAX. Go. Go skiing. Get a dog. Kiss a girl. Shake things up.

SUZANNA. No dogs, but.... Skiing I would try.

MAX. Great. Now let's watch pornography.

SUZANNA. Remember that big...porn superstore we used to drive past on the way to the mall? I remember the day I saw the word "amateur" on the marquees for the first time. You were driving and I said—

MAX. "Who wants to watch sexual amateurs?"

SUZANNA. I thought it meant, like, people who didn't know what they were doing.

MAX. I remember. You ever watch the amateur stuff?

SUZANNA. (*After a beat.*) A little.

MAX. OK, so you know what these "amateurs" look like.

SUZANNA. They're not all fat and ugly, Max. That's just not true.

MAX. It is true. The hot amateurs are being paid, so they're not really amateurs.

SUZANNA. Yeah, I can't watch that—girls in this country illegally and addicted to drugs...

MAX. What consenting adults do to get into this country and stay here is not my problem.

SUZANNA. I didn't say it was. Relax. (*After a beat.*) Well. That's the only porn I can watch. All the rest.... I feel too responsible. You know?

MAX. No. (*A beat.*) See, you are why civilization is gonna end. You would choose a disgusting reality over a beautiful fiction. I don't understand that. I want *The Love Boat.* I do not want a real boat with real lovers.

SUZANNA. *The Love Boat....* Wow. That's just about my happiest memory of our childhood. Remember...

MAX. What?

SUZANNA. The Saturday your mom died, we watched that on TV while my parents got your dad drunk. Remember?

MAX. Not really.

SUZANNA. We did a thousand piece puzzle and watched *The Love Boat.*

MAX. Wait. The puzzle. Was it porpoises or something?

SUZANNA. It was a whale! You remember!

MAX. Not...well.

SUZANNA. I remember *The Love Boat* ending and my dad's footsteps and I remember thinking.... It's over. Max has to go home. And I prayed that wouldn't happen.

MAX. What do you mean, you prayed?

SUZANNA. I prayed. I said please God, don't let this end. I didn't pray for your mom to be alive, or my mom to be...not sick. I prayed for more time with you. And my prayer got answered. Dad came around the corner with hot chocolate. We passed out during *Fantasy Island.*

MAX. I don't remember any of that. Let's watch TV.

SUZANNA. I don't want to watch porn, though.

MAX. Fine. How about horror?

SUZANNA. Oh, yes please. Can you find some?

MAX. I can try.

(*They get cozy on the bed.* MAX *takes the remote, and starts channel surfing. This closeness is scary.*)

SUZANNA. Now I want hot chocolate. Hot chocolate and horror. That is what I want more than anything in the world.

MAX. Don't pray. Or if you do, don't squander it. Pray for money.

SUZANNA. I would never pray for money.

MAX. OK. Here. Look. *Nightmare on Elm Street.* But which one? Hundred bucks if you know.

SUZANNA. It's.... Gimme a second.... It's three! Freddy's about to say, "Where's the bourbon, bitch?"

MAX. You're right. Good call!

(*A beat. They watch* Nightmare on Elm Street. *Then....*)

MAX. "Where's the bourbon, bitch?" Like it's not bad enough he has knives for fingers; he has to be verbally abusive.

SUZANNA. I saw a rock concert at Jones Beach last year.... It was late at night and freezing even though it was summer. And they didn't sell booze, so.... I drank hot chocolate.

MAX. (*After a beat.*) That's it? That's the whole story.

SUZANNA. Yeah.

MAX. That's not a story. That's a set-up for a story.

SUZANNA. It's a snapshot. An exhilarating moment.

MAX. If that was exhilarating, you left a part out.

SUZANNA. I asked the concessions guy why they didn't sell booze and he said that a girl had been struck by lightning the year before. So they stopped serving booze.

MAX. (*After a beat.*) That makes absolutely no sense.

SUZANNA. The guy next to me bought a coke and the concessions guy poured it out of the bottle into a cup. And, again, I asked why. And he said that somebody had thrown a bottle on stage the night before and hit the singer in the head. So no more bottles.

(*A beat. A look. They watch the movie.* SUZANNA *thinks....*)

SUZANNA. OK, I got it. The point.

MAX. Fantastic.

SUZANNA. I had this moment...this wave of exhilaration came over me and the exhilaration was feeling.... It was worth it. People getting struck by lightning and whacked in the head with bottles.... A certain amount of... brutality was worth it to see a rock concert next to the ocean. The night your mom died felt like that, you know? My mother was sick, yours was dead.... But I felt so happy to be with you. Maybe that's how life works, you know? All these hideous things, but you get little pockets of joy to get you through. Rock concerts on the ocean. Puzzles and TV.

(MAX *kisses her and she lets him. She starts kissing back and stops.*)

Max, I can't. You're my brother.

MAX. I'm not your brother. I think your mother hammered that point home.

SUZANNA. OK.... You're my...money manager.

MAX. I am. Keep kissing me, I might take that responsibility seriously.

SUZANNA. I can't.

MAX. You don't want to.

SUZANNA. I really want to.

MAX. So what's the problem?

SUZANNA. It's...epic. It's...

MAX. It doesn't have to change anything.

SUZANNA. Really?

MAX. Really.

(*Leaving the TV on, they start making out. Reluctant at first,* SUZANNA *soon reciprocates with* MAX's *level of enthusiasm. A sense on both sides that this was a long time coming. Lights fade...*)

Scene 2

Eight months later. ANDREW, *and* SUZANNA's *apartment in Providence, Rhode Island.* SUZANNA, *standing, talks on a cell phone.*

SUZANNA. Hi. It's Suzanna. This is my fifth call and I'm worried.... I am worried and my husband is worried. We're afraid you're dead or injured. We just.... No. You know what? I know you're not dead or injured. You're just being you and thinking only of yourself. So.... So fuck you, you know? Just fuck you. Fuck. You. Mom. Call me.

(ANDREW *enters with an open laptop computer.*)

ANDREW. OK, there are no flights tonight out of Providence. Cheapest flight...out of Boston to Key West is...nine hundred seventyfive dollars. Round trip.

SUZANNA. Nine-hundred? What the fuck am I supposed to do, Andrew? She's not answering her phone, we know she used her health insurance...

ANDREW. But that could mean nothing. For all you know, she has, like, a yeast infection...

SUZANNA. Yuck! Andrew, that's my mother.

ANDREW. I think if it were serious, Lester would have called.

SUZANNA. No. If it were serious, Lester would empty her bank account and flee to Mexico.

ANDREW. They've been together almost a year. I think if he was gonna kill her, he'd have done it by now.

SUZANNA. That's not how psychopaths work, stupid! They take time to gain your trust. I love that you're not a psychopath. I view this as the biggest accomplishment of my life: I married a man who is not a psychopath.

ANDREW. Well.... Thank you. But don't call me stupid. And call Lester.

SUZANNA. No! I told you, Andrew. I set a boundary with my mother. She can't just act out and make me reverse myself.

ANDREW. She's not acting out. Something happened to her that required medical attention.

SUZANNA. Wait. You do think it's something bad. When does the flight leave?

ANDREW. Ten o'clock. How 'bout I call Lester?

SUZANNA. Fuck no. You're my husband. If I make a boundary, it's your boundary, too. (*Pause.*) Andrew, what should I do?

ANDREW. That's up to you. I will support whatever—

SUZANNA. Don't throw the decision back to me when I ask you.... Sorry. I'm freaking out. I need you to tell me what to do.

(ANDREW *gets her a glass of wine.*)

ANDREW. First you need to drink some wine and chill.

SUZANNA. (*Overlapping.*) Again— That's not an answer!

ANDREW. Sweetie, I can't be your dad. You're gonna have to participate in the decision—

SUZANNA. (*Overlapping.*) What's that supposed to mean?

ANDREW. You're getting pissy with me because I won't make a decision for you—

SUZANNA. No. I'm asking you to take a firm position. Don't be hurt—

ANDREW. I'm not hurt. I know when you lash out at me, the anger isn't really about me.

SUZANNA. It isn't?

ANDREW. No. It's "why isn't my dad here when I need him?" It's still this really primal rage in you—

(SUZANNA *makes a dismissive gesture: swats the air or crinkles her face.*)

SUZANNA. Now you're being a writer and, like, gilding my motivation to make a crap situation more existential. Which also doesn't help me.

ANDREW. Wow.

SUZANNA. Andrew, if I was in an accident and my head was bleeding, you would have to make a decision for me.

ANDREW. Fine. Right now your head's not bleeding. Your head is fine and capable and…totally cute. Even when obnoxious words come out of it.

SUZANNA. Kiss me?

(*They kiss. It's a good kiss. There's real love and passion here.*)

What I said about you being a writer? That wasn't meant to be bitchy. Is this our first emergency as husband and wife?

ANDREW. I think so. (*Pause.*) Yeah, I think it is. What do you want to do?

SUZANNA. (*After a beat.*) Call Max. (*Remembering.*) Max. Shit! What time is it? We should cancel with Max and Becky.

ANDREW. Max is probably on his way. I can cancel Becky, but…

SUZANNA. No. If we have Max, we need Becky. He's already resistant to the whole "blind date" thing. We can't abort the mission.

ANDREW. I thought you said he stopped being resistant.

SUZANNA. Let's just introduce them and send them off on their date. I can't be social when I'm this worried.

ANDREW. No. If you're backing out of dinner, we need to cancel with Becky.

SUZANNA. Why?

ANDREW. I just…. The plan was a double date, with me there as her friend to, you know, facilitate a supportive—

SUZANNA. Oh, no. Wait. Why does she need support?

ANDREW. Everyone needs support. And she's…sorta delicate.

SUZANNA. Oh, fuck you, Andrew. Are you fixing Max up with a basket-case crazy person?

ANDREW. Whoa. You need to stop it, like, now.

SUZANNA. Stop what?

ANDREW. Come on, Susie, we've been over this. I didn't grow up with people sniping and accusing...

SUZANNA. OK, fine. Tell me the truth about Becky.

ANDREW. She started temping in my office two months ago. I've told you all I know.

SUZANNA. How is she delicate?

ANDREW. She's just at a transition point in her life. She's in a kind of melancholic place...

SUZANNA. Melancholic. Great. You tell me this now.

ANDREW. Can you stop fixating on my words? Becky is a great catch and she's available because she's in a transitional life space.

SUZANNA. I better warn Max.

ANDREW. Don't. I already warned Becky.

SUZANNA. About what?

ANDREW. I told her.... His coarse delivery belies a rich interior life.

SUZANNA. You've met Max—what—twice?

ANDREW. Exactly. He's a tough first meet. Second time, I liked him. You know, I could drive you to Florida. Miss work Monday, back on Tuesday...

SUZANNA. Take off Monday? Bullshit you'll take off Monday.

ANDREW. You want to rephrase that?

SUZANNA. (*After a beat.*) I love you so much. This is the one and only thing that drives me crazy. That you would just blow off work...

ANDREW. Blow off? It's a medical emergency with my mother-in-law.

SUZANNA. You're not working for Jasper and Hermione at the coffee collective anymore. This is a real job.

ANDREW. Oh, this is a "real job" because I wear a suit and it sounds good to your mom and Max. I'm a fucking office manager.

SUZANNA. No. It's a "real job" because you make twice the hourly wage you made at that fucking coffee collective.

ANDREW. When your mom fell down the stairs, Jasper and Hermione—who I know you have no respect for—told me take all the time you need—

SUZANNA. Andrew, you matter more at law firm. Any imbecile can change a filter.

ANDREW. You have class issues.

SUZANNA. No. I have a newly sobering view of how much money it takes to get by in America since my dad died.

ANDREW. (*After a beat.*) OK. I've been thinking about that and.... We don't need two bedrooms. I like having a room to write in, but we could get by in a one bedroom or a studio...

SUZANNA. Studio? Andrew, we talked to Max. With your new job and me picking up extra work, we're living within our means.

ANDREW. Right, but I can't get any writing done and I hate my job.

SUZANNA. So, you want to move us into a studio, so you can serve coffee.... Is that where this is going?

ANDREW. Just until I finish my book and you get your degree. It's not—

(*The phone rings.*)

SUZANNA. Oh, this better be my mother. (*Looking at number.*) It's Max. (*Answering.*) Hey, I can't talk, I'm waiting for my mom to call. (*Pause.*) It's in Andrew's name. Porter. (*Hangs up.*)

ANDREW. OK, before he gets here.... I don't want to leave this unfinished...

(*The buzzer buzzes.*)

SUZANNA. (*Going to buzzer.*) Let's talk about it with Max.

ANDREW. No! Susie, this is private.

(SUZANNA *rushes to* ANDREW *and kisses him hard on the mouth.*)

ANDREW. Is that your way of saying you'll live in a studio.

SUZANNA. No. That means I love you and fighting is OK, it doesn't change that.

(SUZANNA *rushes to the door, opens it, and steps out to look for* MAX.)

SUZANNA. (*Calling out.*) Are you ninety? It's two flights of stairs...

MAX. (*Entering.*) I had to muscle past five generations of Portuguese people frying fish.

SUZANNA. They're our landlords. Don't be racist.

MAX. It's nice to see you, too. What the hell is wrong?

SUZANNA. The usual shit. You want a glass of wine?

MAX. Sure. I brought a bottle.

(MAX *gives* SUZANNA *a bag with a bottle of wine in it. As she takes it to* ANDREW *who will open it....*)

SUZANNA. Our wine is not shit, Max.

MAX. Don't be hostile. I brought a nice wine because it's your...six-week anniversary? Hello, Andrew. Congratulations.

ANDREW. Hey, Max.

SUZANNA. It's three months, asshole. That's not a real anniversary. Next week is, though. We can drink on that. (*After a beat.*) Max?

MAX. What?

SUZANNA. Next week?

MAX. I don't know. What is next week?

SUZANNA. Come on!

MAX. What is it…. Flag Day? I don't know.

ANDREW. (*After a beat.*) Her dad's death…. It's a year…

MAX. OK. Right. You don't celebrate that, though. That's what threw me.

SUZANNA. You acknowledge it. You're coming over, right?

MAX. I…. What day is it?

SUZANNA. Forget it. Andrew and I are gonna commemorate it. If you can't even remember the date, I don't want you here.

MAX. Commemorate? It's not the fucking Bicentennial.

ANDREW. "Commemorate" is probably the wrong word. It was my idea. When I was in high school, a kid in my class died. And when the anniversary came around, people had a lot of feelings about it, so—

MAX. I'm sure they did. They were in fucking high school.

SUZANNA. Max.

ANDREW. We threw a party. It sounds weird, but it really helped shift us from mourning to, you know, celebrating his life.

MAX. OK. I'll come. Should I make a mix tape, or…

SUZANNA. If you're gonna make fun of it, don't come.

MAX. Are you having your period? What the fuck is wrong with you?

SUZANNA. What's usually wrong? My mother…

MAX. Oh. Well, in that case, we should start drinking and change the subject.

SUZANNA. You know, Max…. This is why you don't have a girlfriend.

MAX. Your mother is why I don't have a girlfriend? Actually, there's probably some truth to that.

SUZANNA. No. You don't have a girlfriend because you ask me what's wrong, then when I tell you, you're all "nothin' I can do."

MAX. (*To* ANDREW.) Is it all you hoped and dreamed of…being married to her?

ANDREW. It's great. How do you like Boston? You getting settled?

MAX. Boston is…. For four months, it's fine.

ANDREW. What is it you're doing…again…

MAX. I'm opening a Boston office for my company.

ANDREW. Yeah? Which part of the city—

MAX. (*Overlapping and dismissing.*) That's a whole…. I'm still sorting the details out. (*And changing subject….*) Look. Susie. You and your mother…. It's like the Middle East. Bad situation, not gonna change. So why talk about it?

SUZANNA. Because…. It begins with an "e," ends with a "y." You can't do it…

MAX. Nurture? No. Empathy! Right! Women and empathy, man.... This is just like that date I had last week.... The dance professor who wanted to talk about the Iraq war...

ANDREW. You can't talk about the Iraq war?

MAX. For a few minutes, fine. But there's nothing I can do about it, and there is definitely nothing Annabelle the dance professor can do about it, so—

ANDREW. Wait, you can't really believe there's nothing anyone can do.

MAX. Let me clarify. I send a lot of money to people whose job it is to do the right thing—

SUZANNA. The Democrats?

MAX. No, NAMBLA. Of course, the Democrats, stupid.

ANDREW. So people who don't have money can't exert any impact?

MAX. That's not what I'm saying. I'm saying I do my share.... I give away ten percent of my income to people whose job it is to solve this problem. It's their job. It's not mine. And I don't want my dinner ruined.

ANDREW. So what did you say to her?

MAX. Oh.... She wanted to tell me about this protest at Harvard. Some artists emoting against the war bullshit...

SUZANNA. You told her it was stupid and pointless.

MAX. I did not say it was stupid. I did say it was pointless.

SUZANNA. You're a jerk.

ANDREW. (*To* MAX.) You're probably right, but you don't want to say that on a first date.

MAX. Wait. Did you just agree with me?

ANDREW. It depends on how you said it. I used to go to those protests at Brown, but...I started to feel like they weren't really about the war. No one important was watching, we were just...assuaging our guilt and getting laid. I feel like.... Do something real or do nothing, you know?

SUZANNA. Now, if you say it like that, it's OK...

MAX. Which do you do?

ANDREW. What?

MAX. About the war. Do you do something real or do you do nothing?

ANDREW. Umm.... I don't do as much as I should. There's a group at Brown that sends books to the troops—

MAX. Oh, those poor troops. The Brown kids are sending them books...

SUZANNA. The troops are not illiterate, Max.

MAX. No, they're not. But when you live in fear of dirty bombs and torture, you do not want a used, highlighted copy of *To the fucking Lighthouse!*

SUZANNA. Let's change the subject.

MAX. You throw any sunblock in with the great books?

SUZANNA. Stop it, Max.

ANDREW. Max, I need you to take, like, a mellower tone with Becky.

SUZANNA. She's delicate.

ANDREW. She is not delicate! Just…. Max, it's not, like, emasculating to open yourself to another person's experience…

MAX. I don't know, Andrew. That sounded pretty fucking womanly.

SUZANNA. Tell him what to say. Give him actual words.

ANDREW. You could say something like, "Wow, that's kind of outside my experience, so I would need for you to say more."

MAX. (*To* SUZANNA; *genuine.*) Is that…. Don't tell me he snared you talking like that?

SUZANNA. I love it. It makes me weak.

ANDREW. Or you could say, like…. "Whoa, that's a little heavy for Saturday night" and then segue out…with a question about her life—

(ANDREW's *phone rings; he answers it.*)

ANDREW. Hello? (*Pause.*) Hey! (*Pause.*) Sorry. It's Porter. Just buzz— (*Pause.*) Oh, sure. Stay there. I'll meet you. Bye. (*Hangs up.*) That's Becky. I'm gonna go get her.

SUZANNA. Why don't you just have her buzz?

ANDREW. She was actually calling from the mini mart. She didn't know my last name either.

SUZANNA. Why is she at the mini mart?

ANDREW. She doesn't have a cell phone. I'm gonna go get her.

(ANDREW *grabs his coat and leaves.*)

MAX. Is my date…Amish?

BECKY. No. You're here! I'm so happy!

(SUZANNA *grabs* MAX *and bear hugs him. He enjoys it, if stiffly.*)

MAX. I am here. You…really do live in Rhode Island.

SUZANNA. What's that supposed to mean?

MAX. (*Sniffing his lapel.*) I've got Portuguese fish fry all over me.

SUZANNA. My landlords are so sweet. When we moved in, they made us wedding soup.

MAX. And you ate it?

SUZANNA. Of course. It's not like New York, Max. Landlords don't kill you to end your rent control.

MAX. I'm not rent-controlled. I own my place. I may buy a building, did I tell you?

SUZANNA. Your building?

MAX. No. In Brooklyn. So when you're ready to leave this little Portuguese fishing village, I'll cut you a good deal.

SUZANNA. I don't know if Andrew wants to live in New York. Listen…. I should have asked you this before, and please don't tell Andrew I didn't. You and that woman are totally done, right?

MAX. That woman?

SUZANNA. Christa. It's over, right? You're available?

MAX. I told you it's over.

SUZANNA. I know. It's just…. She was around longer than the others, so I wasn't sure—

MAX. "The others?"

SUZANNA. Come on, Max. You're a short-timer. You get the three-month itch. That was a really long relationship for you.

MAX. It was three months. I love that you're incapable of even simple math.

SUZANNA. It felt longer.

MAX. Well. I don't move as fast as you and Junior…

SUZANNA. If you call him Junior to his face, I'll kill you—

MAX. A four month courtship and a Vegas wedding. That's fast. And he is your junior.

SUZANNA. By four years! Thirty-one/thirty-five…. It's nothing.

MAX. He's thirty-one? I guess he seems younger because he's so…indie rock.

SUZANNA. Stop it.

MAX. It's not bad, it's just a cultural difference. Hey— When he comes back…. Five hundred dollars says he thinks 401k is a band.

SUZANNA. No, don't. That's mean. But speaking of money…. Don't tell Andrew I asked you this…

MAX. I'm keeping a lot of secrets here…

SUZANNA. Andrew is, like, not that happy at his job. He wants to take a pay cut and move us to smaller place.

MAX. What's the question?

SUZANNA. Could we stay in this apartment if our income was…less.

MAX. How much less? Don't answer. Look, you can do whatever you want. You can take a ten-thousand-dollar honeymoon. You can buy a nice car. But when your money's gone, it's gone.

SUZANNA. So the answer is no?

MAX. It's a judgment call. If you'd married a medical student, I'd say go ahead, live a little. But Andrew.... I don't see any guarantee of earning power.

SUZANNA. That's not the measure of a man's worth, Max.

MAX. You didn't ask me about his worth! You asked me about money.

SUZANNA. Sorry. I know it's a judgment call. But your judgment's better than mine, you know?

MAX. Oh, I know. (*After a beat.*) Look at a couple cheaper places. Come back to me with actual numbers and I'll tell you what to do.

SUZANNA. (*Hugging him.*) Thank you.

(*The door opens. It's* ANDREW *and* BECKY.)

ANDREW. Hey! Everyone.... This is Becky. Becky, this is my wife, Suzanna. This is Max. Let me take your coat...

(MAX *stands to shake* BECKY's *hand.* BECKY *takes off her coat to reveal a slightly puffy, pastel-colored cocktail dress. Maybe it's satin and bare. It's a great dress for another occasion...New Year's Eve, for example. For this night and these people, she is overdressed. She realizes this almost immediately. The confidence she cultivated alone in her apartment evaporates.*)

BECKY. Nice to meet you all. Or...both.

MAX. Wow. You look like...a birthday cake.

SUZANNA. No, she doesn't. Ignore him. It's nice to meet you, Becky.

MAX. I was complimenting her! It wouldn't kill you to wear a dress once a year...

BECKY. I'm totally overdressed.

ANDREW. No, you're not. Do you drink red wine?

BECKY. Yes.

(*Awkward, wordless moment between* MAX *and* BECKY. *They check each other out. First looks.*)

MAX. You're very.... Your face is pink. Have you been drinking this evening?

BECKY. No! I just.... I called the cab too early, so I had to walk around and kill some time. It's really cold...

ANDREW. You should have just come over. We weren't doing anything.

SUZANNA. Yeah, we were just fighting. I'm actually not dressed yet. I'm gonna change.

MAX. Why were you fighting?

SUZANNA. I told you. My mom. (*Remembering.*) Shit! My mom! (*To* MAX.) You totally distracted me. I'm gonna try and call her...

(SUZANNA *leaves to change and call her mother. A slight awkward silence.*
This would be the moment for the newly introduced couple to begin a gentle Q
and A....)

MAX. Warming up any?

BECKY. Yes! I guess that was silly of me. It's just.... You know how
Providence cabs are. Or.... You don't; you live in New York.

ANDREW. I should have picked you up. I feel like an idiot...

MAX. Is something wrong with your car?

BECKY. Yeah. I mean, I don't have one.

MAX. Is that...an economic necessity or a life choice?

BECKY. Life choice?

MAX. Are you, like, a militant environmentalist? Do you oppose cars in
theory or...

BECKY. Oh, no. I just don't have any money. (*An awkward moment.*) I mean
I have some. I have money.

(*Awkward.* MAX *can't think of an appropriate retort.*)

MAX. So what's up with Susan? Why is Susie calling her?

ANDREW. Her mother's health insurance company called. (*To* BECKY.)
My wife and her mother have the same name: Suzanna Slater.

BECKY. Oh. That must get confusing.

ANDREW. It's actually pretty manageable with nicknames. Her mother
goes by Susan, Suzanna kinda defaults to Susie. If we have a female child, I
don't know what's left for her.

BECKY. There's...Suki.

MAX. Too Asian.

BECKY. Actually, Edie Sedgwick.... The Warhol model? Her sister was
Suki. Suki Sedgwick.

MAX. Really?

BECKY. Yes.

MAX. Do you know the lineage of all the Warhol models, or just—

ANDREW. So, the insurance people called here. They realized they had the
wrong Suzanna Slater and they hung up. And Susan's in Florida with her
boyfriend, Lester.

(SUZANNA *returns in a dress...more monochromatic and sophisticated than*
BECKY's *dress. The best she could do, having legitimately tried to match*
BECKY.)

SUZANNA. She's still not picking up. And she's in Florida with Fucko the
Rent Boy so God only knows what's become of her.

MAX. You called Lester?

SUZANNA. Hell, no I did not call Lester! It's still early...I think I should fly down there and find out what happened.

MAX. Did you call the hotel?

SUZANNA. I don't know where they're staying.

MAX. So what the fuck are you gonna do when you get there?

SUZANNA. Just...find her. Key West can't be that big.

MAX. Uhhh.... It's big enough. Why haven't you called Lester?

SUZANNA. What kind of stupid fucking question is that? You know why.

MAX. Andrew, why won't she call Lester?

SUZANNA. Max, fuck off. I made my boundary very clear.

ANDREW. You guys.... Becky doesn't know any of these people, so maybe we should stop...

BECKY. Oh, no.... It's OK. Family problems are just.... God, I don't even speak to my family.

MAX. Really? Why is that?

BECKY. Umm.... It's a pretty long story.

MAX. You don't speak to them, or they don't speak to you?

BECKY. It's basically mutual.

SUZANNA. Oh, don't look at her like that's so weird. I wish I could do it. So do you.

MAX. Yeah, but we'd never actually do it; they're our parents. Andrew, call Lester.

ANDREW. Susie says we have the same boundaries because we're married.

MAX. (*Gets out his phone.*) Wow. It's a good thing I showed up. I have no boundaries at all, Becky. Did they tell you that?

BECKY. No...

MAX. (*To* ANDREW.) Did you try to talk some sense into her?

ANDREW. I offered to drive her down...

MAX. And do what when you get there? What the hell is wrong with you two?

ANDREW. I didn't know she didn't know—

SUZANNA. Max, Key West is not that big!

MAX. Correct. It's a small town with about nine hundred bed and breakfasts.

ANDREW. There's probably only one hospital.

MAX. Did you call this one hospital? (*No answer.*) Of course, you didn't. You're both idiots.

SUZANNA. Max—

MAX. (*Dialing his phone.*) Sit down, drink your wine. It's ringing. Lester! Lester, my man, Max Garrett here. How the hell are you? (*Pause.*) I'm very well. How are you and Susan? (*Pause.*) Well, that's great to hear. So the reason I'm calling is that you are a lying sack of shit. What happened to Susan? (*Pause.*) Uh huh. (*Pause; rolls eyes.*) So she's OK? (*Pause.*) Good. I— (*Pause.*) Suzanna? Fuck Suzanna. This is a conversation between men and I am not a snitch.

(*Mouth away from receiver,* MAX *shakes his head, mouths "stupid, stupid, stupid" as he walks into* ANDREW *and* SUZANNA's *bedroom and closes the door.* SUZANNA *moves toward the door.*)

ANDREW. Susie. Don't. Just let him get the whole story.

(ANDREW *and* SUZANNA *meet each other halfway.* ANDREW *refills her wine....*)

SUZANNA. I'm sorry, Becky. This is completely rude.... I just don't know if it's serious or not...

BECKY. It's no problem! Is Max, like, related to you?

SUZANNA. Not exactly. My parents kind of adopted him.

BECKY. Oh! His parents are dead?

SUZANNA. Only his mom. His dad's just...useless.

BECKY. I don't really feel I'm making a good impression.

ANDREW. You're doing great.

SUZANNA. Please. I'm the one making a bad impression. If you're not at your best it's only because I'm not at mine.

BECKY. So you agree I'm not at my best...

SUZANNA. No! I'm just apologizing that my problems are dominating the room. See, my mother would never let that happen. If we had company.... My mother was perfectly poised no matter how much pain she was in.

BECKY. God, I wish I could do that. When I'm hurt, I can't hide anything. How did your mom do it?

SUZANNA. Containment. The way you do it, I think, is to have one or two people in your life you can treat really, really badly. That was my mom's strategy and it worked very well for her.

ANDREW. Not so well for you and your dad.

SUZANNA. True. Do you want some more wine, Becky?

BECKY. A little.... Thanks. Is there anything I should do or not do, as far as Max...

ANDREW. Just be yourself.

SUZANNA. In as much as you can, don't show him any weakness.

ANDREW. No. Susie.... That's not helpful...

BECKY. Do I seem weak...so far?

SUZANNA. No, no, no. All I'm saying is.... First date. Everybody's nervous. We all have a *thing* we fall back on when we're nervous.... Flirting or bragging or whatever. His thing is bullying. Just try not to give him an opening.

(MAX *reemerges.*)

MAX. OK. I really don't like to admit that I'm wrong. But my God he is a loser.

SUZANNA. See????

MAX. They were in the hot tub at the hotel and your mom "forgot" her cane up in the room.

SUZANNA. Because Lester makes her self-destructive.

MAX. Oh, shut the fuck up. If that's what your psychology program is teaching you...

SUZANNA. She forgot her cane and she fell. Is it bad?

MAX. No. She tripped. Her knees are bruised. The hotel overreacted. She is not "self-destructive," Suzanna—

ANDREW. (*To* BECKY.) Susie's mom has MS. Multiple—

MAX. Andrew, give the girl some credit. She knows what MS is.

BECKY. I don't know a lot. I know Jerry Lewis does that telethon...

SUZANNA. That's muscular dystrophy.

BECKY. Oh, my God, I know that! I don't know why I said that...

SUZANNA. Refusing to use her cane is self-destructive.

ANDREW. MS is multiple sclerosis...

BECKY. I know that. I just.... Nerves.

MAX. You're nervous?

BECKY. A little...

MAX. Look, Suzanna. I know you don't want to hear this, but sexual activity releases brain chemicals known as endorphins...

SUZANNA. Stop it right now before I kill you.

MAX. Endorphins make our bodies feel better. Your mother forgets the cane because she's feeling better and she's feeling better because she's fucking Lester.

ANDREW. You guys, this is getting a little personal...

SUZANNA. If she's fine, what did you have to go in the other room for?

MAX. Because.... Sometimes in a crisis, you learn things about people that you didn't know.

SUZANNA. What did we learn?

MAX. Lester's credit cards are all maxed out. He can't use them.

SUZANNA. He's a huge loser. That's not a surprise.

MAX. Well, it surprised your mother. She gave him money to pay off his credit cards and he spent it on something else.

SUZANNA. What—drugs?

MAX. No. Some kind of editing equipment. For his film.

SUZANNA. You fucked up, Max.

MAX. No, I didn't. Your mother called me, she wanted five thousand dollars sent to Lester's credit card company. I said great, fine. Then I sent the money to Lester. You see what I did there?

SUZANNA. Yes. You fucked up.

MAX. No, stupid! I protected you. You should be down on your knees thanking me—

SUZANNA. (*Overlapping.*) How is putting thousands of dollars in Lester's hands protecting me?

MAX. Anyone? Anyone?

BECKY. (*After a beat.*) You set him up to fail. (*Surprised eyes on* BECKY.) Instead of paying his creditors, you paid him. You tested him, knowing he would fail.

MAX. Very good, Becky! So now he has to beg your mother's forgiveness, and that's gonna take forever. That little movie he wants to make.... I just put that baby in turnaround

SUZANNA. You're a genius. I'm so sorry.

MAX. Oh, rest assured I will do whatever it takes to protect you.

SUZANNA. I know. I shouldn't doubt you.

ANDREW. So, if Susan's OK.... Maybe we can kinda start the night over...

SUZANNA. Yes! Let's do that. Let's start over.

MAX. Starting over. Great. So. Becky. What are you doing in Providence? Did you go to Brown?

BECKY. I actually did go to Brown...briefly. But I dropped out.

MAX. So that makes you...smart, but lazy.

ANDREW. Max.

BECKY. No, it's OK. I got into Brown because I lived in Rhode Island—

ANDREW. That's so not true. You're super smart; you were not a regional quota filler.

MAX. So you're actually from here? Congratulations. On losing the accent.

BECKY. We moved here when I was eleven. I was born in North Carolina, actually.

MAX. Well my congratulations holds. That's a pretty fucking awful accent, too.

BECKY. Right. Thanks.

MAX. *(To* SUZANNA.) Wait wait wait…. Tell that story.

SUZANNA. What story?

MAX. The bubbla…

SUZANNA. Andrew's heard it.

ANDREW. Yeah…. I have…

MAX. Becky hasn't. You gotta hear this…

SUZANNA. OK, so I work with a lot of kids at the clinic. I'm a grad student in psychology. And we do these intake interviews…

MAX. I hate how women tell stories. Susie's interviewing a kid and the kid says…

SUZANNA. Wheasdabubbla. And I'm writing my thesis so I'm like…. I'm reading all these amazing cases where the therapist was like Sherlock Holmes cracking the code and saving the day—

MAX. Mother of fucking God, get to the point. Wheasdabubbla.

SUZANNA. So. I wrote it down to analyze later, and then she yells, "WHEASDAFUCKINBUBBLA?!" And I hear a thud…the secretary's chair hitting the wall. I poke my head out the door and the secretary says…

MAX. Givvasomewota.

SUZANNA. Water. Bubbla is bubbler which is Rhode Islandese for water fountain.

BECKY. So did you give her some water?

SUZANNA. Yes. I gave her some water and she threw it at me. And then, I started to get it.

MAX. Please don't tell me you drew some fancy conclusion from a kid throwing water.

SUZANNA. It wasn't "fancy," but…

BECKY. But it gave you this amazing clue. You could see—

MAX. Amazing clue?

ANDREW. Jesus, Max. Let Becky talk.

BECKY. It just seems like she got angry because she wasn't being heard. She didn't ask for water; she asked you where the bubbler was. You weren't listening to her.

SUZANNA. Well—

MAX. That is such horseshit.

ANDREW. It's not horseshit. The kids at that clinic have some pretty serious problems.

SUZANNA. I never said they didn't, Andrew.

ANDREW. Not that the story isn't amusing out of context. I get that.

SUZANNA. We should drop it anyway. Max has a personal bias against psychotherapy.

MAX. It can't be personal. I've never been in therapy.

SUZANNA. I know. Say that a little louder in case Becky missed it.

MAX. Becky, I HAVE NEVER BEEN IN THERAPY.

BECKY. I have.

MAX. And did it cure you of whatever...problem brought you there?

BECKY. Umm.... I went a few times for a few different issues.

MAX. OK. So.... To recap, you dropped out of college, you're not on speaking terms with your family, and you have no money. That sounds to me like the therapy didn't work.

ANDREW. Max—

BECKY. (*Flirting?*) How do you know? You didn't see me before I went.

SUZANNA. Oooh.... She told you.

MAX. She definitely did...tell me. Anything else you want to reveal here... STDS, felony convictions...

BECKY. I just have...mistakes. Family stuff. Don't we all have that? Don't you?

MAX. No, I've led a wholly unblemished and exemplary life. I will, however, own up to being hungry.

BECKY. Hungry? Yeah.... I feel that, too. Do you know what you're hungry for?

MAX. Tonight, I'm thinking lasagna. Can we get out of here?

SUZANNA. Don't kill me...

MAX. Oh, no.

SUZANNA. I want to talk to my mom.

MAX. Susan is fine!

SUZANNA. I want to call and provoke her. If she fights with me, then I'll know she's OK. Give me a pass tonight. Andrew can go.

ANDREW. You know what? The vibe I'm feeling is maybe you two go have a nice dinner; Susie and I will veg out here. Is that too weird and awkward?

BECKY. No, no. It's fine. If it's OK with Max, I mean.

MAX. We don't need you two to have fun. Fuck you two. We're out of here.

(*Everyone rises, coats are put on....*)

SUZANNA. Have fun. Be safe.

ANDREW. You know where you're going?

MAX. I have no idea. But my date lives here, right? She knows restaurants.

BECKY. I do. I mean, I don't really eat out ever, but...

MAX. Of, course you don't. (*Off her mild recoil...he touches her.*) Kidding. Kidding. (*To* SUZANNA.) Did you put any thought at all into this evening or is there a Zagat's New England you can throw at me on my way out?

SUZANNA. I know. I'm sorry. Andrew print out that Federal Hill map...

MAX. I don't need a map; I need a recommendation.

ANDREW. No, this is a map *with* recommendations. It comes in your Brown orientation materials. That's a really good idea. I can also mapquest.... Why don't I show you on the computer...

> (*Awkwardly...MAX follows* ANDREW *to the office. A moment's silence between the women.*)

BECKY. So, what...happened to her—the girl?

SUZANNA. The girl?

BECKY. The bubbla...girl. The girl who needed water...

SUZANNA. Oh! Right. You know, I don't know. I only saw her that one time.

BECKY. Why?

SUZANNA. I...don't remember. We do a lot of evaluations for the public school system. *A lot.* Sometimes we treat, sometimes it just ends there.

BECKY. That must be hard for you.

SUZANNA. Which part? I mean it's all...hard.

BECKY. Seeing them only once. For me, that would be very hard.

> (*Some strange tension here, maybe. Or maybe not.*)

SUZANNA. It is. But.... I mean.... You do what you can.

> (MAX *and* ANDREW *return....*)

ANDREW. Just have fun, you know...

MAX. Fun? Andrew here has given me a list of restaurants so exceptional that one must... (*Reading.*) ...book in advance for commencement and campus dance.

SUZANNA. That just means they're expensive.

ANDREW. I circled the ones that aren't, like, weird and fussy.

MAX. (*To* BECKY.) Andrew's incredibly nervous. Tell him you're OK and you're going to have fun.

> (BECKY *smiles at this and turns to* ANDREW.)

BECKY. I'm OK. And I'm going to have fun.

> (*A beat before* MAX *and* BECKY *leave. The idea is to suggest a frozen moment after which these lives will change. Maybe lights go down last on* BECKY *watching the others, or watching us.*)

End of Act I

ACT II

Scene 1

Downtown Providence (outdoors). Two days later, Monday. BECKY *and* ANDREW *have left the office to get coffee or hot dogs. We begin with* BECKY *alone on stage.*

BECKY. Something bad happened on my date with Max.

(ANDREW *enters and hands* BECKY *her drink/food.*)

ANDREW. Here you go. So…. What I was saying…. Susie is trying to play it cool, not call Max for forty-eight hours after your date. But she's, like, twitching to make the call.

BECKY. Andrew, something happened on my date with Max.

ANDREW. Yeah?

BECKY. We were robbed. We were robbed with a gun!

ANDREW. Robbed? Where?

BECKY. We went to The Decatur for a nightcap. Andrew, I feel so stupid!

ANDREW. Why?

BECKY. I'd never been there! You said it was cool, so I said it was cool. Jesus! I hate myself!

ANDREW. Wait. A stranger robbed you, right? Why would you hate yourself?

BECKY. We parked too far away, and it's a bad area…

ANDREW. It's not bad…

BECKY. It's bad, Andrew! A man came up to us with a gun and we gave him our wallets, but neither of us had much cash, so Max said we should walk back to the car…

ANDREW. Wait. Did the guy ask for more or did Max just volunteer, "I'm rich, I have money in my car"?

BECKY. He…volunteered.

ANDREW. That's really stupid.

BECKY. There was a gun pointing at us! He was trying to keep us alive.

ANDREW. I'm sorry.

BECKY. The guy held the gun on me while Max went into the car…. Andrew, I thought I was going to die! Max gave him two hundred dollars and a camera. Then he left.

ANDREW. He left. He didn't hurt you. Rape you…

BECKY. No. Oh, my God! Don't even say that!

ANDREW. What did you do? Were you at the police station all night?

BECKY. Until two. Neither of us could give a description. At all.

ANDREW. Really?

BECKY. The detective said it's normal. It's called "gun focus." When someone points a gun at you.... (*Demonstrating with hands.*) All your focus goes to the gun. You can't look past the gun to the person holding it or if you can.... You can't see them clearly. All you see is... (*She begins to break.*)

ANDREW. Oh, Becky. I'm sorry...

BECKY. The detective said it's survival instinct: keep your eye on the gun.

ANDREW. That makes sense.

BECKY. Does it? The gun is not.... There's a story behind the gun, right? There's a person. That gun is one night, one mistake. And there's a whole life behind it! A whole life that informs the mistake...

ANDREW. Well—

BECKY. Maybe your best chance of surviving a gun in your face is to look past the gun. Look at the person holding it and say, "I know that you are more and you are better than one bad night."

ANDREW. Don't second-guess yourself. You had no power...

BECKY. What do you mean, I had no power?

ANDREW. He had a gun. You weren't equally matched, you know? Jesus, I'm so glad you're not hurt!

BECKY. Don't tell me I'm not hurt!

ANDREW. I just mean.... Thank God it ended well...

BECKY. It hasn't ended.

ANDREW. Well, of course! Becky, what can I do?

BECKY. Can you give me a hug? Would that be OK?

ANDREW. Oh my God, yes. Here...

(*It's awkward with drink/food. The delay getting into the hug lends a tension, a charge. He pats her back, soothes her.*)

ANDREW. Maybe you should talk to someone about this. You have a therapist, right?

BECKY. I haven't seen her in years. My parents helped me pay for that and now.... They're not speaking to me and I'm uninsured and completely broke.

ANDREW. Call her anyway.

BECKY. People don't work for free, Andrew!

ANDREW. Just.... Tell her you need a few sessions, but you can't pay right away...

BECKY. A few sessions. That's like eight hundred dollars. I can't even afford to buy a meatball sub at lunch. I'm eating peanut butter sandwiches every day. I'm sorry. I have made a mess of my life. It's not your problem. (*Pause.*) No one in my family speaks to me, you know.

ANDREW. I know. I don't know why, but I'm sure they're the problem, not you.

BECKY. You don't know the whole story. We should go back to work.

ANDREW. Let me call Susie and get the name of a clinic with a sliding scale.

BECKY. No...

ANDREW. It's no problem.

BECKY. No, Andrew! I don't want ghetto therapy!

ANDREW. (*After a beat.*) It's not ghetto therapy. Though if that was a sit-com—"Ghetto Therapy"—I would definitely watch it.

(BECKY *laughs.*)

BECKY. There is one thing you could do that would really help...

ANDREW. Anything. Shoot.

BECKY. Max and I haven't spoken since that night. He's the only person who knows what I'm feeling and he won't return my calls.

ANDREW. Maybe he lost his cell phone. He hasn't called Susie either.

BECKY. It didn't happen to Susie! It happened to me. He should call me.

ANDREW. He should, you're right. Susie can make that happen.

BECKY. Tonight? I want it to happen tonight.

ANDREW. OK, tonight. She'll make it happen tonight.

Scene 2

That same evening (Monday). MAX *and* SUZANNA *in* MAX's *Boston hotel room. It's a nicer hotel than the New York hotel in Act I. At least one more star.*

SUZANNA. I just figured I should drive up here, smooth things over face-to-face before they get any worse.

MAX. Your husband's a dick.

SUZANNA. He just asked you to call Becky. Why are you being so weird?

MAX. I'm weird because I won't call her?

SUZANNA. Well...yes. This is *all* really weird, Max. I find out secondhand from Andrew that you were held up at gunpoint. Why didn't you call me?

MAX. Are you the police? Are you in a position to get my camera back?

SUZANNA. You need support, Max. Look, I know from my work that men can experience shame when they're victimized...

MAX. Oh, no...

SUZANNA. OK, I'm gonna say something. Don't cut me off. Both times your father got arrested, I begged you—

MAX. I'm not having this discussion.

SUZANNA. Why? Why don't you call me when your dad gets in trouble? Why don't you call me when you get held up with a gun?

MAX. My father's not in trouble anymore.

SUZANNA. But in New York, you said—

MAX. That was a year ago. I fixed it.

SUZANNA. Well, that's…good. But I still feel like…. God, Max. I know when you're hurting. I can see it. (*She points at him.*) Your eyes go narrow, you clench your teeth…

MAX. That's not hurt, that's frustration.

SUZANNA. Fine! We should talk about it. We're friends.

MAX. My frustration is with you.

SUZANNA. With me?

MAX. Yes. My father is a white-collar criminal. He is an unrepentant repeat offender. This is never going to change. Between my father's stealing and your father's squandering, it's amazing that I have any time or any money for myself. When you force me to talk about things that make me unhappy, you pollute my leisure time. You become part of the fucking problem.

SUZANNA. (*Not what she expected.*) OK, I respect that. I'm sorry I brought it up. Your dad. And if you don't want to talk about the robbery either—

MAX. I'll buy you a steak and a soufflé if you drop the subject.

SUZANNA. OK. Steak and soufflé sounds great. But first will you just please call Becky?

MAX. No!

SUZANNA. It's one phone call. Why—

MAX. Why? Because that's my choice. It's like you marrying Andrew. Friends don't have to agree with each other's choices, but they do have to respect them.

SUZANNA. (*After a beat.*) OK, let's just do this. You're angry at me for marrying Andrew and I don't understand why.

MAX. I'm not angry. I just think it was a shit decision and you should have consulted me.

SUZANNA. If I'd consulted you, you'd have told me not to do it.

MAX. Exactly. You think I should have called you after I was robbed. I think you should have called me before you flew to Vegas and married your ski buddy.

SUZANNA. Wow. You really are angry. Is it because we slept together that one time?

MAX. (*After a beat.*) Well…

SUZANNA. I knew it! You can't say sex won't change anything. It always does.

MAX. Not always. When you've known the person twenty-five years, it....
Yes.

SUZANNA. You told me it wouldn't change anything!

MAX. Sex makes men territorial. Forget it. It's not rational.

SUZANNA. Let's call it what it is, OK? We opened the door. After two decades, we opened the door and neither of us walked through it.

MAX. Well. I turned around, you had a husband in the fucking doorway...

SUZANNA. That was months later! You started dating Christa before I—

MAX. A month after we.... Were you waiting for me to walk through the door? This isn't Jane Austen's England, Susie. You could've walked through it, too.

SUZANNA. Right. We both could have done it and neither of us did. So I think.... There's our answer.

MAX. OK.

SUZANNA. There's our answer. We love each other, but not in the way Andrew and I—

MAX. Fuck Andrew. He is way out of line calling me at work—

SUZANNA. You're angry because Andrew—

MAX. I'm angry that you two morons put me in this position!

SUZANNA. Max, we didn't rob you.

MAX. Oh, fuck the robbery. It's a nonevent and I'm over it.

SUZANNA. Well, Becky isn't over it.

MAX. Clearly. She's been calling me all weekend.

SUZANNA. Max, she had a gun pointed at her. It's traumatic.

MAX. For her, maybe. Not for me.

SUZANNA. Max, that's just insane.

MAX. No. My reaction is not insane. In life.... I'm gonna do this visually because I know you can't do math. This wall is your perfect, ideal, un-blemished life. You and everyone you know living happy lives until you die of old age in your loved ones' arms.

SUZANNA. No one has that life.

MAX. Shut up, I'm still talking. That wall over there is as bad as it gets. Use your imagination.

SUZANNA. *(After a beat.)* Is that rhetorical? Are you asking me?

MAX. Yes! What is that wall for you?!

SUZANNA. You know what it is, Max. The underground sex-torture dungeon.

MAX. Consider these two walls...and the points in between—chair, table, lamp, phone—being all variety of life shit in between *(Indicating walls.)* torture in a dungeon and happy all the time. Where on this trajectory would you place a three minute holdup in which no one got hurt?

SUZANNA. Max, that's not fair.

MAX. It is fair. You and I have been through hell with our parents. Cancer, MS, jail, death.... What happened to Becky and me.... It doesn't even rank.

SUZANNA. Say, for the sake of argument, you're right. What does it cost you to talk to her?

MAX. I don't want to. And I don't have to.

SUZANNA. OK, forget responsibility. How about charity? If you can alleviate her pain—

MAX. Why me? Why? Where are her fucking friends?

SUZANNA. She wants to talk to you because you were there.

MAX. Well, that I don't believe.

SUZANNA. What do you think the reason is?

MAX. She wants a relationship with me.

SUZANNA. Really? After one date?

MAX. Look at her life, look at the dress she wore that night. You fixed me up with a desperate woman.

SUZANNA. She's desperate because she wore a dress?

MAX. She's a thirty-five-year-old office temp with no money, no friends, no relationship, no family.... How the fuck could you set me up with that?

SUZANNA. Wait. You think I set you up with someone who isn't good enough for you?

MAX. I don't think that. That is a fact.

SUZANNA. Max, she's beautiful. She's smart...

MAX. She's a sad person, Suzanna.

SUZANNA. So? I've been sad. Did it make me undesirable or—

MAX. It detracted from your desirability as a mate. Yes.

SUZANNA. You slept with me when I was grieving, Max. You are so full of shit—

MAX. I slept with you. I didn't date you.

SUZANNA. (*After a beat.*) Well. That's you. Andrew fell in love with me—

MAX. Andrew didn't bring a lot to the fucking table. Romantic relationships are the pairing of equals. That woman is not my equal!

SUZANNA. Please call her, Max.

MAX. What the fuck do you care? You met this girl once.

SUZANNA. I'll give you the script. Tell her that this experience—the holdup—has shown you that you're not emotionally available enough to be in a relationship. Let her talk about her experience. Wish her well.... It's over.

MAX. None of that is true.

SUZANNA. No, but it's merciful. Sometimes lying is the most humane thing you can do.

MAX. (*After a beat.*) I'll think about it.

Scene 3

ANDREW *and* BECKY *in* BECKY's *apartment the following night—Tuesday.* ANDREW *has brought beer and a pizza.*

BECKY. I'm so sorry. I heard this weird noise and since the holdup, I'm just... (*Indicates jittery.*)

ANDREW. It's totally OK.

BECKY. But to make you come running over here.... Suzanna must hate me.

ANDREW. No. It's good I got out of the house. She's...studying.

BECKY. Please thank her for speaking with Max on my behalf.

ANDREW. Not that it helped.

BECKY. What did he say—exactly?

ANDREW. A lot of bullshit that has nothing to do with you.

BECKY. Really? If he thinks I'm a loser, I can take it. It's the silence that's so—

ANDREW. It's not that.

BECKY. So what is it?

ANDREW. I think he just can't deal with what happened. He's emotionally a very...stunted man.

BECKY. Then why did you set me up with him?

(*Awkward beat.*)

ANDREW. I'd met him twice before that night. I trusted Susie...

BECKY. Max wasn't at your wedding?

ANDREW. No.... We got married kind of fast. In Las Vegas.

BECKY. Why so fast?

ANDREW. It was just a really intense time.

BECKY. How was it intense?

ANDREW. Susie's life was just.... It was seriously, the most epic, Faulknerian chaos I've ever encountered outside a fictional paradigm. (*Pause.*) Did I just sound like a total tool?

BECKY. No, I understand. Chaos is exciting.

ANDREW. Oh, I didn't mean that. It was awful for Susie—

BECKY. I didn't mean—

ANDREW. I'm not explaining it well. Her dad had just died. We met on a ski trip and…. She was so sad and something about the landscape…. All this whiteness, these huge mountains. Susie's little, you know, and she had this red parka. I would look at her and feel like…. I shouldn't tell you, it's weird.

BECKY. Tell me.

ANDREW. I would see her and think…. She's like blood on the snow. It's like nature is bleeding…and it's wrong and I can fix it.

BECKY. I don't think that's weird.

ANDREW. It makes more sense if you knew her then. She was really different. More…delicate. Or…fragile.

BECKY. Suzanna? That's hard to imagine.

ANDREW. Oh, I know. She's so much healthier now. It's great.

BECKY. She's very lucky she found you.

ANDREW. *(After a beat.)* Look, I want to apologize. Susie is blind to Max's flaws, but I—

BECKY. He takes such good care of her.

ANDREW. Well…. They're family. And on paper, Max looks great. He's rich, charismatic, looking to settle down—

BECKY. He's looking to settle down? He said that?

ANDREW. He told Susie, you know, "I'm thirty-six; I'm ready to… *(Thinking better.)* to, I guess be open…"

BECKY. Wow. I kind of wish you hadn't told me that.

ANDREW. Saying it is one thing. He's never gonna do it.

BECKY. Wait. You fixed me up with someone you think is never going to settle down?

ANDREW. No, no, no—

BECKY. He said he wants to settle down and he meant it, right? You're just trying to save my feelings now by lying—

ANDREW. I'm not lying. I just found out. *(Pause.)* Look. Susie wasn't studying when you called. We were fighting because Susie said that Max is…a short-timer.

BECKY. What is a "short-timer"?

ANDREW. It's a Vietnam War term. It means guys who go into combat for short stints and don't stay. Max, apparently, only dates women for, like, three months.

BECKY. Oh.

ANDREW. I didn't know that until tonight. Susie said it and I just flipped—

BECKY. She should have told you.

ANDREW. I know. And I wasn't gonna tell you, but then you got so upset about the marriage thing…

BECKY. (*Covers her eyes, tears up.*) I'm sorry. This is all really hard.

ANDREW. I know. Susie wanted me to ask if you called the therapist she recommended.

BECKY. Uck. I couldn't stand her. She barely even asked about the holdup. She kept asking what else was wrong… (*Cries/gasps.*) Oh, my God, Andrew. It hurts!

ANDREW. You know what? (*Takes her hands in his.*) Forget the therapist. Tell me what hurts.

BECKY. I had a gun pointed at me!

ANDREW. OK, I know, but…. Not to sound like that therapist, but if you look past the gun, what else is—

BECKY. He was black. And that hurts me! Because I was hurt very badly…twice. It's why I don't talk to my parents…

ANDREW. A black man…hurt you?

BECKY. When I was a freshman at Brown I met a boy who really liked me. He was black…. And my parents said, you know, it's him or it's us. Choose.

ANDREW. Are you serious?

BECKY. And I couldn't face losing my family. So I ended it with Stefan and I learned after I let him go, that he had really loved me and my family really didn't. I tried to go backwards. But he wouldn't…. I had kind of a break-down. I had a scholarship and I lost it.

ANDREW. Shit. I'm sorry.

BECKY. Then…. Last year, I was working at a law firm and I became involved with one of the lawyers who was—is—black. I told him that if I committed to him, I would lose my family, so he had to be very sure he wanted me…

ANDREW. He wasn't sure…

BECKY. No, he was. I cut ties with my family. We got an apartment in Cranston. I was so happy. Then he changed his mind.

ANDREW. Oh, shit.

BECKY. I've been having these terrible racist feelings since the holdup. I've been thinking that black men have ruined my life and I…I can't say it.

ANDREW. Say it. Say anything.

BECKY. Walking to the bus, I get pictures in my mind of black men…being tortured…. God, I fucking hate myself!

ANDREW. Becky, you had a trauma. You're allowed to feel some crazy shit for a while. And you're not gonna act on these thoughts, right? You're small, but you're intense…

BECKY. Don't say I'm intense! Jason said that when he left me.

ANDREW. It's not a bad thing.

BECKY. Yes, it is. Men don't want intense women.

ANDREW. Uh…. Yeah, we do.

BECKY. You think you do, but you don't. Jason left me. You're fighting with Suzanna…

ANDREW. No. Intensity is a good thing. It means you can love. It's just a matter of, you know, how you channel it.

BECKY. I can see where Suzanna might strike out and that would be so much healthier…

ANDREW. Healthier for her, maybe.

BECKY. Sometimes the fantasy isn't enough and I think about cutting myself with a knife.

ANDREW. (*Rallying.*) Then we need to go to the hospital. Tonight.

BECKY. I don't have insurance.

ANDREW. I don't care. If you want to hurt yourself, I have to protect you.

BECKY. I feel that. I feel really safe with you.

ANDREW. (*After a beat.*) Do you have any girlfriends? I mean, I am here for you, but—

BECKY. I lost them when I moved in with Jason.

ANDREW. Wow. Your friends were all racists?

BECKY. They weren't racist at all, actually. It's just…. Jason made me happy and happiness made me mean. To women. Not to Jason.

ANDREW. What did you do?

BECKY. Dumped them. You know what it was like? My mom grew up really poor. In North Carolina. And I asked her once…why she never took me there to see where she grew up. She said (*Hard and sneering imitation.*), "There's nothing to see. We were poor." I felt that way about being single, you know? It was poverty and once I made it out, I couldn't look back.

ANDREW. Why was it so terrible?

BECKY. Oh, come on. You've seen it. The all-female table in the bar? Women drinking fucking Midori sours pretending to like each other while they scan for men.

ANDREW. God, I can't stand women like that…

BECKY. But I am women like that! I got a boyfriend and stopped returning their calls. What Max is doing to me now? I deserve it. (*Pause.*) God, Andrew, I feel like I'm falling in love.

ANDREW. In love?

BECKY. With Max. That's crazy, right?

ANDREW. Umm…

BECKY. Andrew, we slept together.

ANDREW. You…. So he did call you.

BECKY. No. I'm so embarrassed. We slept together that night.

ANDREW. After the…robbery?

BECKY. After the police station, we wanted a drink to calm down. But nothing was open. So we went to his hotel.

ANDREW. You went to Boston?

BECKY. No. He had rented a room here for the night.

ANDREW. He rented a room in advance? Are you kidding me?

BECKY. We had some drinks and…. It turned kind of bad.

ANDREW. Did he hurt you?

BECKY. Not…sexually. He just wouldn't let me stay overnight.

ANDREW. He what?

BECKY. He gave me cab fare…

ANDREW. Cab fare?

BECKY. I told him I didn't want to be alone after what had happened and he offered…. Jesus, I can't say it.

ANDREW. Say it.

BECKY. He offered me his credit card to get my own room in the hotel.

ANDREW. Let me get this straight. He fucked you—

BECKY. Please don't say that.

ANDREW. He had sex with you, then he kicked you out of his bed, and offered you money.

BECKY. Not for sex! For a hotel or a cab.

ANDREW. It doesn't matter! Becky, he's sick! Listen: I will take care of you. You are never to contact him again. Do you hear me?

BECKY. Yes. I hear you. Yes.

Scene 4

MAX *and* SUZANNA *in* MAX's *hotel room in Boston. The following night: Wednesday.*

SUZANNA. You shouldn't have slept with her, Max.

MAX. She initiated it!

SUZANNA. I don't care. You knew you didn't want to see her again and she'd just been held up with a gun…

MAX. She initiated it!

SUZANNA. I don't care. It was selfish and sleazy.

MAX. She grabbed me like this. (*He indicates on* SUZANNA.) She said, "I need this."

SUZANNA. You kicked her out of bed afterwards!

MAX. Oh, come on. I didn't stay in your bed after we...did it. I have a sleep disorder!

SUZANNA. No, Max. You have an intimacy issue that you pay a doctor to call a sleeping disorder.

MAX. Are you a doctor? Have you seen my sleep study?

SUZANNA. Fuck your sleep study. Having sex and then leaving...or kicking out.... It's degrading. You need to get some sleeping pills.

MAX. You think I haven't tried that? They give me a hangover.

SUZANNA. Love, Max, is worth a hangover.

MAX. Do you understand the pressure of my job? I'm not a...a barista... poet...secretary boy like Andrew. I control people's money. I can't be off my game!

SUZANNA. So your clients matter and your women don't?

MAX. Uhhh.... If you're asking me will I jeopardize people's life savings because women need to cuddle, the answer is no.

SUZANNA. (*After a beat.*) Call Becky Shaw. Call her now.

MAX. No!

SUZANNA. She says she's suicidal, Max. Andrew is afraid to leave her alone. I've barely seen him since this happened.

MAX. That's Andrew's bad, not mine. You pulled that suicidal shit with me, I didn't go running.

SUZANNA. Hence me marrying Andrew and not you.

(*A hard silence, then a spike in anger for both.*)

MAX. Say whatever you want, but give me credit. I cured you. And I did it by refusing to enable the Sylvia Plath, post-collegiate bullshit—

SUZANNA. You cured me? No. Meeting Andrew cured me.

MAX. Yeah? Well, you met Andrew because I kicked your ass. I kicked your ass out of bed and onto that fucking ski trip!

(*He's right....*)

SUZANNA. And I am so, so grateful. Are you trying to torpedo my marriage? If you are, please stop.

MAX. Jesus, Suzanna. You let a crazy woman into your life. You let her into mine. How have I become the bad guy?

SUZANNA. (*Breaking down.*) Because you won't help me. That's what loving someone is, Max. It's doing stuff you don't want to do that holds value for the person you love. It's staying in bed all night. It's listening even when you

can't help. And right now...today...this minute.... It is calling Becky Fucking Shaw so I can get my husband back!

(*This all surprises and affects* MAX. *He's momentarily frozen by it. When he
unfreezes, there's a gentleness to his approach.*)

MAX. OK, calm down. Go back to Providence. I'll call her.

SUZANNA. Thank you! Max, thank you.

MAX. I'm also gonna give you some advice. Your husband is not the fucking Red Cross. The last time he started consoling a cute, suicidal chick, he
married her. He hears, "I want to hurt myself" like a fucking mating call.

SUZANNA. No...

MAX. Yes...

SUZANNA. Just make her go away.

(MAX *genuinely wants to ease* SUZANNA's *pain. But the notion of* SUZ-
ANNA's *marriage imploding is undeniably appealing, too.*)

Scene 5

MAX *and* BECKY *in a cafe. Thursday.*

BECKY. I understand your reluctance to see me. What happened to us...on
a first date! It's just so crazy...

MAX. It...certainly was.

BECKY. Did Detective Hogan call you, too?

MAX. Umm.... He may have. I think I told you, I'm opening a Boston office for my company, so...I have a stack of messages I haven't even looked
at. (*Off her expression.*) Your messages...I did receive. I apologize for not returning them. This is a...very busy time.

BECKY. I'm sure.

MAX. But I've...made time. To talk about...whatever you need to talk
about to put this event behind you.

BECKY. I gather from Andrew you feel it already is...behind you. The
holdup.

MAX. I do.

(BECKY *waits for him to say more. He doesn't.*)

BECKY. It's been...upsetting for me.

MAX. Of course.

BECKY. No, I want to apologize. I was very pushy...calling you all the time.
I regret that. I really do.

MAX. Apology...accepted.

BECKY. I'm in the same place you are now. I feel ready to just...be past it
and move on.

MAX. Great.

BECKY. (*Forced lightness.*) Our next date should be like a…daytime visit to the zoo! I don't know. Something completely not dangerous.

MAX. My feeling about all of this, Becky…. We were interrupted. This thing interrupted the normal dating process. Chalk it up to my personal failing, but I don't feel we can get past that. It's just not gonna work.

BECKY. (*She's really thrown.*) OK…. Wow. You're saying…. If not for the robbery, you'd have wanted to see me again?

MAX. Not exactly that—

BECKY. I understand, Max.

MAX. Good.

BECKY. I wondered if this was the reason you weren't calling me. If you're embarrassed about how you acted during the hold up, you shouldn't be.

MAX. Embarrassed?

BECKY. You were scared, so was I. If you're running away from me because you're embarrassed…. My feelings for you are only deepened by that glimpse into your vulnerability.

MAX. Becky, you're not understanding me.

BECKY. And I want to. Max, the detective told me—I'm sure he told you, too—that you shouldn't have led the…perpetrator to your car…

MAX. Now, wait—

BECKY. No, hear me out. If you're embarrassed about that, I want you to know…I think it was the right thing to do. And I was there; the detective wasn't.

MAX. Right—

BECKY. I absolutely understand why you feel the robbery ruined our chance. But it doesn't have to. I'm over it now. I don't need to ever mention it again.

MAX. I didn't say the robbery ruined our chance.

BECKY. Yes…you did.

MAX. OK, yes. I did say that because Suzanna told me to. The truth, Becky is…. I just don't think we're a good match—

BECKY. Because the robbery is clouding your feelings—

MAX. I knew before the robbery.

BECKY. (*After a beat.*) Can I ask when?

MAX. At the restaurant.

BECKY. So you slept with me knowing I wasn't your match?

MAX. I'm sorry if I misread your signals.

BECKY. Can you tell me why…you decided that?

MAX. Oh, for God's sake…

BECKY. I'm not angry. I just want to know what I did—

MAX. Jesus, I'm allowed to not be interested. I'm allowed to walk away from you. I don't owe you an explanation.

BECKY. I don't disagree. I just want to know what it is about me, so I can—in the future—correct it.

MAX. This! I didn't return your calls. Any normal person would have—

BECKY. But you said you knew at the restaurant. What did I do?

MAX. This! You force people to hurt you!

BECKY. I made you feel you could hurt me. That's it? You don't want to be with a woman you feel you can hurt?

MAX. Would you want to be with a man you could hurt?

BECKY. But that's love, isn't it? Caring so much that you hurt—

MAX. Love, Becky. We had one date.

BECKY. I gave you power prematurely. Is that it?

MAX. (*Rising to leave.*) I don't want to do this.

BECKY. This doesn't hurt me! It helps. Please sit for a second. (*And he does.*) I took some wrong turns, Max, and I changed. See, when I was in college…

MAX. I don't…. I don't care. (*Recoiling; back-pedaling.*) I'm sorry. This is starting to feel like the second date I didn't want to have.

BECKY. OK. I just wanted you to know that I wasn't always like this. And I feel I can get back to being myself—my good self—if I'm really fearless in examining—

MAX. Great. Do that with a therapist. Not me.

BECKY. OK. Just one last question.

MAX. No!

BECKY. Just as a favor—

MAX. I don't owe you any favors!

BECKY. (*After a beat.*) Then I don't owe you any then either. Right?

MAX. Are you threatening me?

BECKY. I'm not good enough to date, but I'm good enough to…to fuck and to be trusted with a confidence that you would not like me to betray. (*Off* MAX.) At the police station? I said you have to call Suzanna, she's your family. You said, "She's not family. I don't fuck family." Andrew doesn't know.

MAX. (*Sitting down.*) You're a fraud.

(MAX *leans across the table and grabs her arm.*)

BECKY. (*Loud enough to be heard.*) Stop it! You're hurting me.

MAX. You care, you understand…as long as you get what you want. You just went from trying to date me to blackmailing me in about three minutes. You're a scary person, Becky, and I knew it the minute I met you.

BECKY. Then you shouldn't have fucked me. (*To* MAX, *quieter.*) If I was that person you just described…. I'd have screamed by now and had you arrested for assault. Let go of my arm…and walk away.

(MAX *lets go of* BECKY *and stands up. He takes a moment to really look at her before he walks out.* BECKY *sits, recovers. She thinks about what* MAX *said about her and her choice to end the encounter without making a scene.*)

Scene 6

ANDREW *and* SUZANNA *in their apartment. The same day: Thursday.*

SUZANNA. Max assaulted her? In a cafe full of people? I don't believe that.

ANDREW. Assault is my word, but any time a man raises his hand against a woman—

SUZANNA. Assault is your word? What's Becky's word?

ANDREW. He grasped her forearm across the table, Suzanna.

SUZANNA. He grasped her forearm. You left work…. You made me leave work…because Max grasped her forearm?

ANDREW. It is never acceptable for a man to dominate a woman by force!

SUZANNA. Agreed. But you said this was an emergency.

ANDREW. This is an emergency, Suzanna!

SUZANNA. No…it isn't. Look, you know I find your radical feminist side an incredible turn-on…

ANDREW. This is not a joke.

SUZANNA. Sweetie, I know that. But I just walked out on a patient who has actual, real problems and I need to get back to her. In the future…. A forearm grab is not an emergency.

(*She tries to kiss him. He recoils.*)

ANDREW. Max assaulted my friend, Suzanna. He is out of our lives.

SUZANNA. Out…. He's out of yours, maybe.

ANDREW. You want me to be a man and make the decisions in this marriage? I just made one. You, Max—done.

(*A beat. Is she gonna escalate this or bullshit agreement and go back to work?*)

SUZANNA. You know what? Fuck you, Andrew. Here's a reality check. What Max is guilty of is fuck-and-run. It's not very nice, but it's also not a war crime. He blew her off. He didn't strangle her cat!

ANDREW. Jesus! Why do you and Max have to use such violent examples to make your points?

SUZANNA. Because we have some fucking perspective on life! Becky needs to get over it and you need to stop the Sir Lancelot bullshit. You have spare time to manufacture drama where none exists.... Put it in your writing so you can get published and we can keep our apartment!

ANDREW. Jesus, I feel like I don't know you.

SUZANNA. Why?

ANDREW. When I met you, Max and your mom were telling you to "get over" your dad's death. I listened and I cared. You're OK now because I did that.

SUZANNA. That's true! Your love healed me. But Becky needs to find her own savior, she can't have mine.

ANDREW. She doesn't have anyone else!

SUZANNA. That's not our fault.

ANDREW. Her pain is our fault. You knew Max's record with women. Fixing him up with her was thoughtless.

SUZANNA. I have apologized! What more can I do?

ANDREW. You've done enough. It is up to me now to.... (*Off* SUZANNA's *look.*) I'm not going to abandon this woman when she's drowning!

SUZANNA. Right. You'll save her and then you'll abandon her.

ANDREW. You want to tell yourself I'm turned off by you getting healthy? Go ahead. I'm not turned off by your health, I'm turned off by your character.

SUZANNA. (*Wounded.*) My character?

ANDREW. Max treated Becky like garbage from the moment she walked in that door. And I watched you that night. You didn't care then, and you don't care now. Your lack of compassion for her is incredibly unattractive.

SUZANNA. I do care, Andrew, but...

ANDREW. But what? How could you fix Max up with her? How could you fix him up with anyone?

SUZANNA. Max is a a good man, Andrew. Just because—

ANDREW. (*Overlapping.*) Are you kidding me? Fine. You know what? We've reached an impasse on this Max...thing. I'm gonna stay with friends for a couple days.

SUZANNA. Why?

ANDREW. I need to think.

SUZANNA. Think about...us? Oh, no. No. Andrew, listen to me. When I married you, I married up. I married a better person than I am. I love that you want to help Becky. I love that you don't think the bubba story is funny and I love that pornography makes you cry. You're good like my dad was good—

ANDREW. Your dad was a dishonest, financially irresponsible alcoholic! He left your sick mother with no savings! Jesus, Suzanna! Your dad is good.... Max is good.... Here's a "reality check" for you: Loving Suzanna is not the sole criteria for goodness!

(ANDREW *starts for the bedroom to pack some stuff and leave....*)

SUZANNA. (*After a beat.*) Wait. Andrew, I'm gonna tell you something. Max doesn't know and you can never, never tell him, OK? (*He nods yes; a beat.*) My father bought Max. From his father.

ANDREW. What do you mean, he bought him?

SUZANNA. He gave Max's dad a lot of money not to send Max away after his mom died. It was supposed to be money for his dad to, you know, raise him, but he didn't want to raise him, so.... That's why Max moved in with us. (*A beat.*) My father was good like you, see? Max wasn't his problem, but he saw a child in pain and he just couldn't walk away. I know what goodness is. It's kindness that asks nothing in return. Like you and Becky. It's kindness. You don't have...feelings for her. Do you?

(*A hideously long pause.*)

Oh, no.

ANDREW. I don't.... Our problem isn't Becky. (*Off her devastation.*) Let's... talk in a few days. I think it would be good for you to do some thinking, too.

Scene 7

The living room of SUSAN SLATER's *home in Richmond, Virginia. Saturday.* SUZANNA, *alone, with two big duffel bags, checking her cell phone for messages.* MAX *enters.*

MAX. Your mother is sleeping. We should get our story straight before she wakes up.

SUZANNA. I'm gonna tell her the truth. Andrew and I fixed you up with a woman and you made her attempt suicide.

MAX. Oh, no—

SUZANNA. Yes! That is why my husband isn't here with me now.

MAX. First of all, she did not attempt suicide. She cut herself. If it were at all serious, she would be hospitalized, but she isn't. She's home convalescing with your husband. (*A beat.*) He should be here. This shit you're about to face.... This is way more serious than a cut on the arm.

SUZANNA. If you can't get Lester out of jail before Monday, my mom's gonna freak out.

MAX. Then she can freak out. Your mother needs to understand that this is serious. It's not a bar fight. If Lester was doing what they say.... It's mail fraud. That's big.

SUZANNA. Not as big as cutting yourself. Apparently.

MAX. That's life and you know it. There's two kinds of trouble in life…

SUZANNA. I don't want the "two kinds of trouble" speech right now.

MAX. Yeah, but you need it. Two kinds of trouble. Sexy and not sexy. Your mother's chronic, wasting illness? Not sexy. Pretty girl with knife? Sexy. People like me show up when the trouble's not sexy. Indie-rock writer boys—

SUZANNA. Don't.

MAX. He's not here, honey.

SUZANNA. (*After a beat.*) I thought crime and jail were in the sexy category.

MAX. Not when it's mail fraud. If Lester had shot somebody, your husband would be here now.

SUZANNA. Are you sure what Becky did isn't serious?

MAX. She cut her arm! It's teenager shit. You remember what I told you when you wanted to do it.

SUZANNA. Yes.

MAX. You're too old for it. Cutting yourself over the age of eighteen is just embarrassing. Everyone at the ER will laugh at you.

SUZANNA. You're harsh, Max.

MAX. It worked. You never did it, did you?

SUZANNA. No. I didn't.

(SUSAN *enters. She just woke up.*)

SUSAN. How long have you been here?

MAX. Ten minutes, tops. You hangin' in?

SUSAN. Do I have a choice?

SUZANNA. Hi, Mama. Did we wake you?

SUSAN. (*Overlapping.*) Yes, you did. Where's Andrew?

SUZANNA. He couldn't come.

MAX. (*Overlapping.*) He had to, um—

SUSAN. You've separated.

SUZANNA. We have not separated! Andrew has a coworker who tried to…. You know…suicide. He's helping…her.

SUSAN. (*After a beat.*) So he's had an affair. I'm sorry.

SUZANNA. No! Jesus, Mom!

SUSAN. Max, what is our plan here? Lester needs a very good lawyer and, obviously, I don't know anyone.

SUZANNA. Are we allowed to talk about, you know, what he did?

SUSAN. He didn't do anything.

MAX. Well. It's a concern. Coming on the heels of Florida—

SUSAN. Florida! That absurd hotel was afraid of a lawsuit. It was a non-event—

MAX. I wasn't referring to your injury—

SUSAN. Injury! A bruise the size of a nickel—

MAX. Lester lied about paying off his credit cards. We have to ask if he's lying now, too.

SUSAN. No, he isn't. Now I'd like to hear the plan.

(*Silence. There's no budging her.*)

MAX. I have three names…of lawyers with expertise in this area—

SUSAN. Have you called them?

MAX. It's Saturday. I only have office numbers.

SUSAN. Use my computer. Get their home numbers.

MAX. OK. Fine.

(MAX *leaves to use* SUSAN's *computer, leaving mother and daughter alone. After some silence….*)

SUSAN. I'll give you a piece of advice. Don't let your pride cloud your judgment.

SUZANNA. Excuse me?

SUSAN. If you need money to leave your husband, ask Max for a loan—

SUZANNA. I'm not leaving my husband!

SUSAN. No one respects a woman who forgives infidelity. It kept Hillary Clinton from becoming president.

SUZANNA. Andrew is not cheating on me. We fixed one of his coworkers up with Max and the date went badly, she freaked out.

SUSAN. Did Max rape her?

SUZANNA. Of course, he didn't rape her! Are you insane?

SUSAN. Why does someone attempt suicide after a bad date?

SUZANNA. Forget it. The point is, Andrew has the decency to face the problem, Max doesn't.

SUSAN. Well, that's very gallant of Andrew. It's a good thing Max was available to take care of us.

SUZANNA. I don't want to talk about this. (*A beat.*) Wait a second. You're telling me that one sexual indiscretion merits divorce, but you…you allowed—

SUSAN. (*Whispering close.*) Listen to me. This business about your father being homosexual…. It's absurd. It's Max fabricating in order to dominate and control—

SUZANNA. Whoa. That's not at all where I was going…

SUSAN. I'm sorry. Go on.

SUZANNA. I just…. You tell me to divorce Andrew over an affair, but you let Lester lie and get arrested. Why do I have to play by different rules than you do?

SUSAN. Well, I don't have your assets, now do I? A relationship is a deal between equals. It's a mutually advantageous bargain—

SUZANNA. Oh, my God. Did you teach Max that?

SUSAN. Money is what I have to offer a man…

SUZANNA. You don't really believe that. Your ego is too big.

SUSAN. I am a formidable intellect, yes, but I'm sick. That cancels out my other attributes and my money is what's left—

(MAX *returns.*)

MAX. Well, I just got screamed at for interrupting dinner. But we have a lawyer.

SUSAN. Max, thank God for you. You never fail me.

MAX. I'm gonna meet him for ten minutes, bring him up to speed. You ladies want to come? (*The women grumble "no's" in unison.*) Of course, you don't. That's what you have me for.

(*A beat. He's uncomfortable leaving them alone together.*)

So…. I'll be back.

(MAX *leaves. A beat.* SUZANNA *goes to the window and watches him get in his car.*)

SUZANNA. Mom, this stuff about Dad…. It has messed with my head.

(SUSAN *swats the air dismissively.*)

Why are you giving me the exasperation look? If Max tells me something, I believe him.

SUSAN. Well, that's a mistake. (*Off* SUZANNA's *surprise.*) Please. We all have our flaws. That's his. I love him like a son, but he's a power monger and a liar.

SUZANNA. Max made it up? Dad wasn't gay?

SUSAN. The important point is this: Max has a long history of…embroidering the truth to captivate you. Since you were very young, he has lied and manipulated to foster your dependence.

SUZANNA. Max doesn't lie.

SUSAN. Suzanna, don't be dense. (*Off* SUZANNA's *confusion.*) After Max's mother died…. He was staying with us, but he had keys to his father's house. He knew he was not to go over there and watch horror movies. But more than that, he knew that you couldn't handle those movies. He lied to me and to your father—

SUZANNA. Oh, Mom, that's kids' stuff.

SUSAN. All those nights we let you two sleep in the den in your sleeping bags. He orchestrated that! He showed you those vile, horrible movies until you were afraid to sleep alone.

SUZANNA. You're telling me that Max—at ten—hatched a systematic plan to make me afraid so we could sleep in the den together?

SUSAN. Yes. There wasn't any…sexuality behind it. He just adored you and took steps to hobble you so you couldn't stray.

SUZANNA. If you saw Max doing this to me, why didn't you stop him?

SUSAN. We knew you could never take care of yourself. We saw in Max's devotion a kind of security.

SUZANNA. OK. Wow. So…. Max telling me Dad was gay, this was a lie to "hobble" me?

SUSAN. Probably. Yoshi had a strange adoration for your father. I think it's possible he made some overture. Whether or not your father reciprocated…. I have no idea.

SUZANNA. No idea? You were married to him!

SUSAN. We're a different generation, Suzanna…

SUZANNA. Meaning…

SUSAN. Meaning your father and I allowed for pockets of mystery in our marriage and I would advise you to do the same.

SUZANNA. "Pocket of mystery" sounds like code for gay.

SUSAN. Was he gay? Perhaps. Did he have affairs with men? No. Your father was deeply moral and would never have broken his vows. Also, he was not a very sexual person.

SUZANNA. Well, that's definitely code for gay.

SUSAN. No, it isn't. This graduate program you're in…. They're teaching you that we all have cores of passion and ferocity screaming to get out. It isn't true. Some people don't.

SUZANNA. You're saying dad wasn't…fierce.

SUSAN. Sexuality is like intelligence. We're all born with different…endowments. Some people are retarded and they eat paint, others split atoms and write symphonies.

SUZANNA. Oh, my God…

SUSAN. I'm sorry, Suzanna. When Max told me this about your father and Yoshi…. It was like someone telling me the mongoloid who bags my groceries had found the cancer cure. I have to allow for the possibility while remaining exceedingly dubious.

SUZANNA. God, I'm really confused.

SUSAN. He's gone. What does it matter—

SUZANNA. If it's true, it means I didn't really know him. And I thought we were so close...

SUSAN. You were very close. There are pockets of privacy within "closeness." That's as it should be. My advice to you.... Never mind. You don't want it.

SUZANNA. I do want it.

SUSAN. Your generation is fixated on "intimacy." That's why your marriages don't last. You think marriage and family require absolute honesty. They do not.

SUZANNA. Can you truly know someone when you're lying to them?

SUSAN. Why do you have to truly know them? Why?

SUZANNA. Because that's...love?

SUSAN. It's a prescription for misery. It's like those television commercials for cleaning products where they take a microscope in your kitchen and show you a lot of germs the naked eye can't see. It's stupid. If you look hard enough at anything...*anyone*, you will be revolted by what you see.

SUZANNA. You think if you'd known dad, you would have been revolted by him?

SUSAN. (*After a beat.*) By his weakness. Yes. If you're gay, be gay. Have some guts. (*After a beat.*) Now, you will never hear me buy into any of this new age nonsense about my illness being a gift. It has ruined my life and I hate it. But. It was a gift to me in this one respect. It meant I couldn't leave my marriage.

SUZANNA. And if you hadn't had MS, you would have left?

SUSAN. I would have felt I could do better than your father. And I would have been wrong.

SUZANNA. (*A beat; hard to say.*) I think I'm revolted by Max. But if I were to lose him.... I feel like I wouldn't survive. How is that possible? I can't live without him, but I don't want him.

SUSAN. The heart wants what the heart wants. I want Lester with a ferocity you can't imagine. I see his flaws...

SUZANNA. Max isn't good, Mom. Do you know what I mean? Max isn't good and Andrew is.

SUSAN. Be careful chasing after goodness. Goodness and incompetence too often go hand in hand in men. Your father's financial irresponsibility.... It's unforgivable really.

SUZANNA. Andrew's not incompetent.

SUSAN. He scribbles and brews coffee. He's too old for that! If he's not going to pull his weight financially, he must adore love and care for you in spades to compensate—

SUZANNA. He does.

SUSAN. He isn't here, Suzanna! And Max is. What would you have done, if not for Max? What would I have done?

SUZANNA. I would have driven down here and…dealt with this.

SUSAN. You wouldn't have done a good job.

SUZANNA. I think that's awful for a mother to say.

SUSAN. It's the truth, Suzanna. There's power in knowing where you stand.

SUZANNA. Mom—

SUSAN. I told Max he had to get rich if he wanted women to swoon. And you see? He followed my advice.

SUZANNA. He's an emotional cripple! The women are swooning, but he can't sleep through the night with them. He's a mess.

(The doorbell rings.)

SUZANNA. Do not tell him we talked about this.

(SUZANNA *opens the door, expecting* MAX. *It's* ANDREW *and* BECKY.)

ANDREW. I promised at the hospital I'd take care of her, but I wanted to be here.

SUSAN. Is it Max?

(ANDREW *steps into the house.* BECKY *follows, cautious and sheepish, behind him.*)

ANDREW. Hey…Susan. I'm sorry about Lester. This is my friend, Becky…

BECKY. Andrew is helping me. I hope it's OK he brought me…

SUSAN. Well, you're here now, OK or not. Come in.

(And they're in.)

ANDREW. Where's Max?

SUSAN. Max is meeting with our lawyer. He has the situation in hand. I'm very relieved.

ANDREW. That's great.

(Terribly awkward silence.)

SUSAN. What did you do to your arm?

BECKY. Oh! This? I cut it. *(More awkward silence.)* I should actually maybe change the bandage…

SUSAN. I'll show you the bathroom…

(SUSAN *starts to lead* BECKY *out.* BECKY *looks to* ANDREW *to follow.*)

ANDREW. Maybe I should…. I was at the hospital, so—

SUSAN. I raised two children, Andrew. I can supervise changing a Band Aid. Come on.

(BECKY *looks afraid, but* ANDREW *doesn't intervene.* SUSAN *and* BECKY *leave the room. Awkward beat between* SUZANNA *and* ANDREW.)

ANDREW. I had no choice, Suzanna. She has no health insurance! The only way they'd let her leave was if I promised to be responsible—

(SUZANNA *kisses him suddenly.*)

SUZANNA. I'm so glad you're here!

ANDREW. Of course I'm here. I know what day it is. Are you OK? Are you freaking out?

SUZANNA. About Lester?

ANDREW. About your dad. It's the anniversary.

SUZANNA. You…. You remembered. Even though you hate me, you remembered.

ANDREW. I don't hate you…

SUZANNA. Andrew, I don't want to lose you to Becky. I can change. Just tell me what I have to do, or be…. I'll do it.

ANDREW. I don't want to be with Becky.

SUZANNA. You don't? Really?

ANDREW. No. (*Pause.*) I can't fix her. I can't or…. I don't want to. I don't know which. But I think I led her on and I'm afraid she'll do something if I walk away.

SUZANNA. Did you sleep with her?

ANDREW. No! I wouldn't do that.

SUZANNA. But you almost did. (*Before he can answer.*) No, don't answer that. What do we do now?

ANDREW. I don't know. The whole ride down here, I'm thinking…. And I have no idea.

SUZANNA. Ten hours of thinking and you have no idea? How is that possible? Do you have human waste in your cranium where a brain should be?

ANDREW. Suzanna, don't start. I will get back in that car.

SUZANNA. Don't! I'm sorry. I can do this. I can be the…decider. (*After a beat.*) We'll get Becky another therapist and we'll loan her…. Fuck. We'll give her the money. We can see her together, but you can't be with her alone outside of work. I think to make this marriage work we have to be in it full-time, you know?

ANDREW. I think that's fair, but I think the same should apply to you and Max.

SUZANNA. That's totally different. Just because you don't like him…

ANDREW. It's more than that. Stop pulling this "he's my brother" crap. I know there's more there.

SUZANNA. There isn't more there.

ANDREW. That's a lie, Suzanna. You want to make this marriage work? The two of you need to…stop.

SUZANNA. Can I still have my phone time?

ANDREW. I wish you didn't need it, but…I guess so. OK.

SUZANNA. But I can't see him anymore.

ANDREW. I think…. Same rules for you as for me. You can see Max with me. All three of us together. (*As she takes that in….*) I better go check on Becky. This agreement? We should tell them today.

> (ANDREW *goes to find* BECKY. SUZANNA *sits, thinks.* MAX *returns….*)

MAX. What the fuck is going on?

SUZANNA. Were you…watching the house?

MAX. Did he bring her here? I'll fucking kill him…

SUZANNA. He had to bring her; she's on suicide watch.

MAX. Get her out of here. Now.

SUZANNA. Don't give me orders, Max!

MAX. I'm here taking care of your mother! I'm spending time I do not have and I am not gonna be tortured on top of it.

SUZANNA. You can leave. (*Off his shock.*) I can handle it. You got the lawyer, Andrew is here. You can go.

MAX. No. I used my good name to get us a lawyer. I'm not gonna turn him over to your indie-rock boy toy.

SUZANNA. He's my husband, Max. (*After a beat.*) And that is…permanent.

MAX. Why are you looking at me like you're breaking up with me? I'm not dating you.

SUZANNA. Max, stuff is gonna have to change with us.

MAX. What "stuff"?

SUZANNA. Andrew and I just made an agreement. He can't be alone with Becky, and I can't be alone with you…

MAX. What?!

SUZANNA. It's not appropriate for us to be emotionally intimate when I'm married to Andrew.

MAX. Emotionally intimate? According to you, I'm not capable of that.

SUZANNA. We can talk on the phone, but…. We can't be alone, it just gets too blurry.

MAX. This is because of Becky.

SUZANNA. Not entirely—

MAX. (*Overlapping.*) It is. God, I fucking hate that woman. She's a nutcase, so our relationship has to change?

SUZANNA. Yes.

MAX. How? How does a twenty-five-year friendship change because of her?

SUZANNA. Up until this…. I had doubts. I thought maybe I should be with you instead of Andrew, but…. Now I don't have them. Doubts.

MAX. If you don't have any doubts, then why are we blurry? (*Off her silence.*) I'll rephrase the question. What are your "doubts" about me?

SUZANNA. (*Careful.*) You have always had the ability to tune out other people's pain when it inconveniences you.

MAX. Excuse me?

SUZANNA. Not mine. You have always been there for me and for my parents. I'm talking about other people…Iraq is not your problem, Becky is not your problem…

MAX. That's right. They're not. And I make no apologies. Unless you're Ghandi or Jesus, you have a limited sphere of responsibility. You have a plot of land and the definition of a moral life is tending that plot of land—

SUZANNA. You need new material. I've heard the plot of land speech.

MAX. Becky Shaw is not on my plot of land! You are. And I tend my plot. I will always tend my plot.

SUZANNA. You make me sound like an obligation. Am I more than that to you?

MAX. Yes! If I didn't want you on my plot, I would rip you out and compost you. I want you on my plot. (*After a beat.*) Bring Becky in here and I'll apologize. We'll put this behind us.

SUZANNA. It's not that simple.

MAX. I will apologize! I will pay her damages, whatever you need. I want her erased from our lives.

SUZANNA. This is exactly what I'm talking about, Max! You erase people. That's wrong.

MAX. Give me another example. Aside from the war and Becky, how do I "erase" people?

SUZANNA. You watch pornography.

MAX. What? You watch it, too!

SUZANNA. But I feel guilty when I watch it! You don't.

MAX. Are you fucking kidding me? I'm gonna lose you because I don't feel guilty when I watch porn?

SUZANNA. Pornography makes Andrew cry.

MAX. That is the stupidest thing I've ever heard.

SUZANNA. I don't think it is.

MAX. Does it.... Does pornography make you cry?

SUZANNA. No, but it should and I wish it did.

MAX. This is completely insane. You cannot tell me—

(ANDREW *enters on top of this.*)

ANDREW. Susan really wants to go to Lester's visiting hour, so.... Hi, Max.

SUZANNA. OK. Can you just give us one—

ANDREW. (*Leaving.*) Oh, sure. Sure.

SUZANNA. (*To* MAX.) Why don't we talk...in a few days.

MAX. I can't. I'm busy.

SUZANNA. Max—

MAX. I have a very full schedule between...laughing at rape videos and sneering at the troops.

SUZANNA. That isn't fair.

MAX. No. This. This. Isn't fair. Anything else you want to say, you better say now.

(*He could cut her off and she knows it. The time is now if there's anything left to say.*)

SUZANNA. Today is Saturday, right? It's the third?

MAX. (*Totally perplexed, but he checks his cell phone....*) I don't fucking.... Yeah, it's the third. You need anything else before you wash your hands of me? You want the weather? Stock quotes? Horoscope?

SUZANNA. I don't want to wash my hands of you.

MAX. You just did.

(SUSAN *enters,* BECKY *and* ANDREW *trail cautiously behind her.*)

SUSAN. I want to go to the prison and I want to go now.

MAX. It's not a prison, Susan. It's a jail.

SUSAN. You can call it whatever you like if you drive me there.

SUZANNA. OK. Everybody listen up. Max feels he needs to stay here because he initiated contact with the attorney. Andrew and Becky and I are going back to Providence.

SUSAN. You have a responsibility here.

SUZANNA. I'm aware of that, but Andrew and I have set some new...boundaries for our marriage and.... He's not allowed to spend ten hours in a car alone with Becky.

BECKY. I feel like I've caused so much trouble for you and—

SUZANNA. You have, actually. So that's it. Let's go.

(BECKY *starts to weep, sits down....*)

ANDREW. Becky...

BECKY. I can't. I'm sorry. I'll take the train. I just can't...

ANDREW. When we get back to Providence.... Susie and I talked. We're gonna help you.

BECKY. This is an incredibly uncomfortable situation for me. To get back in that car...with the two of you...

ANDREW. You're right. I think the train is a great idea.... Susie?

SUZANNA. We can look into it.

MAX. (*Leaving.*) I'll do that.

(*Horrible, awkward waiting.*)

ANDREW. You're gonna be OK...

SUSAN. Becky and I had a conversation. She knows what needs to be done.

SUZANNA. I'd like to screen any recommendations my mother—

BECKY. No, it was good advice. I need to get back in school, I do.

SUSAN. The story about the black boyfriends and the racist parents. Write that up and re-apply to Brown. You'll get in.

SUZANNA. Mom, that's a terrible idea.

SUSAN. (*To* BECKY.) You may have been very victimized in your life; you may be a complete con artist. I don't know. My sense is you fall somewhere in the middle. Truth or con.... It's unattractive. We pity Job; we do not fall in love with him.

SUZANNA. Mom, don't.

BECKY. It's OK. I'm not afraid of the truth. Everyone else is—

SUSAN. (*To* BECKY.) Learn to lie. When someone with damage—as we have damage—courts a lover, we must be like the pedophile with the candy. Lure with candy no matter how frightful your nature and your intent.

SUZANNA. Don't listen to her. This is why Max behaves the way he does.

BECKY. She's right. She's absolutely right.

SUSAN. You're a beautiful woman; the only thing broken about you is your timing.

BECKY. I had a chance with Max, didn't I?

SUSAN. We don't look back. We look forward.

(MAX *returns.*)

MAX. She won't make the six o'clock and the next one's four a.m.

BECKY. I don't mind waiting. I won't intrude. I could help.... I could make sandwiches for you to take to Lester.

SUSAN. I think that's a wonderful idea.

BECKY. Max, what would you like—

MAX. I would like you to try harder the next time you attempt suicide. That is what I would like.

SUSAN. Max!

SUZANNA. OK. Becky comes with us. We'll buy a book on tape. Let's go.

(BECKY, *resigned, stands up. The threesome move towards leaving.*)

ANDREW. OK.... Susan, I really hope things work out OK with Lester. And I just wanted to acknowledge...today.

SUSAN. Acknowledge today?

ANDREW. The anniversary of Richard's death. I know it's really hard...

(SUZANNA *and* MAX *make eye contact....*)

SUSAN. Life is hard, Andrew. An anniversary is just a number.

(ANDREW *leads* BECKY *out.* SUZANNA *kisses her mother....*)

SUZANNA. Mama, you're in good hands.

SUSAN. I know.

(SUZANNA *looks at* MAX, *then leaves.*)

SUSAN. This is a very impractical solution, you know. If Lester isn't released Monday and you can't stay—

MAX. I'll hire someone for you. Don't worry about that. (*After a beat.*) It's time for you to sell the house. I want to see you put that in motion before I leave.

SUSAN. Fine. We'll discuss it after we visit Lester. I'll comb my hair and we'll go. I'll buy you a wonderful dinner after—

MAX. And.... I know this game. You don't talk about money over dinner.

SUSAN. (*As she leaves the room.*) That's right. I don't.

(*After a beat,* BECKY *returns.*)

BECKY. I'm taking the four a.m. train...

MAX. No—

BECKY. They're gone.

MAX. We're going out. You can't—

BECKY. I'll just wait here. Until it's time.

(*Stand-off.* MAX *is dangerously angry.* BECKY *sits down, gets settled.*)

BECKY. We've lost them, you know. Suzanna and Andrew...

MAX. Don't.

BECKY. And what I have to tell you.... What I came back to say.... Max, we'll be fine without them.

MAX. There is no "we," Becky—

BECKY. I know your father abandoned you. My parents abandoned me, too!

MAX. (*In her face, stifling fury.*) My father did not abandon me. I am nothing like you—

BECKY. (*A rush to get this out before he stops her.*) Listen to me, Max. We have damage; we have scars. People like Andrew and Suzanna will always run from us when we show them who we are. (*Aim and...fire.*) I see everything you are and I'm still here. (*A beat.*) When I was at the hospital, they asked me for a name...someone they should call in an emergency. A spouse, a parent, a child. I don't have any of those people. You don't either.

(SUSAN *returns and is surprised to see* BECKY.)

SUSAN. You're still—

MAX. We're dropping her at the train station.

SUSAN. I thought the next train was four a.m.

MAX. It is.

SUSAN. Well, we can't—

MAX. (*Snapping.*) We're dropping her at the train! This is fucking over. This is the end of it.

SUSAN. (*Snapping back.*) Max! You are and ever will be a guest in my home. Adjust your tone. (*Composed now.*) Becky will stay with us until it's time for her train. You're a grown man, you can be civilized for a few more hours. (*To* BECKY.) My boyfriend is unjustly incarcerated. That is as much stress as I will tolerate today. If you're going to be disturbed by visiting a prison, stay here.

BECKY. Oh, don't worry. I'm game! I mean.... Life is disturbing, right? It's just a prison.

SUSAN. Nicely put. I'm going to buy you both a wonderful dinner and some really excellent wine. We'll have a nice evening and put all of this behind us. But first we have to go to prison.

(SUSAN *leaves the house—her signal for* MAX *and* BECKY *to follow. And they will. But first...*MAX *and* BECKY *eye one another.* SUZANNA *and* ANDREW *are gone, and a long evening stretches ahead. What are the possibilities?* BECKY *takes a step towards* MAX. *He doesn't flinch. She takes another.*)

End of Play

NEIGHBORHOOD 3:
REQUISITION OF DOOM
by Jennifer Haley

BIOGRAPHY

Jennifer Haley is a Los Angeles-based playwright whose plays include *Gingerbread House*, *Dreampuffs of War*, and *The Butcher's Daughter*. Her work has been presented and developed at Actors Theatre of Louisville (Humana Festival of New American Plays), Brown/Trinity Playwrights Repertory Theatre in Providence, PlayPenn in Philadelphia, and Refraction Arts at the Blue Theatre in Austin. Ms. Haley holds an M.F.A. in Playwriting from Brown University, where she was awarded the Joelson Prize in Creative Writing the Weston Award for Drama. She was a 2008 resident of the MacDowell Colony and Millay Colony for the Arts.

ACKNOWLEDGMENTS

Neighborhood 3: Requisition of Doom premiered at the Humana Festival of New American Plays in March 2008. It was directed by Kip Fagan with the following cast:

father type: steve, doug, tobias..........John Leonard Thompson

mother type: leslie, vicki, barbara, joy................Kate Hampton

son type: trevor, ryan, jared,
zombiekllr14, blake.......................................Robin Lord Taylor

daughter type: makaela, kaitlyn,
madison, chelsea.. Reyna de Courcy

walkthroughs...William McNulty

and the following production staff:

Scenic Designer ....Michael B. Raiford
Costume Designer..Jessica Ford
Lighting Designer... Brian J. Lilienthal
Sound Designer .... Benjamin Marcum
Properties Designer ....Doc Manning
Fight Supervisor .... Lee Look
Stage Manager...Bethany Ford
Production Assistant...Sara Kmack
Dramaturg.. Amy Wegener
Assistant Dramaturg.......................................Charles Haugland
Casting... Cindi Rush Casting
Directing Assistant...Dav Yendler

Neighborhood 3: Requisition of Doom was developed with the assistance of New York University's hotINK International Festival of New Play Readings; Seven Devils Playwrights Conference, a project of id Theatre Company at the Alpine Playhouse in McCall, Idaho; and the Brown/Trinity Playwrights Repertory Theatre in Providence, Rhode Island.

PRODUCTION NOTES

Most of the play should be staged abstractly, in the netherworld of a video game or modern-day suburbia. Realistic elements may be added to Scene 9, so that we feel we are somewhere recognizable, comfortable, and may imagine, for a little while, that none of what's happened previously in the play is real. However, the violence should be dramatic, unbelievable, and loud—perhaps with stupidly spurting blood, like a video game.

A knowledge of MMORPGs, or Massive(ly) Multiplayer Online Role-Playing Games, such as *World of Warcraft*, is helpful in understanding this play.

The language should be spoken as it appears on the page. However, the line breaks represent the briefest of pauses, should be emotionally motivated (not robotic), and sound almost natural. The walkthroughs may be voiceovers or spoken by the actors.

For a look at production photos, or more information about online role-playing, avatars, and gamers gone wrong, visit *http://www.jenniferhaley.com/neighborhood.html*.

PLAYERS

father type	steve, doug, tobias
mother type	leslie, vicki, barbara, joy
son type	trevor, ryan, jared, zombiekllr14, blake
daughter type	makaela, kaitlyn, madison, chelsea

One need not be a chamber to be haunted,
One need not be a house;
The brain has corridors surpassing
Material place.
                              —Emily Dickinson

175

Kate Hampton and John Leonard Thompson
in *Neighborhood 3: Requisition of Doom*

32nd Annual Humana Festival of New American Plays
Actors Theatre of Louisville, 2008
Photo by Harlan Taylor

NEIGHBORHOOD 3: REQUISITION OF DOOM

1 walkthrough

the house you want is third from the left
as you face the cul de sac
all the houses look the same
be careful

move toward the house slowly
you will hear the sound of your
footsteps
in the street
do not walk too fast

as you approach the house
you will see on the sidewalk
a Claw Hammer

pick this up
you will need it later

like all other houses
this house will have a
flesh colored brick façade
and a welcome mat in front of the door

hint: if you kneel down and
take a closer look at this mat
you will see the word
'welcome' becomes
'help me'

enter the house
on your right is a set of
saloon doors
push through these
and enter
the kitchen

1 kitchen

makaela.	you want a coke
trevor.	okay
makaela.	shit we don't have any my brother inhaled them
trevor.	that's okay
makaela.	so then i just have stupid stuff like grape juice want some grape juice
trevor.	okay
makaela.	only he left like an inch in the bottle
trevor.	that's okay
makaela.	no it's not i'm going to rip his balls off
trevor.	i mean i don't need grape juice
makaela.	well nobody needs grape juice it'd just be nice otherwise we've got milk you want some milk
trevor.	no thanks
makaela.	it's Chocolate Milk
trevor.	okay
makaela.	it's like we're eleven again
trevor.	that's the last time i had it when i was over here my mom doesn't buy Chocolate Milk

makaela.   your mom

trevor.   what

makaela.   doesn't she sell
             makeup
             or something

trevor.   vitamin shakes

makaela.   what are those

trevor.   shakes with vitamins

makaela.   can you e lab or ate

trevor.   it's like powder
             you add water
             you make a shake
             you drink it two times a day

makaela.   does it taste good

trevor.   no

makaela.   why do you take it

trevor.   my mom says it gives you
             everything you need

makaela.   does it work
             are you getting
             everything you need

trevor.

makaela.   i always see
             a bunch of cars
             in front of your place

trevor.   she has meetings
             at the house
             she gives
             demonstrations

makaela.   isn't it like a
             pyramid scheme

trevor.   what's that

makaela.   you know
             you get a bunch of people
             there are all these levels

everyone tries to get to the next
level
tries to get to the
top
like scientology
or the mafia

trevor.   my mom
is not
in the mafia

makaela.   she doesn't know
you're here

trevor.   she's gone
this afternoon

makaela.   it's the first time i've seen you
on the bus

trevor.   she drives me

makaela.   i'm getting a car soon

trevor.   what kind

makaela.   the brand new kind

trevor.   but what make and model

makaela.   i don't know
tyler
my brother
just got a hummer
it's actually his second
hummer
he totaled the first one
almost killed someone
so my dad got him another
i want something that costs the same price
as two fucking hummers
like maybe a jag

trevor.   you think your dad
will get you a jag

makaela.   maybe
if i act like a giant jerk
who's totally circling the drain
he'll buy one to try to

	save me otherwise it'll probably be a toyota
trevor.	
makaela.	
trevor.	still
makaela.	yeah then i could drive you to school
trevor.	my mom drives me
makaela.	wouldn't you rather i mean it's high school
trevor.	you don't have the car yet so you can't drive me so there's no point in discussing it
makaela.	no point in discussing it okay dad
trevor.	just didn't you say your brother has an xbox
makaela.	
trevor.	
makaela.	do you want a vicodin my brother's a candy man i know where he keeps his stash
trevor.	won't that slow my reflexes
makaela.	haven't you done it before
trevor.	no
makaela.	you should ask mummy for a sip of her special shake

trevor.   she doesn't make
                     special shakes

makaela.   she doesn't get
                     that many people over for
                     vitamins

trevor.   look
                     i didn't come over here to
                     do drugs
                     or listen to you insult my mom
                     i thought we were playing
                     a game

makaela.   that's the only reason you came over
                     you barely said hello to me in four years

trevor.   so I'm saying
                     it now

makaela.   yeah cuz i have
                     an xbox

trevor.   i wanted to
                     it's just
                     you know

makaela.   what
                     your mom

trevor.   no not my mom

makaela.   she stopped letting you out
                     cuz you got so cute

trevor.   look shut up
                     makaela
                     i stopped coming over
                     cuz you're such a flippin know-it-all
                     i don't have to take this crap
                     i'm leaving

makaela.   we've got Neighborhood 3

trevor.

makaela.

trevor.   you've got Neighborhood 3

makaela.   it's tyler's
                but i know where he
                hides it

trevor.

makaela.

trevor.   okay
               but my mom
               doesn't stop me

makaela.   okay

trevor.   okay

makaela.   i have to sneak into
                his room

trevor.   I'm dying to play Neighborhood 3

makaela.   ha
                that sounds like something out of a horror movie
                like you're about to play this video game
                and you think it's just a game
                but actually it's real
                but these teenagers don't know it
                but the audience knows it
                and this one kid's like
                i'm dying to play
                and it's like ooooo foreshadowing

trevor.   i've been watching cody play

makaela.   so he's your contact

trevor.   he's got all the walkthroughs
               so you know what to look for
               in the game

makaela.   bet cody doesn't have Chocolate Milk
                bet that's why you came over here

trevor.   he came on to me

makaela.   no
                way
                cody came on to you

trevor.   i think so
                he kept saying how good I was with the joystick
                and they're not even called joysticks
                anymore

makaela.   i can't believe it
                he's so hot
                next time i see him
                i'm gonna tell him
                i'm pretty good
                with a joystick

trevor.   are you

makaela.

trevor.

makaela.   i could be

trevor.   well let's turn on the game
                and find out

makaela.   wait
                are you
                what are you

trevor.   the game
                what are you

makaela.   nothing
                i'll set it up and
                you can play

trevor.   you're not going to play

makaela.   nah

trevor.   do some split screen with me

makaela.   no

trevor.   why not

makaela.   this game's fucked up
                it maps out
                your own Neighborhood
                how creepy
                is that

trevor.	are you kidding it's sweet it's the best use of satellite technology i can think of
makaela.	oh now he's excited
trevor.	how can you not think it's sweet
makaela.	there's no point to it
trevor.	sure there is you have to keep getting to the next level you have to get to the top
makaela.	and then what
trevor.	you're out you're free you've beat everything and nothing can hurt you anymore
makaela.	my brother beats the shit out of those things he gets online and plays with his friends the sicker the game they more they like it he whacks those Zombies to smithereens and spends a little too much time with them after they're dead
trevor.	sometimes it's fun to be sick sometimes you need a place to be sick
makaela.	that's not the only place he's sick you don't know much about my brother
trevor.	he plays at cody's house
makaela.	what

trevor.   tyler
he's almost almost at
the Last Chapter

makaela.   have you been
hanging out
with him

trevor.   they won't let me
play the game
they keep calling me
a noob

makaela.   what else
do you do
with them

trevor.   what do you
mean

makaela.   any of that other
sick shit
any of their missions
in the Neighborhood

trevor.   missions

makaela.   maybe your mom
would want to know about this
would want to know about her
beautiful vitamin shake boy
what if i told
your mom

trevor.   you say a fucking word to my mom and i'll

makaela.   what
slice my titties off
like they do the girl Zombies
in the game

trevor.

makaela.

trevor.   you're nuts

makaela.   just leave

trevor.   you're the one
who invited me

makaela.   i didn't know
you'd got so twisted

trevor.   it's only
a game

makaela.   oh right trevor
don't tell me
you've never seen it

trevor.   seen what

makaela.   one of those things
like
reach out

trevor.   what things

makaela.   in the game
while you're hacking it
reach out with what's left of its
hand
and gurgle
i'm coming
to get you
for real

2 walkthrough

drink the
Chocolate Milk
to replenish your
Sugar Rush

exit the house and
advance down the street
slowly
remember
all action
must appear
unhurried
the goal
during the daytime
is to blend in

two blocks down
on your right

> look for the house
> with a Garden Gnome
> in the front yard
>
> use your Hammer
> to break the Gnome
> inside you will find a
> Pink Post-it Note
> with three numbers on it
>
> add this to your inventory
> and proceed
> up the sidewalk

2 front door

steve.   hi there
             hi

leslie.   yes

steve.   i'm sorry i
             accidentally kicked
             your Garden Gnome

leslie.   oh

steve.   it's just
             his head
             i've got some
             superglue

leslie.   no that's

steve.   you might want to keep him
             out back
             i don't think Garden Gnomes are
             acceptable
             to the Neighborhood Association

leslie.   are you with
             the Neighborhood Association

steve.   no i

leslie.   oh i
             thought you were a
             representative

                    come to give me another
                    warning

steve.   no i'm
                    from down the street
                    i'm

leslie.   of course
                    halloween

steve.   halloween
                    yes
                    i was in
                    the gorilla suit
                    until

leslie.   yes
                    i remember

steve.   i sometimes get
                    carried away at
                    block parties

leslie.   well this one was
                    unseasonably warm

steve.

leslie.

steve.   steve

leslie.   leslie

steve.   you have
                    twins
                    right
                    both of them
                    were there
                    the wolfman and
                    cinderella

leslie.   the hunchback and
                    tinkerbell

steve.   tinkerbell
                    oh right
                    my daughter was
                    freddy krueger

leslie.   with
                     the hat

steve.   yes

leslie.   oh i didn't know
                     that was a
                     girl

steve.   sometimes neither do we

leslie.

steve.   uh so
                     i'm home from the office
                     early today
                     i went in the house
                     and couldn't find my daughter
                     chelsea
                     my wife is
                     taking a break from
                     the family
                     so i'm kind of
                     holding down the fort ha ha
                     and
                     well
                     um

leslie.   i'm sorry
                     but

steve.   yeah
                     it's hard

leslie.   no
                     we're having
                     a party
                     for my husband
                     when he gets home
                     i'm making
                     buffalo wings

steve.   a party
                     oh
                     that's nice
                     that's really nice
                     well i won't
                     take up your time

i just um
let me ask you real quick
have you heard about these
online video games
the kids are playing

leslie.

leslie.   why do you
ask

steve.   my only daughter
chelsea
is hooked on one
Neighborhood
something
i don't know
but when i say
hooked
i guess i'm
putting it mildly
she basically plays this
every waking moment
from the time she gets home from school
to the time she goes to bed
if she goes to bed
we bought her a
high speed gaming computer
for christmas
we thought that would make her
happy
we didn't know
we'd never see her again
she gets online
and plays this character
with other people online
playing characters
some of them
are her friends
but some of them
for all i know
could be pedophiles
they conspire for hours
on that instant message
and conference calls

they run around a Neighborhood
that looks very much like
ours
butchering Zombies
who look a whole lot like
us
but let's see
what am i worried about

i'm worried that
she's not making real friends in the
real world
the way she looks
no one at school will
talk to her
when i was a kid
i made bombs out of firecrackers
and my folks thought i was
possessed
and of course they were
overreacting
and
i've threatened to
remove the computer
but i don't know if it is the computer
or if it's

i'm a
corporate manager
i manage people at all levels
and when they're not up to task i just
fire them
but you know
you can't fire your only kid
even when she comes out of her room
looking like some kind of
monster

leslie.

steve.   i'm sorry
of course
your party

leslie.   no let me
come outside
my daughter
madison
plays this game

steve.   really

leslie.   i can't get her to
come to dinner
we used to think it was
anorexia
until i figured out i had to
set the food down
right in front of her

steve.   that's what i do
i pick chelsea up
a burger
everyday
on my way home from work

leslie.   i circle back
for the dirty dishes
she screams when i
make her stop for half a minute
to clean drippings
out of the keyboard

steve.   her mom and i were dating
by her age
but she's never mentioned
a single boy

leslie.   i'd be terrified to see
what kind of date
she'd bring home

steve.   she won't allow me
in her room

leslie.   she calls me
leslie
she won't call me
mom

steve.   what about taking
the computer away

leslie.   she'd just go to
                     someone else's house

steve.   that's what i thought
                     i'd be in our house
                     alone

leslie.   we'd never see her
                     we want to see her
                     it's hard enough
                     with her father

steve.   it's his
                     birthday

leslie.   no
                     no
                     not that kind of
                     party
                     he's a judge
                     a federal judge
                     he has to decide
                     right and wrong all the time
                     it's really quite stressful
                     i'm hoping it will
                     end soon
                     i hear her talking to
                     the other players
                     something about
                     the Last Chapter
                     they're almost at
                     the Last Chapter
                     doesn't that sound
                     promising

steve.   i thought
                     your daughter was
                     tinkerbell

leslie.   it was dark
                     at the block party
                     you didn't notice
                     the hoofprints
                     on her chest
                     she went as
                     tinkerbell bride of satan

steve.

leslie.

steve.   i came home
and found her gone
i looked on
her computer
this game is
quite sophisticated
it uses global positioning
to map out the Neighborhood
there's a key for points of
Zombie infiltration
several houses
including mine
and yours
are red

leslie.

steve.   i want
to talk
to madison

leslie.   she's on her
game

steve.   she may know
where chelsea is

leslie.   i can't
disturb her

steve.   we don't know what they're
really up to

leslie.   tonight is already
very hard

steve.   i don't know anymore
what's serious
what if this is
serious

leslie.   i know serious
i know serious
you think i don't know
serious

steve.   no i

leslie.   they're making me do this tonight
                  his friends from work
                  this wasn't my idea
                  everyone coming over
                  to tell him he's drinking
                  it's so stupid
                  he knows he's drinking
                  he'll think this is
                  my idea and then
                  i don't know
                  i don't know
                  i don't know anything anymore

steve.   i'm sorry

                  i guess
                  this is not a good night
                  here's your
                  Gnome

leslie.

steve.

leslie.   i liked
                  the Gnome
                  everyone else in the family
                  hated him
                  but
                  he was always so cheerful
                  on the front lawn
                  i'd sit down next to him
                  and put my hands
                  on his cheeks
                  when it's warm out
                  they're warm
                  when it's cold out
                  they're cold
                  the logic
                  is so appealing
                  when it's warm out and turns cold
                  his cheeks are still warm
                  so you have a history
                  but only a recent history
                  just the past hour

instead of the crushing history
of your lifetime
or your country
or hominids

steve. i'm sorry i
kicked him
i've got some
superglue

leslie.

steve.

leslie. no

steve. no

leslie. i think
his time
is up

3 walkthrough

enter the house
you will find yourself in a
living room
with white walls and a
white carpet

turn to your left
proceed up the stairs
and enter the
bedroom

across the room
is a closet
warning: do not enter
this closet
unless you picked up the
Weed Wacker
in Chapter Four

instead
on the nightstand
you will see the
Glass of Red Wine

drink this

when you exit the bedroom
and go back down the stairs
you will notice a pool of
blood
on the carpet

you have just moved through
a secret wormhole
in the Neighborhood
you are now in a house
on the opposite side
of the subdivision

3 living room

vicki.   did you get what you were
                looking for

kaitlyn.   yes thank you for letting me in
                his room

vicki.   hopefully he won't find out
                we were in
                his room
                unless he has some
                hidden camera

kaitlyn.   i don't remember
                a camera

vicki.   i'm kidding
                although i wouldn't be surprised
                he's always been into
                gadgets

kaitlyn.   yeah

vicki.   i don't know what he has in there
                he keeps it such a big
                secret
                but we've always pledged
                to protect his
                privacy

kaitlyn.   uh huh

vicki.	well this will be our little secret
kaitlyn.	um i should be going but thank you again mrs. prichard
vicki.	vicki it's still vicki and it's no problem i'm glad you found what you were looking for it's so good so good to see you again
kaitlyn.	it's good to see you too
vicki.	we really miss you around here
kaitlyn.	yeah me too
vicki.	my husband and i thought you were really good for him
kaitlyn.	thanks but i should
vicki.	do you want to sit down for a minute
kaitlyn.	oh
vicki.	i could get you a coke or even a Glass of Wine i'm having a Glass of Wine only if you think your mom wouldn't mind
kaitlyn.	no she lets me have Wine sometimes it's just i
vicki.	i don't expect tyler home anytime soon

kaitlyn.   okay
                      i guess i could
                      for a minute

vicki.   great
                      great
                      sit down
                      let me get you
                      a glass
                      did you notice we reupholstered the loveseat

kaitlyn.   it looks nice

vicki.   thank you
                      it was not cheap

kaitlyn.   no it looks
                      nice

vicki.   i went back and forth on the material
                      i just couldn't decide between
                      stripes or oriental
                      it doesn't seem like a big decision
                      but it affects the whole room
                      these things that seem so small
                      have such enormous consequences
                      here you go

kaitlyn.   thank you

vicki.   so
                      kaitlyn
                      how's school

kaitlyn.   fine

vicki.   what electives
                      are you taking

kaitlyn.   graphic design

vicki.   really
                      on the computer

kaitlyn.   oh yeah

vicki.   wow
                      they teach you such
                      great things now

	how are the grades still good
kaitlyn.	i guess
vicki.	you know even though we got him that hummer tyler's grades took a downturn when you two split up
kaitlyn.	oh i'm sorry
vicki.	no no it's not your fault i just think he was upset
kaitlyn.	
vicki.	i mean you were the one to break up with him
kaitlyn.	sort of
vicki.	that's what he said
kaitlyn.	we weren't hanging out much anyway
vicki.	but when he wasn't on his computer i thought he was with you
kaitlyn.	i mean sometimes
vicki.	almost every night of the week
kaitlyn.	no
vicki.	well where could he have been

kaitlyn.   probably
                   with his friends

vicki.   you mean the olson boys

kaitlyn.   he's not really
                   friends with them

vicki.   those are his
                   best friends

kaitlyn.

vicki.

kaitlyn.

vicki.   it was strange to see his room
                   i haven't seen it in months
                   we bought that bed
                   when he was five years old
                   one morning i went in
                   and his feet were poking
                   off the end
                   and they were

                   hairy

                   i said it was time
                   for a new bed
                   but that was when
                   he sealed off the room
                   and like i said
                   i want to give him
                   a place of his own
                   to be himself
                   isn't that good
                   i'm not the kind of parent
                   to read her son's diary
                   if boys really keep diaries
                   maybe he has a
                   what is it called
                   a blog
                   even if it was online
                   i wouldn't read it
                   not that i'm too savvy
                   with the internet
                   he's playing that

game now
that takes up
all his time
when he's not out with his
friends
or whoever
he goes out with
i'm just trying to
something's different
do you think
gosh
do you think it's
drugs

kaitlyn.   maybe that's
part of it

vicki.   he has those
red eyes
but that's just marijuana
right

kaitlyn.   not like
that kind of
red

vicki.   you mean
something harder
something like
it was on dateline
oxycontin

kaitlyn.   maybe not even
drugs

vicki.   he has a great imagination
he gets into trouble
with the Neighborhood Association
but so would a saint
i mean
who cares about the stupid golf course
it was strange
to see those posters
on his walls
but all the boys
have posters like that
with skeletons

                        and Zombies
                        and blood
                        right

vicki.

kaitlyn.

kaitlyn.   i think you should go through his room

vicki.

kaitlyn.

vicki.   what do you think
                    i might find

kaitlyn.   do you remember
                    that Cat

vicki.   what Cat

kaitlyn.   the hendersons'
                    Cat

vicki.   wasn't it
                    hit by a car

kaitlyn.   you didn't hear
                    how they found it

vicki.   how did they
                    find it

kaitlyn.   it was
                    still alive
                    even though

vicki.   stop

                    i don't know what
                    this has to do with
                    my son
                    we give him
                    everything
                    he needs
                    this Wine is
                    too sweet
                    it's making me
                    sick
                    i suppose i do need to let you

get home
i'm so glad you
stopped by
say hello
to your mother
for me
i see her in the
grocery store
all the time
and we keep making plans to
get together
but we just can't seem to
get together
you only live a few blocks over
so i don't know
what it is
but tell her i really will
call her
and we really will
get together

kaitlyn.   okay
thanks for the
Wine
and letting me
in

vicki.   of course
of course
come back if you need
anything else

what was it
that you needed

kaitlyn.   sorry

vicki.   from his
room

kaitlyn.   just something
of mine
he took

vicki.   something
like
what

kaitlyn.   it's
                     private

vicki.   oh

kaitlyn.   i mean

vicki.   no that's
                     okay
                     of course i
                     respect that

kaitlyn.

kaitlyn.   did you know
                     this house
                     is the mirror opposite
                     of mine

vicki.

kaitlyn.   if you divide the Neighborhood
                     along the line of the sewage ditch
                     and fold it in half
                     my room
                     would be right on top of
                     his room
                     so we'd see each other
                     through the ceiling
                     which is kind of how
                     we got together
                     when i needed to escape
                     my mom
                     i could lie in bed
                     and look through the ceiling
                     down at him in his bed
                     looking up through the ceiling
                     and we just sort of
                     knew each other

                     he started playing
                     that game
                     it uploads floorplans
                     from the Neighborhood Association
                     he showed me a map
                     of the subdivision
                     and the wormhole
                     between our rooms

there are wormholes
all over
the Neighborhood
he said
one of them connects
your imagination
in the game
to what happens
in life
for real
it's not just
the Cat
vicki
i think you should go through his room

vicki.   his father's
a real estate agent
i quit my job
to be home for him

kaitlyn.   if you don't
look at something
it can kind of
blow up
don't you want to know what's in his

vicki.   no

he needs the right
to his own
privacy
and we give him
everything
he needs

4 walkthrough

before you are through
back away
from the Cat
do not let the mewing
deter you

leaving it
half alive
will boost your

Ruthless Ratings
which will help you
in future combat

continue down the street
casually
one block up
you will see a house
with a flagstone path
leading to
the back

take this path
to a wooden gate
use your Hammer
to smash the lock
enter the backyard
and proceed to
the pool

4 pool

doug.   it's okay son
                   things die
                   Snickers had a
                   good life

ryan.

doug.   we don't really know what happens
                   when something dies
                   Snickers could be with us
                   right here
                   right now
                   we could even say
                   hello Snickers
                   you were an awesome Cat
                   i'm sorry you got hit by that
                   hummer
                   at least it happened fast
                   we should all hope to be
                   so lucky

ryan.

doug.   as henry david thoreau said
i went to the woods
because i wished to live deliberately
to front only the
essential facts of life
and not
when i came to die
discover that i had not lived

ryan.   Snickers didn't go to the woods

doug.   well he went into the bushes a lot

ryan.

doug.   look
ryan
we've all been affected
by the death of Snickers

ryan.

doug.   it reminds us of our own mortality
and i know that can be scary
as inderpal bahra said
we are afraid to live
but scared to die

ryan.

doug.   death comes to everyone
think of it as something really democratic
like our country

ryan.   or as warren leblanc said
life is like a video game
everyone must die

doug.   who is warren leblanc

ryan.   he got caught up in this game called manhunt
and killed his fourteen-year-old friend
with a Claw Hammer

doug.

ryan.

doug.   that's not quite
what i mean
look

ryan
we need to do something about this
crying
everyone has had a
good cry over Snickers
now it's time to dry our eyes
lift the shades
and let in the sun
do you think you can do that

ryan.

doug.   you're not a child anymore
part of growing up is realizing
there's a lot of pain in this world
and taking responsibility for your life
means you don't let it destroy you
and you don't let your behavior
increase the pain and fear
for everyone else

ryan.

doug.   your mother wants to put you
on antidepressants
do you want to be put
on antidepressants

ryan.   um

doug.   i didn't think so
we don't need drugs
to repair ourselves
the answer is within us
our personal power
is greater
than we realize
you've always been a good son
we depend on you to keep us in
good spirits
now
we've given you
a break on your chores
since Snickers passed
but i think reinstating them
will help take your mind off things
as henri matisse said

derive happiness in oneself
from a good day's work
so
ryan
you know the grind
clean the filters
skim the leaves
and replace the chlorine tablets
okay

ryan.

ryan. i don't like
the Barracuda

doug. it helps us
keep the pool clean

ryan. i don't like
the way it moves

doug. what are you
ten years old
it's not as though it's
alive

ryan. maybe not the way we think of
life

doug. well i guess we have
two options here
we could turn it off
or
you could practice getting over
your fear of it
which would you rather do

ryan.

doug. which would be the
brave
thing to do

ryan.

doug. look

ryan.   i just don't want it going while i'm cleaning the pool
                    is that so
                    fucking
                    hard

doug.

ryan.

doug.   is there something else
                    besides Snickers

ryan.

doug.

ryan.   it's just
                    something
                    in the Neighborhood

doug.   what

ryan.   i don't know
                    i don't think Snickers
                    was hit by a hummer

doug.   your mom saw it
                    pulling around the block

ryan.   i just don't
                    the way Snickers looked
                    it just
                    didn't look
                    like a car
                    did that

doug.   what did it
                    look like

ryan.   i've been playing this
                    game
                    at blake's house

doug.   we have seen a bit
                    less of you

ryan.   and we
                    there's this part with this
                    Cat
                    and we
                    we

i didn't think
it was
real

doug. what was
real

ryan. that
it would
Snickers
dad
listen
there's something
in the Neighborhood
something's
coming

doug.

ryan.

doug.

ryan.

doug. do you remember
what i was saying
about personal power
being a wonderful thing
well it works both ways
personal power
can do great damage
when it's negative
you're beginning
to remind me
of my sister
every morning
when she woke up
you'd hear this
wail
up above
this wail
would sound
and you'd think
here she comes
she'd appear
at the top of the stairs

with her pigtails all twisted
her mouth wide open and wet
hair sticking to the mucus on her cheeks
she'd come down the stairs
one pajama foot
after another
dragging her yellow blanket behind her
plunking down and
down and
closer and
closer
her howls sounding
louder and
louder
god
nothing will scare you more
than your own family

as charles manson said
from the world of darkness
did i loose demons and devils
let me tell you
son
don't you dare
bring something like that
into this house

5 walkthrough

once you've vanquished
the Barracuda
open the filter
behind its mouth
you will find a
Lime Post-it Note
with four numbers on it
add this to your inventory
and exit the backyard

the only way
to escape the Neighborhood
is to enter the
Final House
you must enter the

Final House
before the Neighborhood
is overrun
by Zombies

proceed past the
pocket park
to the house with the
open garage
if you have any available
light weapon slots
turn to the
gas grill
and pick up the
Barbecue Fork

enter the house
through the back of the garage
and find yourself in
the gameroom

5 gameroom

jared.   come on
             madison
             it's going to start

madison.   i'm coming

jared.   no
             come on
             now

madison.   i said
             i'm coming

jared.   you always say that
             it's never true
             he's on his way home from work
             he'll be here any minute

madison.   i'll be right
             there

jared.   i'm not mom
             don't feed me bullshit
             she went through alot

to pull this together
don't you think it's more important
than your game

madison.   we're almost at
the Final House

jared.   you worked on
what you're going to say to him
didn't you

madison.   did you

jared.   sort of

madison.   what are you
going to say

jared.   i asked you first

madison.   i'll just tell him
he's totally fucked up
and he's fucked
everyone in the family up
so he should fucking stop
fucking everyone up
hey shithole
get off me
fucking Zombie
how about some gut raping
with my garden spade

jared.   you're not
supposed to be
angry

madison.   that's been made
perfectly clear
by that douche
from the facility

jared.   he's trying to get everyone together
in the living room
he told me
to come get you

madison.   well you tell him
i'm coming

jared.

madison.

jared.   i'm going to tell dad
that time he forgot to pick me up
from baseball practice
really
um
hurt
i was standing
on the sidewalk
and all the other dads
were picking up their kids
until everyone was
gone
except for me
with my mitt
and it turns out
he was at that bar
in the strip center
he totally
forgot

madison.   oh he'll cry
with his big red eyes
and everyone
will feel sorry
for him

jared.   don't you
feel sorry for him

madison.   i'm surrounded by Zombies
where the fuck is my team

jared.   what if he
can't help it

madison.   look i stayed home
didn't i
everyone else
is at cody's house

jared.   i think you're like him
i think you're
hooked

madison.   oh who was sleeping like
                 two hours a night to play

jared.   i gave it up

madison.   not until the end
                 you were almost in
                 the Final House

jared.   yeah dude
                 it creeped me out

madison.   what did

jared.   you're almost there
                 you'll see

madison.   i can't get
                 any closer
                 hello
                 chelsea
                 come in chelsea
                 where are you guys

jared.   i think we play
                 to get away from him
                 like he's trying
                 to get away from
                 whatever he's trying to
                 get away from

madison.   like us foreclosing

jared.   what do you mean
                 foreclosing

madison.   hello
                 he drank up
                 all our money

jared.   how do
                 you know

madison.   i went in the study
                 i needed some dough
                 i went through their records
                 mom opened a new card
                 to pay for his fancy rehab
                 where are they

jared.   madison
would you stop
for a moment
playing that

madison.   they better not have
ditched me
why does everyone
ditch me

jared.   for a moment
would you stop
and look at me

madison.   no fucking way
they went in
they went in the Final House
they went in without me
now i'll never
get in
i can't do it
on my own

madison.

madison.

madison.   you have to
log in
and help me

jared.   i'm not playing that
anymore

madison.   jared
i need you
you're my twin

jared.   just stop
and do it
later

madison.   i'm not stopping
anymore
i'm not stopping
for him
you've got the computer
it will only take a second

jared.   there's something
                     wrong

madison.   you've got
                     the circular saw
                     and the lawn darts
                     pleeeeeeeeaaaasee

jared.   no

madison.   pleeeeeeeeeeeeeeeaaaaaaaasse

jared.   no madison

madison.   please please please please please please
                     you have to help me or i'll die

jared.   he'll be home any minute
                     we don't have time

madison.   i don't care
                     i hate him
                     i hate him
                     he's messing even this up for me

jared.   this is nothing
                     don't you care about
                     anything that
                     matters

madison.   hold up
                     chelsea's online
                     why isn't she using
                     oh
                     she says her headset is dead

jared.   besides
                     with the game
                     there's something

madison.   weird
                     tyler found a Zombie
                     in the Final House
                     that looked like
                     his mom

jared.   what'd he do

madison. he pwned her with the Barbecue Fork
they're freaking out
chelsea's logging off
she said
don't go in

jared. don't go in
where

madison. i'm not going anywhere
cuz i'll get creamed
cuz my team ditched me
shit
mother fucker
die
die
die
die
die
die
die
die
die
die
die

jared. listen

madison. what

jared. in the Neighborhood

a siren

madison.

jared.

madison. pleeease

jared. why don't you put
that energy
into this intervention
if not for him
then for us
maybe it would be
good for us
to
tell the truth

don't you ever want to
shout the truth
out the window
shout
this is the truth
this is the truth
this is the truth

madison.   fuckin a
you're gonna get us in trouble with
the Neighborhood Association

jared.   i don't care
come and get me
come and get me
Neighborhood Association
come and get me
for telling
the truth

madison.   you're not even
saying anything
why don't you shout this
every night
on his fifth cocktail
my dad
turns into a Zombie
and basically tells me
what a loser i am
what a loser son i am
so now i
slump
everywhere i go
i'm known at school as
The Hunchback
i still think he's great
way deep down
i'm so glad
the man who deformed me
is taking a month at a spa
to learn he's a
beautiful being
at heart

jared.

jared.

jared.   i don't want to
                  yell that

madison.   yeah cuz it's
                  the truth

jared.

madison.

jared.   okay
                  let me log in

madison.   yaaaay

jared.   have you
                  figured it out
                  have you seen
                  the Final House

madison.   no
                  there's like
                  twenty Zombies
                  in my way
                  if i pop out
                  they'll see me

jared.   where are you

madison.   in the pocket park
                  behind the bench

jared.   i'll distract them

madison.   don't die
                  remember
                  in the Last Chapter
                  you can't resurrect

jared.   you telling me now
                  about this game

madison.   oh my god
                  you're running right out
                  in front of them

jared.   hurry
                  madison

madison.   this isn't a
                 suicide mission

jared.   you wanted to see
                 the Final House
                 go on
                 one block past
                 the pocket park
                 locate the house on the left

madison.   how do you
                 remember

jared.   oh this house
                 i could never forget

madison.   but

jared.   go
                 go
                 go

madison.   i'm going

jared.   a few of them
                 are peeling away
                 they're coming after
                 you

madison.   shit
                 shit
                 i'm almost there
                 house on the left
                 house on the left
                 house on the left
                 is

                 our house

jared.   what did i tell you

madison.   what happens
                 when you
                 go in

jared.   i don't know
                 that's where i stopped

madison.   i'm on the front porch
                 i'm at the front door

jared.   oh man
                 did you hear that

madison.

jared.

madison.   he's home

6 walkthrough

killing Zombies
will alert the Neighborhood Association
to your presence

as the job
of the Neighborhood Association
is to protect
the Zombies
consider the forces they deploy
to be your
enemy

exit through the garage
proceed down the street
two blocks
and take a
right

in the front yard
of the first house
you will see
a newly-planted crape myrtle tree
with a set of
Hedge Clippers
at its base

move toward
the tree

6 front yard

tobias.   excuse me
                 you're in the way of my
                 Weed Wacker

barbara.   you already did this
                  you weed wacked it
                  yesterday

tobias.   i'm weed wacking it again
                  today

barbara.   you do it everyday
                  the grass doesn't need it
                  everyday

tobias.   i have to keep it down
                  i have to keep the ground prepared

barbara.   i can't
                  hear you
                  could you please turn the Wacker
                  off

tobias.

barbara.   thank you
                  i'm barbara
                  i'm from next door

tobias.   i've seen you
                  come and go

barbara.   you know my son
                  cody

tobias.   i've seen him
                  come and go

barbara.   my husband and i
                  just got home
                  cody apparently had some
                  friends over
                  they left the game room a mess
                  a different kind of
                  mess
                  you didn't see any of them
                  come and go
                  while you were here wacking your
                  very short grass

tobias.   i just got
                  started

barbara.   but
you don't work
do you
you didn't see them
this afternoon

tobias.   i heard some
screaming

barbara.   screaming

tobias.   i think they were playing
some kind of
game

barbara.   you mean like
cheering

tobias.   i mean like
screaming

barbara.   like they were
excited

tobias.   if by
excited
you mean
frantic
then
yes

barbara.

tobias.

barbara.   why do you do your lawn
every single day
every day i hear that
buzzing

tobias.   the grass is
unruly
it grows
very fast

barbara.   not in a day
not that fast

tobias.   i notice you have
stones

barbara.   we filled our yard with stones
so we wouldn't have to mow
i am very sensitive
to noise

tobias.   i'm surprised stones
are allowed
by the Neighborhood Association

barbara.   we were one of the first buyers
they wrote our contract
without the grass clause

tobias.   ah the grass clause
you have to have grass
but keep it short
they want it to look like everything
is under control

barbara.   what

tobias.   they want it to look like everything
is under control

barbara.   i can't hear you
over the sirens

tobias.   everything
is under

control

barbara.   they must love you

tobias.   i don't trim my grass
for the Neighborhood Association
i have to keep the ground prepared

barbara.   prepared for what

tobias.

barbara.   you don't work
do you

tobias.   i stopped finding it
important
i stopped finding alot of things
important

barbara.	you did this today to your house why are the windows boarded
tobias.	protection
barbara.	what are we expecting a hurricane
tobias.	have you looked at your son's game
barbara.	how do you know about
tobias.	it's quite popular playing with real people
barbara.	i know some of the people he plays with but some of them i don't it could be someone next door or it could be a pedophile
tobias.	or both
barbara.	what do you mean
tobias.	what do you mean
barbara.	
tobias.	
barbara.	you don't have children do you
tobias.	we had a hard time we took some drugs we got pregnant with triplets three girls dead in the womb at seven months we buried them in the yard under the crape myrtle tree

barbara.   isn't that
illegal

tobias.   no
it's our belief
they were
Ballerinas
they died floating in a
pas de trois
at night they come out
and float through the yard
i cut the grass for their glissades
they move on to your place
to practice their grand jetés
you wake up and hear
their pointe shoes
on your stones

barbara.   i wake up
and hear that
clacking

tobias.   we moved here
to raise children
and then i realized
this Neighborhood
in trying so hard to
deny fear
actually magnifies it
i could feel it
warping them
in the womb
if they'd been born
it would have warped them
into something
unthinkable
instead
they dance
for the Last Chapter

barbara.   the Last Chapter
that's something from
cody's game

tobias.   it was hard
getting it out of him

barbara.   getting it out
i thought you hadn't
seen him

tobias.   not today
last night

barbara.   last night
what were you doing with

tobias.   i caught him in
my yard
he was making
a mess

barbara.   what kind of
mess

tobias.   a different kind of
mess

barbara.   you have to
tell me
i'm his
mom

tobias.   we believe imagination
creates reality
if you fear something
it will manifest
if you don't face it
it will kill you
are you sure you're ready to
face it

barbara.   his father's out
looking for him
his father is
an angry man
if you're not telling us
something we need to know

tobias.   are you sure you're ready to
face it
yes or no

barbara.   i'm not playing
this game
with you

tobias.   then if you'll
                     excuse me

barbara.   don't you dare
                     turn that on

tobias.   are you
                     threatening me

barbara.   yes

tobias.

barbara.   yes

tobias.   cody said
                     in the Final House
                     there's a wormhole
                     once you go in
                     you take your family with you
                     they appear to you as
                     Zombies
                     and finally you can
                     kill them
                     without
                     remorse

barbara.

tobias.

barbara.   do you know what the neighbors say about you
                     they say you killed those girls
                     you killed them and buried them in the yard
                     because you were afraid
                     they were going to be
                     monsters

tobias.   monster
                     who do you think
                     is the monster

                     i'll leave out these
                     Hedge Clippers
                     if you see
                     your son
                     don't hesitate

7 walkthrough

you may pick up the
Hedge Clippers
if you have a proficiency
in garden tools

proceed toward a street sign
that reads 'dead end'
turn left into
the cul de sac

as night
begins
to fall
you may engage the
Run Really Fast Function

your Stealth Talent
increases by
three
Zombie Olfactory Skill
increases by
twelve

turn to the first house
on your right
you will see the
Cell Phone
in the driveway

pick this up
and move toward
the house

7 driveway

steve.   there you are
        i've been looking
        all over for you

chelsea.   not now steve

steve.   don't not now steve me
        chelsea
        get back inside
        the house

234 JENNIFER HALEY

chelsea. i'm not staying
i have to check on
my friend

steve. what friend

chelsea. you don't
know her

steve. it's too late
where have you been all afternoon

chelsea. i was at
someone's house

steve. whose house

chelsea. you come home
every night
in the dark
what do you care

steve. i came home early
to spend some time with you
only to find you
gone

chelsea. i have to check on
my friend

steve. even when
you're here
all i see
is you at the computer
with your big bag of cheetos
well that's about to
end

chelsea. you have no idea
what's going on
i don't need
your permission

steve. why don't you
just call her

chelsea. i can't find
my Cell Phone

steve. that's because i have your Cell Phone

chelsea.

steve.

chelsea.   give it to me

steve.   is this what you came home to look for
                      it was on the kitchen counter
                      'lot of interesting stuff here

chelsea.   what are you
                      talking about

steve.   fascinating
                      photo gallery

chelsea.   you looked through my
                      pictures

steve.   only
                      a few
                      i saw
                      enough
                      your dad
                      may be
                      a lot of things
                      but one thing he's not
                      is a pervert
                      who are these for
                      you got a
                      boyfriend
                      you're not
                      telling me

chelsea.   yeah
                      a boyfriend
                      how fucking
                      quaint

steve.   your mouth
                      when did you get so
                      filthy

chelsea.   my friend's in
                      trouble
                      give me
                      my Phone

steve.   your Phone
                       who do you think
                       paid for
                       your Phone
                       this is a
                       market economy
                       i've paid for
                       this house
                       this Phone
                       this driveway
                       you're standing in
                       right now
                       i got the money
                       to pay for it
                       because i
                       work
                       i have something of
                       value
                       what do you have of
                       value

chelsea.   i am a level 90 gothic cheerleader
                       with a plus 12 proficiency in the Golf Club
                       i suggest
                       you give me
                       my Phone

steve.   my god
                       i let you do
                       whatever you wanted
                       after your mother left
                       i've given you
                       everything
                       why would you take these
                       pictures
                       why chelsea
                       tell me
                       why
                       and i'll give you
                       your Phone

chelsea.   currency

steve.   you mean money
                       i give you

chelsea.   in the game
we have our own
currency
i upload
photos
to other
players
in exchange for
food
armor
weapons
i know all about
the market economy
i know
what i have
of value

steve.

chelsea.

steve.   get inside

chelsea.   you said
you'd give me
my Phone

steve.   i've done something
wrong
i can no longer
trust you

chelsea.   i can't
trust you
you said
you'd give me

steve.   this is not
a debate
this is
an order

chelsea.   you don't fucking
understand
there's something
at madison's
house

steve.   what did you say to me

chelsea.   there's something
                    at madison's
                    house

steve.   you're lucky
                    i can't hear you
                    young lady
                    over all the
                    sirens
                    what's up with
                    the sirens
                    what's going on
                    in the Neighborhood

chelsea.   oh my god
                    go inside
                    and lock
                    the door

steve.   what

chelsea.   give me
                    my Phone
                    and get
                    inside

steve.   you're the one
                    who's going
                    inside

chelsea.   dad
                    listen
                    we were all playing
                    at cody's
                    we went in
                    the Final House
                    tyler found a
                    Zombie
                    that looked like
                    his mom
                    he stuck her through the eyes
                    with the Barbecue Fork
                    freaked out
                    ran home
                    and called us

                    screaming
                    get out of
                    cody's house
                    he screamed
                    cody's father
                    is after him
                    his house is covered in
                    yellow tape
                    there are sirens and
                    swat teams
                    from the Neighborhood Association
                    i'm trying to
                    get to madison
                    to tell her not to
                    go in
                    maybe she can help us
                    if she doesn't
                    go in

steve.   stop it
                    right now
                    something is
                    really wrong with you
                    are you on
                    drugs

chelsea.   keep the Phone
                    i'll go myself

steve.   you're not going
                    anywhere

chelsea.   let go
                    of me

steve.   i don't know
                    why i didn't
                    see this
                    why i didn't
                    see you

chelsea.   let go

steve.   maybe i never wanted to
                    look
                    and this is what happens
                    when you don't

	look your family becomes something you don't recognize
chelsea.	i'm going to scream
steve.	your mouth a wound your eyes a ghoul and those pictures you didn't used to be like this my daughter you used to be so pretty
chelsea.	
chelsea.	
steve.	i'm sorry don't cry i'm sorry i'm a monster
chelsea.	
chelsea.	
steve.	why are you looking at me like that
chelsea.	
steve.	where did you get that Golf Club
chelsea.	
steve.	chelsea wait please no

8 walkthrough

remove the
Pink and Lime Post-it Notes
from your inventory

the numbers on
the Notes
combine to form
a phone number

using the
Cell Phone
text the words
Final House
to this number

you will receive a
return text
that contains your
instructions

as darkness falls
for good
you must use the
streetlights
to track the
Zombies
make sure you have the
Flashlight

and follow your instructions
to the Final House

8 street

zombiekllr14. holy shit man
WTF

barbara. don't kill me
don't kill me

zombiekllr14. what

barbara. i'm sorry i
knocked you down

zombiekllr14. are you a player

barbara.   please don't kill me
                    i'm trying to find
                    my son

zombiekllr14.   i can't kill you
                    if you're a player
                    i'll lose points

barbara.   i'm a player
                    i'm a player

zombiekllr14.   then get down
                    they're alerted
                    to movement

barbara.   who are

zombiekllr14.

barbara.

zombiekllr14.   are you sure
                    you're a player

barbara.   i
                    my name is
                    barbara

zombiekllr14.   barbara
                    your screen name is
                    barbara
                    LOL

barbara.   who are you

zombiekllr14.   Zombiekllr14

barbara.   are you with
                    the Neighborhood Association

zombiekllr14.   do i look like i'm with
                    the NA

barbara.   they're sending out
                    swat teams
                    you're wearing all that
                    armor

zombiekllr14.   if i were with
                    the NA
                    you'd already be

dead
i'm looking for
the Final House

barbara.   no
the Final House
my son
i think
went in
all the sirens
all the houses with
yellow tape
no one will tell me
what's going on
my husband and i
are looking for him
he has to be here
somewhere

zombiekllr14.   WTF
get down

barbara.   WTF

zombiekllr14.   what the fuck
stay out of the
streetlight
i don't know how you got to the Last Chapter
noob
but you better not give me away

barbara.   the Last Chapter
what is it with
the Last Chapter

zombiekllr14.   you're really
pretty
you look like
my friend's mom
i always thought
she was hot
where'd you get
that avatar

barbara.   avatar
you sound like
my son

zombiekllr14. you have a son
               IRL

barbara.   IRL

zombiekllr14. in real life
               are you like
               old

barbara.   what was that
               in the streetlight

zombiekllr14. the streetlights
               are how we
               keep track of them

barbara.   track of what

zombiekllr14. shit
               there's like
               fifty
               heading this way

barbara.   fifty of what
               how do you know

zombiekllr14. on my headset
               one of my team members
               told me
               aren't you on
               a team

barbara.   i mean
               my husband
               my son

zombiekllr14. come on
               keep down
               if i have to kill one
               we're in trouble

barbara.   what
               have you
               been killing
               what's that
               in your hand
               a Hammer
               oh my god
               it's slimy

zombiekllr14. where's your
weapon

barbara. i don't have a
weapon

zombiekllr14. how'd you get
this far

barbara. my neighbor
tried to give me
Hedge Clippers

zombiekllr14. oh wow
you've got the Hedge Clippers

barbara. no
i didn't take them

zombiekllr14. dude
what's wrong with you

barbara. i thought he was
crazy

zombiekllr14. you're the one
who's crazy
get the fuck
away from me

barbara. wait
where are you
going

zombiekllr14. there are fifty of them
hot on our tracks
you're going
to give me
away

barbara. oh my god

zombiekllr14. OMG

barbara. oh my god

zombiekllr14. it's OMG

barbara. OMG
fifty of what

zombiekllr14. fifty Zombies

barbara.

barbara.   i don't believe in
                     Zombies

zombiekllr14.   AFK

barbara.   AFK

zombiekllr14.   away from keyboard

barbara.   keyboard
                     what are you
                     talking about
                     what the hell are you
                     talking about
                     i don't believe in
                     Zombies
                     do you hear me
                     i don't believe in

                     what was that
                     was that what i
                     think it
                     was that
                     did you see that
                     hey
                     did you see that
                     hello
                     what's wrong with you
                     you said there were
                     Zombies
                     so why don't you
                     do something
                     do something
                     do something

zombiekllr14.   i'm back
                     sorry
                     i had to shut my window
                     there was some woman outside screaming
                     now what was i doing
                     oh yeah
                     ditching you

barbara.   wait
                     i saw something

zombiekllr14.   where

barbara.   over there
                        in the streetlight

zombiekllr14.   that's the only way
                        to see them coming

barbara.

zombiekllr14.

barbara.

zombiekllr14.   WTF

barbara.   what happened to
                        the streetlights

zombiekllr14.   the NA must have
                        turned them off

barbara.   it's so dark
                        i can't see
                        anything

zombiekllr14.   where the fuck is my team
                        come in
                        KneelBeforeMe
                        are the lights out
                        where you are

barbara.   my god
                        where am i

zombiekllr14.   KneelBeforeMe
                        where are you man

barbara.   where am i where am i

zombiekllr14.   you better
                        come in
                        you've got
                        the Flashlight

barbara.   i have a
                        Flashlight

zombiekllr14.   you have the
                        Flashlight
                        f 'n a
                        turn it on

barbara.

barbara.   Last Chapter
                    Final House
                    Zombies
                    OMG
                    am i in
                    cody's game

zombiekllr14.

barbara.

zombiekllr14.   you know
                    cody

barbara.   cody
                    is my
                    son

zombiekllr14.   mrs. whitestone
                    it's me
                    blake

barbara.   blake
                    blake
                    you're
                    seven feet tall

zombiekllr14.   dude
                    i thought i recognized you
                    how'd cody find an avatar
                    that looks so much like you

barbara.   where is he

zombiekllr14.   last time i heard
                    he had a fuckload
                    i mean buttload of Zombies after him
                    one of them looked like
                    his dad

barbara.   OMG
                    i've got to
                    find them

zombiekllr14.   where are you going
                    with that
                    Flashlight

barbara.   cody's in
                  trouble

zombiekllr14. i need you
                  i need you to get to the
                  Final House

barbara.   no
                  don't go in the
                  Final House

zombiekllr14. that's the only way
                  out of the Neighborhood
                  i need you to follow me
                  and keep the light
                  in front of us

barbara.   i can find him
                  on my own

zombiekllr14. i'm sorry to say this mrs. whitestone
                  but i will waste you
                  and you know
                  if you die
                  in the Last Chapter
                  you can no longer
                  resurrect

barbara.

zombiekllr14. over there
                  up one block
                  let's go

barbara.

zombiekllr14.

barbara.   ewgh
                  something
                  dripped
                  on me

zombiekllr14. come on
                  come on

barbara.   it felt
                  warm

zombiekllr14. felt
that's some imagination you got there
mrs. whitestone

barbara. what is up there
in that tree

zombiekllr14. don't worry
it's dead

barbara. but it looks like
someone i

zombiekllr14. just keep
the light
in front of us

barbara.

zombiekllr14.

barbara. did you hear that

zombiekllr14. yeah
that was creepy
shine the light
over there

barbara. OMG

zombiekllr14. WTF
it looks like

barbara. Ballerinas

zombiekllr14. what are Ballerinas
doing in the game

barbara. don't you get it
Zombie Killer
this isn't

zombiekllr14. holy shit
they found it
we're at the
Final House

barbara. it's
my house

zombiekllr14. it's
my house

barbara.   cody
i wonder if
what's that on
the porch

zombiekllr14.   careful

barbara.   Post-it Notes
they're covered in

zombiekllr14.   yeah
the blood effects are
killer

barbara.   are these
cody's
where is

zombiekllr14.   i don't know
mrs. whitestone
he may not
resurrect

barbara.   what do you mean

zombiekllr14.   my teammate
just told me
that Zombie that was after him
got him

barbara.   i don't
no
i don't
no
there must be

zombiekllr14.   when my team gets here
we're going in

barbara.   no
no
don't
go in

zombiekllr14.   that's the only way
out of the Neighborhood

barbara.   that is not
the only way
get up

　　　　　　　from your computer
　　　　　　　get up
　　　　　　　from your computer
　　　　　　　and go talk
　　　　　　　to your mom

zombiekllr14.　i don't talk
　　　　　　　to my mom

barbara.　　tell her
　　　　　　　barbara sent you
　　　　　　　she knows me
　　　　　　　from when you and cody
　　　　　　　were boys

zombiekllr14.　she doesn't
　　　　　　　listen to me
　　　　　　　crap
　　　　　　　here she comes

barbara.　　tell her
　　　　　　　to contact
　　　　　　　my neighbor

zombiekllr14.　right when i'm
　　　　　　　about to
　　　　　　　go in

barbara.　　no
　　　　　　　do not
　　　　　　　go in
　　　　　　　maybe
　　　　　　　it's not
　　　　　　　too late
　　　　　　　if some of you
　　　　　　　don't
　　　　　　　go in
　　　　　　　maybe
　　　　　　　oh god
　　　　　　　cody

zombiekllr14.　i can't play with her
　　　　　　　over my shoulder
　　　　　　　fuck
　　　　　　　AFK

barbara. wait
blake
blake
tell her
to listen you
talk
to your mom
talk
to each other
oh god
cody
we thought
when we moved here
we were moving
up
but all the Neighborhoods
are mirror images
all the Neighborhoods
fold onto each other
don't go in
the Final House
there are no levels
there's no moving up
there's no
getting
out

9 the final house

A teenage boy sits at a computer. Light from the monitor shines on his face. He wears a headset and alternately types on the computer keyboard and maneuvers a fancy mouse with a giant tracking ball. Clothes are strewn about his room. Fast food wrappers litter his desk.

BLAKE. I'm here. (*Pause.*) At the final house. (*Pause.*) In the bushes by the front door. (*Pause.*) Well hurry up. (*Pause.*) My Cologne du Corpse is wearing off. They're gonna smell me. (*Pause.*) Please just get your ass over here.

(*The door to the bedroom opens. A woman in a fuzzy bathrobe stands in the hall light, clutching a fast food bag.*)

JOY. Honey? (*Pause.*) Are you still on your game? (*Pause.*) I microwaved your burger since you were too busy to eat it earlier. Do you want it now?

(*He ignores her. She is used to it.*)

I'm watching a little *CSI*. I love how that forensic team figures everything out in the end. This episode is about a dwarf—I mean little person—who

murders another little person because he's about to marry his daughter—
who is normal—I mean, a person of average height. He wants his daughter
to marry another person of average height so she'll have a normal family. I
mean, everyone wants a normal family. So he murders the little fiancée by
hanging him. They even show the vertebrae going snap snap snap. At least,
that's what I think was happening. You know I cover my eyes for the gory
part. It's too, um, real.

*(She hears something downstairs, turns her head for a moment to listen, then
turns back to BLAKE.)*

I know you're busy, but, it's a little lonely downstairs...don't you want to
come sit on the couch with me and watch?

(He ignores her.)

Well. I offered.

(She drops the bag inside the room and closes the door.)

BLAKE. There you are, man! I was getting lonely. *(Pause.)* Yeah, I'm ready.
In a minute. Calm down. Don't you think, um...

*(As he talks he gets up from the computer, retrieves the burger, comes back to
the computer.)*

Don't you think we should wait for the rest of the team? *(Pause.)* Yeah I
know we can, it's just—I have to check my armor one more time. *(Pause.)*
And refill my Sugar Rush. *(Pause.)* And um...hey, get off the porch, get back
in the bushes, I'm not ready yet! *(Pause.)* I am NOT stalling—!

(Door opens.)

JOY. Honey? I thought I heard something by the front door. It sounded.
Strange. I don't know, maybe I'm imagining things. You aren't—up to anything—are you? You can—tell me—if you are. I promise I won't—freak out.
I'd really actually prefer some advance notice to one of those phone calls.
Why don't you come downstairs, I'll make some popcorn, we can—talk—
and maybe you could listen to this noise and see if you think it sounds
strange. Like something coming through the walls. I never used to feel that
way about this place. But now. It's like that movie. Maybe our house is built
on an Indian burial ground. Maybe the neighborhood. Maybe the whole
country. Oh now listen to me—being morbid—I must need another— *(She
stops herself.)* It's just that thing by the front door. You wouldn't know anything about it, would you? *(Pause.)* Hey. I'm talking to you. Look at me when
I talk to you!

(BLAKE turns his head the tiniest degree possible. Pause.)

No, of course you wouldn't. Why don't you get ready for bed. I'll bring you
something to help you sleep.

(She closes the door.)

BLAKE. Fuck, she makes me insane. (*Pause.*) No, I'm not ready yet. (*He eats his burger, talking through the food.*) It's not about being a pussy you fucking douche—listen—there was this woman. (*Pause.*) I wish—no—in the game. I couldn't tell if she was a Zombie or a player. She looked like Cody's mom and kept asking if I'd seen him. (*Pause.*) Yeah, I thought at first it was Cody being a total weirdo, but. Something was off. She kept saying, don't go in. (*Pause.*) I know it's lame, but— (*Pause.*) Look, shut up—I took care of it! That's her on the sidewalk. I bashed her head in.

(*Door opens.*)

JOY. Blake, I'm sure of it. There's something out there. You're the man of the house now—you should come take a look. It's not just the noise, I saw— a shadow. In the porch light. Coming. To the front door. Hey! Are you listening to me? I am asking you a favor! It's the least you can do after everything I do for you. I cook your meals. I wash your clothes. I make sure you don't shrivel up and—die—behind that computer. The computer that was *bought* for you. And can you be bothered to do a single thing for me? (*Pause.*) You! I'm talking to you! I'm not just some drudge who does all your shit work! Look at me!

BLAKE. (*Without turning around.*) What.

JOY. What?

BLAKE. I said what.

JOY. Is that all you have to say?

BLAKE. What do you want me to say, Joy?

JOY. Don't call me that!

BLAKE. It's your name.

JOY. I have told you not to call me that! I have told you and told you, but you don't listen to me! You don't listen to a thing I say! And I have done— everything for you! Well let me tell you, buster, things are going to change around here. Nothing's free in this world, and it's time for you to earn your keep. I'm making a list of after school chores and setting limits on your game time. Starting now. Off the computer in five minutes!

(*She closes the door. BLAKE straightens.*)

BLAKE. Grrrw, I just got the things-are-gonna-change-around-here speech. But nothing ever does. So fuck it—let's go in. (*Pause.*) Get up here and cover me. (*Pause.*) I'm trying the front door…oh weird, weird…it's opening on its own. (*Pause.*) I can't see anything inside. (*Pause.*) You ready? (*Pause.*) Okay. (*Pause.*) I'm in, I'm in! (*Pause.*) I'm behind the sofa come on. (*Pause.*) Shit I saw something move. (*Pause.*) In the light of the television. (*Pause.*) I don't know—just get up the stairs—it's in the bedroom at the top. Bedroom at the top. (*Pause.*) Wait, don't open the door yet. (*Pause.*) Do you hear that? (*Pause.*) Fuck, my heart is pounding. (*Pause.*) Okay, ready man. (*Pause.*) Opening the door…. I'm…opening the door…

(*Door opens.*)

JOY. Honey?

BLAKE. Not now!

JOY. I did it. I looked.

BLAKE. You said I have five minutes!

JOY. I didn't have a choice—the front door just—opened.

BLAKE. Get the fuck outta my room!

JOY. Do you remember Barbara, Cody's mom?

(*Pause. For the first time,* BLAKE *turns to look at her.*)

BLAKE. What about her?

JOY. She's on the sidewalk. With half her head gone.

(BLAKE *stares at her in disbelief. Then he whirls back to the computer and jabs at the keyboard.*)

BLAKE. Get out. Get out of the room get out of the house. Get out get out get out get out get out get out fuck the front door is locked.

JOY. I locked the front door.

BLAKE. Are you there man? We're in trouble!

JOY. All night I've heard sirens.

BLAKE. I'm unarmed. I dropped my hammer somewhere on the stairs.

JOY. Is this what you're looking for? I found it on the stairs.

(BLAKE *turns around to look.* JOY *is holding a bloody claw hammer.*)

BLAKE. Give that to me.

JOY. Does it belong to you?

BLAKE. Look, Joy—

JOY. Don't call me that! Just the fact that you're capable of calling me that…What happened to Barbara?

BLAKE. You tell me.

JOY. No, you tell me. You never tell me anything anymore.

BLAKE. You never ask.

JOY. I try all the time to talk to you.

BLAKE. You don't really want to know.

JOY. You never even look at me anymore.

BLAKE. I'm looking at you now.

JOY. I don't recognize you.

BLAKE. I'm your son. Give me the hammer.

JOY. I have tried to talk to you! I have tried! I want to hear you say, I know you've tried.

BLAKE. Easy, Joy.

JOY. DON'T CALL ME—

BLAKE. OKAY! You've tried.

JOY. Say it like you believe it. Say it like it's the truth.

BLAKE. I. Believe. You've—

JOY. NO. You don't believe me. You don't even see me. You don't see anything outside of your game. You don't see anything that's real!

(JOY *realizes* BLAKE *is cowering from her. She sags.*)

JOY. I'm sorry. (*Pause.*) It's so good...to see you, son. It's so good...to see your face.

(*Touched,* BLAKE *nods. This is their only moment.*)

I just want to...I just want...the two of us.... It's not too late, is it? It's not too late?

(BLAKE *shakes his head.*)

I'm so sorry. So so so so so so so so so—

(*She rushes towards him, arms raised.* BLAKE, *suddenly terror-stricken, wrenches the hammer from her hand and, through her screams, beats her to death.*)

10 bedroom

(BLAKE *shoves himself away from the computer. Shivering. He looks around the empty room.*)

BLAKE. Mom?

End of Play

JENNIFER HALEY

SOME SCENE NOTES

1 kitchen
It is fun for the actress playing makaela to use a whispery, gravelly monster voice on *i'm coming to get you for real.*

2 front yard
There may be a whiff of sexual attraction between Leslie and Steve.

4 pool
Doug is not a calculated sadist; his behavior arises from fear.

5 gameroom
Chelsea is on a PlayStation or Xbox. When her team members' headsets go out, she can use her controller to send text messages to them via the game. Jared logs into the game using a computer.

7 driveway
This is not a case of physical incest.

8 street
Look at the movement of AFK (away from keyboard) characters in World of Warcraft for zombiekllr14.

9 the final house
This is an actual episode of *CSI.*
The violence should be dramatic, unbelievable, loud. Look at the killing of harpies in *World of Warcraft.*

DEAD RIGHT
by Elaine Jarvik

BIOGRAPHY

Elaine Jarvik is a reporter for the *Deseret News* in Salt Lake City, and the winner of numerous journalism awards including Best of the West, the American Association of Sunday and Feature Editors and a national award for feature writing from the Society of Professional Journalists. She is also co-founder of the Senior Theatre Project, a non-profit group that takes original plays on tour to senior centers in Utah. She used to play the drums in the band *Elaine and the Elaines* and now plays conga in church. Because this play is about vanity and the futile desire to be "somebody," she finds it ironic to be mentioning any of these accomplishments.

ACKNOWLEDGMENTS

Dead Right premiered at the Humana Festival of New American Plays in March 2008. It was directed by Marc Masterson with the following cast:

PENNY .... Dori Legg
BILL .... William McNulty

and the following production staff:

Scenic Designer .... Paul Owen
Costume Designer... Susan Neason
Lighting Designer... Paul Werner
Sound Designer .... Benjamin Marcum
Properties Designer .... Mark Walston
Stage Manager...................................... Debra Anne Gasper
Assistant Stage Manager.......................... Captain Kate Murphy
Dramaturg .... Adrien-Alice Hansel
Assistant Dramaturg... Devon LaBelle

Special thanks to the Senior Theatre Project, Salt Lake City, Utah.

CAST OF CHARACTERS
PENNY
BILL

PLACE
In their kitchen.

TIME
The present.

William McNulty and Dori Legg
in *Dead Right*

32nd Annual Humana Festival of New American Plays
Actors Theatre of Louisville, 2008
Photo by Harlan Taylor

DEAD RIGHT

Lights up on BILL *and* PENNY, *each reading a section of the newspaper. Silence at first, turning of pages.*

BILL. Hey, isn't this that woman?

PENNY. What woman?

BILL. The one you knew from your writing group. From a while back. (*Reading.*) Francine Louise Schmidt.

PENNY. What about her?

BILL. She died.

PENNY. Where?

BILL. At home.

PENNY. (*Grabbing the paper.*) Not *where.* Let me see that. Oh. It *is* Francie. "Francine Louise Schmidt died peacefully at home Saturday surrounded by her family." Ohhh. I didn't even know she was sick. (*Reads to herself, interjecting a "huh" and a "hmm" every so often, then throws down the paper.*) That is so tragic.

BILL. Cancer?

PENNY. Her obituary. It's so dull.

BILL. That's no way to talk about the dead.

PENNY. I'm talking about the living. How could they do that? She has no chance to do a rewrite. And this photo.

BILL. That looks like how I remember her.

PENNY. Not at her *best.* She fixed up much better than that. This photo was taken in direct sunlight. In the middle of the day. Look at her wrinkles.

BILL. Hmmm.

PENNY. There must have been other pictures. Look. You can see someone else's shoulder.

BILL. Her husband I bet. Maybe it's the only one he could find on the spur of the moment.

PENNY. "She died peacefully at home surrounded by her family." While she was lingering he couldn't look around for a better picture?

BILL. Maybe he was tending to her.

PENNY. A hundred thousand people will see this obituary and think "Francine Louise Schmidt. That's what she looked like."

BILL. She did look like that. It's a *photograph.* Anyway, the people who know her will think, well, that's not Francine at her best. And the people who don't know her won't care.

262

PENNY. She once wrote a short story in which every sentence began with a different letter, in alphabetical order. Do you know how hard that is? Now she's frozen forever as a woman with bad skin and a dull life. She doesn't want to be remembered that way.

BILL. She's dead.

PENNY. She was a vibrant woman. Sexy. This doesn't do her justice (*Reading.*) "Francie loved reading and hiking and was a deacon in her church." Please.

BILL. What's wrong with that?

PENNY. Everybody loves reading. That's like saying "Francie loved sitting." At least they could have mentioned what kind of books. Specificity! Every writer knows that. Francie liked both Sylvia Plath *and* New Age self-help. She once had a correspondence with Deepak Chopra. They could have mentioned that at least.

BILL. A correspondence?

PENNY. She sent him a letter and he wrote back.

BILL. That's not a correspondence.

PENNY. My point is, there were things about Francie that were a lot more complex and interesting than what they've written here. I bet she had a rich fantasy life.

BILL. You can't write about somebody's fantasy life in an obituary.

PENNY. (*Looking at the obit again.*) Oh no! I didn't even notice this before. "Francie had less faults than anyone we knew."

BILL. It's okay to exaggerate a little.

PENNY. *Less* faults? "Never use 'less' when referring to more than one item." They've put a grammatical error in her obituary!

BILL. Give them a break, Penny. They were grieving.

PENNY. Promise me when you write my obituary you won't make any grammatical or syntactical errors.

BILL. I can't promise that.

PENNY. Have Rachel proofread it. (*Beat.*) Promise me you'll have Rachel proofread it.

BILL. Jeez, Penny.

PENNY. (*Long beat.*) What will you say about me?

BILL. I'm sure I'll die before you.

PENNY. But if you don't.

BILL. I plan to die before you.

PENNY. Don't say "Penny loved reading." Say "Penny loved social commentary and the works of Thomas Pynchon." Say "Penny played the cello."

BILL. But that's not true.

PENNY. Yes it is.

BILL. You haven't touched the cello since we got married. It's been sitting in the basement for 15 years.

PENNY. *"PlayED* the cello." (*Beat.*) Where did I graduate from college?

BILL. Purdue.

PENNY. And?

BILL. What do you mean?

PENNY. My master's.

BILL. Oh. Right.

PENNY. You would have forgotten to mention my master's?!

BILL. It was before we got married.

PENNY. This is exactly what I'm afraid of. How could you forget my master's?

BILL. You were married to James then. I can't remember everything.

PENNY. It's my master's! People will read my obituary and think I only got an undergraduate degree!

BILL. So what? You'll be dead.

PENNY. James would remember to include the master's.

BILL. Ask James to write your obituary then.

PENNY. Maybe I will.

BILL. Fine.

PENNY. He probably knew me better anyway.

> (*Silence.* BILL *goes back to reading the paper.* PENNY *stews.*)

And that poem I had published in *Modern Haiku.*

BILL. What about it?

PENNY. You should mention it.

BILL. I'll make a list. (*Begins writing.*) Cello. Poem. Thomas Pynchon. Master's. Anything else?

PENNY. You're not taking me seriously.

BILL. I'm making a list.

PENNY. You're writing it on the newspaper.

BILL. I'll clip it out and save it.

PENNY. It'll turn yellow and disintegrate.

BILL. So will your obituary.

> (PENNY *picks up the newspaper and begins reading. So does* BILL. *They sit in silence.*)

PENNY. And if I die in some weird way, don't put that in the obituary. That would be just like me. I'll probably get my scarf caught in a power window and strangle to death. Just say "died unexpectedly."

BILL. You're not going to die like that.

PENNY. How do you know?

BILL. Do we have to talk about this? Anyway, I'm sure I'll die before you. I've got cardiovascular disease all over my family.

PENNY. Don't say that.

BILL. It's true.

PENNY. I don't want you to die before me. I can't bear the thought of it. I would just come back to this house and not know what to do with myself.

BILL. You could play the cello.

PENNY. I'm serious.

BILL. You'll be fine.

(BILL *goes back to reading.* PENNY *thinks.*)

PENNY. There's a picture of me you took last year in Hawaii. I want that picture.

(BILL *stares at her, distracted.*)

For my *obituary?*

BILL. What if you die when you're 90?

PENNY. I still want that picture. It was really good lighting. Kind of washed out. I could be 30 in that picture.

BILL. Then it really doesn't look like you.

PENNY. I want to be remembered like that.

BILL. Even if it doesn't look like you?

PENNY. I don't want the kids—and then their kids, and then *their* kids—to remember me wrong. (*Suddenly remembering.*) All those old pictures when I had Farrah Fawcett hair!

BILL. But that was you.

PENNY. I have two pictures of my grandmother. In one she apparently forgot to comb her hair. In the other she's walking down some street in Greensboro and for some reason somebody snaps a picture of her. She has this kind of grim look on her face and I'm not even sure if she was wearing her dentures. I have no idea why those two pictures survived. Why those two pictures and not two others.

BILL. When you start wearing dentures I'll stop taking pictures.

PENNY. I'm going to go through the house right now and get rid of all the pictures I don't like. Just so you won't be tempted. Every last one of them. Because I can see you can't be trusted.

BILL. Fine! Get rid of them.

PENNY. I'm going to.

BILL. Fine.

PENNY. Because sometimes you're totally oblivious.

BILL. I said fine! Make a file called "Penny's obituary." Put a glam shot in it. Put in your resumé. Make up a resumé. I don't care. And tape the whole thing to the fridge!

PENNY. You don't need to get testy.

BILL. No, actually, you know what I'm going to write in your obituary? "Penny was a shallow woman who wanted you to think she was prettier and smarter than she really was."

PENNY. Bill!

BILL. Really Penny! I can't believe you.

PENNY. Well here's what I'm going to write: "Bill was a man who never really knew his wife."

BILL. That's not true.

PENNY. What's my favorite musical group?

BILL. The Rolling Stones.

PENNY. Rolling Stones?!

BILL. You told me that once.

PENNY. I just said that when we were dating because you said they were *your* favorite.

BILL. I never said that. (*Beat.*) That was probably James.

PENNY. Oh, please. James was a Doors fan.

(*Strained silence. They both go back to the paper.*)

What I'm talking about is an accurate portrayal. At the end of your life you've got this one chance to sum it all up. To say, "This is me. This was my life."

BILL. You know what I hope you'll say about me? "Bill was a decent guy."

PENNY. (*Beat.*) That's it?

BILL. Yep.

PENNY. What about your Ph.D.?

BILL. I don't care.

PENNY. You're the president of the State Chemical Society!

BILL. So? It's just a society. Who said an obituary should be a list? Why not a moment? One moment from your life when the sun was shining and you were riding your bike and the world smelled like honeysuckle. (*Small beat.*) I heard this German man being interviewed today on the radio. His English was good but not perfect, you know, and the interviewer asked him something, what he thought about his latest film, and he said "I feel very

CONtent." When of course he meant conTENT. We can't tell the difference. That's the problem with the world.

PENNY. Now *you're* sounding like Deepak Chopra.

BILL. Just put "Bill was a decent guy."

PENNY. (*Beat.*) You *are* a decent guy. That's why I love you.

BILL. And I love *you* because you can make me laugh even when I've had a rotten day. That's how I'll remember you.

PENNY. I'm talking about how everyone else will remember me. How the world will remember me.

BILL. The world won't remember you, Penny. And that's okay.

(*Long silence.*)

PENNY. I got my master's at Boston University.

BILL. I thought it was Northwestern.

PENNY. Just checking.

(*Lights down.*)

End of Play

the break/s

...a travel diary recorded as dream
...lewis and clark at hip hop's Mason-Dixon line
...one last look at Africa
...a decision to love, but not live...

written and performed by
Marc Bamuthi Joseph

BIOGRAPHY

Marc Bamuthi Joseph is an educator, performer, and the artistic director of The Living Word Project, a theatre company dedicated to the aesthetics of post-hip hop performance. In the Fall of 2007, Bamuthi graced the cover of *Smithsonian* magazine after being named one of America's Top Young Innovators in the Arts and Sciences. He is a National Poetry Slam champion, Broadway veteran, GOLDIE award winner, featured artist on *Russell Simmons' Def Poetry* on HBO and inaugural recipient of the United States Artists Rockefeller Fellowship. He has entered the world of literary performance after crossing the sands of "traditional" theatre, most notably on Broadway in the Tony Award-winning *The Tap Dance Kid* and *Stand-Up Tragedy*. His evening-length works have been presented throughout the United States and Europe and include *Word Becomes Flesh, Scourge, De/Cipher* and *No Man's Land*. His work has been enabled by several prestigious foundation awards including grants from the Ford Foundation, the Center for Cultural Innovation, Creative Capital, the National Performance Network Creation Fund, the Wallace A. Gerbode Foundation, the Creative Work Fund, the Rockefeller MAP Fund, the NEA, the Hewlett Foundation, and a Dance Advance award from the PEW Foundation. A gifted and nationally acclaimed educator and essayist, he has lectured at more than 100 colleges and universities, has been a popular commentator on National Public Radio, and has carried adjunct professorships at Stanford University, Mills College, and the University of Wisconsin. A resident at ODC Theater, YBCA, and Intersection for the Arts in San Francisco, Bamuthi's proudest work has been with Youth Speaks where he mentors 13- to 19-year-old writers and curates the Living Word Festival for Literary Arts. He is a currently an Artistic Consultant for the HBO series *Brave New Voices* and is developing *red black and green: a blues,* which performatively documents the eco-equity movement towards green-collar jobs in Black neighborhoods.

ACKNOWLEDGMENTS

the break/s premiered at the Humana Festival of New American Plays in March 2008. It was directed by Michael John Garcés with the following performers:

Marc Bamuthi Joseph
DJ Excess
Tommy Shepherd aka Soulati

and the following production staff:

Scenic Designer .... Michael B. Raiford
Costume Designer .... Jessica Ford
Lighting Designer .... Brian J. Lilienthal
Sound Coordinator .... Paul Doyle
Properties Designer .... Doc Manning
Video Designer .... David Szlasa
Documentary Filmographer .... Eli Jacobs-Fantauzzi
Original Music .... Ajayi Jackson
Choreographer .... Stacey Printz
Arranging and Mixing .... DJ Excess,
Tommy Shepherd aka Soulati
Stage Manager .... Lori M. Doyle
Dramaturgs .... Brian Freeman, Julie Felise Dubiner
Assistant Dramaturg .... Charles Haugland
Executive Producer .... MAPP International Productions
Directing Assistant .... Zoe Aja Moore

the break/s was produced in association with Living Word Project.

It received world premieres at the Humana Festival of New American Plays at Actors Theatre of Louisville (March 8-29, 2008) and the Walker Art Center in Minneapolis (April 10-12, 2008).

Lead commissioning and development support: the Walker Art Center with support from the Joyce Foundation. Additional support provided by The Wallace Alexander Gerbode Foundation and The William and Flora Hewlett Foundation Emerging Playwrights 2006 Initiative, The National Endowment for the Arts, Zellerbach Family Foundation, Creative Capital, The James Irvine Foundation, Rockefeller MAP Fund, Association of Performing Arts Presenters, Youth Speaks, East Bay Fund, Yerba Buena Center for the Arts and Z Space. Artistic Consultation by Jeff Chang and James Clotfelter and production consultation by KelVin Productions, LLC.

MOTIFS

FALLING... "I was in Haiti once at a vodun ceremony and I passed out. I personally think that I just turned chicken shit at the sight of blood and fainted like a little beyoncé, but my whole crew believed I'd been possessed."

The action in this piece sometimes mirrors this line. This falling, not knowing what hit you...I want this piece to have a sense of narcolepsy, and I want to create signatures in the physical environment (light, sound, blocking, gesture) that reflect the sensation of falling over into dark space, thought, or sleep...most of the choreography plays with this idea, but not too literally.

DREAMING... mostly journal entries taken from planet hip hop. That sounds so big *planet hip hop*...really what I mean is my world. Black artist being seen. Whenever I'm feeling too self-conscious I drop into a dream. Race matters less here. I feel safe to laugh at it. There should be a music signature, think music for a dream deferred...super African American "Langston-Spike-Duke Ellington-Dr. Dre"...this basic score takes on the reflection and resonance and character of each international venue we visit in the dream state.

CROSSING... code switching...timetwist as shapeshift...using anything that's happened before in the action and sampling it into the present to compound the metaphor in the present moment. Any one of the four agents on stage can "cross"...mostly scripted, but when we get good at this thing, we can have a little jazz during the last few loops...

There are three folks on stage. One plays words and body. One plays images and recorded music. One makes the music live. They all play time. There are two cameras on stage as well, used by the DJ/VJ to capture the moment and project the feed onto two screens, placed in accordance with the director and set designer's shared vision. One camera is downstage right. The other is directly overhead the action.

KASÉ is a Dance Sequence.

Because negroes can't have success without feelin like they're sellin
    SOMEBODY out.
Because I want a lexus AND justice
Because I'm teaching hip hop in Madison Wisconsin
And *she*'s sitting with the dalai lama in India
Because of jeff chang.

Marc Bamuthi Joseph
in *the break/s*

32nd Annual Humana Festival of New American Plays
Actors Theatre of Louisville, 2008
Photo by Harlan Taylor

the break/s

LOOP 1.

If jazz is the broom Africans jump over to become Americans
Then what is hip hop...?
KASÉ with Text.

KASÉ is a series of "clock walks," quarter-turn rotations performed while a dancer is on his back. Upon completion of the turns, the imprint of MBJ dragging his feet around in a circle "draws" record grooves on the stage surface.

MBJ. Cycles to break
No more lying
Much less flying
Call your grandma
Practice faith.

Don't confuse your art with your life
embody what you write.

Stop contradicting.

Slipped in the groove of institution and reparations

Funk and function equally separating to reveal me in the break

Psychically cycling
I got patterns to shake

Music to make
Culture to love
Guilt to feel
Prayers to say

OVERTURE: **MBJ-EXCESS-SOULATI.**

(OVERTURE is staged like RUN DMC would do modern dance.
All three characters are "introduced" in the span of an eight-bar sequence
A chance to scratch in our tools...
An exhibition of drums, scratch, dance, poetry, vocal percussion, and lights.)

(MBJ sets metronome, a sound like the wind inhaling and exhaling, then eventually becomes the break from "South Bronx" by BDP which SOULATI performs vocally. Closes with the tone that MBJ started with, this time with SOULATI assuming the metronome as MBJ begins to spit.)

MBJ. This is what it looks like right before I fall

(*Three-beat pause as* EXCESS *slowly spins a record backwards, then everyone comes back in on the one...*)

(*MUSIC: "South Bronx."*)

Jackie Robinson swinging under the color line
Jesse Owens hoverin over the hand of the heil
J-Hova
The brown bomber
Obama
Crossover

(*MUSIC: Traditional folkloric rhythm.*)

Legba bring the drama with the lesson
I am an American at the edge
More than less
I keep tryin to push this blackface
In urban high schools
More and more it matters less

I'm straddling the line

Don't push me

cuz I'm close...

I'm trying not to...

FALL

I am trying to believe that loving you
Doesn't mean I'm crossing over
Trying to accept a self-concept that includes being your partner
But every time I think the question of commitment
I fall sleep
A not quite coma
Anxiety driven neuroses
that feels like spending the entire day in a dream

DREAM #1

I was in Haiti once at a vodun ceremony and I passed out. I personally think that I just turned chicken shit at the sight of blood and fainted like a little beyoncé, but my whole crew, all people who honor and respect Haitian culture, believed I'd been possessed. They said I fell like this

(EXCESS *backspins a record hella slowly.* MBJ *performs "suspended possession" [SP] gesture, the animation of a fall in arrested development.*)

A feeble pawn or a priest...either is possible...who knows where the body goes when the consciousness flies away...when you lose your mind who

jumps in to take its place...the Haitians started callin me *neg ginen...ginen* is
the tunnel that connects Haiti to Africa, so when a Haitian calls you *neg ginen*,
that's real respect the really real black shit...that's a stripe...

I wonder what they'd say if they knew my kid was half Chinese and my girl
was white...

> (*FILM #1... If jazz... Interview [series #1].*)
> (*MUSIC:* SOULATI *and* EXCESS *re-create "Bonita Applebum" by A Tribe Called Quest.*)
> (*KASÉ: Hip hop based phrase.*)

LOOP 2.

MBJ. This story begins in the middle
Halfway across the planet
I think...
That I'm awake
Last night at dusk I
Took a red eye across the Atlantic
Landed on the first morning of summer in Europe
For the last 40 sumthin hours it's been day
I think
I might be dreamin
But I'm not sure

I'm in Paris for a festival of
young contemporary choreographers from Africa
By the grace of god, I get to watch
It's one of the perks. I've managed to convince the performing arts machine
    that I am high art AND hip hop...

FALL

sshh don't tell em I've gotten stuck I'm in between
Back row of the audience
Falling up
Waking dream
In Paris I
Represent my country in the flesh
The surrogate for Allen Iverson and 50 cent
But What good is a black man in America if stripped of his right to threat?
How hip hop can I be if they let me onto their set?

RETURN

Anyway as a guest of the institution
I'm at this dance festival and on the first night

This South African soloist does this joint where she wears a tutu and a big easter bunny costume head-thing and contorts herself into a big plastic bag for like 30 minutes...and then she walks through the audience putting saran wrap over people's mouths and kissing them on their plastic dental dammed lips...and then it ends...that's it.

In my head

DREAM #2

(*MUSIC: Dream sig equally touched by kwaito/sarafina and ladysmith mambazo.*)

the image of South Africa is fixed on apartheid, Steven Biko, Robben Island. In my head it is always the late 80s and Mandela is the first person I ever truly truly wanted to be free. The first major metaphor for liberating me...

The triangle of perspective is crazy...
I'm lookin at this African woman for some sense of root
She's lookin at European performance art trading in amandla for a frayed
     pink tutu
And Europeans ALWAYS been lookin at me...

KASÉ WITH TEXT

Ever since my name was satchmo Langston josephine
Since the days when they bred me
I am the descendant of an experiment (*Begin gesture phrase.*) in psyche and body
A fetish taking my place in line
Fractured
wondering when this woman's history stopped being mine
I've been flying for the last forty hours I have no sense of time
I wonder which one of us is sleep, and which one is just tired

and then
Exactly right then
I fall

(*FILM #2—Title: White people in hip hop.*)
(*MUSIC: SOULATI and EXCESS re-create the break of Aerosmith's "Walk This Way."*)
(*KASÉ: A wild abstraction of the "electric slide" social line dance.*)

FALL

Real late at night
just the two of us
in the dark
when my own snoring wakes me up
in the dark

when my history is irrelevant and I am a soul to be touched
when all falls away but words on the page
she is perfect

the woman I want to come home to,
but not always who I want to leave the house with
my perfect match in love
a plague upon my self-perception and politics
she's turning 30
childless
she wants to get married
I present her every day with a ring of silence
And a fat rock of maybe
Cuz MAYBE I can choose love over identity
But maybe…

> (*Gesture phrase.*)

LOOP 3.

> *MUSIC: Dream music sig with a touch of crump…maybe chopped and screwed as a breakdown.*

DREAM #3

MBJ. My cousins are WILDIN OUT!!!
You get PAID to teach hip hop…
Oh hell NO

> (*MUSIC out.*)

My uncle's 60th birthday has brought us all to South Florida
five boys
one a computer guy
every day shirt and tie
one a senior in high school
one did a bid
one has a kid out of wedlock
the fifth don't really get off the block
it's starting to be NOT cool
between my dad and his three siblings
five boys
one generation is all it took for my West Indian fam to resemble the African
    American statistics book
we shaped bell like hooks
one in five
statistically, one of us ain't supposed to be alive past 25 the fourth boy just
    turned 26
I am the absentee godfather of the fifth

I haven't seen him since he was six
So at first when my sister pulls up at the airport with some nigga in the passenger seat
I'm thinking who the fuck is THIS?

Then he smiles
Big braces grin
He's 17 now my cousin
Right at the brink
We get home and first thing
He's in the kitchen mixing himself a drink
I wanna say something but the rest of my cousins is WILDIN out
    (*MUSIC: Krunk Dream reprise.*)
DAMN you get PAID to teach hip hop

How the hell you come up with that hustle…?

Did you go to COLLEGE for that shit

Ay yo Marc let me teach your class yo, you could get me a job?

Who the fuck listens to YOU?

FALL
    (*MUSIC:* SOULATI *and* EXCESS *make "T.R.O.Y."*)
Hip hop's story is the choice to commit to one side of the line or the other
To get so close to the edge
You can smell the afterdeath
In hip hop it smells like cisco and sulfur
Because if you don't commit to spinnin on yo head
You will break your neck
In a dream I'm a puppet being held up by white lines
Dancing for respect

The more I'm accepted by others, the less I accept myself
I am stumbling my way to the line
    (*FILM #3— Invisible icon— How relevant are the pioneers to contemporary hip hop? How relevant is Thomas Jefferson to contemporary politics?*)
    (*MUSIC:* SOULATI *and* EXCESS *make "T.R.O.Y."*)
    (*KASÉ: A "Soul Train" line of sorts. A hybrid of locking.*)
This story begins in the middle
Halfway across the planet
I think…
That I'm awake
Last night at dusk I
Took a red eye across the Pacific

Landed on the first morning of summer in Japan
For the last 40 sumthin hours it's been day
I might be dreamin
But I'm not sure

I am a Living word lost in translation
Guess this is a near death experience

At the club in Japan
      (MUSIC: Dream sig with Far Eastern inflections.)
EVERYBODY in hip hop knows that the culture is HUGE over here
Mostly cuz they heard it on yo mtv rap interviews with the wu-tang clan
It is times square times ten
There are so many lights on in Tokyo at midnight the sky looks like 11 a.m.
      plugged into a socket
My hosts are all hip hop kids that INSIST tired as I am that I roll to the spot
I lead with my ego think, why not
I expect, that when I walk in the club the music will STOP
The rivers will part
The reverence will begin

Behold young Japanese motherfuckas that sweat my culture
Authenticity is IN the building
It's me
Born 1975 in Queens,
Nas, A tribe called quest, RUN DMC
The real hip hop is obviously oozing from my pores for all to see and all
Ignore me
The only black guy in the room except for the ones we're all dancing to
I am either so racist, or self-centered, or so oblivious I think that props are
      due
Head nods
Fists up
Eye contact
None of that

Invisible…race doesn't matter…I'm just another guy who might be a little
too old to be at the club…and in the tradition of the wrong guy at the right
party, I retire to a corner…music thumpin…haven't been to sleep since
yestersumthin…and I fall…
      (FILM: live feed.)
FALL
In a dream I am safe above the menace
I don't know jack about oppression
Mostly I see that shit on TV

Feel it in my skin
Wear it where it winds its way through the corridors of racist establishments
But I am often the face for oppression's disestablishment
Poster boy for the street
Middle class
Buppy assimilationist me

I represent the real hip hop
Where schoolly d becomes school of thought
I am all the urban edge convention's intellect can ingest
I am safe above the menace
Ya boy...

In a dream
I am riding the lightning of my writing
Writing the whitening of my life I am
Lightening

Experiencing a merging
Of divergent selves

American African

Melt I am the bitches brew
Easy to see how a brother could lose his mind
I got two

Double consciousness
Double dutch
Double time
In my life I am always thinking about you...

I plan my words years ahead of the moment
So that maybe you'll hear and be moved

I'm a performer
Looking at self through the eyes of others...
Maybe you can relate

Black people in this country got a special kinda crazy
Cuz we descendants of slaves and there's a little bit in all of us that thinks
Maybe the next time somebody tells us to get over the wound we should
    KILL you
Don't matter who
But there's also a lot a bit in most of us that thinks fuck it
Lil Wayne got a new album out
LeBron got a new pair of gym shoes

Maybe everybody schizophrenic
Du Bois calls this double consciousness

KASÉ (SP)

When your smile is scroll
Skin is a rainbow and sadists have a self-covenant to cap you
A sick hatred your history
Your past is cast as misery
You can't say this without the sadists laughin at you

STUCK

Love to dance
When people watchin your shwoomp turns to shuck
You jim
You buck
You brain

Warring ideals trapped in one body
Abel and Cain

RETURN

This story begins in the middle of the country in the middle of fuckin winter
I am teaching in wiskahnsin for the semester
Twice a week eight weeks 90 minutes a pop
I got 24 hours to open up Madison to hip hop
Instead of broad strokes
I paint pointillist.
My notes:

Last night my baby mama called
she is a fly girl in the buttermilk
I have lied to her enough to slit her wings
it's been six years her fly girl flutterby's still ain't quite stitched
it's always my fault
but we manage

My notes:
I tell my class
Hip hop is not the music you listen to but how you listen to it
It's how you parent

She says
*Bamuthi, What if I came home with some white man and had him helping me raise
     YOUR son?*
She actually didn't say that, but if she were more objective, she would have
     phrased it as a question instead of TELLING me

My notes, March:
I tell my class
Hip hop is form
It is the social norm formerly known as a generation's struggle against social norms

The starting center on udub's basketball team is in my class
Pretty girl light skinned six four
Don imus has just showed his ass
Called women nappy headed ho's and now oprah's blamin hip hop
Danielle spits a poem at the end of the class
Self reflective of how she thinks she is seen
Kinda like me

My notes, April:
I tell the class hip hop ain't a form, it's the generational possibility that a Floridian girl who was born in Taiwan can question whether or not her Haitian baby daddy is still real if he lives with a white girl and teaches in Wisconsin

Danielle

Says
I'm just tryin to do me

I say
Ma I'm just tryin to do me

Baby mama say
You can't just do you you also gotta do your son
think if a white stepmom is what he needs…

The truth is
I'm afraid to commit
It don't matter what friggin color the culture is…
        (EXCESS *backspins us into…*)

LOOP 4.

DREAM #4
        (*MUSIC: Dream sig with hiplife, baaba maal, sabar undertones.*)
MBJ. The first African American woman I may have ever met was a white chick from Lubbock Texas.
Molly melching

Big um'n
Came to Senegal 20 years ago to work for unesco
Has never left
Fell in love with a Senegalese man had a baby

Was happy
Until He left
She speaks wolof, and twi, and is a BEAST negotiator at the marketplace
Fully integrated into and respected by her community
Among the Senegalese I meet, I am often referred to as a black american
Molly An African american

When I get off the plane in Senegal
I have no plans and no real money
I have molly's phone number in my pocket, given to me by a friend of a
friend
And lots of stories in my head, also given to me by friends of friends…

They say

BOY in Africa, they'll love you
Go meet the dancers
Go find the hip hop
Someone will adopt you
You'll be taken care of don't trip…

Three days in
I've been hustled out of my drawers
and am spending money at a pace that will leave me homeless in eight days.
I've got one of those non-transferable, non fuckwitable tickets to be here for
     four months.

In tears I call molly, she invites me to her home in Thiès, says I can stay,
Not quite the African I expected to take me in
She runs an NGO here called Tostan, she's a champion of women's health
Works to eliminate female circumcision in rural villages
Calls it mutilation

I become her roadie
Sit in the backseat gazing at endless stretches of endless flatland and wide sky
     as we drive from one end of the country to the other.

We drive to the middle of NOWHERE yo
NOWHERE, and come to a stop in front of a single stone building with a
     thatched roof.

Three girls come out all smiles and grace
they greet and I think molly is gonna meet with them and we'll be out
within a minute, a little boy produces a drum and begins playing it, which I
think is kind of annoying to have going during the meeting, but WHO THE
FUCK AM I, just KEEP QUIET, and LISTEN FOR YOUR NAME

I sit on a rock and take it all in

All of the nowhere

Africa

Okay, so the boy playing the drum is this village's version of a mass email, And pretty soon, I don't know where the hell the people come from, but the little courtyard with the one building looks like the rose bowl on new year's day, with like 100,000 people come to see the circus in town which is namely, the big white African, and the short clueless American friend, and

Molly is trying to have this meeting with the like head women of the village council, to spill her propaganda about stopping this backward indigenous ritual, but nobody can hear anything cuz of all the commotion and people trying to bust into the building to have a look at the ONE white woman within a 1,000 miles, and finally molly says,

Bamuthi, I need you to distract them...

Uh molly I'm a poet and they don't speak English...and there's no electricity
        and I have no megaphone, microphone radio telephone whatever
How'm I gonna keep them all occupied or whatever
I am wilting I need water I need...

Five minutes later
all the village children
I am surrounded heart pounding
AFRICA

don't have to astound em
only distract
no microphone, no turntables, no language

that's my whole act

to survive

I become hip hop empath
I channel the low beginnings
Fires burning all over the Bronx
Post civil rights glass ceilings
No lights
No loot
You just do what you feel to the groove

A dance floor uprising of youth

(I just pray that they buy it)

KASÉ

(MBJ *breaks it down sound dancing to his own beatboxed groove, until* SOU-LATI *takes over and* EXCESS *scratches on the breaks. Rock a few bars with* MBJ *spitting:*)

The future aesthetic/ the future's not static/ it's movin kinetically manic/ you mimic? You cynic of smith that works with florid words/ the world is THIS *minute/ magnanimous moment/ a future aesthetic/ a mytho-poetic/ cerebral and soulful/ vivid/ kinesthetic/ it's not in your head or your heart or your feet/ it exists in all three...*

they're buying it...

while I make 'em laugh with my shamrocks
molly speaks to the village council in a language that I have never heard of
she convinces them to abandon a centuries old practice
encourages them to modernize their attitude toward women

I think

I know another Texan who came in to the brown people's country and tried
     to get them to adopt a foreign way...

This is how I became an MC...
Without saying a word...

     (*FILM #4: Hiplife in Ghana.*)
     (*KASÉ with FILM #5. Interviews with MC's.*
     "YOU EVER LOST YOUR MIND ON STAGE? Ever lost your mind on the mic?")

LOOP 5.

MBJ. This story begins in the middle
Halfway across the city
I can't think
I'm at a wake
over the last ten years
I've taught thousands of students
I'm losing my first today
He's crossed the line

DREAM #5

When we meet
He is at the edge of his youth
Not quite a man
A beautiful lie
He comes from san francisco's forgotten streets
In 20 years the corner where he cops crack will have a yoga studio on it

By then he'll be ghost
In the moment he haunts me
The kid is at the ledge of bi-polarity

KASÉ
a freebird
Forecasting the murder of his own reality
Feathers caked in stardust freebase high on crystal galaxy

We meet before the drugs swept him over the edge
Back in the day when he was only going crazy
When he was 17 and poetry and prose was his sanity's plea
A kid floating down forgotten streets
Pavement piercing his peace like a needle puncturing bird's wing on dark
    nights
The kid thought he was trippin
He kept hearin death singin
His sleep walk had become sleep flight
When I met him in my workshops
He was writing time tied taut as the turbulence of tumult in his tortured mind
he wrote about thunder clappin clave for death while he rhymed
he wrote about destiny calling the sun spilling red wine into the new day to
    libate the sky
Sacrilege under the sign of Saturn
Patterns of paradise lost
An earth turned in on itself
A core of nuclear frost
Frothing
The universe turned rabid dog
Old conversations spoken in music
Digitized analog
Contradictions and metafictions
Metatexted
Manifested
Metu neter
Disease infested
An epidemic of intellect
snappin
New Orleans takin over
Insurgent like basquiat taggin bush's yacht on a video shoot for hova

Oh this thing
Like a birthplace of jazz trapped in a syringe
Filling my blood with sin

he was goin crazy
last time I saw him was at a poetry slam he was tryin to win a few bucks to
    get by
when I see him my girl was by my side
and he
looked
at me
with disappointment in his eyes
then walked away to get high
as I watched the stride of a walking coffin…
last heard he was snortin holy word
still spittin angel dust
the kid could bust
bullet shots

at his wake
I am losing my mind
Holding back the tears
Before they fall…

> (*KASÉ in silence. At end of KASÉ,* SOULATI *composes original music track vocally using loop station as* MBJ *watches.* MBJ *resumes KASÉ when the track is halfway formed.* SOULATI's *spoken/scratched refrain is:*)

SOULATI. This is what it looks like right before I fall…

> (*At end of KASÉ,* MBJ *picks up with:*)

LOOP 5A.

MBJ. Forrest gump the re-mix
It's 1996 and I'm on the staff of my college newspaper
Arts and entertainment
co-editor thank you
it's the sweetest gig for any 20-year-old to possibly have
Three or four times a month,
I'm interviewing new and established artists as they pass through Atlanta
D'Angelo
Erykah Badu
Donald Byrd
The Roots
Das Efx
OutKast
I have the vague sensation that life might not ever get any better than this
One afternoon my co-editor pages me
(cuz it's 1996)
Tells me he's interviewing this new cat named Jay-Z at a hotel downtown
Do I wanna roll?

And I don't.
Who the fuck is Jay-Z?
And it's the middle of the week
I probably gotta go deconstruct the etymological blah blah of the whatever whatever...
But my co-editor ALWAYS has the good trees
So I say fuck it
And I go and the interview is in his hotel room in midtown and that's all I really
Remember
Except three things...

One...
I remember that I don't remember much because we were already high when we got to Jay-Z's hotel room
But then damon dash offered the blunt
And I didn't smoke cuz he was damon dash the dynasty,
He was just some background nigga in some anonymous rapper's hotel room,
I took the blunt cuz you get looked at funny if you don't
Like it's third grade and YOU the kid that's allergic to cheese or some shit
So of course I took the blunt, because you HAVE to
But what a goddamn mistake, because
MAN
WHOA
Which leads me

Two...
I remember I didn't have a fuckin question to ask this nobody rapper
Homeboy was already the oldest rapper EVER probably 27-28 at the time,
You know he might as well have been smokey robinson
A GROWN man dog, and this was his FIRST album
So I respected him and also felt sorry for him at the same time
And he KNEW it and I remember this because

Three...
The look in his eye
Hunger
Boredom
Business
He wanted his shit to pop and he knew that he was above wasting his time with a blunted ass cub reporter
But he was NOT above the hustle
And if this bullshit interview led to one spin at the local club
Which led to 20 album sales at the mall

Then it was worth it
And everyone in the room knew the deal
And the entourage was in our grill
Both fascinated and completely distrustful as you'd expect Brooklyn niggaz
    to be
And man it would be so dope if I'd commented on it RIGHT THEN
The hunger...

Jay-Z
Head of def jam
Kingpin of the inkpen
Beyoncé's man

I had harry potter before hagrid showed up
I had Jordan in his high school locker room sho nuf
And the first and ONLY question I asked him was...damn is this the
chronic?

In the re-mix I ask him
        (*FILM with gesture-based KASÉ: If you could ask Jay-Z ONE question...?*)
        (*MUSIC:* SOULATI *and* EXCESS *make "Nuthin' But a 'G' Thang" by Dr. Dre.*)

LOOP 6.

MBJ. I am a dreamer who forgets
Wake up mornings covered in caul of lost vision and night sweat
Midnight's child I make moonshine by four's light on my grandfather's clock
Lately I can't dream of nothing but missing my kid and uprocks
Waking up every morning in a different bed in a different city
This story begins in the middle
I am in love (I think)
We are on the run
I'm touring and teaching
She's traveling as well
We won't see one another for months

It's always too late
Shifting time zones
Twelve and a half hour difference
one of us always sleeping while the other waits
from India
she leaves me a poem on my voicemail
listening while running to catch my connecting flight at O'Hare
my heart breaks

when she begins
I first mistake her voice for that of the surrogate lover I'm tempted to take
I've been here before
Lust, infidelity, distance I am raw

her voice hovers
above it all
in harmony
with airport sounds
love is on the line
I daydream the next town

Pushing hip hop from the center of the institute
My art is commuting in
I send my kid to private school
I want a lexus AND justice
I am becoming one of them
negroes can't have success without feelin like they're sellin SOMEBODY out.

Don't push me

Cuz

I'm

Close...

KASÉ

> (*MUSIC:* SOULATI *and* EXCESS *re-create "Paul Revere" by the Beastie Boys.*)
> (*FILM #9: Name as many demographic categories as you can.*
> *Ready?*
> *Go!*
> *WHICH of those demographic categories do you identify with the most*
> *And why?*)

DREAM #6

> (*MUSIC:* SOULATI *"narrates" the perspective of the youth with beatbox.*)

MBJ. A walk through the park in postwar Bosnia
I am scared for my life
It is night
And the guy following me is gaining
I cross sharply across the cobblestone road
Then make a break for it through the trees

The next day he shows up in my workshop
He looks nothing like the Neo-Nazi I thought was trailing me from the
    shadows
He's probably all of thirteen
Sharp blue eyes close cropped hair
All goofball elbows and knees
Speaks no English
Shows up to write every day for three weeks

And then
Begins showing up at my place
every morning at the cock's crow
I need to learn the Bosnian words for
Lil mother fucker I'm still sleep

Until then
I open the door
He smiles his goofy grin
And then starts to beatbox
He is 5 ½ feet deep in ethnic warfare's grave
He's found someone to help him dig
out
His mouth music make like skipping bullets against the wall of first light
    darkness
Still dreaming I begin nodding my head to the beat
In the distance the adan calls
It is dawn
The cipher can't wait for the day to break

LOOP 7.

DREAM #7

MBJ. I was dreaming when I wrote this

Stop me if I go too fast

In the middle of Minneapolis

I'm chillin with prince…

Cuz, when you a freaky scorpio and science has just determined that your
ruling planet isn't really a planet, but like a planetoid you go to prince to set
your freaky cosmology back in order…

So in a dream, I'm with prince, you know rollin through his crib, it's like the
opposite of BET real women, natural beauty, very lovesexy and I come

across this DOPE ass painting...I say prince this shit look JUST like the mona lisa

He says

Dearly beloved

That is the mona lisa...

I say come on fool the mona lisa's at the louvre, I seen the shit last summer in Paris, besides, mona lisa's not really smiling here, she looks more frustrated than anything else...

he says...

Aaahhh...bamuthi I'll tell you the story man but first you're gonna have to purify yourself in the waters of Lake Minnetonka...

I said for real

He said
Nahh nigga I'm just playin, listen...
Prince says, I KNEW mona
She was a waitress on the promenade
She worked the night shift
Legend had it that her smile could make you rich
If only you had the proper math to access it
All the genius numbers motherfuckers tried to tap it...
Galileo Pythagoras Aristotle Banneker brilliant all
Died broke on a boardwalk in Montego Bay moanin 'bout mona secret smile
   is too safe
Til one day my man Da Vinci come through to mona's restaurant, put him-
   self at a booth in the back

He ordered said let me get a fruit cocktail I ain't too hungry
Mona almost laughed
Said you sound like a real man to me
Kinda cute
You wanna take a chance
I got secrets
Coded language flipped in Fibonacci sequence
Leonardo knew this was the chick in which future fortune lay
But first he had to get her to smile just a certain way

Started with visual massage
Rubbed down her body with his eyes
Took hot honey
Painted butterflies inside her open thighs

Then he took a cube of ice
I'll trace that pattern if you like
But before she could decline
Leo's cell phone chimed
She said whoever's callin
Can't be as cute as you

Right then and there leo knew
Da Vinci Deciphered the code
Already saw the movie, didn't have to crack the book first
Took her out of the bath and into the hot tub leapt but didn't look first
Held her ass just above the jet stream in the Jacuzzi
Fucked her let the rushing water be a surrogate for his tongue in her bootie
    the nucka was nasty
I said yo yo prince, keep it real fool, that's some crazy detail, you act like you
    was there…. So then this fool, give me that prince stare…

Let me finish…

Prince continues

Mona was No venus hottentot No nina simone No frieda
Neither Cleopatra not Egyptian nor jones
But Lisa moaned
More
Make Italian monarchs head leaned back
Leo said fuck it Da Vinci conducted his dick like stravinsky symphonically
    stroking the kitty while doin the math
If I twist my hips to 13 seconds past sunset six she'll cream before 3:16 this
    is the tropics
She's a cancer at five I'll make her green iced tea
Started thinking about last suppers lasting love and the lush of mona's
    anatomy
and just then mona left
her eyes move three breaths west of anti climax
couldn't take Da Vinci jackin off his intellect
so here's the secret to mona's smile prince says

it's totally made up…
Mona went to work at another restaurant on the promenade still worked the
    night shift
Heard about leo's portrait
She took to wearing a wig
Dishwater blond
Still tall and fine
She got a lot of tips…

I said prince, how the fuck do you know all this, he said, cuz last year, mona rolled through Minneapolis...

Spent the evening told me the whole story, but when I woke up the next morning,
Mona wasn't there

I looked all over, I didn't find anything but this painting at the bottom of the stairs, on the back was a note that said

Thank you for a funky time...

Call me...

     (*FILM: Women in hip hop...*)
     (*MUSIC:* SOULATI *and* EXCESS *make "Get Ur Freak On" by Missy Elliott with a touch of "Darling Nikki" by Prince.*)
     (*KASÉ: Channel your inner video vixen.*)

LOOP 8.

DREAM #8

MBJ. This story begins in the middle
Halfway across my childhood
I think that I'm awake
Sitting in a South Bronx apartment
The light outside says it's first wink of day
But I can't sleep
Five of us spent the night at our boy's crib
the first one who falls out gets his hand
soaked in water
I can't afford to pee in these jeans

I'm up...
We're all perched around a radio
Like an audio campfire
Listening to Public Enemy

SOULATI/MBJ.

Listen for lessons I'm saying inside music that critics are all blasting me for
They'll never care for the brothers and sisters
Now across the country has us up for the war

We got to demonstrate, come on now, they're gonna have to wait
Till we get it right
Radio stations I question their blackness
They call themselves black, but well see

CROSS
MBJ.
Hip hop's story is the choice to commit to one side of the line or the other
To get so close to the edge
You can smell the afterdeath
In hip hop it smells like cisco and sulfur
Because if you don't commit to spinnin on yo head
You will break your neck
I keep dreamin of being held up by white lines getting high off the wrong
    man's respect

The more I'm accepted by others, the less I accept myself
This story begins in the middle-class black
I am stumbling my way to the line

KASÉ
My Grandmere has been dying ever since I can remember...
Thirty years it's been the big joker
the double six
the shit she rolls out
to MAKE SURE I get in line...

whenever she wants to keep me in check
she reminds me she ain't got much time
come to church with granny, I want to make sure I go to mass with you again...

before I die...

and it's true
On the early morning she makes three calls to my cell
she is 92

on some mornings her spirit shrinks she thinks this might be it
we live 3,000 miles away
the distance makes it urgent
these might be her last words to me...

she's been playing this card ever since I can remember
but I have no choice but to take this seriously

she says be there for your son
we're all very proud of you
but the boy can't be raised by a race man on the run
and if you really love the woman
slow down

(*FILM*: *"Inventos"* by *Eli Jacobs-Fantauzzi*.)
(*MUSIC*: *Dream Cuba*.)
(EXCESS *go off*.)

LOOP 9.

MBJ. Cuba
July
Santiago
Hips moving like moons orbiting planets orbiting suns orbiting god ordering
  it all
On this street the music is the ground beneath my feet
I am thoughts and humidity moistening
Missing my son...

I crack day either still dreaming
Or still drunk...
Last night I fought Cuban rum, and I'm pretty sure the drink won...
But I'm UP
I gotta teach class in 20 minutes but instead of preparing I spent last night
  channeling my inner-fucking hemingway

So when I show up, I have nothing...so I cheat...
My visa's on the line I gotta do SOMETHING so I take them to the beach
say Cuba libre on me...the most singularly American thing I have ever done
...instead of my lecture on hip hop I take a class full of local college students
to the ocean in the middle of the day to get drunk. Fidel is somewhere
fuming...

If things were different, I'd be in Haiti instead...
Back to the ceremony
But civil war and unrest in my ancestral land has driven me here...
Sixty miles west
and yet...
in the skin
high cheekbones
and music sutured to movement it is clear that these too are my people

And then the singing...
          (EXCESS *spins "Song for Eleguá."*)
          (SOULATI *busts "Mona Lisa" by Slick Rick underneath*.)
I'm pretty sure this is sacrilege
But I see something in the break
The kinship of prayer and escape and elixir and ecstasy...I say where do you
  go when you're at the line

And you want to escape?
This is not a simple question to be asked by the turista from the United
        States...
I wheel up and go back to the break

Hip hop is folklore
Is gospel
Is order
Is ocha
In orbit
No bullshit
No doubt...

Old school is a fixed time in history
And its golden age ended 1993, 94
So like Sophocles is classic mythology of golden Greece
KRS is classic folklore of generation me

I'm kinda talking out my ass at this point
They have a whole different paradigm for folklore
It involves deities that frequently visit the earth
Called down by drum, sung bodies and word
But the rhythm never changes
And that's the point I'm making
I may or may not think that that I'm full of shit
All that matters is I'm finally talking hip hop music to these kids
And so right or wrong...
They go with it...

And it's only in the delirium of the dance that things finally make sense
We escape into music like runaway slaves...
Until night falls...
Free form
God calls
Fear falls
Falling into the night
like tongues on fire incinerating the sky shot

fall back

chains break

falling...

red moon

madness

full on

til heart fills

(DVJ *chops and screws B-boy/B-girls with ceremonial footage.*)

(SOULATI *and* EXCESS *trade 8's while* MBJ *busts.*)

MBJ. It's ethereal

Lyrical

Miracle

Biblical

Spiritual

Cyclical

Steerable

Unnearable

Hearable

Liminal

Spherical

Physical

Quizzical

Is it

Is it

Is it

Real...?

Living word...

Future folklore

(*KASÉ/ritual/film...with different interviewees...a duet...a solo for two [many].*)

(*We've seen this movement before, shown on screen in interviews, as shadowy subliminal in slow motion behind molly, double consciousness etc...Stacey teaches the movement to different dancers/groups, everybody in on the act...*)

FALL

I wake up in my own bed and still am somehow in a different state

Break up

mourning

The house is completely still

Silent

Nascent

Like first breath

On the dining room table

Two words

red ink

yellow post-it

Taking space
The movies never get the break up right
In the movies people throw shit and its HELLA loud and SUPER weepy
That happens too, but that's the easy part...
The heart of any break is the silent morning
When the world is new

and the one you would normally call
is the one that's left the door open
and the house quiet
even the birds are taking a moment of silence
before they spread their cardinal wings and fall...

KASÉ WITH TEXT
I choose
My black ego gone blue
Over love
In the big black book
This looks real good
So why do I think I fucked up?

Grandmere say how you love
is what you do
Not what you say
Action is truth
The anchor
Cape Haitian

Just wants to see me settled

Pou pouche before I die

Do what you love
And be still...

        (*MUSIC:* SOULATI *and* EXCESS *re-create "Act Too" by The Roots.*)

FALL/KASÉ
Cycles to break
Don't instill fear in the boy
Pray with full body
practice faithfulness
and faith
cycles to break

there's more than one way to live...
more than one way to believe black is beautiful
more than one way to raise kids
more than one way to love

more than one struggle
more than one answer
more than one way to break

KASÉ/(SP)

Falling in between the cracks of commitment
Loving in the margins between music and manhood

Embracing the silence in the break between beats
In a dream I am bold In love and at peace
God help me I'm falling
Like counterculture cloaked corporate consumed
Like lacking the courage to love you in spite
Falling like the Cuban night
I am an American at the edge…

Don't push me

Cuz I'm close…

I'm trying…

End of Play

In Paris You Will Find Many Baguettes but Only One True Love

by Michael Lew

BIOGRAPHY

Michael Lew's plays, *Tenure* (American Airlines Theatre on Broadway) and *Keep Truckin'* (Atlantic Theatre), were recently produced by the 24 Hour Plays. His one-woman play *Yit, Ngay (One, Two)* is published in *Plays and Playwrights 2006* and excerpted in *The Best Women's Monologues for the 21st Century* (Applause). Other publications include *The Roosevelt Cousins, Thoroughly Sauced* (2007 Samuel French Festival winner) and *Magician Ben vs. The Wizard Merlin* (Smith & Kraus). Mr. Lew received a Sloan commission from Ensemble Studio Theatre and works for New Dramatists. His play *A Better Babylon* was workshopped at Victory Gardens in Chicago. Writing residencies include Ensemble Studio Theatre's Youngblood, Ma-Yi Writers' Lab and Old Vic New Voices. Mr. Lew was a Westinghouse finalist for his work on homeobox genes and graduated from Yale College in 2003.

ACKNOWLEDGMENTS

In Paris You Will Find Many Baguettes but Only One True Love premiered at the Humana Festival of New American Plays in March 2008, and won the Actors Theatre of Louisville's Heideman Award. It was directed by Sean Daniels with the following cast:

LINDY..Brandie Moore
LIZ..Jessica Lauren Howell
RYAN ....Christopher Scheer

and the following production staff:

Scenic Designers.............................. Brenda Ellis & Paul Owen
Costume Designer.. Emily Ganfield
Lighting Designer... Paul Werner
Sound Designer .... Benjamin Marcum
Properties Designer .... Mark Walston
Stage Manager.. Debra Anne Gasper
Assistant Stage Manager...........................Captain Kate Murphy
Dramaturg .... Adrien-Alice Hansel
Assistant Dramaturg..Charles Haugland

This play was originally developed in New York City with Ensemble Studio Theatre's Youngblood Playwrights Group (Graeme Gillis and R.J. Tolan, artistic directors).

CAST OF CHARACTERS
LINDY, an American tourist
LIZ, her best friend
RYAN, a Parisian street mime

PLACE
Paris.

TIME
The present.

NOTE ON THE TEXT
A slash (/) in the dialogue indicates that the next line interrupts at the slash point.

Christopher Scheer and Brandie Moore
in *In Paris You Will Find Many Baguettes but Only One True Love*

32nd Annual Humana Festival of New American Plays
Actors Theatre of Louisville, 2008
Photo by Harlan Taylor

IN PARIS YOU WILL FIND MANY BAGUETTES BUT ONLY ONE TRUE LOVE

LINDY *sits apart from* LIZ *and* RYAN, *who are snuggling.* RYAN *is a mime.* LIZ *has a black beret and rosy circles painted on her cheeks.*

LINDY. (*Loud, ostentatious sigh.*) Ennui.

(*Pause. Looks at* LIZ *and* RYAN, *who ignore her. Sighs.*)

Malaise.

(*Pause. Looks at* LIZ *and* RYAN, *who ignore her. Sighs.*)

Chagrin! Tristesse! Les Misérables!

LIZ. What the hell, Lindy?

LINDY. I know! I'm sorry.

LIZ. If you keep *tristessing* all over the place, you can spend the rest of the trip alone. (*She goes back to snuggling.*)

LINDY. (*Incredibly self-pitying.*) I'm already alone. *Isolement...*

LIZ. Lindy?

LINDY. Yeah?

LIZ. You don't speak French, so shut your baguette hole. You're ruining the trip.

(*To* RYAN, *as though he is deaf.*)

She feels lonely.

(LINDY *nods slowly.* RYAN *nods quickly.*)

Her boyfriend left her.

(LINDY *nods slowly and* RYAN *quickly.*)

Her boyfriend said, "I like you but I'm not *in like* with you." Do you understand?

(RYAN *nods. Mimes tears.*)

Yes! Yes, that's it exactly. Oh my God we have so much in common!

(*They lean in to kiss but....*)

LINDY. Liz?

LIZ. (*Holding in just-about-to-kiss position.*) Yeah Lindy.

LINDY. I don't mean to ruin the trip.

LIZ. (*Pulls away from* RYAN.) For shit's sake. This is PARIS! Grab someone! That's what I did. (*To* RYAN.) Didn't I grab you?

(LIZ *mimes casting a reel to* RYAN, *and* RYAN *mimes being hooked.*)

LINDY. I'd like to. Grab someone. But...it's so hard. You know...love?

LIZ. *(Extremely tender.)* I know sweetie. *(Thumps her forehead.)*

LINDY. HEY!!

LIZ. Look. We came here. What did we say?

LINDY. You...you thumped me!

LIZ. That's right now pay attention. We came here. What did we say?

LINDY. In Paris we'll find the men / of our dreams.

LIZ. We'll find the men of our.... No, dammit. You said it too fast. Do it like we practiced on the plane! We came here. What did we say?

LINDY. In Paris / we'll find the men of our dreams.

LIZ. We'll find the men of our dreams! *(Extremely tender.)* Yeaaaaaaahhhh. Well I did it! I said...what did I say to you?

LINDY. You said, "I've always wanted to bag a traditional French street performer."

LIZ. That's right. And what the fuck did I bag?

LINDY. A traditional French mime.

LIZ. That's right and we love each other. *(To* RYAN *as though he is deaf.)* Don't we? Love each other?

(RYAN *mimes tying a string to her heart and tying a string to his heart. With one hand on her chest and one hand on his, he pulls back and forth on their heartstrings. They move in rhythm.* LIZ *laughs while moving with the heartstrings.*)

See? I said to myself, "In Paris I'll find the man of my dreams. I'll have a bite to eat and I'll find him." So I went to the café and I had a *baguette.* I had a *ficelle.* *(To* RYAN.) Is that how you pronounce it? *Ficelle?*

(RYAN *mimes "I don't know, I can't talk."*)

I had a...*ficelle.*

(RYAN *starts miming being in a bakery.*)

I had a *croissant.* I had a *palmier.* I had a *brioche.* I had a *batard.* Then I...I had another *baguette.* And damned if the man of my dreams didn't walk right up to me. Trapped in an invisible box!

(RYAN *is in an invisible box and* LIZ *unlocks it. He emerges, triumphant. They hold each other.*)

I slapped on a *béret* and some *rouge* and I haven't looked back. And that joy could be yours, Lindy. But get this: you have to find it.

LINDY. I know. But I still miss him. Look, I made a locket out of that bottle of *cologne* he left in my room.

LIZ. Jesus put that away—you've been showing me that all week. Lindy, do you know that in French they spell "bread" the same way we spell "pain"?

LINDY. I don't see what that has to do with...

LIZ. Pain, Lindy. Pain. And I think that means you have to go through a lot of pain...or in my case (*In French.*) *pain*...until you find true love. Speaking of which, it's breakfast time. You think about that while I buy us some breakfast. (*To* RYAN.) I'm going to buy us some breakfast! Breakfast!

> (RYAN *mimes being a fat man.*)

Exactly! We have so much in common!

> (*They kiss.* LINDY *sprays some cologne on her hand and kinda sniffs her own hand.*)

Did I get mime face on me?

> (*She wipes her face.* RYAN *tries to get up.*)

No, no. You stay there. Lindy stop sniffing your hand it's weird.

LINDY. But it smells like him!

LIZ. (*To* RYAN.) Cheer her up for me, will you? I'm getting some breakfast.

> (LIZ *exits.* RYAN *mimes picking a bouquet and gives it to* LINDY, *who doesn't take it. Beats. Lindy stares into space. Mime and Lindy. Lindy and Mime. Beats.*)

LINDY. (*To nobody, really.*) We should start making out or something. That would really freak her out. (*Silence.*) She'd come back and I'd have all this mime face on my crotch. Our clothes spread out across the floor. She'd gasp and you'd make a face like...

> (*Put her hands to her cheeks and makes a surprised face. Beat.*)

Not that I'd do that. She's my best friend.... (*Silence.*) But wouldn't it be funny? (*Beat, mumbly.*) If we made out...

RYAN. (*Canadian accent.*) I'm not about to make out with you Lindy.

LINDY. Holy shit!

RYAN. But I am about to tell you something unexpected.

LINDY. Holy shit you're not a mime at all!

RYAN. I am so a mime.

LINDY. But you can talk!

RYAN. (*Firm.*) Mimes talk, *Lindy!* It's not like we go home to our mime houses, kiss our mime wives and eat silently at the dinner table. It's not like we have noiseless joyless pantomiming mime sex. We *talk*, ok?

LINDY. Ok.

RYAN. But I do have a confession.

> (*Sits her down.*)

I'm not French.

LINDY. Well, obviously. Listen to you! You sound like some backwater hick from Saskatchewan!

RYAN. Actually I'm from Manitoba. And that's exactly why I can't speak to Liz. That's why I mime. I was in the row behind you on the plane. For hours I couldn't even see her face. But I could see between the seat cushions, and I fell in love with the curve that reaches from the back of her shoulder to the side of her arm. Do you know that part?

   (*He traces that part on* LINDY.)

She wouldn't stop talking about finding a traditional French street performer. And I thought, "Well I've had years of clowning experience back in Manitoba. This was meant to be."

LINDY. Clowning isn't mime. Or is it? I don't know much about Canada.

RYAN. Clowning is like the headstrong sister of mime.

LINDY. I see. (*She takes this in.*) So when you say you're a mime, really you're not.

RYAN. Oh. Oh.... I guess not in the strictest sense, no.

LINDY. (*She takes this in.*) You were on the plane with us?

RYAN. Yeah.

LINDY. We landed six days ago!

RYAN. Yeah, so.... I've been stalking you.

LINDY. So you're a fraud. A creepy stalker fraud. This LOVE is.... A FRAUD!

RYAN. (*Firm.*) No! No, Lindy! This is what I've blown my cover to tell you. In Canada we have an expression: No beaver ever made a dam without a whole lot of pining. Do you understand?

LINDY. N...nnoo?

RYAN. That's reasonable. Canada isn't really known for its aphorisms. It means that nothing great has ever been accomplished without a whole lot of desire and pain. It means that love is suffering. Love is yearning. Love is longing for her so deeply that you're willing to sleep in the streets just for the chance to see her walking out of hotel room 32C. Is that not so?

LINDY. I don't know!

RYAN. (*He grabs her.*) I see in you this fantastic pain. Deep, crushing—whiny—but fantastic pain.

LINDY. Thank you?

RYAN. Yes, thank you! It means you're going to find love, because you're pining. One day you're going to stop pining for this man who is already gone and you'll start pining for another man. And then another. And then another. And then perhaps you'll start pining again for the man from two times ago. And then another man entirely. And some day? Some man will also start pining for you. Some man will contort himself just-so for you, while you try, simultaneously, to contort yourself just-so. Is that not lovely?

LINDY. I...I'm not sure I buy that. Liz is happy as a *frite* in mayonnaise. (*High-pitched vaguely French voice.*) "Oh lookit me I'm a little *frite* I'm all swaddled in mayonnaise." And she didn't have to contort worth shit!

RYAN. Of course she did. She had to come all the way to Paris to find me!

LINDY. But you're not French!

RYAN. So what if I'm not French? I have been doing some serious pining! Do you know how hard it is to win someone's heart by being a *mime?* A mime, Lindy. Do you know how much easier it would be if I could just sing to her, or juggle? I had to compete against magicians, acrobats, people on stilts! You think that was easy? That's love.

(*LIZ enters with brown bag, two baguettes sticking out.*)

LIZ. Baguettes! Two of them. *Pâté.* (*Looks in bag.*)

LINDY. Liz, thank God!

LIZ. Yeah, right? Thank God for *pâté!*

LINDY. Liz I have to tell you something.

(*RYAN grabs the baguettes.*)

LIZ. Hey! What are you doing with breakfast?

(*RYAN mimes drumming with baguettes.*)

Oh, he's drumming!

(*She laughs. He uses the baguettes as prison bars.*)

Oh, he's in jail!

(*He uses the baguettes as weights.*)

Oh, look! He's lifting weights!

(*She laughs. He uses the baguettes as a bazooka.*)

Oh, he's pretending to be a rebel insurgent shooting a rocket-propelled grenade at an American Black Hawk helicopter! (*She laughs.*)

LINDY. LIZ! That man is...

(*RYAN gets on the baguettes and uses them as skis.*)

LIZ. Our breakfast! You're ruining breakfast! (*She laughs despite herself.*) Oh he's skiing!

(*While on the skis he mimes shooting.*)

He's racing a biathlon!

(*RYAN gets off the skis, triumphant.*)

Yaaaaaaaaay!

(*LIZ rushes in and hugs RYAN. RYAN stares directly at LINDY. Nobody moves. LIZ breaks the embrace, kissing him.*)

LINDY. (*A quiet utterance.*) But that...

LIZ. (*Tender.*) You ruined our breakfast, my French gold medalist biathlete. (*She turns to* LINDY, *who seems poised to speak. Gently.*) What?

LINDY. That…that's love.

> (*Lights fade as Edith Piaf's "La Vie en Rose" plays.*)

> ### *Fin.*

ALL HAIL HURRICANE GORDO
by Carly Mensch

BIOGRAPHY

Carly Mensch is currently in her second year at The Juilliard School's Lila Acheson Wallace Playwrights Program and is the playwright-in-residence at Ars Nova. *All Hail Hurricane Gordo* was developed at Ars Nova's Out Loud Series, the Kennedy Center's University Playwrights Festival and the Marin Theatre Company. Her play *Len, Asleep in Vinyl* received its premiere in the summer of 2008 at Second Stage Theatre Uptown.

ACKNOWLEDGMENTS

All Hail Hurricane Gordo premiered at the Humana Festival of New American Plays in March 2008. It was directed by Sean Daniels with the following cast:

CHAZ ....Matthew Dellapina
GORDO...Patrick James Lynch
INDIA ....Tracee Chimo
OSCAR ....William McNulty

and the following production staff:

Scenic Designer ....Paul Owen
Costume Designer...Lorraine Venberg
Lighting Designer...Deb Sullivan
Sound Designer ....Matt Callahan
Properties Designer .... Mark Walston
Properties Assistant ....Joe Cunningham
Fight Supervisor .... Lee Look
Stage Manager...Paul Mills Holmes
Assistant Stage Manager............................Captain Kate Murphy
Dramaturg .... Julie Felise Dubiner
Assistant Dramaturg...Devon LaBelle
Casting..Emily Ruddock
Directing Assistant...Michael K. Brooks

All Hail Hurricane Gordo was produced in association with The Cleveland Play House.

CAST OF CHARACTERS
CHAZ, late 20s
GORDO, mid 20s
INDIA, 18
OSCAR, late 50s

SETTING
A ranch-style house in a waning suburb of New York. The living room has been converted into a makeshift office.

Patrick James Lynch and Matthew Dellapina
in *All Hail Hurricane Gordo*

32nd Annual Humana Festival of New American Plays
Actors Theatre of Louisville, 2008
Photo by Harlan Taylor

316

ALL HAIL HURRICANE GORDO

A living room turned makeshift office. Two desks, one neat and organized with a typewriter and carefully arranged stacks of paper and the other a total wreck, purgatory-like, where things half-eaten and half-assed take up residence—opened bags of chips, abandoned Tinker Toy projects, wrinkled WrestleMania magazines, parts of an old Bingo set, a bug collection in a recycled yogurt container, swimming goggles, etc. There is a worn-out couch dead center, covered with piles and piles of phone books and a lone wooden chair in the corner.

CHAZ, late 20s, sits at the neat desk. Shirt and tie. Typing. Enter GORDO, mid 20s. In boxers and a little boy's pajama top. CHAZ continues typing. GORDO watches for a moment.

GORDO. Hey.

(Type type. Type type.)

Hey Chaz.

(CHAZ doesn't respond. GORDO patiently repeats himself.)

Chaz. Chaz. Chaz.

CHAZ. I hear you.

GORDO. You want breakfast?

CHAZ. Already ate.

GORDO. Alright.

(GORDO exits. CHAZ pulls out the sheet of paper from the typewriter and puts it into an envelope. He finds the appropriate address in one of the phone books open on his desk.)

(GORDO returns with some old mush in Tupperware. He loiters around CHAZ's desk while he eats.)

GORDO. Mmm.

CHAZ. What is that?

GORDO. Stir-fry.

CHAZ. From last week?

GORDO. I guess.

CHAZ. You didn't see any cereal?

(GORDO shrugs.)

I bought some yesterday.

GORDO. You bought the bad kind.

317

CHAZ. I bought Cheerios.

GORDO. You bought Shit-e-os. The kind in the plastic bag. The kind you have to crawl on the floor of the supermarket to get. They look like Cheerios but surprise—they're really Shit-e-os. Simple mistake. How long you been working?

CHAZ. Little over an hour.

GORDO. Jeez. That's discipline.

CHAZ. Just finished the fourth one this morning. Oh. And we need to pick up more stamps. We're running low.

GORDO. Look at you. You're like this self-guided missile. Like your brain is on autopilot.

CHAZ. It's after ten by the way.

GORDO. See? You've even got an internal clock.

CHAZ. We start at nine-thirty.

GORDO. *We?*

CHAZ. The household.

GORDO. Yeah…I can't get up then. Sorry.

CHAZ. Why not?

GORDO. Because. You got rid of the TV. That's how I used to tell time— the channel guide. I used to watch the channel guide every morning until breakfast. Do you know you can basically schedule your entire life just by watching the channel guide? It tells you what's on and when and how long, and there's even a little ticking clock in the upper hand corner. But now it's just…nothing. I'm a little ship, lost at sea, all floating around. Where's my compass? Where's my best friend? Oh yeah, Chaz sold it on eBay.

CHAZ. I didn't sell it on eBay. I sold it to Kip Bearman.

GORDO. The guy from the Y?

CHAZ. Yeah.

GORDO. Now what's he gonna do with a TV? Smoke it?

CHAZ. (*Amused.*) Please tell me how you smoke a television set.

GORDO. Oh he'll figure out a way. He'll probably pull out all the wires and try to snort the electricity out of them.

CHAZ. What makes you think he does drugs? We see him at the pool, that's it.

GORDO. And on the bench outside, waiting for the bus. Smoking Lucky Strikes. Every Wednesday, just sitting on the bench. Smoking.

CHAZ. Cigarettes.

GORDO. Cigarettes are a drug, man. They've got nicotine. You smoke one and Bang! your brain is a plate of scrambled eggs. Haven't you seen the commercials? Don't ever smoke Chaz. Promise me you'll never smoke.

CHAZ. It's a little late for me to take up smoking, don't you think?

GORDO. *Promise* me Chaz.

CHAZ. Fine. I promise.

GORDO. Promise.

CHAZ. I said I promise.

GORDO. You can't die on me.

CHAZ. I'm not dying.

GORDO. I'm just saying, you better not.

(*A moment.*)

I'm thinking of writing a letter. To Child Protective Services. With a note that says, "Dear Protective Services. Question: Do you really protect every child in America? Answer: No. You don't. Love, Gordon. P.S. Can you please get me a new TV?"

(CHAZ *just stares at him.*)

CHAZ. Why don't you go get dressed. Your leg hair—it's blinding me.

GORDO. You don't think that's funny? Writing a letter to Child Protective Services?

CHAZ. It's not that funny anymore.

GORDO. You write letters.

CHAZ. That's different.

GORDO. You write like ten a day.

CHAZ. I write inquiries. It's a different thing.

GORDO. I can sign both our names. They might like that—a two for one deal.

(*Noticing.*)

What's up with the tie?

CHAZ. Oh. Right.

GORDO. You look good. You look like you're going to court.

CHAZ. I've…got a meeting today. We both do, actually.

GORDO. Ah…we're auctioning off the couch. First the TV, now the couch. Everything must go!

CHAZ. We're not selling anything. It's—an interview.

GORDO. What kind of interview?

CHAZ. You know, an interview.

GORDO. Okay. But what kind?

CHAZ. You can't get upset.

GORDO. What? Are you getting another job?

CHAZ. Not me. Someone else. Coming here.

GORDO. Someone who?

CHAZ. Someone who's coming here to interview with us.

GORDO. Why would they do that?

CHAZ. Go get dressed and we'll talk all about it. And put on a nice shirt—
you can borrow one of mine if you want. With a collar.

GORDO. No. Tell me now Chaz.

CHAZ. It's no big deal. It's just a meeting.

GORDO. Tell me what's going on.

CHAZ. Not if you're going to freak out.

GORDO. I'M NOT GOING TO FREAK OUT. Just tell me already.

(*CHAZ composes himself.*)

CHAZ. A potential tenant. She's coming in at eleven.

GORDO. Today?

CHAZ. Yeah.

(*GORDO processes all this.*)

GORDO. Okay.

CHAZ. Yeah?

GORDO. Uh huh.

(*Beat. GORDO exits to his room. CHAZ watches the door warily. A few
seconds later, GORDO re-enters wearing a football helmet. CHAZ stares at
him for a moment.*)

CHAZ. Gordon.

(*GORDO stares back.*)

Gordo.

(*GORDO lowers his head like a bull.*)

Don't do this.

(*GORDO kicks invisible dirt as if preparing to charge.*)

I said don't.

(*GORDO charges. Rams CHAZ in the stomach. CHAZ falls down.*)

OFF! Off. Get OFF!

GORDO. AAGGHHH!!!!

CHAZ. Jesus.

(*CHAZ tries to wiggle out from beneath GORDO.*)

I said off.

GORDO. I'M GOING TO BREAK YOUR ARM.

CHAZ. I need my arm.

GORDO. NO YOU DON'T.

CHAZ. Please. I do.

GORDO. NO. NO MORE ARM.

CHAZ. You know what time it is? I think you know what time it is.

GORDO. TIME TO DIE?

CHAZ. What?

GORDO. TIME TO EAT MY FACE!

(CHAZ *manages to break free. Stands up.*)

CHAZ. I think it's time for a time out.

GORDO. No.

CHAZ. Yes. Time out. Go sit in the chair.

GORDO. I don't want to sit in the chair.

CHAZ. You just head-butted me in the goddamn stomach. I've probably got internal bleeding. Go have time out.

GORDO. Fine.

(GORDO *goes to the lone wooden chair and takes a seat.*)

How long?

CHAZ. Two minutes.

GORDO. One.

CHAZ. Fine.

(GORDO *sits in the chair. Counts quietly to himself.* CHAZ *brings* GORDO's *empty container into the kitchen.*)

CHAZ. (*From the kitchen.*) I think you actually ruptured my spleen this time.

(*When he returns,* CHAZ *looks at his watch.*)

58...59...60.

(GORDO *stands up.*)

Are you ready to talk about this like a grown-up?

GORDO. Uh huh.

CHAZ. Are you sure?

GORDO. I'm calm now. See?

CHAZ. Why don't you take off the helmet?

GORDO. It's the San Diego Chargers.

CHAZ. I know.

GORDO. Okay.

(GORDO *takes off the helmet.*)

I don't know why I get so angry.

CHAZ. You've got stuff you're dealing with.

GORDO. But we've both got the same stuff.

CHAZ. I think you've also got some kind of anger management problem, maybe.

GORDO. Like elephants?

CHAZ. Yeah. Like elephants.

GORDO. Goring people in Asia, trampling entire villages in Africa. It's a worldwide epidemic you know. The whole animal kingdom's striking out.

(*Beat.*)

You're not angry?

CHAZ. Not really.

GORDO. I don't want to be so angry all the time.

CHAZ. I know.

GORDO. It just comes out.

CHAZ. Well you've got to work on that. People aren't going to just accept that kind of behavior out in the real world. That's what got you into trouble, remember?

GORDO. Yeah.

CHAZ. You can't just do whatever you feel like. You're a human being. There are certain boundaries.

GORDO. You told me to always be myself.

CHAZ. Well. Not when your self is fiery ball of rage—okay? That's when you make an exception.

(*Beat.*)

GORDO. Can we talk about this person now?

CHAZ. Sure.

GORDO. You're sick of talking to me, is that it?

CHAZ. Yeah. I'm sick of talking to you. That's it.

GORDO. You think I'm boring?

CHAZ. That's not even a possibility.

GORDO. You want me to fade into the darkness like some kind of phantasm.

CHAZ. I want you to be just a little more understanding, that's what I want.

GORDO. I'm very understanding. Trust me, I understand stuff.

CHAZ. I mean more understanding of me. Of what I need. I have needs too you know. I'm not just your babysitter.

(GORDO *chuckles.*)

I'm glad you find that so entertaining. Besides— It's not just that. It's also— money stuff.

GORDO. Why? What happened?

CHAZ. Nothing happened.

GORDO. Are we in the red, Chaz?

CHAZ. We could use the extra income, that's all.

GORDO. You're supposed to tell me when we're in the red, Chaz.

CHAZ. We're not in the red.

GORDO. What about all the money I made at the airport?

CHAZ. You worked there for maybe three weeks.

GORDO. And not just that. I've had a lot of jobs, man.

CHAZ. Oh I know.

GORDO. The library—

CHAZ. Two libraries—you've worked at two of them.

GORDO. Sal's.

CHAZ. I forgot about Sal's.

GORDO. They gave me free meatball subs at Sal's.

CHAZ. Yeah, and it made you fat.

GORDO. What about when I gave people tours of the neighborhood and pretended that Amelia Earhart grew up here? I taught them all how to make paper airplanes so they'd have souvenirs to take back with them.

CHAZ. That doesn't count because you didn't charge them anything. In fact, you actually spent money because of all the paper.

GORDO. That was pretty funny though, right?

CHAZ. It was a little funny.

GORDO. What about you?

CHAZ. Oh—'cause two jobs isn't bad enough.

GORDO. Do three.

CHAZ. Don't you think I'm pulling enough weight here already?

GORDO. You wake up at the crack of dawn. You're up anyway.

CHAZ. I get up early to do my personal business.

GORDO. So I'll do that stuff. What—it's just writing letters and stuffing them into envelopes, right? I can do that.

CHAZ. You can't. It's my personal—it's something I do for myself, okay? It's mine. Besides—we wouldn't be in this situation if someone hadn't gotten himself fired from maybe the easiest job on the entire planet and probably blacklisted from the entire global job market.

GORDO. Hey—

CHAZ. It's true. I don't think anyone's going to hire you now. They've probably tagged you in the system.

GORDO. What system?

CHAZ. The Internet…job system.

(Beat.)

GORDO. So this person. It's a girl?

CHAZ. Her name is India.

GORDO. What? Like the country?

CHAZ. Yeah.

GORDO. That's messed up.

CHAZ. She sounds nice.

GORDO. She's probably a gypsy.

CHAZ. Probably not.

GORDO. So what. Are you going to marry her?

CHAZ. I've never even met her.

GORDO. You said she was nice.

CHAZ. I talked to her on the phone.

GORDO. You can't marry her.

CHAZ. Who said I was? She'd be our *tenant.*

GORDO. Can't.

CHAZ. And who are you to tell me who I can and cannot marry?

GORDO. Can't. Can't do it.

CHAZ. Yeah, you've said that. But why not?

GORDO. Because.

CHAZ. Because…?

GORDO. Because. (*Beat.*) I'm disabled.

CHAZ. You are NOT disabled.

GORDO. I am. I have a social disorder.

CHAZ. You do not. It's all in your head.

GORDO. I have Asperger's. I looked it up.

CHAZ. How many fingers am I holding up right now?

(*He holds up two fingers.*)

GORDO. Four?

CHAZ. You do not have Asperger's.

GORDO. You can't just go off with some girl and leave me alone.

CHAZ. I'm not going anywhere.

GORDO. Promise?

CHAZ. How can I go anywhere? I've got to fucking watch you like a hawk.

GORDO. You don't have to watch me.

CHAZ. Are you kidding? What if you pull another stunt like you just did? What if you grab onto some stranger's ankles at the supermarket? What if you run away and hide out in a tool shed for the next five years eating nothing but paint chips and throwing pebbles at baby animals? Watch you? You might as well be made of cement and glued to the bottom of all my shoes the way things are.

(*Pause. Feels bad.*)

Now how 'bout you go change.

GORDO. I should shower first. If I'm going to put on clean clothes.

CHAZ. Great idea. Why don't you go take a shower.

GORDO. I'm not going to use any soap. You got the liquid kind. There's no lather.

CHAZ. That's fine. Even if you just rinse yourself. That's fine.

GORDO. Okay.

(GORDO *starts to exit.*)

Hey Chaz.

CHAZ. Yeah?

GORDO. You're a good brother. You take good care of me.

(*Pause.*)

CHAZ. Don't forget the pants. Maybe your corduroys. Something nice.

GORDO. Yeah. Okay.

(GORDO *starts to exit.* CHAZ *holds up the envelope.*)

CHAZ. Wait. Mail.

(GORDO *goes over to his desk and picks up a plastic bin from the floor that says U.S. MAIL. He carries it over to* CHAZ *who places the envelope inside.*)

GORDO. I'm on it, bro.

(GORDO *exits with the bin. Blackout.*)

2.

CHAZ *sits at his desk. Across from him is* INDIA, *a self-styled rebel with a blue streak in her hair, in* GORDO's *time-out chair. There is a backpack and an instrument case—a French horn case—on the floor at her feet.*

CHAZ. Can I get you something to drink?

INDIA. Is it appropriate to make drink requests during an interview?

CHAZ. If you're thirsty.

INDIA. I'm not really, but if you have Orangina, I guess I would have that.

CHAZ. I don't think we have any Orangina.

INDIA. Then no. I'm not thirsty.

CHAZ. Alright. How about hobbies?

INDIA. Hobbies?

CHAZ. Yeah.

INDIA. Tough question.

CHAZ. I mean, aside from music obviously.

INDIA. What, because all young people like music?

CHAZ. I just meant, your instrument.

(*Gestures to her instrument case.*)

INDIA. Oh. The horn. Right. I play the horn. Duh. Not all the time though, don't worry. I won't just randomly break out playing the horn.

(*A slight pause.*)

CHAZ. How about movies? That might be easier.

INDIA. Favorite movies?

CHAZ. Sure.

INDIA. Like top ten or just a few?

CHAZ. Just name anything.

INDIA. I like this movie called *The Devils*, how's that?

CHAZ. I've never heard of it.

INDIA. It stars Vanessa Redgrave as a sex-crazed hunchback nun. I guess you'd call it a gothic porno. But there's also this whole historical backdrop too. It's pretty insane.

CHAZ. I'll have to ask my brother—he's really into movies.

INDIA. (*Looking around.*) I thought this place would be dirtier for some reason. Or even just a little seedy.

CHAZ. The house?

INDIA. From the ad. I had this picture in my head—with broken beer bottles everywhere and dial-up that takes thirty minutes just to get onto the Internet. Because it's *so* cheap.

CHAZ. Is it?

INDIA. Five hundred bucks? That would probably get you like a broom closet in Manhattan.

CHAZ. Should I have asked for more?

INDIA. Are you kidding? That's your whole selling point. Besides, I'm like *so* poor right now.

(*Beat.*)

Is this even normal? Being interviewed to rent a room?

CHAZ. I've never rented a room before.

INDIA. It's just that, these questions are getting kind of personal. You're not interviewing me as a person, right? You're interviewing me as a kind of a potential…financial arrangement.

CHAZ. Whoa.

INDIA. I'm just saying.

CHAZ. You want to get a sense of what a person's like—if you're going to live with them.

INDIA. Isn't that weird? That we might live together.

CHAZ. Not together. Next to one another. Across the hall actually.

INDIA. (*Smiling.*) Right.

(*A small pause.*)

What about you? Do I get to ask you any questions?

CHAZ. (*Trying to make a joke.*) Who's conducting the interview, am I right?

(INDIA *doesn't laugh. Just stares at him.*)

CHAZ. I'm kidding. Of course.

INDIA. Okay. Let me think. Okay. How about…. Are you from here originally?

CHAZ. Yes.

INDIA. Do you always wear a tie?

CHAZ. No.

INDIA. What about…how do you feel about the service sector in general?

CHAZ. The service sector?

INDIA. Of the economy.

CHAZ. It's—I guess it's a major part of our economy? Why—how do you feel about it?

INDIA. I hate it.

CHAZ. The whole thing?

INDIA. People groveling on the ground, scrubbing other people's shoes and whatnot. It just seems so demeaning.

CHAZ. That's a very…interesting point of view.

INDIA. No it's not. You don't have to lie.

CHAZ. I'm not. I'm sorry—I don't know what else to say.

INDIA. You don't have to say anything. You can just roll your eyes if you want. When I talk. I won't be offended.

CHAZ. Why would I roll my eyes?

INDIA. I don't know. But if you want to.

(*Beat.*)

Look. Can I level with you, Mr.—

CHAZ. Chaz.

INDIA. This place, Chaz. It's pretty much exactly what I'm looking for.

CHAZ. Well that's great—

INDIA. But the whole set-up—let's just both admit—a little on the creepy side. Two guys working at home. Alone. Asking for someone to come live with them in their weirdo home office slash bachelor pad in bumblefuck, New York. But I'm fine with that. In fact, I kind of like it. The ambiguity. The sense that anything could happen. It's so…exciting. Like there could be dead bodies hidden in the walls, like in that Edgar Alan Poe story with the heart, the one that keeps beating even after the guy is dead, keeps haunting him, haunting his thoughts, his ability to function. And that's totally fine with me. I'm willing to take that risk. But maybe not everyone is, right? Maybe not everyone is as openly adventurous and liberal-minded as I am.

(*Pause.*)

How'd I do? Did I get it?

(CHAZ *just stares at her for a moment.*)

CHAZ. How...old...are you?

(*A slight pause.*)

INDIA. Twenty-four. But I didn't go to college.

(*Enter* GORDO. *Showered, but still wearing his boxers and pajama top, except with a tie and dress shoes.*)

INDIA. Hi. I'm India.

GORDO. You're in my chair.

CHAZ. Come on. We're in the middle of something.

GORDO. She can do it somewhere else. That's my chair.

CHAZ. We don't have any other chairs.

GORDO. She can sit on the couch. It's a perfectly sit-able piece of furniture.

(GORDO *goes over to take the chair.*)

CHAZ. (*To* INDIA.) I'm sorry.

INDIA. It's fine. I didn't mean to take his seat.

CHAZ. You didn't—

(*She gets up.*)

GORDO. (*Taking the chair.*) Thanks.

(*He returns the chair to its usual corner. Doesn't sit in it. Just leaves it there.*)

INDIA. So you're the other brother?

GORDO. I'm Gordo.

INDIA. And you're his brother?

GORDO. I'm not some kind of sideshow. I'm the idea man. I come up with the ideas.

INDIA. The ideas for what?

GORDO. I'm like an electric guitar. Thoughts shoot out of my head like amps and bounce off the walls and hit random people in the audience. And they're like *Help, oh my God, that guy's brilliant idea just zapped me!* And I'm like *Sorry babe, I can't help it for being so electrifyingly brilliant.*

CHAZ. He doesn't actually play the guitar.

GORDO. I used to work at Blockbuster, stocking shelves. I even had my own shelf, "Gordon recommends," which I changed every week so people could follow along. But Chaz thought it was a waste of my talent. That's why

I don't work there anymore. Oh, and I did something kind of bad. Well, not really bad…. But. So now Chaz kind of takes care of me. We're this amazing us-against-the-world dynamic duo. We defy all of Western Civilization's accepted patterns of behavior.

CHAZ. (*To* GORDO.) Why don't you go change so you can join us for the rest of the interview?

GORDO. I already changed.

CHAZ. No. You added a tie.

GORDO. And shoes.

CHAZ. I told you to borrow one of my shirts.

GORDO. None of them went with the tie.

INDIA. I don't care if he wears pajamas.

GORDO. See?

CHAZ. You shouldn't encourage him.

INDIA. I'm just saying—I don't believe in dress codes in general.

CHAZ. It's not a code—it's about getting in the habit of being semi-presentable.

GORDO. I don't believe in dress codes either.

CHAZ. What a surprise. Here, India, why don't we move our conversation over to the couch.

INDIA. Okay.

(CHAZ *and* INDIA *make their way over to the couch.*)

GORDO. Watch out. There's anthrax.

INDIA. Where?

GORDO. In the couch.

CHAZ. He's lying.

GORDO. Bacteria overload—we haven't cleaned it in years.

CHAZ. Just ignore him—really, he's harmless.

GORDO. I'm an elephant. I trample entire villages.

CHAZ. Well then. I guess I stand corrected.

GORDO. I kill civilians with my massive tusks.

CHAZ. That's right. You're an animal Gordo. You're a big fat hairy animal. I'm so glad that you've chosen to tell India about that. You should be really proud of yourself. Really. Bravo.

GORDO. (*A little hurt.*) Yeah, whatever.

(GORDO *takes a seat at his desk. He grinds the ball cage slowly while the others talk.*)

(CHAZ *clears off some phone books from the couch.*)

INDIA. Lot of phone books.

CHAZ. Something I'm working on. You can just throw them on the floor.

(*She does. They take a seat on the couch.*)

So…you were saying you didn't go to college?

INDIA. Nope.

CHAZ. Neither did I. Or rather, I didn't graduate.

INDIA. College is for suckers. It's just a big coming out party for rich kids and conformists.

CHAZ. I made it through most of my first year, but there were extenuating circumstances.

(GORDO *grinds the cage really loudly.*)

(*He stops.*)

GORDO. How come she has bags with her?

(GORDO *gets up and goes over to* INDIA.)

Why did you bring bags to an interview?

INDIA. I thought…you had a spare room.

GORDO. Yeah…but did Chaz already tell you you can have it? He did. Didn't he. Of course he did.

CHAZ. I didn't say anything.

GORDO. Chazenstein, that's what I'm gonna start calling you—Dr. Chazenstein. Cooking up all these schemes like some sort of Mad Scientist.

CHAZ. Fine. Call me whatever.

GORDO. I will.

CHAZ. Good.

GORDO. Yeah, we'll see about that.

(GORDO *exits to his room.*)

(CHAZ *and* INDIA *sit in silence for a moment.*)

INDIA. So you *do* have a spare room, right?

CHAZ. We do. I'm sorry. He's not always like this.

INDIA. I don't mind if it smells like old person or whatever.

CHAZ. It's been empty for about twelve years now.

INDIA. Oh. Okay. Wow.

(CHAZ *stands up and goes over to his desk.*)

CHAZ. I don't really have a contract for you. But I typed up a list of terms…

INDIA. So I got it!?

CHAZ. If you're still comfortable. Given what you've witnessed.

INDIA. Don't worry. I can totally take care of myself. I'm a yellow belt in tae kwon do and I once cursed off this homeless guy who had been following me for like ten blocks.

CHAZ. And you said you can pay by cash, right?

INDIA. I've got it with me now. In my backpack. I can give it to you right now if you want.

(*A moment while he decides.*)

CHAZ. Okay.

(INDIA *pulls out a wad of cash from her backpack.*)

INDIA. Here's the first month. I'll have more later, obviously.

(CHAZ *takes the money.*)

CHAZ. Great.

(*She extends her hand.* CHAZ *shakes it.*)

INDIA. That was easy.

(*She releases her hand.*)

I'm going to go brush my teeth now.

CHAZ. Okay...

INDIA. I'm not compulsive or anything. I just didn't brush them this morning.

CHAZ. Sure. I understand.

INDIA. I don't know where the bathroom is.

CHAZ. The lock's broken. There's a book propping it shut.

INDIA. Thanks.

(*She picks up the instrument case and heads towards the bathroom.*)

And thanks for taking a chance on me. I'll be really good. I promise.

CHAZ. I'm excited to have you here. Both of us. We've never had a roommate before. I mean we've thought about it. I've thought about it. It's been a long time since we've had company of any sort. But. So yeah. It's really exciting. I'm a, we're, very excited.

(INDIA *smiles. Exits.* CHAZ *walks around. Excited.*)

(*Beat.*)

(*A loud crashing noise, like a bull running into a wall.*)

(*Lights fade.*)

3.

The next day.

GORDO *sits at his desk, playing Bingo by himself. This is a difficult maneuver, however, because one of his arms is now in a sling. Something crudely improvised. A bed sheet maybe. Or a tablecloth.*

Enter INDIA. *She stands in the doorway and watches him.* GORDO *seems not to notice. He spins the metal cage.*

Spin spin. Spin spin.

GORDO. B5.

(Puts a plastic marker on one of his cards. Spins the cage.)

N36.

(Puts plastic markers on two of his cards. Spins.)

G52.

(Consults his cards. Doesn't have it.)

Hmmm. What about...G...53? Oh. Will you look at that?

(Puts a marker on G53.)

(Without looking up.) I see you standing there.

INDIA. Oh. I— Is Chaz here?

GORDO. He's gone.

INDIA. Gone?

GORDO. Out.

INDIA. Out where?

GORDO. He's stocking up on nuts for winter. Want in?

INDIA. On Bingo?

GORDO. Here. I'll give you a head start.

(GORDO passes her one of the cards he's been playing with. They play.)

G47.

(Neither one has it. GORDO spins again.)

O75.

INDIA. Can you please pass me a chip?

GORDO. You don't have it.

INDIA. Uh. Yes I do.

GORDO. No. I said G 75.

INDIA. You said O.

GORDO. No. I said G. As in Guantanamo. Or Gypsy.

(GORDO puts a marker on his board.)

Which gives me.... Oh look. Bingo.

(GORDO clears off his board so that she can't contest it.)

It's not your fault. I'm really good at this.

INDIA. I thought Bingo was one of those luck games.

GORDO. Lies. I beat Chaz every time.

INDIA. Oh. Does he usually play with you?

GORDO. Sometimes. Not lately. But. You know.

INDIA. I'm an only child.

GORDO. Okay.

INDIA. I used to pretend I had an older brother. You know how kids create imaginary friends for themselves? I named him Macintosh because we had just gotten this computer—an Apple IIGS—and I spent *hours* playing this game called Number Munchers where this little green monster eats away at really basic math problems. My parents were really worried for a while—they thought naming a make-believe person after a computer operating system wasn't "imaginative" enough. But then I was really good at painting so that made them happy.

GORDO. Me and Chaz. This one time— We painted a dog.

INDIA. You what?

GORDO. We took this dog and we painted it.

INDIA. Oh my god.

GORDO. We found all this yellow paint in the garage so we just covered it all over our neighbor's Rottweiler, Einstein. He looked like a giant Egg McMuffin.

INDIA. That's pretty intense.

GORDO. We used to get into a lot of mischief. Like for example, this other time, we stapled bologna to all the trees in the neighborhood. Oscar Meyer All-American Beef. Because we were so sick of having to eat the same crappy bologna and Kraft sandwiches every day for lunch. See, our mom didn't know how to cook. Or didn't believe in it. It wasn't like a feminist thing. It was like a nurturing thing. She was anti-nurturing in general.

INDIA. Well…. At least you had Chaz as some sort of partner in crime. Not everyone has that sort of thing.

GORDO. Yeah. But then one day he just stopped doing all that stuff. Like it was cut out of him. Now he's so serious all the time. Daddy Chaz. I don't know if you've noticed.

INDIA. He's a little uptight. I was secretly hoping to show up here and find some guy all covered in tattoos and maybe even like moderately illiterate, instead of just some nice normal person wearing a tie. But Chaz seems cool. In his own semi-nerdy way.

GORDO. He's the best. He basically raised me by himself.

INDIA. What about your parents?

GORDO. You mean "Those of which we never speak"? They might be dead. We don't know. It's one of those where-are-they-now? situations. Like on VH1.

(*Beat.*)

INDIA. What happened to your arm?

GORDO. I hurt it.

INDIA. How?

GORDO. Wrestling my demons. They were hiding under the bed so I just, grr, you know.

(INDIA *looks at him—really?*)

I ran into a wall. Busted my shoulder.

INDIA. For fun?

GORDO. It's just something I do.

INDIA. You just run into things?

GORDO. I have trouble controlling my emotions sometimes. That's why I keep getting fired.

INDIA. Do you have...

GORDO. A helmet?

INDIA. No. I mean...have you seen anyone about this?

GORDO. No thank you. Me and Chaz, we don't need anyone else. We operate outside the social order. Plus, we figure they might take me away. If we tell somebody.

INDIA. Who would take you away?

GORDO. ...The authorities.

(*Beat.*)

I don't know where Chaz is.

INDIA. Do you usually keep tabs on his whereabouts?

GORDO. You said you were looking for him.

INDIA. Not *looking* for him.

GORDO. Everyone thinks it's The Chaz Show—All Chaz, All the Time. But I'm the brains of the operation. I'm the guy hiding behind the velvet curtain. (*Beat.*) Boo!

(INDIA *jumps.*)

That was me, coming out from behind the curtain.

INDIA. You got me.

GORDO. We're like one of those famous teams. Butch Cassidy and the Sundance Kid. Mick Jagger and Keith Richards. Beethoven and Beethoven's brother.

INDIA. I didn't know Beethoven had a brother.

GORDO. See? He had two. Caspar and Nikolaus. I forgot Caspar's story, but Nikolaus was an apothecary who collected people's brains in glass jars.

(*Beat.*)

Do I scare you?

INDIA. Not really.

GORDO. Are you sure?

INDIA. Why do you want me to be afraid of you?

GORDO. I don't wear deodorant. Sometimes I wear the same clothes for weeks. Months maybe.

(INDIA *stares at him.*)

INDIA. You're pretty weird, you know that? Both of you. The way you talk about yourself and then Chaz, being this mysterious writer guy.

GORDO. Chaz isn't a writer.

INDIA. He's not?

GORDO. No. He just writes letters. He goes through these phone books and writes letters to people. Hundreds and hundreds of letters.

INDIA. And who are the people he writes letters to?

(GORDO *doesn't respond.*)

So what— Do you just sit around this house all day?

GORDO. I'm pretty busy.

INDIA. Do you do any chores?

GORDO. Not really.

INDIA. Not at all?

GORDO. We abolished them a long time ago.

INDIA. So who cleans your house?

GORDO. It self-cleans. It's a self-cleaning house.

(INDIA *lifts a pair of goggles off of* GORDO's *desk.*)

GORDO. Goggles. For swimming.

INDIA. Where do you swim?

GORDO. At the Y. Mondays Wednesdays and Fridays. I get to use the pool for free because Chaz works there. He teaches random stuff. But mostly tennis. To disabled kids. What about you? Do you swim?

INDIA. He teaches tennis?

GORDO. To disabled kids.

INDIA. That's really sweet.

GORDO. Nah. It's just 'cause he's not so good anymore. And, it's close to home. It's like a ten-minute drive.

INDIA. Did he used to be really good?

GORDO. Yes. No. I don't know.

INDIA. But you just said—

GORDO. I take it back. I don't know. He got a tennis scholarship but then he didn't take it. Stop asking me so many questions. Okay?

INDIA. I was just curious—

GORDO. Why— Do you want to have sex with him?

INDIA. Why would you think I want to have sex with him?

GORDO. Because you're both lonely. Or confused. I don't know. Chaz has never been with a girl before.

INDIA. Why not?

GORDO. I'm thinking maybe he has scabies.

INDIA. He probably just hasn't met the right person yet.

GORDO. Maybe.

(*Beat.*)

I have a girlfriend.

INDIA. You do?

GORDO. Uh huh. Her name is Ivy. She's really hot.

INDIA. That's wonderful.

GORDO. It is. Wonderful. She's wonderful.

INDIA. Where did you meet her?

GORDO. ...Wal-Mart.

INDIA. Wal-Mart?

GORDO. Uh huh.

INDIA. Well I hope I get to meet her sometime.

GORDO. We'll see. She's pretty intimidating. You might be too intimidated by her.

(*A moment.*)

I destroyed the entire "Family Movies" aisle at Blockbuster Video. Two weeks ago. The entire genre—CRASH. Right there on the floor. Cartoons. Disney classics. That one with Robin Williams.... All lying in one big heap on the floor with me right there in the middle. I remember—there was this one girl, a redhead, one of those dopey-looking kids with really thick glasses, standing there, next to her mother, just staring at me. Like I was some sort of car crash on the highway. They told me I had to leave Blockbuster after that. They said I was a "danger to myself and to other people." It was pretty rough.

(GORDO *suddenly bangs his head against the desk.*)

Why did I do that? Why? Why?

(*Does it again. Does it a few times.*)

INDIA. Oh my god— Stop!

(GORDO *stops.*)

GORDO. I'm such an idiot.

INDIA. You're not an idiot.

GORDO. I am. I don't know how to behave like a normal person.

INDIA. Should I...call someone?

GORDO. No.

INDIA. Can I get you something? Water? Do you take Adderall or something?

GORDO. No. I need more discipline.

INDIA. Oh. Okay.

GORDO. Can you tell me to go sit in Time-out?

INDIA. Time-out?

GORDO. Just say. Gordo— Time. Out.

INDIA. Just say it?

GORDO. Now!

INDIA. Okay. Uh...Gordo. Time-out.

GORDO. NO!

INDIA. What?

GORDO. I DON'T WANT TO!

INDIA. (*Confused.*) But—

(GORDO *grabs* INDIA's *wrist. It's a bit scary.*)

I...I really think you should go sit in Time-out.

(*They stand like this for another moment.*)

GORDO. Fine.

(GORDO *releases her wrist and goes over to the chair in the corner.*)

How long?

INDIA. Uh...

GORDO. One minute?

INDIA. Sure. One minute.

(GORDO *sits in Time-out.* INDIA *waits. After about ten seconds,* GORDO *stands up.*)

GORDO. Better. See?

(INDIA *just stands there.*)

What were we talking about? The Y? Did I tell you about my friend there? Kip.

(*No response.*)

Hey.

338 CARLY MENSCH

(No response.)

Hey India. Did I tell you about Kip?

*(A moment—*INDIA *is a bit fazed.)*

INDIA. You'll uh…let me know when Chaz gets back?

GORDO. What?

INDIA. I'm sorry. I don't think I should be here right now.

GORDO. Why not?

INDIA. What you just did—it's awkward now. You'll tell me when he's back?

*(*INDIA *stands to go. Beat.)*

GORDO. He's back.

INDIA. What?

GORDO. I heard his car pull into the driveway. About a minute ago. I just didn't tell you.

INDIA. If you're just messing with me…

GORDO. Count to ten and I bet he'll be here.

(Beat. Enter CHAZ, *carrying a tennis racket and a box of Dunkin' Donuts.)*

See?

CHAZ. Hey.

*(*CHAZ *holds up the box.)*

Donuts!

GORDO. Since when do you buy donuts?

CHAZ. I don't know. I was in a good mood this morning. I woke up and I thought to myself—I should buy something. Celebrate.

GORDO. Celebrate what?

CHAZ. Us. India. Our new little humble household.

INDIA. Oh, I—

CHAZ. No, come on. You're one of the family now. One of the Flynns.

INDIA. Okay. Thanks.

CHAZ. We're rolling out the red carpet—

GORDO. With donuts.

CHAZ. Yes. With donuts. All kinds except for coconut, because I know you hate the texture Gordo. Oh—and I was thinking we could all go out for dinner tonight. Somewhere in town. I thought that might be nice. Maybe Chinese.

GORDO. We never go out for dinner.

CHAZ. Which is why I'm suggesting it now. India—do you like Chinese? I didn't even ask.

INDIA. Sure.

CHAZ. General Tsao's Chicken—is that Chinese? I used to love that stuff. I don't know why we never think to get it anymore. It's so good, right? That sauce. It's settled then. Tonight—General Tsao. Tomorrow—who knows, right?

(*To* GORDO.)

How's the arm?

GORDO. Hurts.

CHAZ. I got you Tylenol.

GORDO. Too late. Damage is already done.

CHAZ. It's P.M. It'll help you sleep.

GORDO. I'm a broken toy on Christmas morning. Nobody wants to play with me. India tried. But she gave up halfway through. She said she can't stand being around me.

INDIA. I didn't say that.

CHAZ. Wait—what happened?

INDIA. Nothing; it's fine.

GORDO. She gave me a Time-out. Ask her.

CHAZ. You gave him a Time-out?

INDIA. Yeah…but, he told me to.

CHAZ. (*Hard.*) You shouldn't do that.

INDIA. He asked for it.

CHAZ. I'm the only one who can say that to him.

INDIA. Okay.

CHAZ. Just me. No one else.

INDIA. I'm sorry. I didn't know.

CHAZ. You're not his parent, okay? He can't have everyone just screaming things at him.

INDIA. I said okay.

(*A slight pause.*)

CHAZ. (*To* INDIA.) I'm sorry. It's delicate.

GORDO. What about me? You should apologize to me too.

CHAZ. I'm sorry. To everyone.

(CHAZ *tosses him the bottle.*)

Here.

(GORDO *struggles to open it.*)

It'll be much easer if you ditch the sling.

GORDO. I just made it this morning.

CHAZ. I know.

(*Pause.*)

GORDO. Yeah, okay.

(GORDO *takes off the sling. Takes a pill.*)

CHAZ. So...

INDIA. So...

CHAZ. So...I taught this kid today.

INDIA. Right. Gordo was telling me you teach tennis.

CHAZ. Uh huh. Jeremy—he's on Sundays. Real cute. Maybe nine. Ten, tops. Totally deaf. Like—nothing. And he does this thing. Okay—so basically he plays every single shot from the baseline. Like even if the ball drops three inches from the net, he just stands there and waits for it. Literally, I'd drop it right over the net just to see if he'd budge, and guess what, he doesn't. He just stands there. Staring at the ball—like it's a UFO coming down to abduct him. And by the time the ball finally does bounce on over, it's basically dribbling on the ground. He would be better off *kick*ing it back to me. I kept wanting to scream MOVE! MOVE JEREMY! JUST MOVE YOUR LITTLE FEET! But. You know. Wouldn't exactly work. (*Pause.*) So that was my morning...

INDIA. Actually. I think it's really noble what you're doing.

CHAZ. It's just the Y—they create all those programs.

INDIA. Yeah. But not a lot of people would go do that with their time.

(CHAZ *shrugs dismissively.*)

(*Throughout the following conversation,* GORDO, *feeling a bit left out, slowly gravitates to the window.*)

CHAZ. It can be pretty frustrating actually. Working with people you can't always fully connect with.

INDIA. Me—I couldn't do it. I'd probably just give up after the first day.

CHAZ. You get used to it. It's like training for a marathon—you have to build up stamina.

INDIA. Well—you're pretty good at it.

CHAZ. Good at what?

INDIA. Connecting with people.

GORDO. (*Looking out the window.*) Holy...shit.

CHAZ. What?

GORDO. Chaz—you have to come see this.

CHAZ. What is it?

GORDO. Come here.

CHAZ. Tell me.

GORDO. Come and look.

(CHAZ *goes over to the window.*)

CHAZ. Oh, the car.

GORDO. You knew about it?

CHAZ. I saw it when I came in.

GORDO. You don't think that's weird?

CHAZ. I guess.

GORDO. It's just sitting there.

CHAZ. It's probably waiting for someone. One of our neighbors.

GORDO. What is that? A Mercedes?

CHAZ. Bentley, I think.

GORDO. It's watching us.

CHAZ. I wouldn't worry too much about it.

(GORDO *paces a bit.*)

INDIA. Did you see anyone. In the car?

CHAZ. Nah. Windows are tinted.

(GORDO *stops pacing.*)

GORDO. OH MY GOD. Chaz. You know who it is?

CHAZ. Who?

GORDO. You know who.

CHAZ. No.

GORDO. Yeah. Uh huh.

CHAZ. I don't know what you're talking about.

GORDO. Three words.

(CHAZ *thinks a moment.*)

CHAZ. It's not Child Protective Services.

GORDO. Yeah man.

CHAZ. No way.

GORDO. They finally came. After all these years. Like we always talked about.

CHAZ. Why would they just be sitting out there?

GORDO. They're spying on us. Taking footage. Collecting evidence.

CHAZ. I don't think government officials drive around in Bentleys.

GORDO. Bill Gates—he gives money to them. The Gates Foundation.

CHAZ. What?

GORDO. He gives money to everyone. Oh my god. I'm going to get dragged off to the asylum by Bill Gates himself. Holy shit.

CHAZ. (*To* INDIA.) You okay?

INDIA. Uh huh.

CHAZ. (*To* INDIA.) Sorry about before.

INDIA. It's fine.

CHAZ. I should have given you a heads up.

INDIA. It's fine, really.

> (GORDO *tries to duck away from the window.*)

GORDO. Wait— Chaz— Did you do this? Did you call them up?

CHAZ. What are you talking about?

GORDO. You did. Didn't you.

CHAZ. I didn't call anyone Gordo.

GORDO. Adopt India, get rid of me. The symmetry. It's beautiful.

CHAZ. You need to relax dude. Take a deep breath.

GORDO. "What ominous black car outside? I didn't notice anything."

CHAZ. I have no idea what you're talking about.

GORDO. Bullshit.

CHAZ. Enough with the cursing already.

GORDO. Fuck. Shit. Motherfucker shit-pants ass-face.

CHAZ. You're disgusting. Why don't you take a walk.

GORDO. What? So you and India can talk about me? Talk about how messed up I am?

CHAZ. You're out of control.

GORDO. Yeah?

CHAZ. Yeah.

GORDO. I'll show you out of control. Just remember—you brought this one upon yourself.

CHAZ. Brought what?

> (GORDO *stares at him. Storms out. A brief pause.*)

India—

INDIA. Yeah.

CHAZ. Hide. Now.

INDIA. What?

CHAZ. Go. Duck under my desk.

INDIA. Uh—okay.

> (INDIA *ducks under the desk.*)
> (GORDO *returns with the football helmet.*)

CHAZ. Gordo—

> (GORDO *stands there.*)

I'm trying to help you.

(GORDO *stares at him.*)

What else am I supposed to do! Tell me. You can't keep doing this.

GORDO. One.

CHAZ. Really. I'm running out of options.

GORDO. Two.

CHAZ. You have to start listening to me.

GORDO. Three!

(GORDO *charges.*)

CHAZ. Ah!

(GORDO *hits* CHAZ *in the legs. They both fall to the ground.*)

GORDO. NO LEGS! NO MORE LEGS FOR YOU!

CHAZ. Stop it! Stop!

(*They struggle.*)

GORDO. AGGGHHHH!!!

CHAZ. Get off! NOW.

(*The doorbell rings.* CHAZ *and* GORDO *look up.*)

(*The doorbell rings again.*)

GORDO. They're here. Say goodbye. This is the last you'll ever see of me.

CHAZ. I'm not saying anything—

GORDO. Don't try to visit.

CHAZ. Visit where?

GORDO. You know.

CHAZ. I DIDN'T FUCKING CALL ANYONE!

(*The doorbell rings again.*)

(*This time,* INDIA *scuttles out from beneath the desk. Without looking at either of them, she exits offstage.*)

(*The sound of a door opening and then closing.*)

(*Enter* INDIA, *followed by* OSCAR, *50s. He wears a cashmere sport coat over a golf shirt and jeans.*)

(OSCAR *looks at* CHAZ *and* GORDO *on the ground, confused. They stare back, also confused.*)

(INDIA *glares at* OSCAR.)

INDIA. AGGHHH!!!

(INDIA *storms off.*)

(*The sound of a door slamming.*)

(*Blackout.*)

End of Act I

ACT II

1.

A few minutes later. GORDO *sits on the couch, a bit frazzled, staring at the football helmet on his lap.* CHAZ *hovers nearby. After a moment.*

OSCAR. *(Offstage, pounding on door.)* INDIA! INDIA!

(Enter OSCAR *from the direction of the pounding.)*

CHAZ. Was there a lot of traffic?

OSCAR. Traffic? No.

CHAZ. That's the worst. Sitting there. Just—waiting.

*(*OSCAR *checks his watch. Then digs into his pockets and pulls out an unopened pack of cigarettes. He holds the pack uneasily.)*

OSCAR. Would it be alright—

*(*GORDO's *eyes open wide.)*

GORDO. Chaz—

CHAZ. Uh—

GORDO. Tell him.

CHAZ. We don't— I'm sorry.

GORDO. This is a strictly non-smoking zone.

OSCAR. Oh, of course.

CHAZ. You understand.

OSCAR. No. You're right, it's a disgusting habit. That's why I quit in the first place.

*(*OSCAR *puts the pack back in his jacket pocket.)*

How long has she been in there?

CHAZ. A few minutes maybe?

OSCAR. And there's no master key? No special trick to the locks in this house?

CHAZ. Maybe she'll come out…if you ask her nicely.

OSCAR. No. Not my daughter. She's very stubborn. She gets that from me.

CHAZ. I take it she wasn't expecting you then?

OSCAR. Oh…she was expecting me.

CHAZ. She seems a bit reluctant to see you.

OSCAR. No…trust me, she wanted all of this to happen. That's what you need to understand about India. She's calculated this exact scenario. Me driving however many miles just to have a door slammed in my face. Sitting here incapacitated while she—I don't know. She's probably watching TV— that's what she's probably doing. She's probably laughing her ass off watching some idiotic reality show on MTV!

(*Beat.*)

GORDO. We don't have a TV.

OSCAR. Mind if I take a seat?

CHAZ. Please.

(OSCAR *sits down on the couch next to* GORDO.)

GORDO. Nice jacket.

OSCAR. Thank you.

GORDO. Can I touch it?

OSCAR. Go ahead.

(GORDO *touches it.*)

GORDO. Feels expensive.

OSCAR. My wife got it for me.

GORDO. Feels like someone ripped it straight off the back of a Himalayan mountain goat.

(GORDO *sniffs the jacket.*)

OSCAR. What are you doing?

GORDO. Nothing.

(OSCAR *takes his arm back. Stands up.*)

OSCAR. So what, you boys just out of school?

CHAZ. Us? No.

OSCAR. Your place. It has that feel.

CHAZ. We grew up here. There used to be more stuff.

OSCAR. I lived in filth after I graduated. A dingy apartment under a bridge. With three guys and a parakeet.

(*Noticing.*)

Why do you have so many telephone books?

CHAZ. It's a hobby. We collect them.

OSCAR. Odd thing to collect.

CHAZ. It's this project we're working on.

GORDO. Chaz's project. He's on a quest.

CHAZ. I'm sorry, I'm just a little confused. So she still lives with you?

OSCAR. India?

CHAZ. Yeah.

OSCAR. Of course she lives with me. Where else would she live?

CHAZ. I don't know. I just find it strange that she would go looking for a room if she's got a nice place to stay.

OSCAR. Right? (*Calling out.*) Did you hear that India? This man says he doesn't understand why anyone would run away from such a nice family!

(*They all listen for a response. Nothing.*)

OSCAR. IF YOU COME OUT RIGHT NOW I WILL NOT GET ANGRY AT YOU! THERE WILL BE NO CONSEQUENCES—WE CAN JUST GET IN THE CAR AND GO HOME.

(*Nothing.*)

India?

(*Nothing.*)

FINE. I'M JUST GOING TO SIT HERE AND HANG OUT WITH YOUR NEW FRIENDS! I HOPE THAT'S ALRIGHT WITH YOU!

(*Nothing.*)

See what I'm dealing with?

(*Pause.*)

GORDO. She probably just hates you.

OSCAR. Excuse me?

GORDO. She probably just, hates you.

OSCAR. Hate is a very strong word, Son.

GORDO. She blames you.

OSCAR. For what?

GORDO. For having all this extra anger.

OSCAR. She's angry at me?

GORDO. She's got lots and lots of anger. She carries it around with her like a cape on her back. Like a big heavy cape.

OSCAR. Did she say that? Has she said that to you?

GORDO. No. But I know.

OSCAR. I don't understand.

GORDO. It's pretty obvious.

OSCAR. (*To* CHAZ.) What is? What is he talking about?

CHAZ. He's just talking to talk.

GORDO. No. She hates him. She's paralyzed by it. It's like a poison from a rare African spider.

OSCAR. You better start thinking about the words coming out of your mouth. Because what you're saying, young man, it could be interpreted as pretty damn offensive.

GORDO. I'm a prophet—I speak only the truth.

OSCAR. Yeah, now you're just making a bunch of noise.

GORDO. I've come down from the Mount to speak with all the little people.

OSCAR. I think you're mixed up, Son. I think you're very mixed up right now.

CHAZ. He's right—you're not making any sense.

GORDO. I make sense. Ask India—she gets me.

OSCAR. India?

GORDO. We're like the same person.

OSCAR. You are *nothing* like my daughter.

GORDO. Wrong. We both like Bingo.

OSCAR. You are nothing like her. You are rude. And…and…immature.

GORDO. What about her?

OSCAR. India. She's—I don't know. Misguided.

GORDO. I'm misguided!

CHAZ. (*Re: the helmet.*) Gordo—why don't you go put that back in your room.

GORDO. I don't want to.

CHAZ. So you don't lose it.

GORDO. I'm not going to lose it.

CHAZ. Please. I really need you to go put that away. I really need that right now.

(GORDO *looks at* CHAZ. *Sees the desperation on his face.*)

GORDO. Okay.

(GORDO *exits with the helmet.*)

OSCAR. Jesus—that kid.

CHAZ. I know.

OSCAR. He's going to get himself in a lot of trouble someday.

CHAZ. I know.

OSCAR. You can't just say those kinds of things. Not in front of strangers. I could have been what—someone with a really bad temper? Knocked his front teeth right out.

CHAZ. Yeah.

OSCAR. Is he like that all the time?

CHAZ. No. He's—well. Not all the time. Just sometimes. More so lately I guess. Maybe it's some kind of phase.

OSCAR. If he were my child, I wouldn't let him talk like that. Not in a million years.

(OSCAR *checks his watch. Exits offstage.*)

OSCAR. INDIA!

(OSCAR *bangs on the door.*)

INDIA!

(*He returns.*)

348 CARLY MENSCH

CHAZ. What would you do? If you were—his parent.

OSCAR. I'd let him know that that was unacceptable, end of story. I wouldn't tolerate it. Not like that. No way.

CHAZ. Yeah. Yeah.

(*Pause.*)

Can I ask you a kind of weird question?

OSCAR. What do you want to ask me?

CHAZ. I know India means a lot to you—

OSCAR. She's my daughter.

CHAZ. Right. Exactly. So I guess what I'm wondering is if you came here to get her because you thought you had to or if maybe it was something else.

OSCAR. Something more like what?

CHAZ. I don't know. It's a stupid question.

OSCAR. What did you mean by *because I thought I had to?*

CHAZ. Because—you have no choice?

OSCAR. Look kid. It's pretty simple. My daughter takes a giant sidestep from reality and it's my job to reel her back in. It's not exactly rocket science.

CHAZ. Right, sure.

OSCAR. You'll understand one day.

CHAZ. I don't know.

OSCAR. You will. When you have your own family.

CHAZ. We'll see.

OSCAR. Come on, didn't one of you boys ever act out at some point? Try to run away?

CHAZ. Us? No.

OSCAR. I did. Run away.

CHAZ. Really?

OSCAR. Sure. But it was different. What India is doing is—well, it's different. Me—it was what everybody did. It was part of the times.

CHAZ. Where'd you go?

OSCAR. Carmel Valley. The northwestern corner of San Diego.

CHAZ. Our mom is from California.

OSCAR. Oh yeah? Whereabouts?

CHAZ. We don't know. We think she was a "hippie" though. We once found an old photograph of her with flowers in her hair.

OSCAR. Why don't you ask her?

CHAZ. She's uh—she's not really a part of our lives anymore.

OSCAR. I'm sorry to hear that.

CHAZ. It's fine. We're—fine now.

OSCAR. It's a beautiful state. California. Beautiful people. Great wine.

CHAZ. And so what—you just packed up one day and moved out there?

OSCAR. Something like that. Me and a few guys, we convinced this friend of ours to steal his parents' station wagon and drive us to this commune we had read about in a magazine. Summer of 1965, the summer before my senior year in high school.

CHAZ. And what about your parents? They must have been pretty pissed.

OSCAR. Oh they were. I was supposed to be working for my uncle that summer. Selling sporting equipment—jock straps and whatnot.

CHAZ. I think I could sell equipment.

OSCAR. You looking for a job?

CHAZ. An opportunity. Some sort of change I guess.

OSCAR. You and I, we should talk. I run a whole string of them now— sporting goods stores. Expanded my uncle's shop across all five boroughs. We're always looking for young, energetic kids.

CHAZ. In the city?

OSCAR. Eight stops on Metro-North, it's an easy commute.

CHAZ. And—the pay?

OSCAR. What about it?

CHAZ. Is it—um, livable?

(OSCAR *eyes him, confused at the question.*)

OSCAR. You got to work your way up. That's how these things work. Start behind the counter for a few months and see what happens. Maybe you'll hate it, I don't know. I'll give you my number, how's that?

CHAZ. Are you sure?

OSCAR. It's no big deal. I do this kind of thing all the time. Plus, this could be a sort of token. For your hospitality. Here. Take a card.

(OSCAR *hands* CHAZ *a business card.*)

You give me a call when you're ready to talk.

(GORDO *returns, sans helmet. He stands in the doorway.*)

GORDO. Hi.

OSCAR. Gordon—that's your name, right?

(GORDO *nods.*)

Gordon. I need to know if you're ready to start behaving like an adult.

GORDO. (*Unconvincing.*) Okay.

OSCAR. No. Not okay. I'm asking you.

GORDO. I'm ready.

OSCAR. One more outburst like that and that's it. There will be serious consequences.

GORDO. I put the helmet away.

OSCAR. Look at me.

GORDO. I said okay.

OSCAR. (*Very firm.*) I said look at me.

(*He does.* OSCAR *stares back. Firm.*)

I'm serious.

(*Beat.*)

CHAZ. India's dad, Mr.—

OSCAR. Waterman.

CHAZ. Mr. Waterman was just telling me about this time when he ran away. Do you want to hear about it?

GORDO. He ran away?

CHAZ. He went to California.

GORDO. Did he go to Disneyland?

CHAZ. He went to a commune actually.

GORDO. What—like a cult?

OSCAR. No. Like a commune.

GORDO. And?

OSCAR. And so I ran away. I wasn't always just some suit and tie, you know. I got my fair share of stories.

(GORDO *goes back to his seat on the couch.*)

I was telling your brother—it's not like how it is with India. Our parents— they were from a very different world than us. My dad used to sit up listening to Jackie Gleason albums and Gordon Jenkins. He was I guess what you'd call "square." I never really talked to him. But India—me and India, it's not the same thing. She knows she can talk to me. We shouldn't be having this sort of misunderstanding in the first place. I'm a very reasonable man. We should be able to reason with one another.

GORDO. What'd you do there? At the commune.

OSCAR. Oh, man.

GORDO. Did you run around naked all the time?

OSCAR. No.

Just try to imagine that for a second. The rush. Kids from all over the country looking for some kind of escape, retreating from the terrible violence and confusion of the world around them. Driving their parents' cars and carrying nothing but the clothes on their backs.

CHAZ. Sounds like such a release.

OSCAR. Yeah…. But it's funny. Hearing myself talk about it like this—like I had it all figured out back then. The reality of it was a very different thing. That place, the so-called commune, it was really just a run-down building in the middle of nowhere. An old abandoned shotgun-shell manufacturing plant left over from World War II. We pretty much just sat around all day smoking dope and eating potato salad out of little plastic cups. Not really doing anything in particular, just kind of sitting around waiting for something to happen. And of course there was no running water. No toilets. No medical facilities. A lot of kids got hurt and had to leave. We weren't getting the riffraff just yet, people with missing teeth and things like that, but it wasn't exactly the Garden of Eden we went there expecting it to be.

CHAZ. So that's it?

OSCAR. Pretty much.

CHAZ. Sounds a lot like this.

OSCAR. How's that?

CHAZ. A bunch of people waiting around for something to happen.

OSCAR. Ha. That's very clever. Very funny.

(*Checks his watch.*)

Jesus. Long day, eh?

(*Plops down.*)

I'm exhausted. I am. I am sick and tired of having to wait for my own daughter to grow up and think about someone else for a change.

(*A moment.*)

(GORDO *scootches next to* OSCAR. *He very slowly and very gently rests his head on his shoulder.* OSCAR *is a bit confused. They sit there like this for a moment.*)

OSCAR. You tired too, Son?

GORDO. A little.

OSCAR. I hear you. I hear you.

(GORDO *continues to rest his head on* OSCAR's *shoulder. Enter* INDIA, *fuming.* GORDO *lifts his head as soon as he sees her.*)

INDIA. God you're such a cliché. Telling stories about your outlaw days in the sixties.

OSCAR. Are you ready to come back now?

INDIA. No.

OSCAR. There's a sandwich from Balducci's in the car for you.

INDIA. I'm not hungry.

OSCAR. India—get in the car.

INDIA. No.

OSCAR. I said get in the car.

INDIA. No.

OSCAR. This isn't a discussion— I'm telling you to get your things and come outside.

INDIA. I'm not coming.

OSCAR. Do you want me to make a scene? Throw you over my shoulder like a toddler and carry you out?

INDIA. Go ahead.

(OSCAR *doesn't budge.*)

OSCAR. India—I did what you wanted. I came all the way out here. Now it's your turn to make a few concessions.

INDIA. I said I'm not coming with you.

OSCAR. You left the address sitting right out in the open. Obviously you wanted me to come to this place.

INDIA. No I didn't.

OSCAR. It was right there. On your bedstand.

INDIA. That was an accident.

OSCAR. Do you have even the remotest idea of how scary that is? Waking up to find out that your child has gone missing? Thinking she might be passed out in some drug lord's bathtub in Queens?

(INDIA *shrugs.*)

Right. Of course. It's all just *whatever.*

(*A moment.*)

You know—Mom was too angry to come. She wanted to call the police and have you stay in a jail cell overnight. Figured that might teach you a lesson. I at least convinced her to let me come instead.

INDIA. Thanks.

OSCAR. Jesus India. I'm really trying here.

INDIA. It's not about you.

OSCAR. Then what is this about?

INDIA. I don't know.

OSCAR. I think you do.

INDIA. Nope. Sorry.

OSCAR. I think you have something you need to tell me.

INDIA. I already said I don't have anything to say.

(OSCAR *gives her a look.*)

What?

OSCAR. Come on.

(INDIA *doesn't respond.*)

Regarding…something you've taken?

(*No response.*)
Something that belongs to me?
(*No response.*)
Something that is my personal property.
(*No response.*)
India.
(*No response.*)
India.
(*A long silence.*)
OSCAR. Where's Bob?
INDIA. Bob who?
OSCAR. (*Slowly, deliberately.*) Where. Is. Bob?
CHAZ. Who's Bob?
INDIA. I don't know anyone by that name.
OSCAR. You both just disappear—on exactly the same day? I find that hard
to believe.
INDIA. Doesn't seem so unbelievable to me.
OSCAR. India—
INDIA. Maybe my leaving opened the door for him. Or maybe he finally
jumped out the window. It's only three flights up. He might have actually
made it.
CHAZ. Who's Bob?
OSCAR. You've hidden him. You've locked him in a closet.
INDIA. Check all the closets.
OSCAR. The garage maybe. Or one of the bathtubs.
GORDO. What's in our bathtub?
INDIA. Nothing. Go check for yourself.
OSCAR. It would be a lot easier if you would just tell me where he is.
INDIA. Maybe you should check the toilets then. And the oven. You should
definitely check the oven.
OSCAR. Okay. You want me to look around? I'll look around.
(OSCAR *storms off to the bedrooms.*)
CHAZ. What is it that he's looking for?
INDIA. Beats me.
(OSCAR *returns carrying* INDIA's *French horn case.*)
OSCAR. Look what I found!
INDIA. So?
OSCAR. You haven't played the horn since fifth grade.

(OSCAR *sets the case down. Opens it up. It's empty.*)

INDIA. Oooo…. Scary.

(OSCAR *sniffs the case.*)

OSCAR. It smells like him.

(OSCAR *puts his hand into his coat pocket and pulls out a handful of loose pet food—small pellets. Holds it out. Crawls around the room.*)

OSCAR. Here Bob. Here.

(OSCAR *makes a clicking sound with his tongue.*)

Daddy's got some food for you. Some foodie woodie.

INDIA. You make it sound like he can actually understand what you're saying.

OSCAR. So he *is* here?

INDIA. I didn't say that.

OSCAR. He is. I smelled him. I can smell him.

(OSCAR *makes more clicking sounds.*)

Here boy. Here.

INDIA. OH MY GOD. This is so embarrassing. Stop!

(OSCAR *gets up from the ground.*)

OSCAR. (*With increasing frustration.*) You're right. It is. Embarrassing. Having to beg my own daughter to give me back something that is mine. Something that obviously has a lot of meaning to me!

(*Pause. Takes a deep breath.*)

But if you tell me he's not here, he's not here. Right? I have to be able to trust you. Now, and in the future. I'm your family, India. I'm not going anywhere. Whether you like it or not. (*Beat.*) So? Which is it?

(*Pause.*)

Is he here or not?

INDIA. He's not here.

OSCAR. Is that your answer?

INDIA. …Yes.

OSCAR. You're sure?

INDIA. Yes.

OSCAR. You're *sure.*

INDIA. (*Averting eye contact.*) Yes.

(*A slight pause.*)

OSCAR. Well okay. If that's what you're telling me. But how about this. Let's say I give you a bit more time to think about it—to think over your answer—and then we'll try this again.

INDIA. You're going to leave?

OSCAR. How much more time do you think you need? A day? A week?

INDIA. Seriously?

OSCAR. I'll give you a day, how's that? That seems fair.

INDIA. You're just going to let me stay here?

OSCAR. You're a big girl. You need to start making your own decisions. I'll come back tomorrow. After lunch.

INDIA. ...Okay.

OSCAR. Just one day though. That's all.

(*Beat.*)

Chaz. Gordon. Very nice to meet you.

CHAZ. Nice to meet you too Sir. Really.

OSCAR. Take good care of my daughter.

CHAZ. We'll do our best.

OSCAR. India—I'll see you soon.

INDIA. Bye.

(OSCAR *heads to the door.*)

OSCAR. Think about everything we talked about. About what it means to be a family.

INDIA. I heard you.

(OSCAR *turns. Goes over to* INDIA—*kisses her on the forehead. Exits.*)

(INDIA *stands as the lights fade.*)

2.

Later that day. INDIA *sits alone on the couch holding her French horn case on her lap. Looks around to make sure no one's there. Opens the case, slowly. Pulls out...a rabbit. Live. Docile. Really cute. Well, cute enough to elicit some oohs and ahs but not enough to upstage the actors. The kind you'd want to take pictures with at a petting zoo. Wears a collar.*

INDIA. You better not pee on me.

(*Holds him up in the air.*)

Sorry for stuffing you in a sock drawer—that was just temporary. So Dad wouldn't find you.

(*Puts him on her lap. They stare at one another.*)

Yeah...I know. You don't like me either. It's okay. We don't actually have to like each other. God, who would even think to shackle a rabbit? Yeah. No need to answer. We both know who.

(*Enter* CHAZ. INDIA *quickly stashes* BOB *back in the [perforated somehow] music case. She rushes offstage to get rid of it.*)

INDIA. (*On her way out.*) I'm not leaving tomorrow.

CHAZ. (*Calling after* INDIA.) Your dad seems to think you are! It's funny you never mentioned him before. Or that you still happen to live with him.

(INDIA *re-enters.*)

You're not really twenty-four, are you?

INDIA. No.

CHAZ. How old are you?

(*Beat.*)

INDIA. Eighteen.

CHAZ. Right.

INDIA. I'm legal.

CHAZ. You're in *high* school.

INDIA. Yeah? So.

CHAZ. So—it's a problem.

INDIA. Not really.

CHAZ. You…should go back. Finish your classes.

INDIA. But you heard my dad—he said he was fine with me being here.

CHAZ. That's not the point. It's a big decision. Probably the wrong decision. I can't be responsible for you deciding something like that.

INDIA. You're not—I'm the one making the decision.

CHAZ. You're too young. You don't have enough—perspective.

INDIA. What are you—like five minutes older than me?

CHAZ. I have a bit more experience than you do.

INDIA. In what—living like a hobbit?

CHAZ. In living out certain consequences.

INDIA. God, you sound like my dad. Consequences, responsibility. Bla-bla-bla.

(*Pause.*)

You know what's so frustrating? Everyone keeps telling me I can't do things because I'm *soo* young. I'm *soo* naïve. I'm so inexperienced. Bullshit. So many famous people did so many cool, revolutionary things when they were young. Mozart. Orson Welles. Bob Dylan ran away three times. He even joined the circus.

CHAZ. It's not like I want to do this. Throw you out.

INDIA. So don't.

CHAZ. You're really nice to have around. To talk to. And to share stuff with.

INDIA. But…

CHAZ. But school is really important. It's where you set up your whole future.

INDIA. Look at you— You didn't even graduate.

CHAZ. I went to high school.

INDIA. And what about college?

CHAZ. College isn't for everyone.

INDIA. Gordo said you got some sort of tennis scholarship.

CHAZ. Yeah. So?

INDIA. So— If you're so *pro*-academia, why didn't you take it?

CHAZ. I did take it.

INDIA. I don't understand.

CHAZ. I took it. I went.

INDIA. So what happened?

CHAZ. I went. It was okay. I took some classes. Played on the team. And then I left.

INDIA. Why'd you leave?

CHAZ. It's complicated. Gordo was having a hard time. I took a term off. One off term turned into two, into three, and so on.

INDIA. That sucks.

CHAZ. No—it was my choice. I made the call. It was the right thing to do.
(*Pause.*)

INDIA. So where should I go now?

CHAZ. You have a pretty nice home, it sounds like.

INDIA. Ew. No.

CHAZ. And a family.

INDIA. Are you kidding? You met my dad.

CHAZ. He seemed pretty nice to me.

INDIA. He's a bourgeois lump of boringness. Ugh. I wish I had been left in a cardboard box on some desert highway. You guys are so lucky, you have no idea.

CHAZ. Don't say that.

INDIA. I mean it. You guys got a blank check handed to you. Someone gave you a fucking blank check. And what? You've just been sitting here in this room, wallowing.

CHAZ. Hey.

INDIA. Sorry. But it's true. You're obsessed. Your brain is like a haunted house.

CHAZ. We've been through a lot, me and Gordo.

INDIA. I know. But so have a lot of people, right?

CHAZ. We were left in a parking lot. Think about that. A parking lot. Our parents drove us there one morning and just never came back. All they left us with is a house full of stuff. That was like our consolation prize—all their stuff.

INDIA. So—you got a lot of stuff. That's cool at least.

CHAZ. We've mostly sold it all by now. Furniture, my mom's jewelry collection, the TV.

INDIA. Why not the house?

CHAZ. You mean sell the house?

INDIA. Yeah. Why not?

CHAZ. What do you mean?

INDIA. Why do you still live here?

CHAZ. It's our *house*. It's where we live.

INDIA. Do you think they're still coming back for you? Is that why?

(*A pause.*)

(CHAZ *stands up. He goes over to the mail carrier and takes out a handful of letters. Hands the stack to* INDIA. *She looks at the top envelope.*)

INDIA. Mr. and Mrs. Norman J. Flynn. 1070 Taramac Trail. Englewood, Colorado.

GORDO. Only eight Flynns in all of Englewood.

(INDIA *flips through the other envelopes.*)

INDIA. Dr. Margaret Flynn. 3 Quintree Lane.

CHAZ. I'm thinking maybe a step-aunt or a third cousin moved out to Colorado sometime in the nineties, and they're just sitting on their porch, whittling a bar of soap, waiting to receive a letter about their forgotten family back on the East Coast.

INDIA. You write to all these people?

CHAZ. Uh huh.

INDIA. What do you say?

CHAZ. Hi. How's it going. Are you related to me?

INDIA. Seriously?

CHAZ. It's more formal than that.

INDIA. And so what—you need to stay here until you get a response?

CHAZ. (*Suddenly embarrassed.*) I don't know. It's silly. It's just—something I do.

(CHAZ *puts the letters back in the box.*)

(INDIA *watches in silence.*)

INDIA. Come with me.

CHAZ. Where?

INDIA. I don't know. California.

CHAZ. What's in California?

INDIA. Something. I don't know. I think I'm supposed to go there.

CHAZ. Not everyone can just up and leave their family like that.

INDIA. Gordo's not your family. He's a pain in the ass.

CHAZ. He's my responsibility.

INDIA. Is there something actually wrong with him? Like seriously actually wrong? He seems pretty smart.

CHAZ. I don't know. I don't think so. I mean, everyone has something wrong with them, right? It's a sliding scale?

INDIA. I'm pretty messed up, but I'm not like running into walls or anything.

CHAZ. Yeah...

INDIA. And he's got his girlfriend, right? Ivy?

CHAZ. He told you about her?

INDIA. Yeah. He said she was "wonderful."

> (*Beat.*)

CHAZ. Ivy is a character from *Soul Caliber*. It's a video game. They have it at Wal-Mart. He plays it on this console they have there.

INDIA. He said...she would intimidate me.

CHAZ. That's because she has a sword that turns into a whip and can do back flips.

INDIA. Wow.

CHAZ. And she has breasts the size of killer whales.

INDIA. Okay. Now I'm intimidated.

> (*Beat.*)

Seriously. You should come.

CHAZ. I thought you didn't like me.

INDIA. What?

CHAZ. I just got that feeling.

INDIA. I don't even know you.

CHAZ. I thought you just thought I was awkward and like, crushingly boring.

INDIA. I don't think you're boring. I think you're gallant.... In an old-fashioned kind of way. How you're always putting other people before yourself—it's just. I don't know anyone like that. You're like a dying breed or whatever. Except, well, it's just that it's weird that no one really notices. Like your brother. Or anyone really. But I do. I mean, notice.

> (*No response.*)

And besides—I don't have a license.

CHAZ. A driver's license?

INDIA. I live in Manhattan. No one knows how to drive there.

CHAZ. So you want me for my car.

INDIA. No...

CHAZ. You want me to drive you across the country.

INDIA. I want you to drive yourself across the country, and bring me with you. I'm really fun to travel with. I promise. Like really, really fun. And I'm a master at the radio. I can find radio stations that you never even knew existed. The stations *in between* the stations.

CHAZ. Why are you so intent on me driving there? To California.

INDIA. Because...I don't know. We're like, the same. We're both kinda stuck I guess.

CHAZ. I'm not stuck.

INDIA. You're not exactly living it up.

CHAZ. I could leave.

INDIA. That's what I always said. Back home, sitting on my bed. *I could leave whenever I want; I could just get up and walk out.* And then, about a year ago, I just started doing it. Getting up and leaving right in the middle of things. Like if I was watching a movie and it was absolutely god-awful, I'd just get up and leave. Or if I was having dinner with a bunch of friends and the conversation just sounded like empty white noise gossip talk, I'd just get up and go eat by myself. Because life is short, right? We're all going to die so we might as well do what we want while we're here. That's what all the philosophers tell you. All those dead French guys. And look—they're dead, right? So they must have been onto something. I guess I'm kind of cobbling together my worldview as I go along. Right now I'm in a very dead French guys/James Dean outlaw place. But tomorrow—who knows? Right?

(A slight pause.)

It's my birthday by the way.

CHAZ. Today?

INDIA. Yesterday, actually. This was my birthday present to myself. Coming here. A sort of Emancipation Proclamation.

CHAZ. Well, Happy Birthday.

INDIA. Thanks.

(Silence.)

CHAZ. What would we do? In California.

INDIA. You could...go back to school. Right?

CHAZ. No, I'm too old.

INDIA. Yeah, you're a regular Old Man River.

CHAZ. And so what—I'd live with you?

INDIA. Why not?

CHAZ. On a beach in California?

INDIA. We could live on the beach. Or Berkeley. I hear Berkeley's pretty cool.

CHAZ. And—just—live there? Like—people?

(*Pause.* INDIA *looks at* CHAZ. *He holds her glance for a moment and then looks away.*)

INDIA. I think your subconscious was calling out to me, when you invited me to come live here.

CHAZ. I think you're projecting.

INDIA. That ad you posted? Your commas were basically typographical teardrops, crying out in desperation.

CHAZ. Now you're just blatantly making stuff up.

(*A moment.*)

INDIA. Okay. Okay. I don't want to force you to do anything. I'm not going to get down on my knees and beg. If you and your car want to come along, then that would be really cool. If not, I would really appreciate it if you could drive me to the train station. I was thinking of leaving tomorrow morning. Early.

CHAZ. Okay.

INDIA. Okay you'll come with me?

CHAZ. Okay I'll drive you to the train station.

INDIA. But you'll at least think about it?

CHAZ. I can't—I'm sorry.

INDIA. Just think about it.

(*Enter* GORDO. *Stretches and yawns.*)

GORDO. Best— Nap— Ever.

INDIA. I'm gonna go start packing my things.

(*Exit* INDIA.)

(GORDO *plops down on the couch. Puts his feet up.*)

GORDO. Wasn't that scary? Back then? When I thought it was you-know-who at the door?

CHAZ. Uh huh.

GORDO. Oh man. Close call. We've got to come up with some kind of plan in case that ever happens again. Stop, drop, and roll. That sort of thing.

(*Pause.*)

CHAZ. She's taking off.

(GORDO *sits up.*)

GORDO. India?

CHAZ. Yeah.

GORDO. I knew it. From the minute she walked in, I knew she was trouble.

CHAZ. It's probably better...

GORDO. Right? Oil and vinegar. Cowboys and Indians...

CHAZ. With her situation...

GORDO. She's a dirty homewrecker, that's what she really is.

CHAZ. She needs to go back to school, figure things out.

GORDO. Back to the status quo. Back to the way it should be. Chazzie and Gordo—The Reunion Tour. Tickets on sale now.

(*A moment.*)

CHAZ. Gordo?

GORDO. Hit me, *mi hermano.*

CHAZ. Do you ever.... Do you ever think about that whole day at the parking lot?

GORDO. *Whoa.* Where did that come from?

CHAZ. Just—go with me for a minute.

GORDO. Wow. Okay.

CHAZ. What do you remember?

(*A slight pause.*)

GORDO. Uh. I remember coupons. Lots and lots of coupons, all over the ground where we were sitting. I remember that.

CHAZ. Do you remember what Mom did?

GORDO. Mom?

CHAZ. Before she got in the car.

GORDO. She...I don't know. Tripped over a fire hydrant?

CHAZ. She put your hand in mine.

GORDO. Oh, right.

CHAZ. She didn't say anything. She just gave me your hand.

GORDO. Yeah. I remember that.

(*Pause.*)

CHAZ. You used to be pretty good at stuff, remember? You were good at English—you even got that story published in the school literary magazine—the one about me and you in the underwater castle.

GORDO. It was a fortress. Not a castle.

CHAZ. I don't know what happened. It's like I didn't give you the right vitamins.

GORDO. You didn't give me any vitamins.

CHAZ. You might have turned out different, that's all I'm saying.

GORDO. What are you talking about?

CHAZ. Mom and Dad. You would have been different.

GORDO. Yeah—so? I would have become some boring grown-up. I would drink coffee and talk about my taxes all the time. I'm my own person. I'm a force of nature.

CHAZ. But maybe—

GORDO. What?

CHAZ. I don't know.

GORDO. Look at me—I'm fun. I'm the funnest guy on the block.

CHAZ. But.... The way you act.

GORDO. That's just me dude. It's who I am.

CHAZ. Right. But—

GORDO. The whole animal kingdom is acting out—remember? I'm just obeying my natural biology.

CHAZ. But I mean—what if I wasn't here? To clean up after you all the time.

GORDO. Why wouldn't you be here?

CHAZ. I might meet someone someday. I might, I don't know, get a job offer.

GORDO. No you wouldn't—don't even joke about that man.

CHAZ. Come on. You must have at least considered that I might not... always be here.

GORDO. Why would I consider that?

CHAZ. I'm just trying to broach the topic. To have a civil conversation with you.

GORDO. Well maybe you should try being a little less *aggressive* about it. You're basically mauling my soul with your so-called civil behavior.

CHAZ. Better than mauling an entire video store.

(GORDO *puts his fingers in his ears.*)

What? I have to be able to talk to you about these things at some point.

GORDO. (*Frantic.*) I said I'm sorry, okay!? What else do you want me to say?

(*A long pause.*)

How about I take out the mail? Okay?

CHAZ. It's Sunday.

GORDO. So? Let me do my job. I'm good at that, right?

CHAZ. Fine.

(GORDO *picks up the mail container.*)

GORDO. Let's see what we've got this week—

(*He looks at the letters inside.*)

Englewood, Colorado.

CHAZ. Yup.

GORDO. You think we've got relatives all the way out there?

CHAZ. I don't know. Worth a shot.

(*Pause.*)

GORDO. It's weird that no one ever responds.

CHAZ. Got to keep trying—

GORDO. Sure, sure. It's just interesting, that's all.

(GORDO *picks up the mail bin. Heads outside.*)

(CHAZ *returns to his desk. Opens up a phone book. Begins typing a letter.*)

(*Enter* GORDO. *Still carrying the mail container.*)

Oh my god. Chaz. Oh my god.

(*Enter* INDIA, *frazzled. Carrying* BOB *in one hand and a plastic bag in the other.*)

INDIA. It's not what you think.

GORDO. Oh my god.

INDIA. You need to stop spazzing out.

GORDO. Chaz—

CHAZ. What's going on?

GORDO. I found her outside. With— With—

INDIA. Bob. His name is Bob.

CHAZ. *That's* Bob?

INDIA. He's a Polish dwarf.

CHAZ. That thing's from Poland?

INDIA. It's the name of the breed.

GORDO. She was trying to kill him.

CHAZ. WHAT?

INDIA. I wasn't—

GORDO. She put a plastic bag over his head.

CHAZ. You're lying.

INDIA. I took it off. I put it on but then I took it off. I wimped out—see? That's the point.

(INDIA *heads to the bathroom to drop off* BOB.)

GORDO. (*Running in circles around the room.*) She was outside by the garbage cans. All sneaking around. I'm telling you, Chaz, if I wasn't there she was going to suffocate that thing. She's a criminal. She's probably wanted by the FBI at this point. She's probably plotting to kill us from the bathroom right now, prying the faucet off to use as a weapon.

INDIA. (*Returning from the bathroom.*) I told you. I didn't go through with it.

CHAZ. Why were you trying to kill it in the first place?

INDIA. You don't understand. It's just so ridiculous— See, my dad actually *walks* him. On a leash. He actually puts a rabbit on a leash, like he's one of those little toy dogs, and the two of them go bouncing up and down Lexington Avenue. Every day. Every morning. It's the most offensive thing you've ever seen. With those little beady eyes. And that sad little nose. It's just. AGGGHHH. It makes me so angry. Because I didn't ask for it. I didn't ask to be associated with all this. This—this—stuff. It was just given to me. Like a tattoo. Like a giant birth mark on my face that everyone can see. UGH—I HATE THE WORLD. I hate it.

(*A moment.*)

CHAZ. Can't you just—let him go.

INDIA. I can't. He's a house pet. He wouldn't survive.

CHAZ. Oh.

INDIA. He'd get eaten by a hawk.

CHAZ. Hawks. Forgot about those.

INDIA. He's pathetic. He's just this helpless little thing my father bought from a breeder in Vermont.

CHAZ. Maybe you should just give him back.

INDIA. I can't. I know it sounds stupid but, it's just something I've got to do. For my own sanity and independence.

GORDO. Your sanity is a little suspect right now. It's in a different solar system.

INDIA. (*Slightly under her breath.*) At least I wasn't dumping letters in the trash.

GORDO. NO!

CHAZ. What?

INDIA. He was pouring that box into a garbage can. I totally saw it.

GORDO. No.

(CHAZ *stares at him.*)

CHAZ. What were you doing Gordo?

GORDO. I—

CHAZ. Tell me.

(*A moment.*)

GORDO. (*Meek.*) I was throwing them in the trash.

CHAZ. Why would you do that?

GORDO. I don't know.

CHAZ. Stop mumbling. Tell me why?

GORDO. She was trying to kill an innocent creature and you want me to explain why I was tossing out a few pointless letters?

CHAZ. They're not pointless to me. You know that.

GORDO. Yeah, but—

CHAZ. But what?

GORDO. Why do you want to discover some mystery relative of ours who doesn't even know we exist? It's stupid.

CHAZ. To you.

GORDO. To everyone.

CHAZ. It doesn't matter why. It's just something I want to do.

GORDO. So you can tell them about me?

CHAZ. What?

GORDO. So you can ask them to come take care of me?

CHAZ. Why does it always come back to you?

GORDO. Why else then?

CHAZ. I DON'T KNOW—OKAY. I don't know.

GORDO. That's right. You don't know.

CHAZ. So. Wait. All of them? You've been doing this to ALL OF THEM?

(GORDO *doesn't respond.*)

HOLY…I'm gonna…all of them? For the past…

(GORDO *just nods.*)

FUCKIN'—AGGHGH.

GORDO. I'm sorry.

CHAZ. YOU ARE SO…

GORDO. I'm sorry Chaz.

(CHAZ *goes over to* GORDO's *desk. After a moment of hesitation, flips it over. Toys go flying. Things break. It's a mess.*)

CHAZ. I need to go.

GORDO. Chaz—

CHAZ. I need to take a walk.

(CHAZ *exits.*)

(GORDO *and* INDIA *stand in silence.*)

INDIA. You are soooo dead.

GORDO. Shut up.

INDIA. You tried to sabotage your own brother.

GORDO. You're an animal killer. You have no soul.

INDIA. I thought it would be so easy. You know, to get rid of him. Stick a plastic bag over his head and not have to look at him ever again. But it's so different in reality—doing something like that—it's so different than just the idea of it.

> *(Beat.)*

Wanna hold him?

GORDO. Bob?

INDIA. Yeah.

GORDO. *(Looking in the direction of CHAZ.)* I—uh.

INDIA. I can't look at him anymore. He knows how I feel about him.

GORDO. What if I drop him?

INDIA. He'll land on his feet. He's pretty good about that.

GORDO. Okay.

> (INDIA *hands* GORDO *the rabbit. It's awkward at first.... He pets* BOB *uncomfortably.*)

INDIA. See?

GORDO. He's soft.

INDIA. I know.

> (GORDO *pets* BOB.)

You wanna keep him?

GORDO. *Keep?*

INDIA. Yeah. I'm not bringing him with me.

GORDO. But what about your dad? Won't he be upset?

INDIA. Probably. But don't worry—he's not going to have to check into a psycho ward or anything. He'll probably just buy another weird pet/symbol of perversity. Like a cobra. With a tiara.

GORDO. I don't know how to take care of something like this.

INDIA. Well. You'd need to feed him.

GORDO. Feed him what?

INDIA. Carrots. Raisins. Hay.

GORDO. Carrots. Raisins. Hay.

INDIA. And he doesn't like to be left alone all the time.

GORDO. Doesn't like to be left alone.

INDIA. Have you ever watched *Animal Planet?*

GORDO. I used to.

INDIA. See? You're perfect.

> *(Beat.)*

GORDO. Could I sleep with him sometimes?

INDIA. With Bob?

GORDO. Yeah.

INDIA. I don't think so. You'd probably smother him. You're a pretty big guy.

GORDO. Oh.

INDIA. And you've got to make sure to cover the floor. He poops all over the place.

GORDO. (*Sympathetic.*) Yeah?

INDIA. Uh huh.

GORDO. Poor Bob. Nobody likes him.

(GORDO *pets* BOB.)

(*Singing.*) Nobody likes you, everybody hates you why don't you go eat worms.

INDIA. So you're okay? You think you can handle him?

GORDO. What?

INDIA. I've got to finish packing. I just want to make sure you're okay.

GORDO. Okay...

(INDIA *exits.*)

(*Singing.*) Fat ones, skinny ones, smart ones, stupid ones, worms that squiggle and squirm.

Hi. My name is *Gordo.* Rhymes with *Board-o.* What's your name? Oh yeah. Bob. Maybe we can name you something else. If you're going to live with us. Guess what? I did something bad to my brother. Chaz. You'll meet him. He watches out for me—just like I'm gonna watch out for you from now on. He's great. He's very patient with me. Very patient.

(GORDO *pets* BOB *as the lights fade.*)

3.

Very early. In pre-dawn darkness. The living room is empty. Enter INDIA *with all her bags. She goes over to* CHAZ's *desk, picks up a piece of paper and a pen, and starts writing him a note. While she's writing,* CHAZ *enters. Fully dressed, with an overnight bag draped on his shoulder.*

INDIA. I was just writing you a note.

CHAZ. Here I am.

INDIA. I was going to try to hitchhike or something. Since you didn't seem—

CHAZ. Last-minute decision.

INDIA. Yeah— No— It's great.

(INDIA *crumples up the note.*)

CHAZ. I didn't take that much stuff. I packed in the dark.

INDIA. We can pick up stuff along the way, that could be fun.

CHAZ. Sure.

INDIA. Maybe like—cowboy hats. Some sort of festive disguise.

CHAZ. Do you have a road map? Any sort of itinerary planned out?

INDIA. No. Why— Do you think we need one?

CHAZ. I guess we could just keep driving west?

INDIA. See? You were totally harboring all this secret spontaneity, I knew it. Plus—it'll be harder for my dad to find us if we're just zig-zagging from one random place to the next.

CHAZ. Right.

INDIA. We should go. Before he wakes up.

CHAZ. Okay. I'm ready.

INDIA. Okay.

> (*She puts her backpack on.* CHAZ *takes one last look around the room. They exit.*)
>
> (*The sound of the front door closing.*)
>
> (*In the darkness, we hear* GORDO *stirring.*)

GORDO. Chaz!?

> (*Some rumbling. A few moments later,* GORDO *emerges from his room wearing a pair of corduroy pants and a tie. He struggles to tuck in his shirt as he dashes from one room to the next looking for* CHAZ.)

Chaz?

> (*He checks* CHAZ's *room.*)

Chaz?

> (*He checks the kitchen.*)

Chaz?

> (*He checks out the front door.*)
>
> (*A moment of realization and then panic.*)
>
> (GORDO *goes to his Time-out Chair. He sits, trying to find the sense of calm and comfort it once provided him, but this no longer works.*)
>
> (GORDO *gets up from the chair. He looks around the empty room. Finally, his legs collapse under him. He sits in one big tangled mess for a moment and then very slowly, very delicately lowers the rest of his body to the floor. He lies like this for a long time.*)
>
> (*Time passes.*)
>
> (*Lights shift to dawn.*)
>
> (*More time passes.*)
>
> (*Then—the sound of the front door.*)
>
> (GORDO *sits up.*)

Chaz!

(*After a moment, enter* CHAZ, *still carrying the overnight bag.* CHAZ *looks at* GORDO *in a loss for words.* GORDO *looks at the bag.*)

Chaz?

(CHAZ *looks at the overturned table. He flips it back over and begins picking up stray parts from the ground. While he works:*)

Sorry about the letter thing. I'll be a lot better from now on. You'll see. A brand new Gordo. I'm gonna make an effort now. The Little Engine That Could. Things are going to be different around here. I promise you. No more bad things okay? They're in the past. They're *so* over with. No more just running around like a crazy man.

CHAZ. Yeah?

GORDO. Yeah. For real.

(*Beat.*)

CHAZ. Here. Come help me with this.

GORDO. Okay.

(GORDO *starts to move—then stops himself. Goes over to his Time-out Chair. Brings it over to the restored table and replaces his makeshift stool.*)

(*Together they pick up the stray pieces on the floor—Bingo chips, etc. Once* CHAZ *sees that* GORDO *is engaged in his task, he returns to his own desk. Unplugs the typewriter. Sets it on the ground.*)

GORDO. Hey Chaz.

CHAZ. Yeah?

GORDO. You're a good brother. You take good care of me.

(*Pause.*)

CHAZ. We might have to get you a new desk. Something more stable. With actual legs.

GORDO. Yeah. Okay.

(GORDO *and* CHAZ *continue to straighten up their respective desk areas as the lights fade.*)

End of Play

ONE SHORT SLEEPE

by Naomi Wallace

BIOGRAPHY

Naomi Wallace's work has been produced in the United Kingdom, Europe and the United States. Her major plays include *One Flea Spare, In the Heart of America, Slaughter City, The Trestle at Pope Lick Creek, Things of Dry Hours* and *The Fever Chart: Three Short Visions of the Middle East.* Her work has received the Susan Smith Blackburn Prize, Kesselring Prize, Fellowship of Southern Writers Drama Award and an Obie. She is also a recipient of the MacArthur "Genius" Fellowship. Ms. Wallace's award-winning film *Lawn Dogs* is available on DVD and her new film, *The War Boys* (co-written with Bruce Mcleod) will be released in 2009.

ACKNOWLEDGMENTS

One Short Sleepe premiered at the Humana Festival of New American Plays in 2008. It was directed by Marc Masterson with the following cast:

BASHEER .... Ramiz Monsef

and the following production staff:

Scenic Designer ....Paul Owen
Costume Designer.. Susan Neason
Lighting Designer.. Paul Werner
Sound Designer .... Benjamin Marcum
Properties Designer .... Mark Walston
Stage Manager... Debra Anne Gasper
Assistant Stage Manager...........................Captain Kate Murphy
Dramaturg.. Adrien-Alice Hansel
Assistant Dramaturg..Charles Haugland

Written for the Global Play Project, University of Iowa.

CHARACTER

Basheer, a young Lebanese man in his early twenties.

SETTING

Lebanon, Then and Now.

Ramiz Monsef
in *One Short Sleepe*

32nd Annual Humana Festival of New American Plays
Actors Theatre of Louisville, 2008
Photo by Harlan Taylor

ONE SHORT SLEEPE

A young Lebanese man, BASHEER, *early twenties, dressed casually, is digging a hole in the ground with a shovel. He digs at different times during the scene but often breaks for periods while speaking to the public.*

BASHEER. At the end of her body. Yes. At the end of her. Body. There are six spinning fingers, called "spinnerets," which make a spinning machine so intricate nothing can match it. These fingers, or spinning tubes, have tiny holes at the end of each one through which spills the thread. Spills. I like that word. And I say spills as the spider's web is actually liquid until it comes into. Contact. Into contact with the air. On the feet are tiny claws to guide the thread, three different kinds. And the pilots. Let me tell you about the pilots: when they are very young they climb to the highest points they can find and then turn to face the wind. And there are various kinds of wind. Today, for instance, is the kind of wind the shapes of jets leave behind. When the jets disappear, their silver hangs in the air, their cold fuel floats like blue threads over the city. Nothing to do with beauty, everything to do with precision. For the spider then stands on tip-toe, raises its *opisthosoma,* its abdomen or end, as high as it can in the air and sends out a stream of silk from its youthful spinnerets. The air takes up the thread and the spinner pays out its line until it is long enough to tug the spider, and hold its weight. Then the spider lets go—and pilots the craft through the breeze. And the spider is not at the mercy of the wind but can haul in its thread or lengthen it to rise and fall in the air.

(He lets out a celebratory call.)

This tiny, perfect aircraft may travel long distances, even out to sea, perhaps to end up on foreign soil. Or if unlucky, to spin its thread on a wave. A wave. That's how they came for us.

Wave after wave, the pilots, covering the ground. Covering the ground with four. Covering the ground with four million. Covering the ground with four million cluster munitions. Covering our streets, our roofs. The bombletts lay their hard fruit in the broken road. And they were made not by God, as the spiders are, but by hands: soldering, cutting, screwing, polishing, testing. And I studied. I studied. Up until the moment of spinnerets, the spiders and their wonders. Of all the studies I could have chosen at Beirut University, I chose entomology because spiders have eight eyes, arranged in two rows on the front of their heads. Eight eyes, imagine it. Eight opportunities to witness an event at a different angle.

It was summer. In the year 2006. The jets took off just outside Tel Aviv and Haifa, perhaps even Jerusalem. And my enemy, my brother the pilot pulled the night smooth and tight across our garden while my sister Ghada examined an ant on her finger. She held the creature up to my face. 'Get lost!' I said.

(*He holds up the blade of the shovel and talks to it as though it were his sister.*)

"Get lost, Ghada! I'm reading. I have exams tomorrow little girl! You know nothing about spiders and soon I will know everything!" We were cruel to each other, my eight-year-old sister and I, because we loved each other absolutely. I was turning the page of my book on spiders. The sirens were sounding. The leaflets were dropping. The kindness of warnings: "You are ordered to evacuate your villages immediately." We had no weapons in our home. But ah the wonder, the wonder of those tiny spinning tubes, of the liquid, of contact with the air.

It was the second raid. My mother couldn't get back home. She was with her mother, safe, across town. My dear father was on our roof. His legs were at the bottom of the stairs. And Ghada had an ant at the end of her body. At the end of her body, on the end of her finger. And she was singing or weeping, singing or weeping and I told her to stop but she just kept on:

(*He sings, first in Arabic, then in English.*)

Little Ant, little Ant
God lives in you.
Take me to your home,
The sky's no longer blue.

I *said:*

(*He speaks to the shovel-blade again.*)

"Shut up. Sing about spiders, you stupid girl! Not ants. Not ants. Ants can't be pilots."

The noise of jets is silence. Until they are done. And when they are done, grace closes its door.

(*He has finished digging.*)

I was going to be an expert on insects. I read all the books in English. I knew the Latin names for silence, for silly girls, for the numbers that surround the number eight.

The bomb that was falling towards our house, the bomb that was fabricated in Nevada or Wisconsin or Indiana, was dreamt into being through a good day's labor and a good day's work.

And then we were hit.

I wish I had been born a spider. *Chelicera. Epigastric furrow. Spigots.* Such eloquent names for small pieces of the body. And to have eight eyes. Eight eyes to see the world from different vantage points in that half second before death when the sky is clear as cold weather, when the sun is tiny in our throats and we kneel at our graves but cannot not warm the dirt, cannot gather our pieces again, nor explain the absence of the love of strangers whom we have never met, only what they have touched.

My sister Ghada and I. We couldn't hold it together. No. We could not hold it together. Our bodies went in different directions. We were. Dispersed. Yes. We "kicked the bucket," we "bit the dirt," we "battened down the hatches." No. That last one is wrong. Maybe… "Croaked"?

(*He now puts down the shovel and speaks sharply to the grave.*)

Oh, it wasn't like that, was it? Hey, I've been to University, sister. I know a thing or two. You've got no sense of humor, kid. …Then you tell me, what were we like when we died?

(*He listens to her answer some moments.*)

You are a brat!

(*He listens to the grave.*)

Alright! Alright! (*Beat.*) Ghada says she has eight eyes. Even though she didn't go to University. Even though she never studied spiders! And she says she saw eight things:

One: that we were, both of us, standing side by side, two clear armfuls of water.

Two: that when the bomb dropped down into us, our water leapt from its hold.

Three: that the wind caught us as our liquid made contact with the air.

Four: that we played out our lines, Five: we played out our lines of gossamer thread with the time we had left to us.

Six: that there was a tug at our lines.

Seven: so we let ourselves go.

(*He hesitates.*)

What is the eighth thing you saw, Ghada?

(*He listens.*)

Huh. She says she won't tell me because I raised my voice.

(*He sits on the edge of the grave/hole and examines his work.*)

I have made a good hole. Though not, perhaps, just for us. Not just for myself and Ghada.

(*He listens to his sister again.*)

Alright. You can have one of my special ink pens if you tell me. But just one.

(*He listens again.*)

With the eighth eye my sister says she did not see anything. With the eighth eye in that moment she heard a song. (*To sister.*) How can you hear with an eye, silly? (*He listens.*) Oh. That's how. Though I am forbidden to tell you. Yet. (*He winks at the public.*)

But I can tell you what she says she heard.

> (*He listens. Then he sings.*)
> *Spider, spider, little boy.*
> (*To grave.*)

Oh. Sorry. My ears are no longer so good from the blast.

> (*He speaks to us.*)

Its not "boy." I try again:

> (*Sings first in English, then in Arabic.*)
> *Spider, spider, little joy*
> *Who lives in your eyes?*
>
> *It was so long ago.*
> *It was just yesterday.*
>
> *Eight times I saw love.*
> *Eight times love saw me.*

End of Play

GAME ON

by Zakiyyah Alexander, Rolin Jones, Jon Spurney, Alice Tuan, Daryl Watson, Marisa Wegrzyn, and Ken Weitzman

BIOGRAPHIES

Zakiyyah Alexander's plays include *Sick?* (Summer Play Festival); *The Etymology of Bird* (Hip Hop Theater Festival); *Blurring Shine* (Market Theater, Johannesburg); *Sweet Maladies* (Rucker Theatre); *After the Show: A Play in Mask, Pralya, Elected* and *ghost* (Keilworks Theater); and *(900)*. She has received developmental support from The Bay Area Playwrights Festival, Rattlestick Playwrights Theater, Hartford Stage, The Providence Black Repertory Company, 24/7 Theater Company, Hip Hop Theater Festival, Vineyard Theatre, Women's Project & Productions, GAle GAtes et. al, La Mama E.T.C., and Greenwich Street Theatre. She's a resident member of New Dramatists, the Dramatists Guild and Partial Comfort Productions. A graduate of the Yale School of Drama (M.F.A. in playwriting), Ms. Alexander is a native New Yorker and was raised in Brooklyn.

Rolin Jones' play *The Intelligent Design of Jenny Chow* was a finalist for the 2006 Pulitzer Prize in Drama. It received the 2006 Obie Award for Excellence in Playwriting and the Elizabeth Osborne Award for an Emerging Artist (American Theatre Critics Association). His full-length play, *The Jammer*, received a Fringe First Award for Best New Writing at 2004's Edinburgh Fringe Festival. His short plays, *Sovereignty*, *The Mercury and the Magic* and *Ron Bobbie Had Too Big a Heart* were produced at previous Actors Theatre Humana Festivals. He currently writes and produces for Showtime's award-winning original series *Weeds*. Mr. Jones is a Yale School of Drama alumnus, class of 2004.

Jon Spurney was co-musical director for the new musical *Passing Strange*, which opened on Broadway in February 2008. At Actors: *Hedwig and the Angry Inch*. Regional Theatre: *Passing Strange* (Berkeley Repertory Theatre). Off-Broadway: *Passing Strange* (The Public Theater), *Hedwig and the Angry Inch* (Jane Street Theater). He has performed/recorded with David Byrne, Lou Reed, They Might Be Giants, Laurie Anderson, John Cale, Natalie Merchant and Jewel. He composed incidental music for *The Colbert Report* and *The Daily Show with Jon Stewart* and a feature film score for *Where in the World is Osama Bin Laden?* (The Weinstein Company) which premieres at the Sundance Film Festival and opened nationally in April 2009. Mr. Spurney was awarded a Bronze Lion at Cannes Film Festival.

Alice Tuan was seen in the 2007 Humana Festival with her collaboration on *Batch* with New Paradise Laboratories. She also authored *Last of the Suns* (Ma-Yi Theater Company, Berkeley Repertory Theatre), *Ikebana* (East West Players/Taper, Too), *Some Asians* (Perishable Theatre, University of Massachusetts at Amherst), *The Roaring Girle* (Foundry Theatre) and the hypertext play

380

Coastline (Serious Play! Ensemble, Edinburgh Fringe). *Ajax (por nobody)*, presented by New York's Flea Theater, performed at Melbourne Fringe in 2001, and is archived in the Billy Rose Collection at Lincoln Center. *F.E.T.C.H.* and *Coco Puffs* were seen at previous Humana Festivals. She received emerging artist notice from the Colbert Award for Excellence for as well as the Richard E. Sherwood Award. Ms. Tuan holds an M.F.A. in creative writing from Brown University.

Daryl Watson graduated with honors from New York University in 2002 with a B.F.A. in drama and a second major in English and American Literature. His other plays include *Prime Time* (co-produced by Real TheatreWorks and PSNBC at the Abingdon Theatre in 2003; read at Lincoln Center Theater in 2005), *The Blueberry Hill Accord* (performed at Stella Adler Studios and published in the Vintage play anthology *Laugh Lines: Short Comic Plays*) and *Snap* (published by Playscripts, Inc. in *Great Short Comedies: Vol. 1* and winner of the Celebrity Judge Panel Award and the Audience Favorite Award at the 2005 *Battle of the Bards*). Mr. Watson also co-created and wrote for the Disney show *Johnny and the Sprites*, starring Tony Award nominee John Tartaglia.

Marisa Wegrzyn's recent productions include *Psalms of a Questionable Nature* with Lucid by Proxy in Los Angeles, *Hickorydickory* at Washington University in St Louis, *Killing Women* and *Diversey Harbor* at Theatre Seven of Chicago and *The Butcher of Baraboo* at Steppenwolf Theatre Company and off-Broadway at Second Stage. Other theatres that have presented her work include Geva Theatre Center, Magic Theatre, CenterStage, Available Light Theatre, Nice People Theatre Company, Hourglass Group, and Rivendell Theatre Ensemble. She is working on commissions from Steppenwolf Theatre Company and Yale Repertory Theatre. Ms. Wegrzyn is a resident playwright at Chicago Dramatists and is a founding member of Theatre Seven of Chicago.

Ken Weitzman's plays have been presented and developed at Actors Theatre of Louisville (2007 Humana Festival), Atlantic Theater Company, Alliance Theatre, Dad's Garage, Arena Stage, New York Stage and Film, Steppenwolf Theatre Company, Playwrights Horizons, The Mark Taper Forum, Williamstown Theatre Festival, Bay Area Playwrights Festival and the Summer Play Festival. He has received commissions from Alliance Theatre, Arena Stage and South Coast Repertory. Prizes include the 2003 L. Arnold Weissberger Award for his play *Arrangements*. Mr. Weitzman received his M.F.A. from University of California, San Diego. He has taught playwriting at UCSD, Emory University, and currently at Indiana University. Prior to writing for the theatre, Mr. Weitzman wrote and produced sports documentaries and narratives for television.

ACKNOWLEDGMENTS

Game On premiered at the Humana Festival of New American Plays in March 2008. It was directed by Will MacAdams with the following cast:

The Majesty of Sport (pt. 1), Jon Spurney
SPORTSCASTERS ....Jesimiel Jenkins,
Andy Lutz, Emily Scott
CHEERLEADERS AND LOUTS ....Ensemble

Multiball: Por que no hay 'cheerleaders' en futbol, Alice Tuan
CHEERLEADERS ....Cheyenne Christian,
Nicholas Combs, Bing Putney,
Ashley Robinson, Sarah Sexton,
Yuko Takeda, Dara Jade Tiller

Welcome to the Life, Ken Weitzman
JOY...Brandie Moore
KATIE...Theresa Wentzell
SAM... Genesis Doyle
ROWDY WOMEN.............Yuko Takeda, Cheyenne Christian
LEE .... Christopher Scheer
TODD ....Nicholas Combs

Hey Batter Batter, Marisa Wegrzyn
THE UMPIRE ....Jay J. Lee
THE CATCHER ....Jessica Lauren Howell
THE BATTER....................................Nicholas Combs
SPECTATORS...Ensemble

Eat This, Zakiyyah Alexander
MA.. Dara Jade Tiller
PA .... Nathan Gregory
BABE .... Katie Gould
EATERS............................ Jessica Lauren Howell, José Urbino

The Best, Daryl Watson
CHRISTINE....................................Ashley Robinson
ANGELA...Emily Scott
TOM...Jay J. Lee
ERIC ....José Urbino

The Majesty of Sport (pt. 2), Jon Spurney

Land of the Underdog, Marisa Wegrzyn
MISS BARKER.. Sarah Sexton

I Hate Lacrosse, Ken Weitzman
JACK...Bing Putney
RANDY...Matthew Sa
STACY...Elizabeth Gilbert
RICK..Jay J. Lee

Extremely, Rolin Jones
JOHNNY...Andy Lutz
JOSH.. Christopher Scheer
JUMP CAPTAIN...Nicholas Combs

Half-Time Show
Performed by the Ensemble

Signature, Daryl Watson
BRANDON..Genesis Doyle
JIMMY..Nicholas Combs

Multiball: The Birth of Rugby, Alice Tuan
THOMAS... Dara Jade Tiller
WILLIAM...Jesimiel Jenkins
FIELDSWORTH ....José Urbino
BOLLINGER.. Nathan Gregory
BLAXON... Thomas Jerome Ferguson
TODD ....Nicholas Combs
CHEATERS .... Bing Putney, Katie Gould,
Jessica Lauren Howell
SQUARES................. Cheyenne Christian, Christopher Scheer

I'm Just a Cubs Fan, Jon Spurney
SINGERS...........Matthew Sa, Yuko Takeda, Theresa Wentzell

The Ultimate, Zakiyyah Alexander
MORGAN ....Brandie Moore
DAR ....Yuko Takeda
LEWIS .... Nathan Gregory
TARA...Cheyenne Christian
LIPPY .... Dara Jade Tiller

GREGORY .... Thomas Jerome Ferguson
DANIEL .... Jay J. Lee
LINDA .... Sarah Sexton

Superfecta, Marisa Wegrzyn
ROSIE ROCKET .... Jessica Lauren Howell
STING LIKE A BEE .... Thomas Jerome Ferguson
SOLID TRIP (#2) .... Jay J. Lee
WAYLAY (#5) .... Cheyenne Christian
TACTICAL JANE (#8) .... Sarah Sexton
JOCKEY DAVE STUPINSKI .... Bing Putney
VOICE .... Genesis Doyle

Multiball: Inside Federer's Head (right now), Alice Tuan
FEDERER .... José Urbino

Chronicles Simpkins Will Cut Your Ass, Rolin Jones
CHRONICLES SIMPKINS .... Elizabeth Gilbert
RACHEL MELENDEZ .... Katie Gould
JESSICA .... Jessica Lauren Howell
BILLY CONN .... Thomas Jerome Ferguson
MR. FINKEL .... Jesimiel Jenkins

The Majesty of Sport (pt. 3), Jon Spurney

Robot Sports Song, Jon Spurney
Performed by the Ensemble

and the following production staff:
Scenic Designer .... Paul Owen
Costume Designer .... Susan Neason
Lighting Designer .... Nick Dent
Sound Designer .... Matt Callahan
Properties Designer .... Adriane Binky Donley
Musical Director .... Scott Anthony
Movement Coordinator .... Nicole Marquez
Stage Managers .... Mary Spadoni, Silka Phyllis Werness
Dramaturg .... Julie Felise Dubiner
Assistant Dramaturgs .... Charles Haugland,
                                                        Devon LaBelle
Directing Assistant .... Wendell Summers

Game On was commissioned by Actors Theatre of Louisville.

384

The Ensemble
in *Game On*

32nd Annual Humana Festival of New American Plays
Actors Theatre of Louisville, 2008
Photo by Harlan Taylor

GAME ON

THE MAJESTY OF SPORT, PART 1
by Jon Spurney

SPORTSCASTERS.
SOMEWHERE IN DEEPEST AFRICA, ABOUT TEN THOU-
SAND YEARS AGO
AN ANCIENT MAN PROPOSED A CONTEST
WHO THE FARTHEST A ROCK COULD THROW,
AND THAT AUSPICIOUS OCCASION, I AM HAPPY TO
REPORT,
MARKED THE END OF OUR ANIMAL NATURE
FOR ON THAT DAY WE GAVE BIRTH TO SPORT.

SPORT ALLOWS US AN ARENA TO RELEASE OUR ANI-
MAL WAYS,
TO RITUALIZE OUR AGGRESSION AND AVOID UN-
COUTH DISPLAYS.
AS WE WITNESS ATHLETIC ENDEAVOR ON THE COURT,
THE RINK, OR FIELD,
WHERE GOOD SPORTSMANSHIP IS PRACTICED, OUR
HIGHER NATURE IS REVEALED.

CHEERLEADERS. YOU SUCK, YOU SUCK, YOU SUCK!

LOUTS. HEY REF, GO BACK TO FOOTLOCKER
AND AS FOR YOU, UMPIRE:
I WOULDN'T EVEN PISS ON YOU IF YOUR HAIR WAS ON
FIRE.
YOUR TEAM'S A BUNCH OF PANSIES, YOU COULD BE
THE WORST EVER,
AND SPEAKING OF YOUR COACH'S MOM,
SHE SHOULDA KEPT HER LEGS TOGETHER.

End of Scene

MULTIBALL: *Por qué no hay estan 'cheerleaders' en futbol.*
by Alice Tuan

CHEER CAPTAIN. READY: OK!

386

CHEERLEADERS. OFFENSE, GET FIRED UP,
　　　　　　HEY HEY GET FIRED UP!

CHEER CAPTAIN. Two more!

CHEERLEADERS. OFFENSE, GET FIRED UP,
　　　　　　HEY HEY GET FIRED UP!

CHEER CAPTAIN. Last time!

CHEERLEADERS. OFFENSE, GET FIRED UP,
　　　　　　HEY HEY GET—

　　　(Sound of a kicked ball.)

CHEER CAPTAIN. DEFENSE!—

CHEERLEADERS. —DEFENSE, WHAT MAKES THE GRASS
　　　　　　GROW?
　　　　　　DEFENSE DEFENSE, WHAT MAKES THE
　　　　　　GRASS GROW?
　　　　　　DEFENSE DEFENSE

　　　(Sound of a kicked gut.)

CHEER CAPTAIN. OFFENSE GET FIRED UP!

CHEERLEADERS. HEY HEY—GET FIRED UP!

CHEER CAPTAIN. 2 more!

CHEERLEADERS. OFFENSE, GET FIRED UP, HEY HEY GET
　　　　　　FIRED UP

CHEER CAPTAIN. Last time!

CHEERLEADERS. OFFENSE GET FIRED UP HEY HEY GET
　　　　　　FIRED UP!
　　　　　　WOO HOO YEAH

　　　*(They do their spirit jumps, when they are suddenly interrupted by
　　　A huge HUGE, amplified mega-sound of a kicked ball.
　　　A couple of 'em [SURVIVALISTS] wanna get the hell out.)*

CHEER CAPTAIN. DEFENSE!—

LOYALISTS. —DEFENSE WHAT MAKES THE GRASS—

　　　*(And then another huge, amplified mega-sound of a kicked ball, possible
　　　bomb—)*

CHEER CAPTAIN. OFFENSE!

LOYALISTS. GET FIRED UP HEY HEY GET—

　　　(Boom.)

SURVIVALIST CHEER CAPTAIN. OFF!

　　　*(More SURVIVALISTS wanna leave the field, and urge the LOYALISTS
　　　off.)*

LOYALISTS. FIRED UP!

SURVIVALIST CHEER CAPTAIN. GET OFF
SURVIVALISTS. THE GRASS!
SURVIVALIST CHEER CAPTAIN. GET OFF!
LOYALISTS. FIRED UP!
SURVIVALIST CHEER CAPTAIN. GET OFF
SURVIVALISTS. THE GRASS!
SURVIVALIST CHEER CAPTAIN. GET OFF!
LOYALISTS. FIRED UP!
SURVIVALIST CHEER CAPTAIN. GET OFF!
LOYALISTS. FIRED UP!
SURVIVALIST CHEER CAPTAIN. GET OFF!

> (*The* SURVIVALISTS *have left the stage.*
> *The remaining* LOYALISTS *climb atop each other's shoulders.*)

LOYALISTS. FIRED UP!
> FIRED UP!
> FIRED UP!
> FIRED UP!
> FIRED UP!
> FIRED UP!

> (*They hold up a huge Butcher Paper Cheerposter:*
> *HEY HEY GET FIRED UP!* [*on one side.*]
> *WHAT MAKES THE GRASS GROW?* [*on the other.*])

End of Scene

WELCOME TO THE LIFE
by Ken Weitzman

A man and woman seated at a baseball stadium. KATIE *bites her fingernails.*

SAM. He's up this inning.
KATIE. I know, I know.
SAM. You have the camera? (KATIE *nods.*) I got the scorecard.
KATIE. Oh good. (KATIE *gnaws. Nervous.*) He hits lefties well.
SAM. He does.
KATIE. .332 against them last season. Of course that was triple-A this is not triple-A of course it's not triple-A this is the show.

> (*She gnaws.*)

SAM. I'm getting you a hot dog.

KATIE. I'm not hungry.

SAM. You're nervous. And before you stuff your whole hand in your mouth I'm getting you food. Food calms you. So give it up. Hot dog and what else.

KATIE. Giant-sized cracker jacks.

SAM. There we go.

(*He starts off.*)

KATIE. And nachos with cheese. (SAM *goes up the stairs.*) And a soft pretzel! (*To herself.*) Thanks Sam.

(*As the between-inning music plays,* KATIE *watches a player enter the on-deck circle. She refers to her scorecard.*)

KATIE. Todd Curtis.

(*A* ROWDY WOMAN *in a very tight-fitting jersey jumps up.*)

ROWDY WOMAN. Todd! Todd Curtis! Up here. I love you Todd!

(*A* WOMAN *moves over a couple of seats to sit next to* KATIE *who watches the* ROWDY WOMAN, *transfixed.*)

Sign my jersey Todd! Sign it right here, (*Indicating/specifying each breast.*) left to right!

WOMAN. Joy.

KATIE. Looks like it.

WOMAN. No, that's my name. Joy. Curtis. As in the wife of Todd Curtis, the man that bimbo wants to autograph her boobs.

KATIE. Oh. Sorry.

JOY CURTIS. I'm cool. You the new guy's wife?

KATIE. Yes, hi, I'm Katie. Fields. My husband, he got called up Wednesday.

JOY CURTIS. Well it's nice to meet you. Welcome to The Life.

PA ANNOUNCER. Now batting number 23, Todd Curtis, number 23.

(*As* TODD *crosses to home plate [which is offstage], the* ROWDY WOMAN *lifts her jersey revealing her phone number written across her midriff.*)

ROWDY WOMAN. Todd, call me! Call me Todd!

KATIE. (*To her feet, exploding.*) HE'S MARRIED YOU TAWDRY BIMBETTE!!!

(JOY *gently guides* KATIE *back down to her seat.*)

JOY CURTIS. Easy girl, easy.

KATIE. Sorry, I'm a little...on edge. I drove seven hours to get here. And I find out the wives can't stay with their husbands on the road, team rules, so now we'll be driving seven hours back, and that's fine, that's fine, he's here, in the majors, I mean it's amazing, but everything's so different and—

(*The* ROWDY WOMAN *has a big foam #1 finger.*)

ROWDY WOMAN. You're my number one Todd. Let's go all the way.

KATIE. —how in the world does that not bother you!?

JOY CURTIS. You stick around a while, you learn some coping mechanisms. Tricks of the trade. Don't worry, you'll get it. You're off to a good start.

KATIE. I am?

JOY CURTIS. You're not alone. You're here with a friend, right? The guy you're sitting with?

KATIE. Sam, yes, he's terrific. Drove with me, keeps me calm.

JOY CURTIS. There you go. You see? That's important. To have a friend. A friend of your own. My husband, he has his friends, that's unavoidable. So it helps for me to have one or two of my own.

KATIE. (*Not at all getting it.*) Oh well Sam's my husband's friend too. He's a best friend to both of us really.

JOY CURTIS. That's often the case. Familiarity, proximity, convenience. Those are all compelling forces. (*Spelling it out for* KATIE.) Someone you like. Who cares how you're doing. You're not following are you? (KATIE's *not.*) Okay. Look over there. Dawn Allensworth? The guy she's with, that's her husband's college roommate. And over there—Cassie Davis, with her husband's lawyer. Celia Fernandez, she's with her husband's second cousin. And over here, with me, my husband's sister. I switch hit.

KATIE. Are you…are you saying that the entire team, that all of the wives are…

JOY CURTIS. Not all. Just the happy ones.

KATIE. My husband and I…we're monogamous.

JOY CURTIS. Sweetheart, we all start off that way.

KATIE. No. I would never.

JOY CURTIS. Of course you wouldn't. You love your husband. You drove seven hours to get here. And you'll be driving seven hours back home. While your husband goes on another road trip. But you'll watch every game on TV of course. And so will your friend Sam. You'll watch together, curse the umps together, analyze the minutiae of your husband's swing together. And in between those moments, and my god in baseball there's lots of in-between moments, you and Sam will have a few beers and talk about life, how you're both doing, then bam!, your husband hits a triple and you're both on your feet, celebrating, whooping it up, you hug, the hug lingers, you feel a little buzzed, a little lonely and…it just happens.

(*The crack of the bat, a cheer.*)

JOY CURTIS and ROWDY GIRL. That's my man!

(KATIE *remains seated, dazed, utterly overwhelmed.*)

JOY CURTIS. Get your camera.

KATIE. (*Dazed.*) Huh?

JOY CURTIS. Here comes your guy.

> (LEE *enters the on deck circle.* KATIE *quickly stands with her camera. She calls out but is immediately drowned out by a* SECOND ROWDY WOMAN.)

KATIE. Lee—

ROWDY WOMAN 2. Lee Fields! New guy! Sign my jersey! Sign it right here. (*Indicating each breast.*) First name. Last name.

> (KATIE *sits.*)

KATIE. They're everywhere.

JOY CURTIS. There's a lot of temptation up here. And it's unrealistic to expect they'll never yield to it. And let me tell you, that's the thing that really breaks up marriages…unrealistic expectations.

PA ANNOUNCER. Now batting number twelve, Lee Fields…number twelve.

> (KATIE *stands again to take a picture.* ROWDY WOMAN 2 *is up on cue.*)

ROWDY WOMAN 2. Call me Lee! Call me! Here's my number!

> (ROWDY WOMAN 2 *lifts her shirt. Her number is written across her bra—first three digits on one side, other four on the other.* LEE *just shakes his head and keeps walking. But then, before exiting, he sneaks a peek back at her.* KATIE *sinks into her seat.*)

KATIE. Oh my god.

JOY CURTIS. Relax. (*She sees* SAM *coming down.*) You're gonna be just fine.

> (JOY *exits [or returns to her seat] as* SAM *arrives, excited.* KATIE *makes sure to only look out at the game.*)

SAM. There he is. There's our boy. Come on Lee! I got you a Coke too. Good to have a little sweet with your savory. (KATIE *tries hard not to look at him.*) Man this is exciting. I wish we could go to San Diego for the next series. Well, at least it'll be on TV. Hey, I'm off at six tomorrow. Why don't I get some beer, come by. It's too nerve-wracking to watch alone. What do you say? We'll hang out, talk, holler for our boy. Sound good?

> (*Slowly,* KATIE *turns to look at* SAM.)

KATIE. (*Quietly.*) Yeah. Ok. Sounds good.

End of Scene

Hey Batter Batter
by Marisa Wegrzyn

BALLPARK ANNOUNCER. Now batting. Number thirteen. Joey Who.
THE FANS. Hey Batter Batter
   Hey Batter
   Batter batter batter batter batter
   Hey batter batter batter
   Heeyyyyyyyyyy
   Batter batter batter
   Suh-wing!
   Suh-wing batter
   Suh-wing batter
THE UMPIRE. Ball!
THE FANS. You look like a dork on your baseball card
   Yeah you look like a dork
   He looks hot on his baseball card
   He looks like a douche on his baseball card
   Well I think he looks hot
   You would
   You get paid two million a year to suck at your job?
   I suck at my job but I only get seven bucks an hour I'm *allowed* to
      suck at my job
THE UMPIRE. Strike!
THE FANS. You suck!
   Can't hit the broadside of a barn
   Can't hit a nail with a hammer
   Can't hit yer wife when she nags you about your road schedule
   When she complains about your cold feet in bed
   When she's all like "Stop leaving globs of toothpaste in the sink!"
   She's such a bitch about that
   You love her but she's unreasonable
   Hey batter batter batter
   Suh-wing!
THE UMPIRE. Ball!
THE FANS. She's cheatin on you anyway, ya know?
   Deep down she likes it you're on the road so much
   I mean she probably feels guilty about feeling like she likes you're
      gone so much on the road so much, ya know?
   Heyyyyyyy batter batter batter
   Suh-wing

Batter batter batter
Hey batter swing batter
Swing miss!

THE UMPIRE. Strike!

THE FANS. You missed that like you missed your son's birthday!
What kind of father are you?
You don't tell him you love him enough
You'd play catch with him but he hates baseball
He wants to be a dancer
Over your dead body he'll be a dancer
Would it really be the worst thing in the world your kid wants to be a dancer?
I mean have you seen *Billy Elliot*, that movie's awesome
Why can't he like good sports movies like *Raging Bull?*
He's five
So?
It'll toughen him up like his old man.

THE UMPIRE. Ball!

THE FANS. Lucky break
You lucky duck
That was a strike
The ump is blind
Yer sittin in a stinky crap-load a luck in your pants ya bum
Your whole career is luck
Doesn't last long
Doesn't last forever
Luck runs out, muscles atrophy, arthritis descends, and then you die
Statistics live forever
Yeah statistics are forever
Full count
FULL COUNT!
Hit something!
Make them remember you!
OhhhhhhHHHhhhhhhh!!!

BALLPARK ANNOUNCER. And that's the game.

THE FANS. He looks sad
Yeah he looks sad
He doesn't get paid to look sad
Oh c'mon, batter, it's just a game
Yeah it's just a game
Cheer up, asshole!

Cheer up, batter
Hey batter batter
Suh-wing batter!

End of Scene

EAT THIS

by Zakiyyah Alexander

In the dark a voice is heard.

BABE. In some ways, seems like my whole life was fated before it even really began. Maybe, it's like the Bible says, some things were just pre-destined. One thing's for sure, I always had the taste for life.

(*Lights up on a very pregnant* MA. *She looks around. No one's watching. She bends down and begins to shove handful after handful of dirt in her mouth. Finally satiated, she pauses. Smiles, and pats her belly.*)

(*Light change.*)

(*Sound of baby crying.* MA *rocks the wailing babe.* PA *paces around.*)

MA. I just don't know what to do. Try as I might I can't get the little critter to stop.

PA. Well, Rib, we got to figure out something. We can't keep on the way we been keeping on.

MA. Done everything I knowed how to do. Rocked her, fed her, burped her, but still she won't let up. Go on and eat your supper before it gets cold.

PA. Man wants to be able to eat in peace, he does.

MA. Woman wants peace just as much as a man, maybe even more the way I see it.

(PA *begins to eat.* MA *rocks the* BABE. *Every time she walks past* PA *the Babe's crying changes.*)

PA. Wait a second. Bring her this way again. Now, take her away, again.

MA. What do you think that's about?

PA. Could be she's hungry.

MA. This littlest bit's just been suckling milk. She gotta full belly.

PA. Maybe she's craving something more.

MA. She ain't got no teeth.

PA. Lemme just give her a little bite, and we'll see.

Just a taste. Can't hurt.

MA. Well, alright, but just a bitty little taste.

(PA *sticks a piece of meat in the* BABE's *mouth. She stops crying for as long as it takes to finish it. Then she wails again, for more.*)

MA. Well, I'll be.

PA. Give her this drumstick to suck on.

MA. She'll choke.

PA. She ain't gonna bite it; just suck on it like a sugar tit.

(MA *gives the* BABE *a drumstick. A couple seconds later the* BABE *shoots back a clean bone.*)

MA. Pa, you seeing what I'm seeing?

PA. Damn skippy, Ma. Think my biggest dreams is finally coming true.

(*Light change.*)

(PA *and* MA *stand with* BABE *who is now a young girl.* MA *stands with a stopwatch.* BABE *has a plate of hotcakes, and a glass of water in front of her.*)

PA. You ready, Babe?

BABE. Pa, you ain't spozed to ask. Judges won't be asking no questions at competition time.

PA. Then I'm gonna count you off. On your mark, set, eat.

(BABE *begins eating; truly it is a feat to watch.*)

PA. Now, when you get tired, that's when you start dipping. That's right, you got it now.

That's it. Keep up your form.

How she doing?

MA. A full ten seconds off her best time.

BABE. Done!

PA. Open up let me check.

(BABE *opens her mouth.*)

PA. That's it. That's it. We're going all the way!

MA. Babe, wash up and get yourself to bed, we got us a big day tomorrow.

(BABE *exits.* MA *and* PA, *alone.*)

PA. Ma, I never told you this before, but I was always hoping that you and me we could have ourselves a little piece of that apple pie.

MA. You still hungry?

PA. No, the America pie. Me and you we ain't done much. But, with Babe, well, I think we're gonna finally get ourselves on that map. Family name gonna be remembered. Can almost taste that apple pie. Sure do sound sweet.

(*Sound of cheers. In the dark a voice booms.*)

VOICE. La-deeze and Gennntle-man welcome to the thirtieth annual eat-off competition!

(*Light on* PA *massaging* BABE's *shoulders.*)

PA. Sure you're ready?

BABE. You're more nervous then me, Pa. But, don't worry. You trained me well. Can handle hotcakes, hot wings, potato salad, key lime pie, fish sticks, tacos, seven-layer salad, fried chicken, Philly cheese steaks, burritos, Jell-O salad, and French toast in a pinch. I'm ready, don't you worry 'bout a thing.

(MA *comes running in.*)

MA. Lord, we in it now.

PA. Woman, don't be bringing that nervous energy round here now. We just cleared out all the bad chi.

MA. There's been a change. For this, the thirtieth year of the competition, they have decided to go green.

BABE. What's that mean, Ma?

MA. Well, they ain't just talking bout food, honey bun.

PA. We ain't trained for that.

BABE. Don't worry bout me, Pa. I can do this. Why, sometimes I think it's why I been put on this god's green pasture. To eat whatever's put in front of me. I can do it. I'm ready.

(*Light change.*)

(BABE *and two other champion eaters sit at stand with plates.* MA *and* PA *stand off to the side.*)

MA. Maybe we should take her home. She's just a little girl.

PA. Rib, our baby girl done got all growned up on us. We got to let her go.

VOICE. Take your positions.

(EATERS *ready themselves. On a platter, a heaping pile of remains is brought out. Bones, rinds of fruit, coffee grounds, etc. Really, it's garbage.*)

(*The* EATERS *steady themselves, a little shocked.*)

MA. Oh Lord, this ain't right. Let's bring Babe off of that stand.

PA. Now hold on, Rib. Look at Babe, why, I think she can take it.

(*Indeed,* BABE *looks, well, confident. She cracks her knuckles, and stretches her mouth. The other* EATERS *look less confident.*)

VOICE. On your mark, get set, eat!

(*The other* EATERS *tentatively go to work, but* BABE, *well she's no match. She eats at a frightening speed.*)

MA & PA. Go, Babe, go!

(*One* EATER *can't take it, and hurls into a bucket.*)

VOICE. Disss-qualified!

PA. We got this in the bag now.

(BABE *swallows every last drop with her signature moves, sure she's got some, why not?* BABE *finishes, opens her mouth wide.*)

VOICE. And, the winner and champion is—

MA & PA. Babe, it's our Babe!

(*Suddenly,* BABE *grips her chest in pain, and falls to her knees.*)

MA. Babe! Someone help! Call a doctor! Call an ambulance!

BABE. Pa, I did it. Had us a taste of the dream, Pa. Don't worry bout me. See, that's why I was put here. So, we could have ourselves a taste—!

(BABE *passes out, exhausted.*)

PA. …That apple pie, it sure ain't as sweet as I thought.

(*Blackout.*)

End of Scene

THE BEST

by Daryl Watson

A skating rink; evening. CHRISTINE, *dressed in figure skating wear, stands at the edge of the rink, tying the laces of her skates.*

ANGELA, ERIC *and* TOM *enter.* ANGELA *and* CHRISTINE *make eye contact.*

ANGELA. Christine?

CHRISTINE. Angela? Oh my God!

ANGELA. Hey!

(ANGELA *walks over to* CHRISTINE, *and they embrace.*)

What are you doing here? I mean, you're here for the Championships, obviously—congratulations!—but what are you doing here?

CHRISTINE. Oh, I don't know. I thought it'd be nice to come back to my old "stompin' ground." Mr. Hinkley let me in.

ANGELA. Just like in high school.

CHRISTINE. I can't believe he's still here! What about you? What are you doing here?

ANGELA. I come here a lot. Just to…oh, this is my husband Eric and my friend Tom.

ERIC. Nice to meet you!

TOM. Yeah! We're big fans.

CHRISTINE. Oh, thank you. Nice to meet you too.

ERIC. (*To* ANGELA.) Honey, we're just gonna be a minute…

ANGELA. Okay.

(ERIC *and* TOM *exit.*)

ANGELA. I've saved all your articles, your photos. You got robbed in Oslo, by the way.

CHRISTINE. God. Don't remind me…

ANGELA. I'm serious. That judge from Switzerland had shit for brains.

CHRISTINE. Well, I am over it. Trying to look ahead to Vancouver. Let the past be the past, you know?

ANGELA. Right.

(*A beat.*)

CHRISTINE. What about you? Do you still skate?

ANGELA. No. I'd like to, I really would, but…you know, my therapist is always telling me that it takes time to heal all the places where we've been hurt. So…

CHRISTINE. Angie. If there's anything I can do…let me know. (*A beat.*) I should probably get going. It was so good seeing you again. I want to catch up. Will you be there on Saturday? I'd love to see you afterwards—

ANGELA. I know it was you.

(*A beat.*)

CHRISTINE. What?

ANGELA. This doesn't have to turn into a thing. But…I know it was you. And I want an apology.

(*A beat.*)

CHRISTINE. I don't understand.

ANGELA. I want you to apologize.

(*A beat.*)

CHRISTINE. You think I had something to do with that?

ANGELA. I know you did.

(*A beat.*)

CHRISTINE. I don't know what to say.

ANGELA. Say, "I'm sorry."

CHRISTINE. It wasn't me. I don't know how much more…emphatic I can be about that. It was not me. I swear to you. I wasn't even at that party.

ANGELA. You knew I'd be there…

CHRISTINE. Angie, look…

ANGELA. …you told those guys what I looked like…

CHRISTINE. This is crazy.

ANGELA. …you had them wait for me…

CHRISTINE. I can't believe you think…

ANGELA. …they shattered my leg so that you could go to Sectionals. I was the only competition you had, and—

(TOM *and* ERIC *enter, behind* CHRISTINE.)

CHRISTINE. Look: I know you're hurting right now, and you want someone to blame and I'm the obvious target. But I can't believe that you think that I would even be capable of doing something like that. What kind of person do you think I am? You think I would break your leg just to get into Sectionals? I didn't need to do that, Angie because the truth is, I would have beat you anyway.

ANGELA. I'm going to ask you one more time to apologize.

(*A beat.*)

CHRISTINE. I'm not apologizing for something I didn't do.

(ANGELA *nods to* ERIC *and* TOM, *who grab* CHRISTINE *from behind.*)

Hey! HEY! What are you...let go of me! Let go! HELP!!

(TOM *pulls a crowbar from underneath his coat and hands it to* ANGELA.)

ANGELA. I really don't want to have to do this.

CHRISTINE. MR. HINKLEY! MR. HINKLEY, HELP!

ANGELA. He's gone for the night. He left me the keys. It's just you and me.

CHRISTINE. Angie. Please, please, please don't do this.

ANGELA. I won't if you tell me the truth.

CHRISTINE. I am telling you the truth!

ANGELA. Christine—

CHRISTINE. It wasn't me!

ANGELA. DON'T LIE TO ME! (*A beat.*) Don't lie to me, Chrissie. Don't do it.

CHRISTINE. I swear. I swear to God. I swear on my mother's grave...

(ANGELA *gives a nod to* TOM. TOM *grabs hold of* CHRISTINE's *leg and tries to hold it out.* CHRISTINE *squirms and kicks, wiggling it out of his grasp.*)

No! NO!

ANGELA. Tom, would you...come on!

TOM. I'm trying. She's moving all over the place!

ANGELA. Eric!

(ERIC *pulls out a switchblade and brings it to* CHRISTINE's *neck.*)

ERIC. You're gonna wanna stop moving that leg.

(CHRISTINE *goes still.* TOM *grabs her leg and holds it out for* ANGELA.)

CHRISTINE. Please...please...

ANGELA. (*To* TOM.) You got it now?

TOM. Yeah. Just don't hit me.

ANGELA. How am I going to hit you if I'm aiming right there?

(*She pokes* CHRISTINE's *knee with the crowbar.*)

CHRISTINE. OKAY! Okay, okay...

ANGELA. Okay what?

CHRISTINE. I'm sorry.

ANGELA. You're sorry what?

CHRISTINE. I'm sorry I asked them to hurt you.

(*A beat.*)

ANGELA. How could you do that?

CHRISTINE. I had to get out of here. I had to get into a good school...

ANGELA. A what?

CHRISTINE. I needed this scholarship, and I had to make it to Sectionals in order to qualify—

ANGELA. You fucked up my life so that you could get a scholarship?

CHRISTINE. My family had nothing! You know that. You know that our whole lives we've barely been able to make ends meet—

ANGELA. Yeah? Where do you think I was? In the Ritz Carlton every day eating caviar off of Ricky Martin's ass? You don't think I wanted to get out of this shithole? I wanted to go to college too! I wanted to go to Oslo too! I wa... (*A beat.*) You were my friend. I trusted you.

CHRISTINE. It wasn't personal, Angie. Only one of us was gonna qualify for Sectionals and it needed to be *me.* You would have done the same thing.

ANGELA. But see...I didn't!

CHRISTINE. Only 'cause you were already better than me.

(*A beat.*)

ANGELA. You're just saying that. (*A beat.*) Say it again.

CHRISTINE. You were better than me.

ANGELA. Again.

CHRISTINE. You were better than me. And everything I got, you deserved.

(ANGELA *raises the crowbar and brings it down.* CHRISTINE *screams... but* ANGELA *only hits the ice, inches away from her leg.* ANGELA *nods to* ERIC *and* TOM, *who drop* CHRISTINE *on the ground.* ANGELA *kneels beside her.*)

ANGELA. Fifty percent. Prizes, endorsements, appearances, whatever comes from this. I get fifty percent.

CHRISTINE. You can't—

(ANGELA *pulls out a tape recorder, hits "rewind" and then "play.")*

CHRISTINE. (*Voice Over.*) "I'm sorry I asked them to hurt you. I just…"

(ANGELA *presses "stop."*)

ANGELA. Or I can send this to the Association. And then I can press charges.

(*A beat.*)

CHRISTINE. Okay.

ANGELA. It was good seeing you again, Christine. I'm glad we had this talk.

(ANGELA, ERIC *and* TOM *head toward the exit.* ANGELA *turns around.*)

Oh, and I'll be there on Saturday. Cheering you on, okay?

CHRISTINE. Okay.

ANGELA. Cool. Break a leg!

End of Scene

THE MAJESTY OF SPORT, *PART 2*

by Jon Spurney

SPORTSCASTERS.
SPORT DELIGHTS IN THE MASCULINE, AND YOU DON'T
HAVE TO BE A FAN
TO APPRECIATE AND REVEL IN THE WONDER THAT IS
MAN.
AND STRIPPED OF FEMININE WEAKNESS, MEN CAN
FINALLY BE THEIR BEST
AND CAPTURE GLORY ON THE FIELDS OF UNBRIDLED
MANLINESS.
CHEERLEADERS.
GIVE ME AN L-A-T! GIVE ME AN E-N-T! WHAT'S THAT
SPELL?
LATENT HO-MO-SEX-U-A-LI-TY!
LOUTS. I LIKE TO PAT THE FANNY OF MY FAVORITE TIGHT
END,
AND GRECO-ROMAN WRESTLING'S A GREAT WAY TO
MAKE A FRIEND.

AND WHEN I'M AT THE STADIUM IT'S CERTAINLY
ROUTINE
TO HEAR THEM PLAY "YMCA" OR MAYBE SOME OLD
SONG BY QUEEN.

I'M NOT SURE WHAT YOU MEAN...

End of Scene

LAND OF THE UNDERDOG

by Marisa Wegrzyn

MISS BARKER. I was friends with Jack who worked processing and feeding dogs at the pound. Strays. Dogs dumped along the road. Family pets too big to flush. Jack lit up every time I strolled through those doors, every few months or so, like clockwork, or so. I was going to adopt, and it was nice for Jack to release a dog who'd be put down anyway. I take the dogs nobody wants. I'm the Daddy Warbucks who takes the hard-knock-life Li'l Orphan Annie. And Jack would ask, "How's that last doggy you picked up doing?" Real fine, Jack, thanks. Settled down and settled in. I take my time at the pound. Strolling through the barking serenade. God, I love it there. So much potential rattling those bars. I see the wily and wild-eyed mutts, those loveable loser pups who'd do anything for a second chance in life. I can't say no to that ambition. (*Points.*) That one. I want that one. He's mine. Jack processes the adoption, looks the other way. I used to pick dogs with a long strong snout, a snout that would take a couple wraps of duct tape so he wouldn't bite my fighter. But then I thought—no. No. What if one of these mutts is a fighter, and I'd never know treating him like training bait—which is what he was. My boyfriend Rick—we met at the fights last year, locked eyes through the kick-up of sawdust, very romantic—Rick says, "Can't teach a worm on a hook to swim like a fish" and that I have watched *Rocky* too many times. God, Rick, there is no such thing as watching *Rocky* too many times! He also says that compassion is not financially responsible. He's right. But so what? I pick my bait dog with some fight and give it a shot at something better, and if a dog pound mutt takes a bite out of my first string fighter in training, God bless, 'cause America's heart pumps fast and hot for the underdog. Now you go to those fights, concrete and blood and fluorescent lights, fat men with fat wallets and beer cans sweating in their hands, might make you sick to think these dogs are fighting to make it to tomorrow. But we're all fighting to make it to tomorrow. It's just a little more fun to think we're fighting to win.

End of Scene

I HATE LACROSSE
by Ken Weitzman

Lacrosse field and bleachers.
JACK, short and thin, sits.
RANDY enters.

JACK. Dude, welcome to senior year.

RANDY. Not till tomorrow. Don't rush me.

JACK. Looking forward to it are you?

RANDY. To it ending and to my getting the hell out of here. Why'd we have to meet here? *This field.* Worst moment of junior year hands down. And the stupidest thing you ever convinced me to do. Trying out for the lacrosse team.

JACK. It wasn't that bad was it?

RANDY. Rick the Dick on the P.A. announcing to the whole school that I was cut because my "stick" was too small? Public ridicule, the end of my sex life which had never begun? You're right, not that bad. (*Bellowing out to the field.*) I hate lacrosse! I hate lacrosse players! I hate Rick the Dick! I HATE HIGH SCHOOL!

JACK. Breathe. (RANDY *does.*) Sit. (RANDY *sits. Calms. A beat.*) It's going to be better this year. I promise you.

RANDY. Don't. Don't start.

JACK. What?

RANDY. I can't do it, Jack. I can't.

JACK. What can't you—

RANDY. The hope. The promises. The big day-before-school-starts *Revenge of the Nerds* master plan. "This is our year, Randy, we'll show 'em." No. Whatever it is you've dreamed up, whatever it is you are going to try to convince me of, I'm not doing it. Not this year.

JACK. Take it easy. Jeez, school hasn't even started and you're all worked up. Come on, sit down. You haven't even asked me about chemistry camp.

RANDY. Sorry, I…I'm sorry. How was chemistry camp?

JACK. Awesome. Let's try out again.

RANDY. For the chem team?

JACK. For the lacrosse team.

RANDY. Are you on drugs?

JACK. Steroids mostly. Anabolic. A little HGH thrown in. (*Off* RANDY's *unsure look.*) Gotta love chemistry camp.

RANDY. What?

JACK. It's completely easy. Get online, order the raw material from China, add water. It's working wonders already. Check it. Watch me jump over stuff.

(JACK *jumps over stuff.*)

By the time lacrosse season rolls around, forget about it.

(JACK *pulls out a syringe with a bow on it.*)

Tada. For you.

RANDY. You made me steroids?

JACK. Deca-Durabolin. Good starter steroid.

RANDY. Jack.

JACK. Last year I…well, I feel bad about what happened. Responsible. Especially with Rick the Dick and that P.A. announcement. But this year—

RANDY. Jack, are you really taking this stuff? There are serious side effects.

JACK. For long-term use. I'm talking just a few months. Dude, it's our senior year. And it's just a little testosterone boost. Adjusting our levels to what Rick the Dick is lucky enough to be born with. And maybe a little boost is all you need—to finally ask out your beloved Stacy Lynn. You know, I could put in a good word for you if you want. Seriously, we're friends now.

RANDY. Yeah right. I bet she's on her way right now to say hello.

(*On cue,* STACY *enters. She does so athletically.*)

STACY. Kick-ass, this stuff really works. My man Jack-attack.

(*They do a nifty high-five.*)

JACK. Hey, you remember Randy.

(STACY *turns.*)

RANDY. H…hi. Stacy.

(STACY *walks to* RANDY, *looks right at him.*)

STACY. Randy, remember this: it's not the size of the lacrosse stick that matters, it's how you wield it. (*Hold a beat, then she turns abruptly, tone shift.*) Jack-attack! Hook me.

(JACK *gives her her stash.*)

JACK. Good luck with your floor routine.

STACY. Don't need it. Not anymore.

(STACY *exits athletically.*)

RANDY. You put her up to that. You totally did.

JACK. I think she likes you.

RANDY. Right. She's Rick the Dick's girlfriend.

JACK. For now.

RANDY. Do you really…you really think she might like me?

JACK. You had her at h…hi.

RANDY. (*Fighting off temptation.*) No. No. I am not doing steroids. I am not. I am not, I am not, I am not.

(JACK *takes down his pants.*)

What are you doing?

JACK. The *gluteus medius* muscle, it's the recommended site for injection. Dude, taking it orally is a no-no, it seriously taxes your liver. (*He takes out an alcohol swab and cleans a patch of skin.*) It's no big deal. You'll see.

(RANDY *holds out the syringe, unsure.* RICK THE DICK *enters with his lacrosse stick.*)

RICK THE DICK. Excuse me boys. I believe GLAAD meets on the badminton court.

RANDY. What? No, we—

RICK THE DICK. And here I thought you two couldn't get any lower on the social food chain. Now you two run along, I'm meeting Stacy here. A little beneath-the-bleachers rendezvous. Boo-yeah.

JACK. She's not coming.

RICK THE DICK. Oh no, little Jackie. And why is that?

JACK. Because she was here already. With Randy.

RANDY. (*Panicked.*) Jack.

RICK THE DICK. Randy? My girl was with dandy-Randy and his little needle? I don't think so. Not when she can have (*He pokes his stick out from between his legs.*) RICK THE STICK—!

(*On "Stick," JACK grabs the stick and jams it up into* RICK's *crotch. RICK goes down. JACK takes the stick and beats RICK repeatedly with it. Then he stops. Then he beats RICK some more. Or maybe he chokes RICK unconscious. Overkill. Way over-the-top overkill. Then he stops and stands over a thoroughly beaten, perhaps unconscious RICK.*)

JACK. That was for the P.A. announcement.

(JACK *drops the stick and turns to walk away, but decides to kick RICK in the gut first.*)

(*Finally JACK moves away and over to an awed and a bit freaked out* RANDY.)

JACK. (*Matter-of-fact.*) 'Roid rage. Some say side effect, I say perk.

(*A beat, then RANDY slowly hands back JACK's syringe.*)

(*But it's not to return it, it turns out. Because RANDY now lowers his pants, and offers his gluteus for injection.*)

End of Scene

EXTREMELY

by Rolin Jones

The opening to Metallica's "St. Anger" in the dark. Lights up, music out.
The sound of wintery wind.
JOHNNY (suited up for wintery fearlessness) stands at the top of a mountain,
an extreme snowboard under his feet. That look in his eyes, please. You never
had that look. You don't even know what that look is about.

JOHNNY. Broke my collarbone riding a mountain bike in Death Valley.
Dislocated my shoulder on a category six rapid. Went cliff diving in Costa
Rica, punctured a lung, shattered eight ribs. Had a finger sewn back on. Even
tried something called lava hockey. Yeah. Pretty fucked up. But that's how I
live. I'm an extreme sportsman.

(JOHNNY's best friend, JOSH, walks up with an extreme snowboard
tucked under one arm, squeezing an extreme hand grip, working his extreme
forearm.)

I don't belong to a gym. I don't play beer league softball with the guys at
work. I don't have a fantasy football team. I live. Extremely.

JOSH. Who you talking to, Johnny?

JOHNNY. Them.

JOSH. Tsup.

JOHNNY. This is Josh. Tell them why we board.

(JOHNNY reaches into his snowsuit, grabs an extreme drink. Pop. Chug.
Crush. Hyped.)

JOSH. We fucking board because we're fucking bored. Tsup. No, I don't
know man, I got into extreme boarding because I was tired of the fucking
system, you know what I mean? Nine reasons to blow your fucking head off
five times a day, seven days a week, get old, shit in a bag, look over at your
old lady, she's growing a mustache. Fuck that.

(JOSH hands JOHNNY the forearm grip. JOSH pulls out a beer. Chug.
Guzzle. Crush. Buzzed.)

JOHNNY. I met Josh at AA. Bunch of sob stories with that crew. Hi, my
name is Dickhead and I'm weak. Hi, Dickhead. I've been sober for three
days. Way to go, Dickhead. Group therapy, pity party, circle jerk, call it what
you want. I needed something else. So I locked eyes with Josh here and we
dedicated our lives to living on the edge.

JOSH. I love beer.

JOHNNY. Josh still drinks.

JOSH. I fucking love beer.

JOHNNY. I do too, but not before I board. You end up pissing in your snowsuit and the ladies ain't fucking feeling that back at the lodge.

(JOSH *locks into his snowboard.*)

JOSH. Beer don't break your heart.

JOHNNY. See y'all down at the bottom.

JOSH. Suck it.

(*Cue Metallica. They push off, begin boarding. [This should be quick and fairly cheesy—they pivot around in the relatively same place, shit flies past them.] They pass trees [actors in black wearing branches.] They skid snow into a skier [bucket of "snow" throw at skier, wipe out.]*)

SKIER. Assholes!

(*They maneuver around a couple of slalom flags [actors in black carrying flags]. They board straight down, gaining speed. JOHNNY takes out hand gun. A deer runs by [actor in black carrying deer]. JOHNNY shoots the deer.*)

JOSH. Tsup.

(*They skid some snow the opposite way [bucket of "snow" thrown into the face of Chris Isherwood conveniently seated in the front row]. They dismount.*)

JOSH & JOHNNY. Exxttrreeemmmeeee!

(JOHNNY *puts away his gun.* JOSH *takes out a beer and a bowie knife, stabs the beer and "shotguns" it.*)

JOHNNY. It's kinda extreme. Mildly extreme. And I could do that mountain all day if I wanted to but Josh here is on parole. And they got all these goddamn rules about firearms. And well, we stole these snowboards. We work at the Simi Valley Sizzler. Not that bullshit Sizzler off the one-eighteen. Those dudes suck. We're at the one near the Reagan Library.

(JOHNNY *rips off his snow gear. He's wearing his preppy best.* JOSH *finishes the beer and belches.*)

JOSH. Protein.

JOHNNY. What's wrong with a power bar?

JOSH. I don't know, what's wrong with being gay?

(JOSH *hits him in the nut sack.* JOHNNY *falls to his knees.* JOSH *rips off his snow clothes. Underneath he's wearing chinos and a gold shirt.*)

What Johnny's taking forever to say is you don't need a board and a fucking mountain to be extreme. Extreme's a state of mind, man. It's guide for living. It's like the other day. We get invited to a work party. We work at the Sizzler over by the Reagan Library.

JOHNNY. I told them that already.

JOSH. Dude, that bitch had Alzheimer's. You think that's easy?

JOHNNY. No one cares.

JOSH. You think it's easy waking up one morning you're the President of the United States, the next you're taking a shit, pointing at the bowl, saying look I made apple pie. Tsup.

JOHNNY. So corporate throws this party for both the Sizzlers in the Simi Valley area.

> *(A badminton net, a cooler are placed on stage. The faint sound of Mariachi music in the distance.)*

JOSH. Tsup.

JOHNNY. It's at some jerk-off public park. The fry cooks are playing their Mariachi.

JOSH. I like them Latinas, man. They call you Papi n' shit.

JOHNNY. Typical Sizzler reach-around. Thanks for making the cheese toast, sorry you don't have health insurance. But here's some pizza and Heineken and a badminton set. Fuck you.

> *(They are handed badminton rackets. An actor in all black holds a black pole with a shuttlecock at the end of it.* JOSH *and* JOHNNY *begin playing. The shuttlecock bounces back and forth over the net.)*

JOSH. Shuttlecock.

JOHNNY. You'd think it was extreme 'cause of the name.

JOSH. Shuttle like the space shuttle. And cock. Says it all.

JOHNNY. But it's just some racket and a net and you could practically put together one of them IKEA chairs and play at the same time.

JOSH. Even if you're playing against some hot girl and her boobs are knocking up and down, it's boring.

JOHNNY. So we take it up to another level.

JOSH. We throw in another shuttlecock.

> *(Another actor in black with another shuttlecock pole.)*

JOHNNY. Two cocks.

JOSH. Four if you're counting ourselves.

JOHNNY. Good one.

JOSH. Tsup.

JOHNNY. And that's cool for about thirty seconds but it gets fucking boring again. So we get another racket, throw in another cock.

> *(They are each handed another racket, another actor in black with another shuttlecock pole. Extreme shuttlecock ballet.)*

That's four rackets, three cocks.

JOSH. Five if you're counting ourselves.

JOHNNY. Funny the first time.

JOSH. Bor-ing.

JOHNNY. And he's right. It ain't extreme.

JOSH. So, we each take a handful of icy hot and wipe it on our balls.

(All the shuttlecocks freeze in mid air. They set down their rackets and start rubbing....)

JOSH & JOHNNY. *(As they rub.)* Exxxttttrrreeemmmeeee.

(They pick up their rackets.)

(Cue Metallica.)

(Extreme badminton with extreme pain in the groin region. The game builds quickly. JOHNNY *and* JOSH *are nearly brought to their knees before* JOHNNY *summons the uber-extreme within him, takes out his gun and shoots* JOSH *in the leg.* JOSH *falls to the ground and* JOHNNY *slams all four shuttlecocks into* JOSH's *face. Metallica cuts out. Faint Mariachi back in.)*

JOHNNY. Beg for the ice. Beg for the ice.

JOSH. COME ON! COME ON!

JOHNNY. Beg for it!

JOSH. PLEASE! PLEASE!

(JOSH opens the ice chest. They both plunge ice into their pants.)

You fucking shot me, man.

(There's a beat. A friendship hangs in the balance.)

Extreme.

JOHNNY. Extreme.

JOHNNY & JOSH. Eexxttrreeemmmeee.

(They are handed helmets. They put them on. They rip off their pants. They are wearing nothing but their shoes and a red sock for a fig leaf [JOSH should be bandaged in the thigh]. We hear the faint sound of an engine.)

JOHNNY. Gonna own my own business one day.

JOSH. We got fired from Sizzler.

JOHNNY. I'm taking night classes in accounting over at Cal State Northridge.

JOSH. Cal State Nowhere.

JOHNNY. Beats Cal State Radio Shack.

JOSH. Fuck you.

JOHNNY. And Cal State Outback Steakhouse.

JOSH. Yeah, you're the smart guy.

JOHNNY. Or Cal State Glory Hole.

JOSH. Let's move on.

JOHNNY. That girl was a dude.

JOSH. I had like eight Long Island ice teas, man.

(A JUMP CAPTAIN *enters.*)

JUMP CAPTAIN. You two idiots need to strap on your chutes now.

JOHNNY. We don't use parachutes.

JOSH. Yeah, fuck parachutes.

JOHNNY. Parachutes are for John Q. Public and his back-up band, the Pussies.

JUMP CAPTAIN. Idiots.

(The JUMP CAPTAIN *opens the cargo door. He exits. The sound of extreme high altitude wind and an airplane engine. They look down.)*

JOHNNY. We're extreme. You don't know what we know. Josh and I? We're the beard hiding the weak chin of America. So in twenty years when China takes to the Pacific and does its best Kimbo Slice on your corn-syrup bodies, don't come crying to us.

JOSH. *(Pissed.)* And if you see our old shift manager, tell him I'm real sorry I forgot to re-up the taco bar.

JOHNNY. And when you tell him that have him crane his fat fucking neck up to the sky, 'cause we're about to fucking bomb his ass.

JOSH. It's cold up here man. Rarified air.

JOHNNY. Don't tell me, man. Tell them.

JOSH. Tsup.

JOHNNY & JOSH. Eexxttrreemmmeee!

(They dive. Extremely.)

Extreme Ending of Scene

HALFTIME!

As JOSH *and* JOHNNY *splatter…*

YMCA begins to blare…

Four apprentices with brooms enter as a marching band and sweep the stage clear from the Extreme mess. Each is a letter Y M C A as they reach center or just past center stage…

Streaker?

As the sweepers reach their exits, they stop and remove their hats, bowing their heads in reverence as the lights drop way down and Navy planes flyover in missing man formation.

As the planes clear, a tight light reveals players in a huddle, getting a pep talk from their coach.

COACH. Are you trying to kill me? You think you can just go out there and be a little funny, a little thought-provoking, and that's how you win this show. I DON'T THINK SO! This half, I want to see hustle from Weitzman, Watson and Alexander. I want to see Wegrzyn, Jones, Tuan and Spurney ready to kill. I want to see 110%. I want to see you leave it all out there on that stage. We are not going to let up, we're going to keep coming at 'em. We're gonna get 'em with our own brand of Actors Theatre of Louisville game. Do you hear what I'm saying? Do you?

PLAYERS. YES!

COACH. What are we gonna do?

PLAYERS. ACT BETTER!!!

COACH. That's right! There's only two ways this is gonna turn out: 1. You win, and we go to Dairy Queen. 2. You lose, and you're changing over rep sets until I say you're done.

> (*Lights shift as "Rock and Roll Part Two" or some other fabulous sports song plays.*)

> (SPORTSCASTER ANDY *is on the sideline giving the halftime update.*)

ANDY. It's a strange night here in the Bingham Theatre even—or because —the first half played out exactly how they worked it in play practice…

> (*As he addresses the camera, from behind him comes a* MASCOT. *The* MAS-COT *jumps around behind him. Maybe devil horns on his head? Maybe waving to mom? Until, she/he comes around to stand next to* ANDY, *pretending he's interviewing him, being a jerk.* ANDY *tries to ignore the* MASCOT *as long as he can, but then he can't.*)

ANDY. (MASCOT *begins to imitate him.*) …word is the team is ready… (MASCOT *belly laugh.*) …and, um psyched. What can we, um, expect from Alexander, Jones, Spurney, Tuan, Watson, Wegrzyn, and Weitzman in the 2nd? (MASCOT *falls to the ground laughing.*) Do you have something you'd like to add? (*Shakes head.*) Really? 'Cause you seem to have something you want to say? (*Laughs again, rolling over banging fists on the floor in glee.* ANDY *kicks the* MASCOT—*hard.*) You want to get up and say something to my face? C'mon, what? You want a piece of me? I'll give you a piece of me! I have a hard job you costumed piece of crap!

> (*The* MASCOT *is pissed, but* ANDY *is more pissed. They fight—he's postal. It's a smack down. Until….*)

> (*Lights go to black as* ANDY *is ready to right [or left] hook the* MASCOT. *We hear the ding ding ding of a boxing bell.*)

End of Scene

SIGNATURE
by Daryl Watson

A boxing studio. Two men, JIMMY *and* BRANDON, *are practicing.* BRANDON *holds a punching bag while* JIMMY *wails on it. After a few punches…*

JIMMY. You wanna grab some Chinese or something?

BRANDON. We just got here.

JIMMY. I know. I'm hungry.

    (A beat.)

BRANDON. You're just hungry all of a sudden?

JIMMY. Not all of sudden. It's been building.

BRANDON. How come you didn't eat before you left?

JIMMY. Look, if you don't wanna go, just say, "No."

BRANDON. All right. No.

JIMMY. Fine.

    *(*JIMMY *goes back to hitting the bag.)*

(Points to the bag.) You wanna hit this for a while?

    (A beat.)

BRANDON. Are you all right?

JIMMY. Yeah. Why?

    (A beat.)

BRANDON. I don't know. *(A beat.)* You seem…

JIMMY. Seem what?

BRANDON. Distracted. A little bit.

JIMMY. I'm fine.

    (A beat. JIMMY *goes back to hitting the bag.)*

BRANDON. 'Cause if…you know…you're worried about Saturday…if you were…nervous or whatever…I mean, that would be…you know…that would make sense. That would be cool. That would be understandable.

JIMMY. Would it?

BRANDON. Forget it…

JIMMY. Naw. You got something you wanna say…

BRANDON. Jimmy…

JIMMY. Something you need to get off your chest, obviously. *(A beat.)* You think 'cause of Rick Bauer? You think that's making me nervous?

BRANDON. Well, I could see why it would.

JIMMY. You're projecting.

BRANDON. I'm what?

JIMMY. Projecting. It's a psychology term. You're worried, and you're projecting that worry on to me, saying I'm worried, so you'll feel better about being worried. (*A beat.*) I'm taking a class on it. I know what the fuck I'm talking about. That's what it is!

BRANDON. All right!

JIMMY. And, either way, the guy's dead, and there's nothing I can do about it. So there's no point in making a scene.

BRANDON. You're already making a scene.

JIMMY. How am I making a scene?

BRANDON. The way you're talking now. And the whole Chinese food thing.

JIMMY. I'm hungry. I can't be hungry?

BRANDON. In the three years we've trained together, you have never skipped out of here to get something to eat until you were done working out. So no, I don't think you're hungry. I think you're fucking scared, and all I'm saying is that it's cool.

(*A beat.*)

JIMMY. Put your gloves on. (*A beat.*) Put your gloves on!

BRANDON. Why?

JIMMY. I wanna spar.

BRANDON. No thanks.

JIMMY. Naw, naw. You're right; you're right. I'm afraid. I'm fucking scared to death…so you're gonna help me get through this. Come on.

BRANDON. No.

JIMMY. Are you afraid?

BRANDON. No.

JIMMY. You scared of me?

BRANDON. I'm not scared. Nobody's scared here.

JIMMY. You sure? You know what? Maybe we shouldn't until you sign a waiver. I don't want to be responsible if something happens to you.

(BRANDON *puts on his gloves. They climb into the ring and start to circle one another. The fight starts off slow, a few jabs and crosses here and there. They ad-lib insults at one another.*)

(*Soon, the fight gets more ferocious. It's hard to tell if they're just sparring or if it's personal.* JIMMY *throws a left hook into the side of* BRANDON's *head.*)

BRANDON. (*Clutching his eye.*) Ah, fuck! Fuck me! Fuck! Ah, fuck!

JIMMY. What? What? Are you okay?

(BRANDON *climbs out of the ring, still holding his eye.*)

BRANDON. Jesus fucking Christ...ah man. Hold on. Aw, shit.

JIMMY. What is it? Are you okay?

(BRANDON *throws his gloves off. He reaches into his eye with one finger, then blinks rapidly.*)

Can you see?

BRANDON. Yeah, I can see. It's just...my friggin' contact lens.... Ah! It was...like...right underneath my eyelid. I was afraid it was going to slide all the way in. You ever heard those stories—

JIMMY. Are you kidding me?

BRANDON. No, man. I've read about it online.

JIMMY. Contact lens? Your contact lens? WHAT THE FUCK ARE YOU DOING WEARING CONTACT LENSES??? You don't even wear glasses!

BRANDON. I'm experimenting. I'm trying to make my eyes look darker. You know?

(JIMMY *takes off his gloves and throws them at* BRANDON.)

JIMMY. You stupid fucking idiot!

BRANDON. What the hell is the matter with you? Stop it!

JIMMY. You know how freaked out I was? Jesus Christ...you can't fucking do that shit.

BRANDON. I'm sorry, all right?

(JIMMY *sits down on the side of the ring. A long beat.*)

JIMMY. Look at me: I'm shaking all over the place. (*A beat.*) I gotta call Pete and tell him to cancel the fight. I can't do it like...not like this.

BRANDON. Hey. It's gonna be all right, okay? It's gonna be all right. (*A beat.*) It's gonna be all right.

(*A beat.*)

JIMMY. Do I gotta click my heels three times or something?

BRANDON. I'm just saying, man, it's not your fault—

JIMMY. Naw...

BRANDON. It's not! He signed the waiver, just like everybody else. So he knew. He knew that he might not—

JIMMY. HEY! We're not doing this!

BRANDON. I don't understand what your problem is. I'm trying to help you.

JIMMY. I don't need your help! I was fine before you started in on me—

BRANDON. No, you weren't—

JIMMY. I wanted Chinese food! If you're that concerned about my well-being and shit, then why don't you just let me have some muthafuckin' lo mein, instead of riding my ass about it? It ever occur to you that that's how I need to deal with it?

BRANDON. So that's it, huh? You're gonna eat some lo mein and that's gonna make everything all right?

JIMMY. Nothing is gonna make it all right! This ain't the Lifetime Movie of the Week where I break down in front of you, and you give me some speech about how it wasn't my fault but I'll get through this 'cause time heals all wounds! Fuck you! He's dead. I gotta carry that around with me, and guess what? You get to watch! Nobody said it was fair, but that's how it is. (*A beat.* BRANDON *starts grabbing his things.*) What's this? You leaving?

BRANDON. You wanna carry it? Carry it. But I don't get to or got to or need to watch a goddamn thing. This ain't *Passion of the Christ* either...

JIMMY. Nice.

BRANDON. ...so when you're done carrying your cross...

JIMMY. Nice. Real nice! Real good friend, you know that?

BRANDON. ...holla at me!

JIMMY. Way to stick by me! Way to really be there for me, you fucking coward! You piece of shit!

BRANDON. What'd you call me?

JIMMY. You're a coward.

BRANDON. You know, if you weren't my friend...

(JIMMY *steps out of the ring and walks up to* BRANDON.)

JIMMY. What? What would you do? Hit me? Is that what you think you'd do? You're a coward, Brandon. Cowards don't hit people. They run and hide in corners, with their hands over their eyes until the scary part is over—

(BRANDON *punches him in the jaw.* JIMMY *falls on his butt and stares up at* BRANDON *blankly. He starts laughing helplessly...but it's hard to tell if he's laughing or crying. A beat.* BRANDON *reaches out a hand to him.*)

BRANDON. Come on. Get up. (*A beat.*) Get up, man!

(JIMMY *takes his hand and* BRANDON *pulls him up.*)
You all right?

(JIMMY *nods. A long beat.*)

JIMMY. Are we gonna make out or are we gonna get some lo mein? What's up?

BRANDON. You're a fucking asshole.

(*As they exit...*)

JIMMY. You been workin' on that upper cut, man. That shit was solid.

BRANDON. Thanks.

(*They exit. Blackout.*)

End of Scene

MULTIBALL: *birth of rugby*
by Alice Tuan

THIS STONE
COMMEMORATES THE EXPLOIT OF
WILLIAM WEBB ELLIS
WHO WITH A FINE DISREGARD FOR THE RULES OF FOOTBALL
AS PLAYED IN HIS TIME
FIRST TOOK THE BALL IN HIS ARMS AND RAN WITH IT
THUS ORIGINATING THE DISTINCTIVE FEATURE OF
THE RUGBY GAME.
A.D. 1823

>　WWE *is playing futbol with his cronies. As they pick teams,* WWE *holds a round football which he squeezes into an oblong shape, every once in a while.*
>
>　BLAXON *chooses* THOMAS, WWE's *brother.*

BLAXON. You.

THOMAS. I'm not playing against Willy. He cheats.

WWE. Rather inclined to take unfair advantage, I'd say.

BLAXON. So you're on the cheaters' team, then.

THOMAS. Cheaters will always win.

BLAXON. What's the point of good ball then?

WWE. Exactly. One can't depend on the whims of a little sphere and how it wishes to resist or submit to gravity. Let's play!

FIELDSWORTH. The brothers shouldn't play on the same team now—

BOLLINGER. Let them. We have no fear!

WWE. I wouldn't think fear is involved in amusement—

THOMAS. Leave the squares in geometry class—

FIELDSWORTH and BOLLINGER. We're with you Blaxon.

CHEATERS. We're with the cheaters.

SQUARES. Defeat the defeaters!

BLAXON. Cheat all you want, William Webb Ellis, but at least apply the noggin to appeal to the wit of flexing rules rather than the base breaking of them.

WWE. Play ball already! (*Kicks the ball in.*)

BLAXON. Cheaters are impatient. Show me how one can stretch the rules while going against them. *That* is the real challenge.

WWE. Squares really are no fun! Let's kill them.

(CHEATERS *go full force.*)

CHEATERS. Revolution! Buck the system!

SQUARES. Rules give order! Perfect the system!

(They kick the ball back and forth. [Maybe some "GET FIRED UP" and "GRASS GROW" from off stage.] The SQUARES *are dominating. One kicks up the ball, "landing" in* WILLIAM WEBB ELLIS' *hands.)*

SQUARES. Drop the ball! Drop it, c'mon!

WWE. Don't come near. As long as I'm behind the scrimmage line, you can't touch me. Those are the rules.

BLAXON. Eat my sod! Fieldsworth, take it from out of bounds.

FIELDSWORTH. Give the ball here.

BOLLINGER. One thing to cheat, another to hoard.

SQUARES. Hand it!

CHEATERS. Don't cross the line!

SQUARES. Hand it!

CHEATERS. Don't cross the line!

THOMAS. Throw it here, Willy!

WWE. That's the spirit, Tom!

(Squares cross the line and chase the TOM.*)*

Throw it back Tom!

(He does and WWE *charges through the* SQUARES *and runs carrying the ball in his hands. He scores. All breathe hard.)*

That would not have been as fun if it were allowed now, would it have been?

(They chase him down.)

End of Scene

I'M JUST A CUBS FAN

by Jon Spurney

I'M JUST A CUBS FAN;
I'M JUST A JERK, WHERE DO I BEGIN?
MUCH TO MY CHAGRIN, MY TEAM JUST CANNOT WIN.

I'M JUST A CUBS FAN;
I'M JUST A VICTIM OF FICKLE FATE.
THAT'S WHY I'VE HAD TO WAIT SINCE THE YEAR 1908.

AND OH, OH, OH, I HATE IT SO,
EVERY MISSED CATCH AND BAD THROW.
BUT OH, OH, OH, SOME DAY, I KNOW,
THE OTHER TEAMS WILL YIELD
AND OVER WRIGLEY FIELD
A BEAUTIFUL PENNANT WILL FLY HIGH.

I'M JUST A CUBS FAN;
I THINK I PROBABLY HAVE A SCREW LOOSE.
'CAUSE THERE'S NO EXCUSE
TO SUFFER THROUGH THIS ABUSE.

BUT OH, OH, OH, I HATE IT SO,
EVERY MISSED CATCH AND BAD THROW.
BUT OH, OH, OH, SOME DAY, I KNOW,
THE OTHER TEAMS WILL YIELD
AND OVER WRIGLEY FIELD
A BEAUTIFUL PENNANT WILL FLY HIGH.

I'M JUST A CUBS FAN;
I'M JUST A JERK, WHERE DO I BEGIN?

End of Scene

THE ULTIMATE
by Zakiyyah Alexander

MORGAN *in light.*

MORGAN. A stroke of genius hits like lighting. Boom. Gift from god. Divinity, yeah, I believe. What, you think I don't go to church? Fuck you, I'm a goddamned Christian. Gotta believe in something in these fucked up times. We're scraping the bottom of the barrel; reruns and game shows and shit. SHIT. It's true. But, the brain stroke of amazement that I had, oh, it's magic. Hang on to your hard on, kids. Reality, that's the word, but it's even bigger than that. Life and death, that's what we're selling. Now, we have to prepare ourselves for controversy, but that only fuels the fire, we know that. And, the teasers we're gonna run are gold. 'Cause, see, everyone is gonna tune in. And, everyone (every one) is gonna want to play: politicians, the soccer moms on Xanax, the guy who works at the fucking newsstand for Christsakes. What do they want? What do they all want? (This is too good, so good I'm coming in my pants, shit.) Here's what they want: they want to pull the trigger first.

(DAR *and* LEWIS *with rifles and gear.*)

LEWIS. This is…wow. I'm here. Can't believe I'm actually here.

DAR. Nervous?

LEWIS. A little. Don't get me wrong; I want to do this…it's just…

DAR. Newbie.

LEWIS. Yeah. Gotta say, I'm a little surprised to be paired up with you.

DAR. What, you think chicks can't shoot?

LEWIS. Uh, no, it's just, uh, you don't seem like the type.

DAR. Don't let the manicure fool you. They put you with me because I'm the best.

LEWIS. So then…you've caught one before?

DAR. Once. A girl. Got her in the back. All the blood made me sick. But, after that…the rush was, well got me hooked.

LEWIS. On the website they say it's hard to catch one.

DAR. Odds are against you, but that's also because most of the folks on this range aren't really hunters. It's a tough shot. Been on a range before?

LEWIS. No.

DAR. Paint-ball? Ever shoot anything, before?

LEWIS. Played *Buck Hunter* in this bar last week.

DAR. This isn't *Buck Hunter.* This is very real…. How'd you get here, anyway?

LEWIS. I took the car service.

DAR. That's not what I mean. All of us out here, we're here for a reason. Me, I'm the youngest partner in the history of my firm. A prodigy. Always had my eye on the prize, knew where I wanted to go. Then I got there. And, you know what I realized?

LEWIS. …That you weren't happy?

DAR. Not only that. I felt nothing inside. Until I started coming here. Every few weeks for a couple hours I'm alive again.

What brings you here?

LEWIS. I spent every last dime I had to afford this. Took loans from people I'll probably never pay back…. Couple years ago the doctors finally figured out was wrong with me. Then they realized there was nothing they could do. And, that was it. I mean there's treatment options, and tests (so many tests.) But, basically, all I can do is wait.

Guess I'm here because…. I got tired of waiting for something to happen. I want to be the one in charge. I want to decide who gets to live and who gets…

DAR. To die?

So, you ready?

LEWIS. I think so.

DAR. Keep you eyes and ears open, and don't point that gun at anything until I say so.

Wait. There. See that? This might be the day for you. Let's go.

LEWIS. I'm ready.

        (MORGAN *in light*.)

MORGAN. So, where are we today. A time of fucking change right, am I right? Obama and Hillary. Right? Following me now? Black man. White woman. That's the sport of it all.

That's the money shot.

        (*Light change.* LIPPY *applies makeup.*)

        (TARA *enters, a little trashed.*)

TARA. Come on. I mean come the fuck on, you're not. You are not seriously going to do this. I mean what the fucking fuck is wrong with you, Lip? Are you on now? You better be fucking on something because that's the only explanation because let me tell you, you are acting crazy. I mean it was funny when we first got here, and the open bar and stuff, but you're not really going through with this.

LIPPY. How do I look?

TARA. Like you've lost your mind. Tell me this is a joke. Are there friggin cameras in here? If there are, I'll kill you myself. Now, that was a real joke.

LIPPY. If anything happens make sure they don't call my mother first, she'll freak. Call my father and tell him to make her drink something first, or better yet, get her stoned. You ever seen my mother stoned? She's a wild one that lady.

TARA. This isn't funny.

LIPPY. Two hundred fifty thousand dollars. That's a lot of fucking money.

TARA. Not enough.

LIPPY. Pay off my loans. Fix up the apartment. Go on vacation. Still have more. Invest and everything.

TARA. It's not enough for your life.

LIPPY. That's more than I might ever make if I work every day for the rest of my life and you add it all up forever and ever.

TARA. What they're talking about. Lip, you would be bait. They want you to run through the fucking forest naked—

LIPPY. Nope, I get to wear sneakers. Look, I ran track in high school. I'm in good shape. I can do this. I know it.

TARA. What are you putting on makeup for?

LIPPY. They said the girls have to look good.

TARA. This is so crazy. I mean who the fuck would even want to try and shoot actual human beings, Lip? It's totally sick.

LIPPY. It's good money, Tara. And, it's a chance. A chance to make something out of nothing. Plus, they've got cameras; this is going to be on television. It's a whole reality situation. Who knows, this could turn into something real.

TARA. If you live.

LIPPY. It's not the first time I've been chased, Tara. Just the first time I've gotten paid for it.

(*Light change.* GREGORY *holds a baby.*)

GREGORY. Dah. Say Daaaah. Daaaaaah. That's me. You are my one good thing. They said we were too young. They said, how is he going to support a baby when he don't have a job, all he knows how to do is run fast with a ball. Just another baby daddy, that's what they said. But, they don't know. The website said they wanted men just like me. Imagine that? See, I been running all my life. But, this time they're gonna pay me for it. Just like the streets, don't get caught. I'm not scared. They can't catch me. Your Mama doesn't know nothing about this, little man, but you can keep a secret for Dah Dah, can't you? Me, I don't matter too much. But, this is for you. It's you I'm running for now. All that money we gonna get, that's for the future. For you. I am yours and you are mine. Now, you tell Daddy good luck. Can you say that? Say Daaaah.

(MORGAN *in light.*)

MORGAN. And, who's the audience? That's the brilliance of it all: we all are. Every single one of us. We can't turn it off. We eat it for breakfast, wipe our asses after we shit it out. We're the fans and the fucking mascots. 'Cause what do we all want? We want to play the fucking game.

(LINDA *and* DANIEL *read the paper.*)

LINDA. Honey, did you read about this? It must be a joke.

DANIEL. Oh, in the sports pages. I read about that. That's that ultimate thing that costs like five thousand bucks a round. But, who could afford that?

LINDA. It's horrible. And, look who's getting hunted. Black men and white women. What is that about?

DANIEL. Socially it makes sense. I mean the totem pole thing. Survival of the fittest, and all that.

LINDA. Tell me you're not serious.

DANIEL. I don't know if I would do it, and we can't afford it anyway. But, there is something about popping someone off like that. I don't know. Could be fun.

LINDA. You're actually telling me if you could afford it, you would kill a human being?

DANIEL. In a supervised setting, maybe, who knows? I'm just saying all your aggressions, all your fear, all your anger. Just like that. Bang. Bits of bones and insides splattered against the carpet.... I understand that. That feeling. It's human.

LINDA. I don't understand it at all. I mean this country, where are we going?

DANIEL. It's just a game, babe.

LINDA. But, the fact that anyone would want to play with life like that. I mean where are we? Where the fuck are we if this is what we do for fun?

DANIEL. We're home.

...Are you coming to bed?

LINDA. In a minute.

> (*DANIEL exits. LINDA looks at the paper...Then, she turns to go.*)
> (MORGAN *in light.*)

MORGAN. Who's ready to play?

> (*Blackout. Sound of loud gunshot.*)

End of Scene

SUPERFECTA

by Marisa Wegrzyn

ROSIE ROCKET *and* STING LIKE A BEE *are in their own area.* WAYLAY, TACTICAL JANE, *and* SOLID TRIP *are in their stalls getting ready to race. They wear their numbers on front. Maybe we think those three are marathon runners.*

ROSIE ROCKET. Rosie.

STING LIKE A BEE. Sting.

> (*They shake hands. Pause.*)

ROSIE ROCKET. How fast are you?

STING LIKE A BEE. How fast are you?

ROSIE ROCKET. Faster than you how many races you won?

STING LIKE A BEE. Like a million.

ROSIE ROCKET. Bull.

STING LIKE A BEE. You?

ROSIE ROCKET. Most races I win most races.

STING LIKE A BEE. Won. Past tense.

ROSIE ROCKET. You tryin' to be a jerk?

STING LIKE A BEE. No no, just that neither of us are running anymore. Can't win if you don't run.

SOLID TRIP. Track's all sloppy just like a mess of slop this race, always before I run, always always rains, it always rains.

WAYLAY. I thrive on slop.

SOLID TRIP. I really suck really bad in the slop.

WAYLAY. Slop slop sloppy slop.

SOLID TRIP. Forget the slop, it'll be fine, I'll be fine I just gotta run fast, gotta run fast, gotta run fast STOP RAINING!

TACTICAL JANE. Shut up I'm trying to focus!

SOLID TRIP. I can't get any less than first. Maybe second. I'd settle for third.

TACTICAL JANE. How bout you settle for my hoof up your ass.

SOLID TRIP. I got this phobia of mud flying in my eyeballs and I take a spill and shatter my bones, and the truck pulls up and the men with the death needles end me!

WAYLAY and TACTICAL JANE. Hey hey hey! / Whoa! / Bad talk! / Geeeeez! / etc.

(JOCKEY DAVE STUPINSKI *enters. He mounts* SOLID TRIP.)

SOLID TRIP. Ohhhh no I don't wanna race today in the mud, I'll fall down and break stuff!

TACTICAL JANE. Buck the little man and jump the fence. You do that they'll scratch you from the race.

SOLID TRIP. Yeah?

WAYLAY. Doooooo it!

TACTICAL JANE. Do it now!!! Go now!

WAYLAY. Are you a horse or are you glue?!

SOLID TRIP. I'm a horse!!!!

(SOLID TRIP *bucks.* TACTICAL JANE *and* WAYLAY *cheer.*)

JOCKEY DAVE. Whoa, whoa, easy now, easy, just, okay, just, okay, settle down.

(JOCKEY DAVE *falls off* SOLID TRIP.)

SOLID TRIP. (*Sprints away, exiting.*) WOOOOOO YEAH!!!!!

WAYLAY. Run Forest!

TACTICAL JANE. Born free.

JOCKEY DAVE. Godammit. Fifth time this week.

VOICE and LAUGHTER. (*Offstage.*) Ha ha look who lost his pony ride!

JOCKEY DAVE. Shut up.

      (JOCKEY DAVE *exits.*)

WAYLAY. Way to knock out the competition. Well done.

TACTICAL JANE. You gotta do what you gotta do. Thank god Rosie Rocket isn't racing today. I mean she's fast and she makes me a better racer and blah blah but I am goddamn sick of losing to her.

WAYLAY. You didn't hear?

TACTICAL JANE. Hear what?

WAYLAY. Rosie busted her leg at Arlington last month, and rumor round the stable—oh this is good—you ready for this? Rosie Rocket's having a little blastoff on the stud farm.

TACTICAL JANE. Nawww. Who's her stud?

WAYLAY. Sting Like a Bee. (*Gratuitous slow motion pelvic thrust.*) "I pleasure you as sloooow as I race."

TACTICAL JANE. What a loser.

WAYLAY. But his parents were racing royalty.

TACTICAL JANE. That's all he's got.

WAYLAY. Moment of silence for Rosie Rocket, shacking up with a big disappointment.

TACTICAL JANE. Huge disappointment.

WAYLAY. Oh yeah.

TACTICAL JANE. The day I can't race is the day they're going to have to put me down. I don't want to get stuck with a loser and I don't want to live if I can't race.

WAYLAY. …Might be changing your tune for a plate of horse cock.

ROSIE ROCKET. You're here. I'm here. We got people watching, so, let's just get it over with before our owners get impatient and decide to just wank you off and do me with a rubber hose.

      (STING LIKE A BEE *approaches* ROSIE ROCKET. *Awkward.*
      STING LIKE A BEE *exits.*)

ROSIE ROCKET. What? You don't think I'm pretty? Ass.

      (STING LIKE A BEE *returns, holding something behind his back.*)

STING LIKE A BEE. Hey.

ROSIE ROCKET. What?

(*Holds out a bouquet of hay.*)

STING LIKE A BEE. Hay.

(ROSIE ROCKET *is not impressed.* STING LIKE A BEE *sadly lowers the hay.*)

ROSIE ROCKET. Gimme the stupid hay. (*Takes it, smells it.*)

STING LIKE A BEE. Sorry about your leg.

ROSIE ROCKET. Least I can move on it, y'know. Could've been worse. I'm lucky.

STING LIKE A BEE. Well you got a bunch of horseshoes nailed to you, so that's a lot a luck right there. (*Crash and burn.*) I'm sorry, I'm such a fan of yours. You're very fast.

ROSIE ROCKET. Was. Past tense.

STING LIKE A BEE. Yeah, but you *were* fast! You were amazing. I was nothing. I was *pptthhhthth*!

ROSIE ROCKET. I saw you win a race. At Arlington, two years ago.

STING LIKE A BEE. That was the only race I ever won.

ROSIE ROCKET. That was a tough race. The odds on you were, what, 15 to 1?

STING LIKE A BEE. 20 to 1.

ROSIE ROCKET. You got some serious heart. Not just the beating bloody muscle of it, but that desire. You want to win, right?

STING LIKE A BEE. More than anything.

ROSIE ROCKET. That's the most important thing to pass down. Let's make the most of our sorry situation with what we got left.

(ROSIE ROCKET *approaches him. He's very shy and nervous now.*)

There's only one thing I need to know about you before we get down to business.

STING LIKE A BEE. Wh—what?

ROSIE ROCKET. Can you dance?

(*Oh, he can dance. Tango music! They dance. The bouquet of hay is the rose. A short and sexy little tango ending on a dip.*)

Let's make a champion.

End of Scene

MULTIBALL: *inside federer's head*
by Alice Tuan

FEDERER *enters the court, ready to return serve from the Deuce Court (right side.)*

The net is a row of folks, kneeling, with heads down. A let ball or fault will cause the head to bob up and then resume netness.

Each syllable uttered while "playing" punctuates a tennis motion. So, "Yo" is prep, "de" is swing, "lay" is ball contact. "Hee" and "Hoo" are each ball contact, the pauses giving time to efficiently run back and forth across court. The "heehooheehoo..." is rapid volleying at the net.

FEDERER. Yo de lay.

    (A winner.)

    (He goes to the Ad Court [left side.])

FEDERER. Yo de lay
yo delay... he hoo

Hee *(Pause pause.)* Hoo *(Pause pause.)*_
Hee *(Pause pause.)* Hoo *(Pause pause.)*_
Hee hoo hee hoo hee hoo hee hoo

Yo *(Pause pause.)* delay *(Pause pause.)*
hee *(Pause and.)* hoo *(Smash.)*

    (Cheers.)

    (Game Federer.)

    (He changes sides and chants.)

A game so ripe to rally foreva game
so ripe to rally foreva game so ripe
to rally forevea game so ripe to rally—

    (While chanting, he stops to towel himself off and sip some water, never missing a beat. These movements are done with balletic grace.)

—foreva game so ripe to rally foreva
game so ripe to rally foreva game so
ripe to rally forev— A game so ripe to
rally for:

(Pre-serve ball bounce.) Yo yo yo. Yo yo yo. Yo yo yo.

    (He serves from the Deuce Court [right side.])

Yo delay...ace!

    (He moves to the Ad Court [left side.])

Yo yo yo. Yo yo yo

Yo delay—

NET 1. (*Super out-of-control loud.*) FAULT!

(*A little leap from the* FED. *Second serve.*)

FEDERER. (*Lightly sing-song.*) Yo delay…second ace!

(*He moves to the Deuce Court.*)

Yo yo yo.

Yo delay…

NET 2: LET!

NET 3. Let ball, first service.

FEDERER. Yo delay…slice right…third ace!

(*He moves to the Ad Court: Match Point. In silence, he bounces the ball three times.*)

(*And three more times. And three more. He serves yet another ace.*)

(*Tamely.*) Game.

(*Falls to his knees.*) Set.

(*A long-ass note held as long as possible, to show full might and endurance.*)

Maaaaaaaaaaaaaaaaaaaaaaaaaaaaaaaaaaaaaaaaaaaaaaaaaaaaaaaaaaaaaaaaaaaaaaaaaaaaa-aaaaaaaaaaaaaatch.

End of Scene

CHRONICLES SIMPKINS WILL CUT YOUR ASS
by Rolin Jones

We hear Nina Simone's "Children Go Where I Send You," then a recess bell and sounds from an elementary school playground. Lights up.

Three fourth grade girls and a tetherball pole. CHRONICLES SIMPKINS, *all pigtails and attitude, eating Fun Dip.* RACHEL MELENDEZ, *pre-pubescent, gum-chewing hootchie mama.* JESSICA, *barely coordinated, plays with her iPhone. She is burdened by a backpack and dental head gear (which also makes it impossible to understand anything she says).*

CHRONICLES. Sydney Burrows gonna get hers.

RACHEL. Walking around in them cute little boots like she's someone.

CHRONICLES. Did you see the way she gave up Reggie?

RACHEL. Saying he copied her long division.

CHRONICLES. The girl's a snitch.

RACHEL. She's got to get got.

CHRONICLES. That's right I'm talking at you, Sydney.

RACHEL. Don't pretend like you ain't hearing her.

CHRONICLES. That's right. Walk away.

RACHEL. Walk away.

JESSICA. (*Unintelligible.*) Walk away.

CHRONICLES. She just jealous 'cause her mom packs her them natural snacks. Carrots and celery.

RACHEL. She wants your Fun Dip.

CHRONICLES. And my ever-lasting lick-a-stick. Who don't?

RACHEL. What flavor you on?

CHRONICLES. Cherrybomb. Saving the aren't you glad you eating orange for after.

RACHEL. For after what?

CHRONICLES. For after I cut her ass. (*To* SYDNEY.) That's right, pretend like you deaf.

RACHEL. You still going get got, Sydney.

CHRONICLES. What time is it?

RACHEL. What time is it, Jessica?

JESSICA. (*Unintelligible.*) 10:42.

CHRONICLES. What?

       (JESSICA *shows* RACHEL *her watch.*)

RACHEL. (*To* CHRONICLES.) 10:42.

CHRONICLES. Running out of time. Recess gonna be over soon.

RACHEL. How 'bout it Billy Eugene? Wanna get your ass whooped?

CHRONICLES. (*Watching him walk on.*) Didn't think so.

RACHEL. Katrina Cook?

CHRONICLES. Ain't she retarded?

RACHEL. Nah, just a slut.

      (*Enter* BILLY CONN, *a sixth grader. A large boy.*)

BILLY CONN. I'll play you.

CHRONICLES. And who are you?

BILLY CONN. I'm Billy Conn.

CHRONICLES. I don't know no Billy Conn.

BILLY CONN. I'm a sixth grader.

CHRONICLES. Big whoop.

RACHEL. Billy Conn runs with that dirty boy, Kennard.

CHRONICLES. Ah, that boy is nasty. Always trying to sneak a look at my boobs.

BILLY CONN. What boobs?

RACHEL. I know you did not just say that.

CHRONICLES. Say it again I'll cut your ass.

BILLY CONN. With what knife?

CHRONICLES. I don't need no knife. I got a rope and a ball. I'll slice you back to Miss McKinley's room and your head can read *Wrinkle in Time* to your neck.

RACHEL. You a punk.

JESSICA. (*Unintelligible.*) You a punk.

BILLY CONN. Freaks.

CHRONICLES. A punk with no game. You need to learn. (*To* RACHEL.) Make it happen.

RACHEL. Alright, Billy Conn of the sixth grade, whatcha got to put up? The champ don't ball for free.

BILLY COHN. Huh?

RACHEL. What's in the sack lunch?

(BILLY CONN *hands* RACHEL *his sack lunch.* JESSICA *peers over* RACHEL's *shoulder.*)

CHRONICLES. Count it down.

RACHEL. Half a subway. Bag of Fritos. Juice box. Pickle.

(JESSICA *likes pickles.*)

CHRONICLES. Not bad.

RACHEL. Seen worse.

JESSICA. (*Unintelligible.*) Pickle. Pickle.

CHRONICLES. You gonna put up the whole bag?

BILLY CONN. You gonna put up your Fun Dip and everlasting lick-a-stick.

CHRONICLES. What did he say?

RACHEL. You did NOT just say that.

JESSICA. (*Unintelligible.*) You did NOT just say that.

CHRONICLES. Billy Conn of the sixth grade, what makes you think I'm gonna give up my ever-lasting lick-a-stick?

RACHEL. You lucky she even letting you look at her.

CHRONICLES. Do you know who I am?

RACHEL. Doubtful.

CHRONICLES. Tell him who I am.

(CHRONICLES SIMPKINS *starts to warm up in the circle. She smacks the ball clockwise, lets it wind and then smacks the ball counterclockwise.* JESSICA *swats at it hopelessly.* CHRONICLES *is simply the fiercest fourth-grade tetherball player in the world.*)

RACHEL. This is Chronicles Simpkins, Billy Conn. This is the Woodlake Avenue Elementary Recess, Lunch and After School Undisputed Unified Tetherball Champion.

CHRONICLES. Tell Billy Conn about the streak.

RACHEL. Seventy-eight games in a row, Billy Conn. You're standing outside a circle of pain.

CHRONICLES. You're standing there with your half a Subway, bagga' corn chips and a pickle thinking you're all that, but all I see on your forehead, in bright Technicolor Crayola is the number seventy-nine.

JESSICA. (*Unintelligible.*) Seventy-nine.

(JESSICA *hands* RACHEL *the Hannah Montana Trapper Keeper of world records from her backpack.*)

RACHEL. This is the Hannah Montana Trapper Keeper of World Records. Do you know what we write inside here, Billy Conn?

CHRONICLES. The names of seventy-eight victims.

RACHEL. The grade they were in when they died and how long it took Chronicles Simpkins to send their butt back to hopscotch…

(CHRONICLES *catches the ball.*)

CHRONICLES. …or kickball or Pokemon or whatever irrelevant shit is going on outside my sacred ten feet. You lucky my girl Jessica likes pickles or I wouldn't waste my time. (CHRONICLES *smacks the tetherball.*) Feel the breeze.

(CHRONICLES *walks away and takes off her glove.*)

RACHEL. (*To* BILLY CONN.) It's on, Billy Conn.

(RACHEL *hands* JESSICA *the Trapper Keeper,* CHRONICLES *hands* RACHEL *the glove.* RACHEL *holds the glove up high and circles around announcing.* CHRONICLES *blows on her hand [it's hot].*)

RACHEL. (*To the schoolyard.*) Alright recess. Gather around. Circle it up. The Woodlake Avenue Elementary Unified Tetherball Championship is about to drop.

(KIDS *gather around [or sounds of kids gathering around.]*)

Chronicles Simpkins versus Billy Conn. Lunch sack for the Fun Dip. No Ropies. No Catchies. No Blind Willies. And no chance you gonna win Billy Conn.

CHRONICLES. What's my record time against a sixth grader?

(JESSICA *shows the Trapper Keeper to* RACHEL.)

RACHEL. January 24th, 2007. Chronicles Simpkins versus David Gardley. 6 point 3 seconds.

CHRONICLES. You ready to make history, Billy Conn.

BILLY CONN. Yeah, like I'm gonna let some fourth-grade girl beat me. Bring it on.

CHRONICLES. Clock this shit.

(*She serves the ball.* BILLY *blocks it and begins hitting it his way.* CHRONICLES *quickly takes out a pepper spray shot and sprays* BILLY CONN *in the face.* BILLY CONN *falls to his knees, clutching his eyes, screaming.* CHRONICLES *stops the ball, smacks it over his head. It winds around the pole at a blinding speed. Smack, smack, game.*)

RACHEL. Five point two four.

(CHRONICLES *takes a victory strut around the circle. She blows on her hand [it's hot], puts back on her glove, picks up her Fun Dip.* JESSICA *grabs the pickle out of the sack lunch and begins licking it.* RACHEL *drops the Hannah Montana Trapper Keeper of records and gives the blind, screaming* BILLY CONN *the world's most intense wedgie.*)

RACHEL. See that's how it rolls here, Billy Conn. You tell that to all them sixth graders. And tell your nasty friend to stop looking at my bra.

(*She takes her foot and shoves* BILLS CONN's *butt all the way back to sixth grade. Exit a forever-altered* BILLY CONN.)

CHRONICLES. Watch you all looking at? You move along Joy Grinell.

RACHEL. Ain't nothing to see here.

CHRONICLES. You look somewhere else Roy Steinbock.

RACHEL. Move along. Here comes the po-po.

CHRONICLES. Play it right.

(*They strike poses of innocence.* CHRONICLES *hides the pepper spray behind her back.* MR. FINKEL *comes running in blowing a whistle.*)

MR. FINKEL. Where is it?

CHRONICLES. Where's what?

MR. FINKEL. The pepper spray, Chronicles.

CHRONICLES. I don't have any pepper spray, Mr. Finkel.

(*She drops the pepper spray to the side.*)

MR. FINKEL. And what's that?

CHRONICLES. What's what?

MR. FINKEL. That thing you just dropped.

CHRONICLES. Says who?

MR. FINKEL. Ms. Melendez?

RACHEL. I didn't see anybody drop anything, Mr. Finkel.

MR. FINKEL. Jessica?

JESSICA. (*Unintelligible.*) Mr. Finkel I didn't see nothing. I don't even see it now. I don't know anything about any pepper spray and even if I did, which I don't, there's a context to everything and…

MR. FINKEL. Enough.

(*JESSICA shuts up.*)

Billy Conn is in the nurse's office right now, Chronicles. That boy can't open his eyes, he can barely breathe.

CHRONICLES. God must have done that to him, Mr. Finkel.

MR. FINKEL. There's an ambulance on the way. You young lady have terrorized for the last time.

(*He picks up the pepper spray and grabs CHRONICLES by the wrist. JESSICA takes off her head gear. She speaks clearly. Maybe a tiny lisp.*)

JESSICA. You can't do that Mr. Finkel. There's a context for these things.

MR. FINKEL. Save it, Jessica.

(*She gets in front of MR. FINKEL.*)

JESSICA. She'll be expelled. Principal Cody will ship her to another school and she'll rule the tetherball court there and the same jealousies will conspire to break her spirit. Pretty soon she'll be selling her body for crack. Is that what you want? You want Chronicles smoking crack? You want to ruin her life? Did you run out here to this small little bit of asphalt, blowing your whistle, making wild accusations because you're trying to justify your existence, Mr. Finkel? Because you have failed to prepare your students, students like Billy Conn for the coming world? A world that is surprising, and scary and yes, occasionally unfair? It's something he can't find in the books you make us read. And the lessons you draw up on the chalkboard. You have to let children fall, Mr. Finkel. You have to let them fall and get back up on their own. Chronicles is an outcast here, Mr. Finkel. In exile everywhere she carries her Fun Dip. But from ten thirty-five to eleven o'clock and twelve thirty to one fifteen she feels safe. When Chronicles steps into this circle, when she's hitting her high arcing serves, and flying that ball over the heads of children more privileged than her, for a brief moment in space and time, Mr. Finkel, Chronicles Simpkins is immortal. And just witnessing it is a thing of beauty. And you want to take that away from her. From us. Shame on you, Mr. Finkel. Billy Conn was weak. That's what happened here.

(*She puts her head gear back on.*)

MR. FINKEL. What grade are you in?

(*Quickly CHRONICLES takes off her shirt and RACHEL puts MR. FINKEL's hands on CHRONICLE's breasts. JESSICA takes a picture of this with her cell phone. CHRONICLES puts her shirt back on. JESSICA throws the cell phone to RACHEL.*)

MR. FINKEL. Hey!

RACHEL. But then again. Maybe we could tell Principal Cody you're a pedophile.

MR. FINKEL. Huh?

CHRONICLES. I'll get expelled. But you'll go to jail.

RACHEL. And you know what they do to predators in jail, Mr. Finkel?

CHRONICLES. They fuck you in the ass and don't ask permission.

(CHRONICLES *returns to her Fun Dip, waiting for* MR. FINKEL's *next move.* RACHEL *waves the cell phone.* MR. FINKEL *begins to back off.*)

You might want to drop that.

(*He drops the pepper spray.*)

Walk away.

RACHEL. Walk away.

JESSICA. (*Unintelligible.*) Walk away.

(MR. FINKEL *runs off. The three of them watch him.* JESSICA *hits the tetherball.*)

CHRONICLES. Feel that breeze.

End of Scene

THE MAJESTY OF SPORT, *PART 3*

by Jon Spurney

SPORTSCASTERS.
THE HUMAN BODY IS A TEMPLE, AND SPORT IS JUST LIKE A PRAYER.
MAKING BODIES BIGGER AND STRONGER, MAKING MINDS MORE AWARE.
IN PURSUIT OF A HEALTHIER BODY, WE ATTEMPT TO EMULATE
THE ATHLETE AND HIS GOAL OF PERFECTION EVERY TIME WE PARTICIPATE.

CHEERLEADERS. EXTRA CHEESE! EXTRA CHEESE! GIMME SOME EXTRA CHEESE, PLEASE!

LOUTS.
WE'LL START WITH MOZZARELLA STICKS THEN KICK IT INTO GEAR
WITH ALL THE WINGS THAT YOU CAN EAT AND SIX PITCHERS OF BEER.

AN OREO PIZZA MY FRIEND IS HIGHLY RECOM-
MENDED.
MY BODY'S GETTING BIG ALRIGHT, BUT NOT THE WAY
THAT I INTENDED.

End of Scene

End of Play